Quantitative Measures and Warranty Coverage of the Risk of Misinforming

Dimitar Grozdanov Christozov
American University in Bulgaria, Bulgaria

A volume in the Advances in Linguistics and Communication Studies (ALCS) Book Series

IGI Global
PUBLISHER of TIMELY KNOWLEDGE

Published in the United States of America by
IGI Global
Information Science Reference (an imprint of IGI Global)
701 E. Chocolate Avenue
Hershey PA, USA 17033
Tel: 717-533-8845
Fax: 717-533-8661
E-mail: cust@igi-global.com
Web site: http://www.igi-global.com

Library of Congress Cataloging-in-Publication Data

CIP Pending
ISBN: 978-1-6684-8800-3
EISBN: 978-1-6684-8801-0

British Cataloguing in Publication Data
A Cataloguing in Publication record for this book is available from the British Library.

Advances in Linguistics and Communication Studies (ALCS) Book Series

ISSN:2372-109X
EISSN:2372-1111

MISSION

The scope of language and communication is constantly changing as society evolves, new modes of communication are developed through technological advancement, and novel words enter our lexicon as the result of cultural change. Understanding how we communicate and use language is crucial in all industries and updated research is necessary in order to promote further knowledge in this field.

The **Advances in Linguistics and Communication Studies (ALCS)** book series presents the latest research in diverse topics relating to language and communication. Interdisciplinary in its coverage, ALCS presents comprehensive research on the use of language and communication in various industries including business, education, government, and healthcare.

COVERAGE

- Computational Linguistics
- Forensic Linguistics
- Discourse Analysis
- Language Acquisition
- Sociolinguistics
- Media and Public Communications
- Language and Identity
- Computer-Mediated Communication
- Language in the Media
- Non-Verbal Communication

IGI Global is currently accepting manuscripts for publication within this series. To submit a proposal for a volume in this series, please contact our Acquisition Editors at Acquisitions@igi-global.com or visit: http://www.igi-global.com/publish/.

The Advances in Linguistics and Communication Studies (ALCS) Book Series (ISSN 2372-109X) is published by IGI Global, 701 E. Chocolate Avenue, Hershey, PA 17033-1240, USA, www.igi-global.com. This series is composed of titles available for purchase individually; each title is edited to be contextually exclusive from any other title within the series. For pricing and ordering information please visit http://www.igi-global.com/book-series/advances-linguistics-communication-studies/78950. Postmaster: Send all address changes to above address.

Titles in this Series

For a list of additional titles in this series, please visit:
http://www.igi-global.com/book-series/advances-linguistics-communication-studies/78950

AI and Its Convergence With Communication Technologies
Badar Muneer (Mehran University of Engineering and Technology, Pakistan) Faisal Karim Shaikh (Mehran University of Engineering and Technology, Pakistan) Naeem Mahoto (Mehran University of Engineering and Technology, Pakistan) Shahnawaz Talpur (Mehran University of Engineering and Technology, Pakistan) and Jordi Garcia (Universitat Politècnica e Catalunya, Spain)
Information Science Reference • © 2023 • 308pp • H/C (ISBN: 9781668477021) • US $250.00

Combining Modern Communication Methods With Heritage Education
Lia Bassa (Budapest Metropolitan University, Hungary & Foundation for Information Society, Hungary)
Information Science Reference • © 2023 • 317pp • H/C (ISBN: 9781668462171) • US $215.00

Handbook of Research on Socio-Cultural and Linguistic Perspectives on Language and Literacy Development
Angela K. Salmon (Florida International University, USA) and Amparo Clavijo-Olarte (Universidad Distrital Francisco Jose de Caldas, Colombia)
Information Science Reference • © 2023 • 500pp • H/C (ISBN: 9781668450222) • US $270.00

A Social-Scientific Examination of the Dynamics of Communication, Thought, and Selves
Seif Sekalala (Drexel University, USA)
Information Science Reference • © 2022 • 277pp • H/C (ISBN: 9781799875079) • US $205.00

For an entire list of titles in this series, please visit:
http://www.igi-global.com/book-series/advances-linguistics-communication-studies/78950

IGI Global
PUBLISHER of TIMELY KNOWLEDGE

701 East Chocolate Avenue, Hershey, PA 17033, USA
Tel: 717-533-8845 x100 • Fax: 717-533-8661
E-Mail: cust@igi-global.com • www.igi-global.com

Table of Contents

Section 4
Warranty of Misinforming

Preface

The problem of measuring the probability of the risk of misinforming appeared to me for a first time in an Information Systems class in 2001. I tried to convince students how important is to design interface that considers the recipient's or end-user's background, professional jargon, and the way how obtained information is mapping to recipient's problem. The purpose of the exercise was to contrast the information provided from the sender to the problem domain of the receiver or what information the receiver needs to address the uncertainty in solving problems. To illustrate this issue of designing Information Systems I provided students with an advertisement describing a personal computer and a list of reasons to use it that the students may need (activities to accomplish with the use of the advertised product). Practically, the majority of students in their sophomore year faced the problem to purchase PC and they were prepared regarding what they want to do with this device. I modified a bit of the PC description from an advertisement, published in a newspaper in the following way: more powerful CPU, more primary and secondary memory, but black -and-white (BW) monitor, practically no network capability. Additionally, I listed a set of activities a PC was used at that time:

- develop and edit text.
- make complex and even sophisticated computations.
- use of e-mail.
- easy access to the Internet.
- organize personal data.
- play games.
- watch movies.

The PC as described, allows us to easily accomplish some of these tasks, but some of others – not at all. Students were asked to define what they are going to do with the PC, and whether the proposed one suits their needs, if the price is attractive.

Rough evaluation shows that about 40% of students will make wrong decisions in purchasing a device they need. The description of the PC provided was fully correct and complete, but results in misleading 40% of potential clients. This result shocked me, and I realize that the problem of evaluating the risk of misinforming deserves attention. At the emerging times when world faces dominated by indirect communication via IT informing, it appeared as a valuable research topic.

Looking back on human history, we can discover many evidences of misinforming. Many people believe that the Bible is a divine message, but for more than 3000 year this message is a subject of interpretation in a way to reveal the true meaning in a way to shape the human behavior. Many people contributed by sharing their own interpretation of the Biblical texts. Talmud is probably the most famous example. In all these cases, probably we have to exclude Moses, the communication is indirect. Bible scholars are trying to reveal the meaning by studying the message without having the opportunity to get direct feedback from the source. Translations from Hebrew also added potential for misinterpretation. And the history is full of evidences of misinterpretation of those messages leading to bloody conflicts and other disasters. The attempts to interpret this message occupy a great volume of efforts of the most brilliant representatives of the human race as Moses ben Maimon (Rambam) and Isaak Newton, and still are on-going. Today these efforts even explore sophisticated computer technologies.

Nowadays, indirect communication prevails in the way people are becoming informed, and the risk of becoming misinformed grows in an unprecedented scale.

This book attempts to discuss some issues related to the phenomenon of misinforming. It not pretended for completeness of covering the issue, but its objectives are to discuss some aspects of misinforming, ideas of how the risk associated with misinforming can be quantified and managed, how the warranty, as risk transferring technique, is applied in case of misinforming. This is made by a special form of warranty – warranty of misinforming, which may be represented by the slogan "if you are not fully satisfied – money back".

Dimitar Grozdanov Christozov
American University in Bulgaria, Bulgaria

Acknowledgment

Several people have contributed to building my understanding about this complex phenomenon – misinforming. In many of the topics presented here, their contributions were critically important.

I am obliged specially to recognize contribution of Prof. Stefanka Chukova from Victoria University at Wellington, New Zealand and Prof. Plamen Mateev from Sofia University "St. Kliment Ohridski" for the fruitful discussions related to information theory, nature of the risks associated with misinforming and how to quantify it, and warranty of misinforming. Contribution of both resulted in coauthoring many papers addressing problems with quantifying the risk of misinforming and advancing the understanding of the role warranty of misinforming plays. Their deep knowledge, understanding of theory and practices can be seen throughout the entire book. They were the first to assess whether the topic is worthy of considering and research. Without their knowledge, wisdom, and professional attitude toward problems this book would never have been possible.

Many other colleagues play significant role in building my vision regarding problems associated with information sharing, learning, and use of computer technologies for informing:

Prof. Michael Buckland was the first who had structured my vague experience in the area. Discussions on his book "Information and Information Systems" allowed me to understand that the trend of developing information systems is switching from efficiency in technology toward increasing efficiency of using technology.

Dr. Eli Cohen moves a step further realizing that one cannot investigate "informing" within limited boundary of established disciplines as computer science or information systems. It needs new way, new paradigm, and this broad area is essentially trans-discipline. His deep understanding about the evolution of the informing processes shaped my current view on the field.

Prof. Stoyan Denchev developed the concept of information environments in case of uncertainty by distinguished uncertainty in decision making from uncertain environments. His vision of an uncertain information environment is what we are living in now. Nowadays, we are exposed to become informed by a mixture of true facts, opinions presented as facts, and a flood of fake news, without clear indicators to distinguish between them and informing is mostly dominated by interpretation causing misinforming.

There are many others to whom I am obliged, but I cannot list all of them here without assuming the risk of missing somebody.

Introduction

We are living in a world where the behavior of everyone depends gradually on the information received. Being informed is becoming more and more important nowadays. The stage the human civilization reached is described by names as "knowledge era" and "information society" that mark the major properties of society nowadays, but also the major challenges the people and other social entities face. The advancement of computers merged with communication's technology, named Information Technology (IT), leads to so called "fourth industrial revolution". Becoming informed via IT, as the mutual today's practice changed completely the way people of using data and information, learning, trading, socializing. Practically all human activities now are shaped by using Computer and Communication Technologies (CCT). Learning via communication has many forms, and its variety and heterogeneity challenged people in making decisions on any level of human activities.

All this leads to an extremely increasing role information plays in our entire activities, and as a result, the harm of becoming misled by obtained information. The risk of becoming misinformed increases in likelihood and impact. The magnitude of effect caused by wrong actions because of misinterpretation of received information places the issue of misinforming among the topics needed deeper investigation and understanding to address the huge variety of becoming informed nowadays. The variety of aspects in interpreting information requires developing managerial tools to address rationally the risks associated with misinforming hazards.

Nowadays, we all are living in a highly uncertain information environment. We are exposed to become informed by a mixture of true facts, opinions presented as facts, and a flood of fake news, without clear indicators to distinguish between them. Informing is heavily dominated by subjective interpretation, subjective selection of what information to trust for, and even a subjective assessment of own competences for understanding and assessing available information. All those are causing circumstances leading to the misinforming phenomenon. This book is addressing this phenomenon in a very narrow aspect – the rational decisions made by a careful "cost-benefit analysis" in the case of honest contribution of information providers.

There are two aspects of current state of how individuals, groups or entire societies operate – desperate needs to relay on complete, correct, precise or, on general, comprehensive, and quality information; and shorter time to comprehend available data in a way to obtain needed knowledge. IT allowed globalization of economy and nowadays practically every business, despite its size, is able to operate globally. This challenges the potential to assess in full the correctness of decisions made as result of interpretation of received information. Using quantitative measures of the impact of misinterpretation allows to improve rationality and to mitigate the risk associated with the misinforming hazard.

From this perspective, the informing or learning is the process of creating acting knowledge, knowledge applied immediately to action, knowledge acquired via communication. And more specifically, knowledge resulting by obtaining information via indirect communication, and by using different kinds of computer and communication technologies. These technologies are now called Information Technologies in a way to stress their critical role in processing information in a way to inform their users.

This book is dedicated to misinforming. The meaning of this term is a bit misleading representing two different aspects of the phenomenon of becoming misled by received information. The first use is when one provided intentionally wrong information aiming to deceive the receiver. This meaning of the word is described also by terms as dis-informing or simply lying. The second meaning covers the case when the receiver is misled, because of wrong understanding, wrong interpreting, or wrong applying the received, otherwise correct, information to the problem needed solution. This book explores the second aspect of the term misinforming. The clear distinction is made according to sender's "intention" when providing information. The case when sender intentionally provides wrong information to harm receiver, or lying, is not subject of this book. The case, when sender provides incorrect information, but assuming it is correct and useful to the receiver, this case also can be described by the term misinforming, is within the scope of the book as well.

There are many issues related to the misinforming phenomenon. The book is trying to answer some of them, or at least to initiate and to attract further investigations of how to model, quantify, and explore the measures of risks associated with misinforming. Some of the questions addressed in this book are:

- Why the phenomenon of misinforming is possible?
- What are factors or circumstances contributing to misinforming?
- Is it possible to consider misinforming as a hazard and to address this phenomenon by following the risk management approach?
- What does misinformation cause in the world of business?
- Is it possible to evaluate the magnitude and impact of the misinforming risk?
- How to monetize this kind of risk?
- What are different origins and therefore different types of misinforming?
- How to mitigate different categories of the risk of becoming misinformed?
- Are there any positive aspects of misinforming?

Special attention is given to the warranty covering the risk associated with misinforming – warranty of misinforming. Warranty is a risk sharing technique. In case of misinforming warranty is used mostly as a promotional tool now, but to manage sharing the evaluation of the exposure of these risks is essential.

Nowadays, business is influenced by information as never before. The business aspects of misinforming are leading in addressing the above issues. Business and management rely on rational, quantified assessment of costs and benefits. Addressing the misinforming hazard does not represent an exception and the management of the risk of misinforming needs techniques allowing to quantify the probability and impact of such hazard. Equally important are the possibilities to assess and financially justify measures applied to mitigate these risks. Special attention is given to only two of these broad areas – models for quantifying the risk are proposed and transferring risk via applying warranty – the second and fourth parts of the book. The first part discusses multiple scenarios leading to misinforming and defines several types of misinforming that need different kinds of attention. The third part describes some practical issues associated with those risks.

The book is organized in four parts:

Part 1 discusses the nature and origin of hazards leading to the risk of becoming misinformed.

Part 2 is dedicated to modeling risks of misinforming, identifying factors, and quantifying the likelihood and impact of misinforming.
Part 3 presents some practical issues related to managing misinforming risks and the use of models proposed in Part 2.
Part 4 introduces warranty of misinforming as a special form of the risk sharing and discusses different aspects of the warranty of misinforming policies.

The book is oriented first to the business practitioners who use warranty of misinforming as a promotional tool but need to evaluate the cost of the warranty policy and to assess its feasibility. Additionally, the book may be of interest to researchers in the field of building mathematical models to quantify real life phenomena usually studied by using qualitative measures.

Section 1
Misinforming

Section 1 Introduction

SUCCESSFUL INFORMING PROCESS

Learning via communication is the dominant mode to reduce uncertainty nowadays. With advancement of Information technologies (IT) the variety and diversity of ways people are learning grows and this exposes opportunities, challenges, and risks. Becoming informed allows a person to behave adequately under given circumstances, to gain advantages, and to avoid harm and extra costs. The book is dedicated to one of the aspects of communication related to the risk of misleading caused by misinforming. The simple case of rational use of information in decision making by assessing cost and benefit. Quantifying the likelihood and impact of the misinforming risk allows to avoid or mitigate the negative outcomes. The ideas of modeling the risks are considered in relatively narrow settings. Many important aspects related to communication are not considered here. Especially factors related to communication such as psychology, intuition, or beliefs are not addressed. Readers interested in these aspects of communication can refer to publications of authors like Jonathan Haidt (2001,2006), Hugo Mercier (2011, 2012, 2016), Hugo Mercier and Dan Sperber (2009, 2017), and Daniel Kahneman (2011). These are factors that are impossible to quantify and are out of the scope of this book. Some of these aspects of communication are discussed briefly in this section of the book only to illustrate different circumstances of occurring the misinforming hazards but they are not explored further in the book.

An oversimplified description of the communication used here is that the objectives of communication process are to transfer data, information, and ideas from one party, sender of information, to another party, receiver of information. When the receiver of information faces solving a problem under uncertainty and the sender possesses information that might be useful in reducing the receiver's uncertainty. The aim of communication is to reduce the receiver's uncertainty.

Communication is important for every species on the earth, but it is essential for human beings, and it is in the foundation of human civilization. Communication may result in successful informing the receiver or not. Unsuccessful informing may happen when the sender intentionally lies to the receiver in a way to achieve some kind of advantages – this kind of communication is marked with the term dis-informing. Another case of unsuccessful informing is when the sender provides the best possible information she or he possesses, but the receiver misunderstood it or misinterpreted it in the context of receiver's needs. This case of failure of informing is called misinforming. The two terms dis-informing and misinforming are often used as synonyms, but in the book, they are clearly distinguished by the existence of intention of the sender to correctly inform the receiver or to lie to the receiver. Disinforming or lying is not among the objectives of this book. The unintentional misinforming, as the nowadays cultural phenomenon with wide impact, is well described by Frankfurt (2005).

Becoming misinformed or misled by received information is a natural side-effect of any form of communication. Nowadays, because of the growing and overwhelming dependence on received information, assessing the potential risk of becoming misinformed is becoming a necessity. Also, computer and communication technologies created an environment with dominance of indirect, technology mediated, communication, which has become an additional important factor contributing to the growing impact of the risk of becoming misinformed.

The Bible story of construction of Babylon Tower tells us that the problem of misunderstanding has been recognized for millenniums.

Why can't people understand each other?
Why was what said by one is understood differently by other?

Better understanding the origin and nature of hazards causing misinforming is the way to reduce the negative impact of the risks of becoming misled.

This book explores the phenomenon of misinforming from decision making perspective. The result of becoming informed is to make decisions for solving the problems in a rational, information driven fashion. This perspective allows us to establish criteria for success – when the problem is solved well and provides clear incentives from the receiver to use provided information.

The objectives of becoming informed or the informing activity are learning, creating acting knowledge, and shaping behavior based on information obtained. Knowledge is generated by own experience or via communication by learning from shared information. Learning by communication includes several activities as receiving information, interpreting it, and merging the understood meaning with existing knowledge – the background. And mapping this enriched knowledge to the problem domain in a way to solve it; and acting accordingly.

This section of the book is trying to identify and discuss different aspects or scenarios of the way people are learning, obtaining knowledge, interpreting information, assessing data describing circumstances in a way to become informed to solve their problems, but are exposed to become misinformed. The risks caused by the hazard of becoming misinformed is common and significant to deserve attention and management. One's behavior is driven by tacit knowledge, which is composition of background knowledge, experience from the past, beliefs and bias, combined with newly obtained, interpreted, and adopted information. The transferred information is an explicit, written representation of the provider's knowledge. Transforming explicit to tacit knowledge is the area where hazards leading to misinforming occur.

Risks associated with informing exist in every phase in the communication process. This is especially valid in indirect communication, where sender and receiver communicate via technologies. Practically, receiver acquires data and informing is via exploring acquired data in form of messages, texts, visuals, etc. Such process starts with acquiring new data, extracting, and structuring it into a useful form of manageable information, toward transforming it to knowledge, transforming explicit or written knowledge to tacit or knowledge leading to actions or shaping receiver's behavior, and building wisdom or understanding regarding causes and effects.

The success of the informing process can be considered only as successful completion of every phase in presenting sequence of activities. According to Christozov et al. (2009) the success of informing can be described also as the following hierarchy, defining the meaning of "success" from very essential stages of communication process from initiation to the outcome:

Level 1. The process is successful if relevant data is successfully transmitted to the receiver: identifying the sources, getting access, and retrieving data. This level corresponds to success according to technical aspects of communication.

Level 2. The process is successful, if the receiver is able to read, understand and present the transmitted data in a meaningful form. It may include translation from a foreign language, understanding formulae, in some case aggregating, summarizing, visualizing, and other techniques aiming transforming data to information.

Level 3. The process is successful, if the receiver does not ignore the information included in the message, but rather accepts and adopts the meaning embedded in it as the receiver interpret the obtained information. The result is that the receiver acquires new tacit knowledge. This process has potential to match the discovered patterns and relationships communicated as data with receiver's expectation, bias, and prejudices. Challenging the knowledge exposed on those data with background knowledge is a critical step in the process of learning. Confidence toward acquired meaning is the outcome of this level.

Level 4. The process is successful if the acquired knowledge is proven to be correct in practice or the obtained via the process knowledge does not mislead the receiver. This completes the process of learning – obtaining knowledge from data according to Plato's definition that knowledge is a trustful and verifiably truth (justified and believed truth).

The next level of learning, level 5, is to obtain "wisdom" or ability to behave properly in solving similar problems. This stage is outside of the scope of the book, but it is essential for learning and developing and utilizing the acquired knowledge.

Level 5. Obtaining wisdom from verified knowledge requires that the knowledge is generalized by abstracting the valuable, common, long term valid cause-and-effect relationships from those data, proven valuable only in given circumstances and specific conditions.

Upper level of success is possible only if all lower levels have been pasted successfully.

The risks associated with any of these levels of success are as follows:

1. The risks on the first level are associated with solely technical problems.
2. The risks on the second level address encoding-decoding problems, linguistic problems and problems caused by insufficiently or incompletely comprehensive expertise or competence of the receiver to understand the message as it was provided by the sender. Also, because of lack of ability to deal with data provided by using appropriate tools for data processing – insufficient systems' expertise.

3. The failures on the third level are caused mostly by the trust/credibility problems. Trust toward the sender and motivation in providing information. If the receiver does not accept the information, s/he will not use it and, of course, will not create or utilize the knowledge associated with this information. The problem of trusting machinery generated information or provided as result of manipulation and complicated processing by technology needs further understanding and trusting to the data source, the data processing algorithms, and technology.
4. The risks on the fourth level are the risks of misinforming. The obtained knowledge regarding cause-effect relationship may differ from the actual one encoded in provided message by the sender. Such misunderstanding or misinterpretation mislead the receiver in making correct decision and act accordingly.
5. Inability to generalize the obtained knowledge may prevent converting it into wisdom and to shape future behaviour.

Not recognizing that data is simplified, codded representation of reality; missing to acknowledge that "lack of evidence is not evidence of lack" as well as that data represents the past reality, and the context of following events may be changed significantly, may cause misinforming. Many factors and circumstances may lead to misinforming in learning from data within a communication process and the acquired knowledge may lead to significant harm for the receiver. The presented hazards in this section of the book illustrate their variety but do not pretend for comprehensive and exhausted coverage.

The "learning from data" process includes gaining access to data, obtaining data, data assessment, cleaning and verification, data analysis, synthesis, and presenting it in an understandable, informing way. All those aspects, representing the complexity of the current information environment, set a number of barriers in obtaining the necessary expertise to learn from data, going well beyond traditionally recognized expertise needed by a person to be called "literate".

Next section of the book is dedicated to defining quantitative measures of the risks associated with misinforming. Risk management requires quantifying the likelihood and impact of a hazard and the ability to quantify the hazard's parameters is a necessary condition for effective management. The risk of misinforming is a specific case of a failure in a communication process as presented above. It is not under the control of any of the two parties involved in the process and its evaluation requires the development of special approaches and techniques for collecting and processing the relevant data. The primary data source is the customer's feedback on the satisfaction with the result achieved with information acquired in the assessed communication process.

The evolution of understanding of what represents success of information services originated in the area of Information Sciences discipline as early as in 1970s and evolve with the evolution of available technologies and corresponding services. The two major milestones – development of personal computers in late 1970s and introducing the World Wide Web protocol in 1990 – marked the revolution of the way of informing and constituted the current state of human society named as information society.

Misinforming is associated mainly with the negative effect of misleading, making wrong decisions, errors. But there are also cases when misinforming plays a positive role creating opportunities for innovations and creativity, for finding "out-of-box" solutions.

In this section of the book the origin of misinforming is discussed as a natural result of evolution of human societies – evolution of language as communication tool; evolution of diversity and complexity of environments; evolution of expertise and experience needed for living in a world with growing complexity; evolution of diversity of backgrounds marked by the term "Information Asymmetry"; evolution of complexity of competences to succeed in increasing sophistication of circumstances surrounding us nowadays; and evolution of Information Technologies – the technologies used in communication to enhance informing.

The second aspect discussed here is what are the factors contributing to the appearing of hazards leading to misinforming. Different cases of mediated informing are discussed from the point of view of their potential to misinform. Trust to the source, and trust to provided information is discussed in the light of converting information into acting knowledge.

The following origins or circumstances creating favorable conditions for misinforming are the subject of discussion in the following chapters:

1. Origin of misinforming
    a. Polysemy of natural languages.
    b. Information Asymmetry.
    c. Lack of adequate competence to understand correctly provided information.
2. Factors, supporting misinforming:
    a. Mediated access to information
        1. Mediated access to information – information brokerage. Relying on mediators increases complexity in assessment

regarding validity and usefulness of information. Also, it added another level of interpretation and assessment of what is relevant and what is not.

2. Informing via Information Technologies: Internet, Big Data, Machine Learning or Artificial Intelligence are phenomena associated with inability of human to comprehend directly accumulated vast amount of data. Indirect communication via computer and communication technologies excludes several well-established practices to verify information, such as body language, environment of providing, and feedback possibility.
3. Machinery generated data: effect caused by inaccuracy of measuring tools. It is quite often nowadays to obtain data by using tools such as microscopes, telescopes, and much more sophisticated devices.

b. Self-misinforming: the short-list selection paradox or Danning-Kruger effect are examples of unrealistic over or under estimation of own potential that often leads to misinforming.
c. Over trust Vs. Under trust. Credibility of received information is essential for its adoption and transforming into acing knowledge. Different attitudes in dealing with information are the origin of different misinforming hazards.
d. Rational Vs. Emotional decision making: a discussion about and contrasting Rational and Emotional decision making is initiating in a way to address the dominant factor in assessment of information and learning and resolving potential conflict between evidence and trust.
e. Transforming information into acting knowledge requires the ability to map received information to specifics of the given problem and transforming cause-and-effect knowledge into action.

Current advancement of Information Technologies makes people to depend much more on information delivered via Internet and often ignore to pay attention to the way of how information is created, captured, and delivered, and informing and learning is achieving.

This section of the book is dedicated to identifying and exploring circumstances leading to misinforming, contributing factors and conditions. It organized by the following chapters:

Chapter 1.1. explores linguistic factors that cause misinforming. It presents the origin of misinforming as building in the polysemy of the natural languages.

Natural languages reflect human life with specific properties of surrounding nature, climate, food, etc. They are developed historically and correspond to the way of formation of a group of people as a society. The language is a key component of group's culture and is a tool to facilitate informing within the group and may serve as a barrier in communication between members of the group with members of other groups. In the computer information systems era, communication via technology added complexity and as well as the risk of misinforming.

Chapter 1.2. is dedicated to the role of competence as the major factor in becoming informed or misinformed. Complexity of communicated information requires corresponding competences to understand, comprehend, and correctly apply the received information. The role of competences, expertise in both subject or problem domain area, and the system for accessing and processing information are discussed.

Chapter 1.3. is dedicated to the phenomenon of Information Asymmetry. The chapter presents misinforming hazards by adding the issue of asymmetric competence and double-sided asymmetry. Information asymmetry is a necessary condition for communication, but also as a source of misunderstanding.

Chapter 1.4. addresses problems caused by informing via mediators and introduces information mediators as a risky factor for misinforming. The two-sided asymmetry and adding mediators' subjective assumptions in a multi-steps process from original data source toward end-users are discussed in the context of human mediators – information brokers. The issue of technology mediated informing is also addressed by emphasizing different categories of nowadays technologies. This chapter also explores different topologies of communication processes according to their potential to mislead receivers. Topologies are contrasted according to their cardinality and feed-back availability.

Chapter 1.5. introduces the reader with a variety of other cases leading to misinforming as negative outcome but also the cases, when misinforming may come out with positive effect.

In conclusion, the nature, origin, risks and contributing factors are summarized. Also, the scope of the next three sections is defined as reflection of hazards discussed in chapters of this section of the book.

REFERENCES

Christozov, D., Chukova, S., & Mateev, P. (2009). The risk of misinforming for competing messages. *Journal of Issues in Informing Science and Information Technology*, *6*, 351–364. doi:10.28945/1064

Frankfurt, H. (2005). *On bullshit*. Princeton University Press.

Haidt, J. (2001). The emotional dog and its rational tail: A social intuitionist approach to moral judgment. *Psychological Review*, *108*(4), 814–834. doi:10.1037/0033-295X.108.4.814 PMID:11699120

Haidt, J. (2006). The happiness hypothesis Finding modern truth in ancient wisdom. Perseus Books Group.

Kahneman, D. (2011). *Thinking fast and slow*. Farrar, Straus and Giroux.

Mercier, H. (2011). Reasoning serves argumentation in children. *Cognitive Development*, *26*(3), 177–191. doi:10.1016/j.cogdev.2010.12.001

Mercier, H. (2012). Looking for arguments. *Argumentation*, *26*(3), 305–324. doi:10.100710503-011-9256-1

Mercier, H. (2016). The argumentative theory: Predictions and empirical evidence. *Trends in Cognitive Sciences*, *20*(9), 689–700. doi:10.1016/j.tics.2016.07.001 PMID:27450708

Mercier, H., & Sperber, D. (2009). Intuitive and reflective inferences. In J. St. B. T. Evans & K. Frankish (Eds.), *In two minds: Dual processes and beyond* (pp. 149–170). Oxford University Press. doi:10.1093/acprof:oso/9780199230167.003.0007

Mercier, H., & Sperber, D. (2017). *The Enigma of Reason*. Harvard University Press.

Chapter 1
Natural Languages as Origin of Misinforming

ABSTRACT

This chapter explores linguistic factors that cause misinforming. It presents the origin of misinforming as building in the polysemy of the natural languages. The evolution of natural languages reflects the needs of human life according to its specific properties such as surrounding nature, climate, food, etc. They are developed historically and correspond to the way of formation of a group of people as a society. The language is the key component of the group's culture, and the society is usually identified by the language. The language is a tool to facilitate informing within the members of the group and may serve as a barrier in communication between members of the group with members of other groups. In the computer information systems era, communication via technology added complexity and as well as the risk of misinformation.

INTRODUCTION

Language is the natural way of communication. Over millennials languages evolve to serve given group of people to communicate effectively. Different groups experienced different challenges and problems that resulted in developing different ways to communicate the meaning subject for communication. Evolution of languages follows the growing need for richer communication results from evolution of complexity in life and societies.

This chapter discusses two aspects of natural languages from point of view of misinforming – natural languages used to present qualitative information as text,

DOI: 10.4018/978-1-6684-8800-3.ch001

wording, sentences; and also, quantitative information as numerals. Diversity of the languages to express meaning is preserved. On the other side the people reached agreement to use the same numerals to present quantities. The efficiency of so called "Arabic numerals" is accepted globally as standard, reducing the probability for misinterpreting.

The following issues are discussed: next section discusses polysemy as a result of evolution and growing the society; the following addresses the evolution of communication between groups and the need of translation from one language to another; development of "jargons" to serve specific domains is introduced in the following sections, including developing of "formal" languages designed to avoid polysemy. The last section discusses the evolution of what is understood by "literacy".

POLYSEMY OF NATURAL LANGUAGES

Natural languages evolved during the history of civilization to serve as a tool for communication. A language is composed of words, used to code particular objects, facts, activities or their properties. Languages evolve to serve the growing needs of details to communicate. This long evolution led to polysemy, as a phenomenon creating misinforming hazards. Polysemy is a misinforming factor in communication between parties using the same language. Communication between parties originally using different languages, a typical case in our globalizing world, includes translation, or interpretation of words in one language to looking for corresponding word in another language.

Polysemy, multiple and often diverse meaning of words and phrases, of natural languages representing the richness of expression is natural nowadays. The language as a reflection of life is developing by constructing terms to mark human activities or observed phenomena in the surrounding nature. With the evolving complexity of life and learning more about nature the languages also evolve to allow representing the nuances in diverse environments. Originally, human life was simple, and people needed a few words to describe and communicate facts, events, actions. Within small groups – family, tribe, village – there was almost no polysemy. By growing complexity of life, and by growing connectivity between different groups, the complexity of language grows and understanding between groups with different experience is becoming more difficult. Uniting tribes includes creating a common language to allow communication, but different meaning of given word used by a separate groups or tribes remain in use and have been preserved. This enriched the language and diversified the meaning assigned to a single word.

Another aspect of using languages is that a word or phrase actually codes the real meaning. A human eye may distinguish about 4000 nuances of colors, but in a language, we are using just a handful different color names – white, yellow, red, blue, etc. By adding adjectives such as dark, light, or similar we may increase the number of codes used, but it is still far from those 4000 nuances. And even more, the actual number of colors – frequencies in the spectrum – is much larger and by using special equipment a human may distinguish them. Or, by using language we are not able to present completely the reality and even what a human, creator of the message, observes or knows. Choosing the level of granularity in describing details of entity's properties is subject to a trade-off decision – choosing low level of granularity allows better view on the properties of a particular instance but provides low possibility for meaningful generalization and classification, as well as correct interpretation, translation, or sharing.

Covering cultural or practical issues into language also provides tools to enrich the vocabulary, but also added possibility for misunderstanding or hiding the actual meaning. We are saying xerox, the name of a commercial entity, often as a synonym of copy machine and vice versa. The name of a literature or historical character is often used to represent in a compact form a particular human property (brave, cowardly, cunning), not necessarily familiar to outsiders. Civilization created another phenomenon, known as euphemisms, by replacing words considered "dirty" with other "clean" for everyday usage. Utilizing euphemisms is an on-going process. The more developed is a given language the more euphemisms are incorporated.

TRANSLATION FROM ONE LANGUAGE TO ANOTHER LANGUAGE

The process of uniting populations has reached its extreme nowadays. Globalization, resulted on advancement of the transportation and communication technologies, challenges languages in an unprecedented way. Communication in the global world requires translation and interpretation between different languages, often lacking the needed experience to correctly understand the actual meaning and to find an equally informative corresponding term. Having in mind that such term may not exist in the language. There are at least four words in Hebrew representing different kinds of "desert": מִדְבָּר, עֲרָבָה, חָרָבָה, יְשִׁימוֹן. Each of them represents a specific living conditions – in מִדְבָּר (midbar) people may survive with their herds (in English this word is translated as "wilderness"), and in חָרָבָה (harava) – no. For me, as a person born and grow in Europe, understanding this difference was almost impossible until visiting Israel and observing different kinds of deserts. But I had not experienced what means to live in those conditions by observing deserts from the window of an air-conditioned vehicle. The language only cannot reveal the actual meaning in case the reader has no right experience to interpret it. Northern nations have many words describing different types of snow, tribes living in a jungle have multiple words for "jungle", etc. Translating such linguistic constructs always leads to losses of information by using more general terms instead of a specific one, holding the meaning of the specific properties of the object.

Today, English became globally the common communication language, but now communication by using English is much easier between "not-native speakers" than between "natives" and "non-natives". Simply because studying English as a foreign language follows almost everywhere similar pathways, slightly dependent on the selected textbook used and teachers' background. Even the native English speakers are divided, based on their origin and sometimes British people cannot fully understood what a New Zealander or Australian wants to say. Dialects and jargons added nuances and enriched the language for insiders (members of the group) but creates barriers for correct understanding by outsiders.

In general, translating from one to another language may generate misinforming hazard. There are two general options of translating – one can apply literal, word-by-word conversion, and other – dynamical – by trying to preserve the meaning. Either may result in losing information, or at least important details. Translation from a language A to language B usually targeting users fluent in language B. Interpreter must use words or phrases typical or understandable in the context of population of language B. And each of the four Hebrew words mentioned in above example are translated as "desert" and eliminate specific details regarding living conditions. This does not allow complete, deep understanding of the message. In a globalizing world translation is becoming a usual everyday activity that adds to likelihood of misinforming hazards. Interpreting messages presented in a natural language, especially in a foreign language, is always exposed to the risk of misinterpretation and may lead to misinforming.

DOMAIN SPECIFIC ASPECT OF NATURAL LANGUAGES

Learning via communication, or sharing is always for purpose and both parties communicate by having in mind particular circumstances. The next chapter is dedicated to information asymmetry and the problem of different backgrounds and competences will be addressed in more detail. From linguistic point of view the two parties may use different "jargons" to express the same meaning. Professional background often leads to use a language with specific terms with well-defined meaning for people with appropriate training but have different meaning for the rest. Instead of being more informative, the message presented in such a way can misinform.

The meaning of the message created by sender is generated in given domain and interpreted by the receiver in domain of the problem, which could be completely different. Despite that the information provided could be useful and relevant.

NATURAL VS. FORMAL LANGUAGES

With the establishment of linguistics as a scientific discipline, and the development of computing machinery, the need of languages to support human-computer interaction appeared. The need for non-polysemic languages resulted in design of so-called formal languages to implement it according to formulated in advance specification. Noam Chomsky pioneering works (Chomsky, 1957, 1964) open the systematic study of formal languages, grammars, and construction of algorithmic languages – languages designed to write software. These languages do not suffer from polysemy and do not create hazards of misinterpretation.

LITERACY, AS THE ABILITY TO LEARN FROM COMMUNICATION

Misinforming is a result of wrong understanding of otherwise correct information. Understanding is usually associated with "literacy" – a person is literate if she or he can understand the meaning of a message. A message can be presented as text, written in a natural language; as a number – by using certain form of numerals – Arabic, Roman, Sumerian; as a formula – written in language of mathematics, etc. If we look on the message as "data" – explicit representation of given meaning – literacy can be considered as the ability to learn from particular type of data: "reading" is associated with learning from a written in a natural language text; "writing" addresses an ability of sharing data in a way to externalize the knowledge, assuming the term used by Nonaka's in developing SECI model, (Nonaka et al, 1995); "doing arithmetic" is related to the ability to understand and process numerical data in a way to learn quantitative properties and relationships.

Recently, literacy was related to the ability to learn from extensive data resources: "information literacy" addresses the ability to locate, identify and retrieve relevant data in available sources. Use of information technology added a new dimension in learning from data - "computer literacy" refers to the ability to use computer technology in data processing in a way to learn. Currently we may speak about "informing literacy" with ability to verify information and to identify "fake news", "social network literacy", or Big Data literacy. A definition regarding "Big Data

Literacy" assuming the use of information technologies available at a time is proposed in Christozov & Toleva (2013).

Any of those literacy types can divide human society into two categories, of course with quite fuzzy boundaries, the category of literate and the category of illiterate members of society. The history of evolution of the human civilization over centuries can be considered as overcoming those divisions by spreading competence of learning from data within the society. Literate members of society are less exposed to misinforming risk, compared to the illiterate members. Any of those literacies offer advantages to the group of literate and disadvantages to others, but also some members of the society may possess one category of literacy and lack another.

The history of civilization can be viewed as the evolution of human literacy. Several stages in this evolution can be identified so far, as presented in Figure 1. Any period of evolution of civilization can be considered from "informing literacy" point of view. How well society as a whole or just only a few – members of society's elite – are capable of obtaining and learning from available data, to become informed, as well as an ability to share information and knowledge – to inform. This evolution can be divided into two major periods: the period of basic, classical literacy covering reading, writing, and doing arithmetic; and the period of "digital literacy" including computer literacy, internet literacy, and data processing literacy. Information literacy can be considered as a transition from the classical period toward the computer era. It emphasizes the ability to locate, assess, retrieve, and classify data objects. These competences were identified and developed well before the design of the first electronic computer. The last stage presented in the diagram places Big Data literacy as the next round of the evolution of Digital literacy. The further stages in IT influence on human life – as Artificial Intelligence or Machine Learning– is on its way to transfer human competences to computers and it is too early to analyze and identify what competences people will need to prevent misinforming at that stage.

Figure 1. Evolution of literacy
(adopted from Christozov and Toleva, 2013)

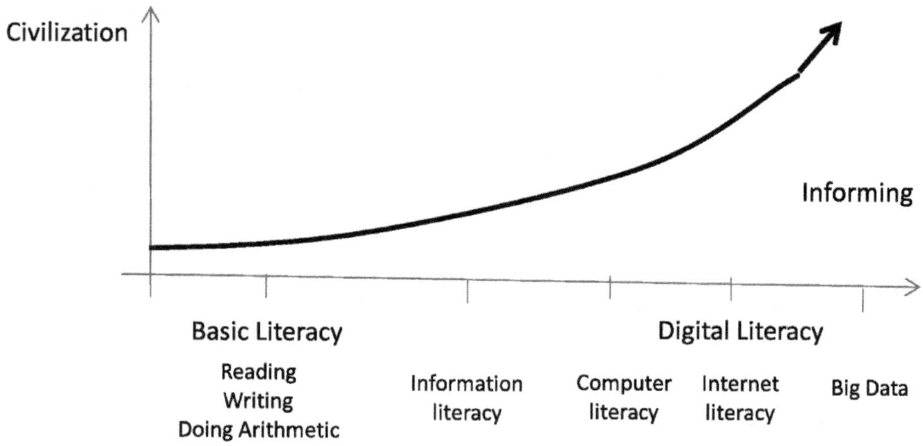

Data Science, Big Data, Information Society are terms used to mark current state of dependence of people on data and the ways people manage data. Nowadays all aspects of classical literacy are influenced by computer-based Information Technologies as well. The triad "data-information-knowledge" characterizes the process of learning from data. Modern information technologies changed completely the way how data is collected stored, organized, accessed, and processed. But the slogan "drowning in information but starved for knowledge", written about 40 years ago by John Naisbitt (1982) is becoming more and more valid. The result of growing volume and variety of information with inability to comprehend it results with higher risk of misinforming. The three Vs – Volume, Variety and Velocity – as properties of current Big Data represents the nowadays round of challenges that required specific literacy to learn via using computers as mediators.

CONCLUSION

The chapter presents the origin of risk of misinforming as result of communication between provider – sender, and user – receiver of information in using natural languages and impact of polysemy as a result of evolution of natural languages. A language reflects the experience of the specifics in life of a human group according to surrounding nature, climate, food, etc. They are developed historically and correspond to the way of formation of a given group of people as a society, building their own culture. The language is a key component of a group's culture and is a tool to facilitate informing within the group and may serve as a barrier in communication between members of the group with members of other groups.

Misinforming is a side effect of using natural languages in communication. The risks vary from wrong understanding the meaning of the received information to missing details. In all those cases, misinforming may result in misleading the receiver in making rational, information driven decisions, and to act according to those wrong cause-effect assumptions.

The other aspect addressed in the chapter is informing in the computer era. Computer information systems, or informing mediated by digital technologies, is the phenomenon marking the current stage reached by our society. The current commonly accepted way is to use natural languages in human computer interaction, or in design of user interface. In the context of technology dominated society, user interface has become a key impact factor for becoming misinformed or to mitigate the risk of becoming misinformed. Computer information systems served for communication via technology, added complexity in informing people by increasing the number of involved parties with including designers of information systems and especially designers of user interface. Increased complexity in communication added new dimensions in human literacy essential to become correctly informed, adding technology as mediators also added to the risk of misinforming.

The unidirectional use of information systems was observed by Calvin Mooers (1950) „… In information retrieval, the addressee or receiver rather than the sender is the active party. Other differences are that communication is temporal from one epoch to a later epoch in time, though possibly at the same point in space; communication is in all cases unidirectional; the sender cannot know the particular message that will be of later use to the receiver and must send all possible messages..." From this perspectives, communication with computer information systems can be considered as communication with past or the meaning communicated with the message is composed without knowing the actual circumstances and needs of its users.

Accepting that misinforming is natural in communication is just the first step in mitigating this risk. Identifying the circumstances and factors leading to misinforming, as well as quantifying its likelihood and impact is the way to allow managing it.

Next two chapters of this part of the book explore different topologies of informing processes, the role of mediators, as well as competence misbalance, or information asymmetry, as the necessary conditions for informing, but also as the critical factor causing misinforming. Acknowledging the positive role of misinforming in creativity, trans-disciplinary innovations, and finding "out-of-box" solutions is also important component of the nature and outcomes of misinforming.

REFERENCES

Chomsky N. (1957), Syntactic Structures, *Mouton & Co.*, 1957

Chomsky N. (1964), Current Issues in Linguistic Theory, *Mouton & Co.*, 1964

Christozov, D., & Toleva, S. (2013) Knowledge diffusion via social networks: The 21st century challenge, International Journal of Digital Literacy and Digital Competence (IJDLDC). IGI-Global. 2013

Loundon, K., & Laudon, J. (1996). *Management Information Systems*. Prentice Hall.

Mooers, C. N. (1952). Information retrieval viewed as temporal signaling. *Proceedings of the International Congress of Mathematicians* 1, (pp 572-573). IEEE.

Naisbitt, J. (1982), *Megatrends*. Warner Books. https://www.brainyquote.com/quotes/john_naisbitt_382513)

Nonaka, I., & Takeuchi, H. (1995). *The Knowledge-Creating Company: How Japanese Companies Create the Dynamics of Innovation*. Oxford University Press. doi:10.1093/oso/9780195092691.001.0001

Chapter 2
Lack of Adequate Competences

ABSTRACT

Chapter two is dedicated to the role of competence in correct interpretation of the information provided in communication. Competences of the receiver is the major factor in becoming informed or misinformed by the message. Complexity of communicated information requires corresponding competences to understand, comprehend, and correctly apply the received information. Role of competences, expertise in both subject area or problem domain area, and the informing system and corresponding information infrastructure for accessing or delivering information are discussed.

INTRODUCTION

In the previous chapter personal literacy in dealing with natural languages was considered as an important factor influencing the correct informing and the opposite, lack of adequate literacy may lead to misinforming. Some aspects of literacy evolution were considered as well. This chapter goes further by the impact of a receiver's expertise on the success of the informing. Competences are forms of literacy, but usually literacy is considered as the very basic, essential competence to deal with information. With the introduction of computer technology and development of computer information systems the expertise needed for success in becoming informed via the processes used today has become more complicated.

The role of expertise in its multiple forms is the objective of this chapter from point of view of misinforming hazards. The two areas of expertise – expertise in

DOI: 10.4018/978-1-6684-8800-3.ch002

problem domain and system's expertise are critically important for success in every area of human activities. Here, the discussion will be limited to analyzing the role of competences in likelihood of misinforming hazards in the context of the market of e-commerce. Commerce provides a natural way to assess relevance, success, risk, or opportunities. And the need for quantifying the output of decisions made based on received information via indirect communication is critical in assessing success of a form of communication, its provider, and the information processing applied.

This chapter attempts to identify competences, literacies, and skills influencing the way people become informed nowadays – the era of Internet, era of globalization, era dominated by indirect informing via Information Technology, as well as essential competences needed to mitigate the risk of becoming misinformed. Nowadays we are witnessing massive introduction of computer delivered services, application based on Machine Learning, Big Data, Artificial Intelligence, and smart devices to everyone's everyday life. Competences, considered as required only for a narrow group of professionals just ten years ago, now are needed to everyone who does not want to become misinformed and outsider.

TWO MAJOR CATEGORIES OF EXPERTISE IN COMPUTER INFORMATION ENVIRONMENTS

Success of informing in the computer information system era are dependent on receiver competences in two areas as identified by Michael Buckland (1991) – subject expertise and expertise to use efficiently the information system providing the service. The impact of the receiver's expertise on both aspects are of crucial importance for the success in information retrieval and are also critically important in e-commerce, which appeared a decade later.

Lack of expertise in using the computer information system or Internet simply excludes such customers from the e-commerce market. The level of receiver's expertise in the subject area affects the success of e-commerce in contrast with the expertise of provider. The difference in the expertise between sender and receiver has impact on success of communication is known as information asymmetry (see next chapter). A high expertise in the subject area reduces information asymmetry and reduces the likelihood of misinforming. Information asymmetry is the major factor for misinforming. Also, the asymmetry in system's expertise may result in misinforming.

Possessing adequate competence reduces the possibility of becoming misinformed, and lacking the needed expertise increases it. Buckland's view reflects the stage of understanding about success of informing acquired by technology provided information services at that time. 1991 is a significant year, when the World-Wide-

Web (WWW) protocol was introduced. In this way 1991 can be viewed as the official start of the Internet revolution. Accumulated technological development since the introduction of Internet protocol in 1974 can be considered as pre-history or preparation for the use of computer-based communication we have experience now. The Internet increased tremendously the ways and varieties people may get access to information, but also exposed problems which were unknown before. WWW changed completely the way people are becoming informed. Nowadays, becoming informed is much more challenging, needs a larger variety of competences, than just 30 years ago. It is almost impossible nowadays for one individual to possess all needed competences for becoming successfully informed in all aspects of life or even to address a single problem. This causes high grow of risk of becoming misinformed and opens many possibilities for disinforming. For solving complex problems in a holistic way, collective wisdom is required. For more information about cooperation in decision making see Chapter 3.4. in the third part of the book.

CATEGORIES OF COMPETENCES RELEVANT TO MITIGATE THE RISK OF MISINFORMING

Natural question is what are the competences needed by a person today beyond those already recognized as "literacy"? Those are competences related to acquire knowledge by exploring data and information obtained via computers and computers' mediated communication. Competences to work with on-line available information and related to the risk to become misinformed.

Several group of relevant competences can be distinguished. Among them are Efficient Data Retrieval from huge heterogenous repository, Data Assessment and Verification, Data Cleaning or Cleansing, ability to analyse and ability to generalize and synthesise new knowledge. Almost all of those competences are considered under the umbrella term of "Analytical Competences". Firstly, analytical competences include "critical thinking" and secondly to apply any of available tools to check and justify not only whether obtained information is correct, precise, and trustful, but also whether the meaning receiver acquired are correct and useful in the problem domain.

Analytical Competences

When we ask what is needed to extract useful value from accumulated data to reproduce the true picture of the observed reality? The easy answer is "data analytics". Data analytics offers those tools that are designed to explore data and to extract value from data. But what constitute "data analytics"? Great majority of people simply understand it as a set of software applications and use them as "black boxes". In many cases this approach works, but the risk of being misled remain significant if those tools are applied solely as "black boxes". Data acquired by public sources are polluted in many ways. Available data is created under given circumstances and reflect objectives of those engaged in capturing and storing facts. Also, analytical techniques implemented in the software are valid only when certain conditions are fulfilled, and specific assumptions met. The level of sensitivity toward data of such techniques varies, and also may result in wrong and misleading inferences. Also, most of data processing applications always produce results, even in cases where the application is not suitable to process the data set.

Analytical competences are recognized as critical (Christozov, Rasheva-Yordanova, and Toleva-Stoimenova, 2018) in learning from data or to avoid misinforming. Critical thinking, setting "problem first" and rational rather emotional assessment of acquired information are essential to avoid the risk of becoming misinformed.

Competences in data analysis allow user to answer questions like the following:

- Whether the available and retrieved data are truly relevant to the problem?
- Whether the set of obtained data is comprehensive and lack of internal conflicts and logical contradictions?
- What data processing tool is the most suitable and what are limitation or conditions in applying a tool to given data set.
- How to interpret and apply results, computed by the data processing tool, to solve the problem?

What competences a user needs in a way to avoid the risk of being misled by the results obtained via use of data analytical tools? What represents a comprehensive set of abilities and skills to explore data? How to structure such set of competences?

Analytical skill is the ability to visualize, articulate, and solve both complex and uncomplicated problems, and to make decisions that are sensible and based on available information.

Mastery of this competence involves developing a set of skills such as:

- Identifying, in the unordered description of a situation, the informative elements it contains, classifying them according to the degree of reliability or certainty attached to them.
- Recognizing existence of information gaps and identifying them. To do this one must have a prior theoretical model to sort out information elements into categories and to assess relevance and sufficiency of information in each of them. Lack of sufficient or not sufficiently reliable information can lead to decisions to search for new information or to posit reasonable hypotheses or estimates before attempting to reach conclusions.

- Using analytical tools to organize available information and show the relations between different components. Such tools include visualization to describe data in a meaningful, structured way as figures, outlines, tables, concept maps, graphs, etc.; and inferring from data by using statistical and other techniques.

Data Science, as a newly introduced umbrella term, supports and encourages shifting between deductive (hypothesis-based) and inductive (pattern-based) reasoning. This is a fundamental change from traditional analysis approaches. Inductive reasoning and exploratory data analysis provide a means to formulate or refine hypotheses and discover new analytic paths.

Taxonomy, developed and published in Christozov, Rasheva-Yordanova and Toleva-Stoimenova (2018), addresses specific objectives and defines meaning, priorities and hierarchies of analytical competences. (see the Appendix A of this chapter). Different objectives may result in different classifications. It presents a view regarding the set of competences composing the so called “analytical inquiry” category by following the publications of Lumina Foundation (2014) regarding Degree Qualification Profile (DQP), here this taxonomy is adjusted to address the misinforming phenomenon.

The general framework used here includes three categories of variables, described by data collected, subject of analysis:

- Controlled variables,
- Uncontrolled variables,
- Outcomes.

The first two are called also factors, predictors, inputs; and the third one – results. A simplified goal of data analysis is to find the relationship between those three categories of variables. Or knowledge generated is an explicitly defined model describing this relationship.

Having those competences allows an analyst to reach correct understanding about “causes and effect” driving development of particular circumstances, and to present this understanding in a useful form.

This taxonomy is designed to address efforts to reduce the risk of misinforming, but it is more generally applicable. To address each of those categories, data relevant to the problem, must be available and its properties known. Following this leading principle, the categories of Analytical Competences can be classified as ability to accomplish the following activities:

A. Identify and Analyze the Existence of a Problem.

Identify the Existence of a Problem.

Identify What Cause the Problem.

Identify Whether the Problem is Decomposable.

Assess Whether Factors with Impact on Problem's Solution are under Control.

B. Identify and Assess Information Needs, Data Quality, and whether Data is Relevant to the Problem.

Identify what Information is Needed.

Where relevant information can be found (sources)?

Ability to access, to retrieve, and to structure relevant data.

Ability to clean and to explore the acquired data (Transformation stage).

Ability to verify and to assess credibility of obtained information.

Ability to assess data quality.

C. Choosing and Applying Data Processing Tool.

Understanding Limitations of Applied Analytical Tool.

Map Obtained Data to Analytical Tool. Assessment of relevance.

Synthesizes solution.

Setting Assumptions and checking their validity.

Comparing Different Applicable Courses of Action.

Verifying Obtained Model.

D. Communicating results.

Informing competences.

Detailed description and explanation of categories of Taxonomy of Analytical Competences is given in the Appendix to this chapter.

Trans-Discipline Competences: Culture of Sharing

There are two tendencies in development of science and generating new knowledge – from one side the time of "encyclopaedists" passed and the volume of accumulated knowledge in every scientific field grew to the level that a single human is not able to comprehend it; from other – complexity of most of the problems faced by society requires holistic approach, combining knowledge, expertise, and scientific methodologies mastered by different disciplines. Trans-discipline team is the only known way to approach and solve such problems. Also, with its development, society reached the point where humans are unable to comprehend available data, term "Big Data" marks this, without heavy use of Computer Information Technologies. The last couple of decades are characterised by emerging new scientific areas by combining fields such as computing, mathematics, statistics, algorithms, machine learning, artificial intelligence, and so forth, with other disciplines engaged in study of specific domains. Terms like "interdisciplinary" or "multidisciplinary", widely used to emphasize mutual penetration of needed knowledge to solve problems, do not fully explain the specifics of such cooperation. These terms define cooperation preserving relative independence among the fields. The new realities require integration of specific knowledge possessed by different fields on a much higher level – the term "trans-discipline" explains this fusion of expertise (Lotrecchiano & Misra, 2018) to create the necessary synergy.

Generation of new knowledge is always associated with solving problems, where the most essential is to understand different aspects associated with the circumstances, the nature, how problem was identified, what caused the problem, what is the effect, etc. Complexity of problems, number of factors, data, and rules needed to investigate, and constrained human cognitive capacity to comprehend all those aspects leads to unsuitability of uni-discipline analysis as the way to search and generate innovations.

Informing Science and Data Science are examples of trans-disciplines, built on a synergetic contribution of diverse areas of knowledge – from pure technological achievements to process Big Data via intensive use of data analytical techniques toward different methodologies, defined by scientists in the data domain, toward presenting and visualizing results in a compact and informative way. In Chapter 3.4. the trans-disciplinarity is discussed withing the context of cooperative decision making and the culture of sharing as the necessary circumstances for success in building trans-discipline solutions.

"Classical" areas of Information Systems address mostly efficiency of storing retrieved data, but they do not support extracting useful patterns and relations – learning – in the needed level of convenience. In order to gain knowledge from the accumulated complex and complicated data, a special class of computer applications are developing. This, in turn, limits the number of people who possess the necessary expertise to take advantage of the available data resources (Christozov & Rasheva-Yordanova, 2017; Christozov & Toleva-Stoimenova, 2015; Christozov, Toleva-Stoimenova, Rasheva-Yordanova, & Vukarski, 2016). Thus, the Big Data phenomenon imposes a new social divide between those capable of benefiting from Big Data (members of the so-called "Big Data Elite") and those relying on intermediaries in order to "study" from data. This new divide adds new aspects to the already existing digital divide in society (Christozov & Toleva-Stoimenova, 2015). To benefit in full by exploring Big Data requires combining and applying multidisciplinary expertise and diverse competences. Both fields – Informing Science and Data Science – address these emerging challenges.

The following features of the nature of a trans-discipline are:

- Holistic view of problems and solutions: viewing problems and considering all factors influencing the problem, assessing their impact, their interrelation and interdependence. Also, the combined effect on the entire area of related to the problem entities.

- Broader perspective in solving problems: solution is searching by combining expertise, methodology, facts and experience belonging to different knowledge domains.
- Multidimensional nature of reality: understanding and exploring complexity.

Emphasis was given to competences and skills, problem-solving attitude, agility, flexibility, and adaptability rather than knowledge in the form of memorized facts. The following aspects of training professionals capable of contributing to innovative transdisciplinary teams, must be addressed. The major one is migration from transferring knowledge towards developing skills and competences. With the rise of availability of information resources and easiness to acquire information via the Internet, the need for memorizing facts, formulas and techniques is becoming less and less important. Memorizing is switching with abilities to find relevant information, understand it, map it to the problem, and apply information in an appropriate way. This is recognized globally, and education gradually is moving toward training those competences rather than forcing students to "know by heart" facts. This attitude leads to increasing the impact of informing and abilities to identify, access, interpret, and apply information, and therefore, the exposure to the risk of becoming misinformed. The second one is to develop respect toward others' opinions – professional "ethics". Overcoming the natural arrogance of a narrowly trained expert towards the "illiterate" others is one of the major obstacles for the success of trans-discipline teams. The third aspect is the ability to understand correctly the arguments presented in the professional jargon used in other disciplines.

Misinforming is among the major risks for the success of transdisciplinary teams, but it may serve to reach an innovative, out-of-box, solution (Lotrecchiano, 2017). Misunderstanding of particular recommendation, but the acquired meaning is logically sound and applicable.

In a nutshell, those challenges are associated with the inevitability of migration from a narrow and rigid professional training based on knowledge transfer, towards training competences allowing flexibility in adapting to emerging vulnerable circumstances, life-long learning, and agility. Designing the two programs by applying the ideas of trans-disciplinarity, aims to achieve these objectives. The major problem was to find the right balance between mastering competences in a given field and developing skills of acquiring the needed knowledge and developing abilities to apply them when needed in cooperation within a diverse team.

USERS' ROLES IN CURRENT INFORMATION ENVIRONMENT: COMPETENCES NEEDED

Current information environments are associated with two phenomena. From one side the phenomenon of Big Data and from the other side the impact of Internet based social networks. Big Data, defined as 3Vs – volume, velocity, and variety – is associated with data sets that users can observe only via using computer technologies and only in aggregated summarized form. Social networks established an over democratic society where creating, sharing, and using information is allowed to everyone excluding mediator as editors, correctors, censors, etc.

Considering competences associated with these two aspects of informing via Big Data and informing via communicating in social networks, two categories of information expertise, associated with digital literacy, are recognized, and two roles in this communication environment are available to practically every participant – passive user of information, and active creator of information. The current information environment allows every participant to play both roles. Passive role is when user explores available and accessible information – the role of receiver, and active role – is the role of producer and distributor of information. Both need competences as described above, but different roles need also specific competences.

Passive Role

Passive role is associated with learning from data. This includes an efficient use of computer or digital technologies, sophisticated analytical techniques, and a variety of techniques to visualize and represent in a compact form the major properties of data. More specifically, this includes:

- Extracting useful data in appropriate form – retrieval competences. Understanding heterogeneous character of data accumulated in today's organizations; using database technologies – SQL and NonSQL; applying programming languages to specify what is needed and in what format; exploring "modern" technologies such as Data Warehouses and understanding the Extract-Transform-Load (ETL) process, data cubes and OLAP.
- Summarizing and presenting extracted data into useful information – information competences. Competences to understand and use technologies, including tools to extract and present the embedded knowledge in a useful format. This requires an understanding of what a given analytical technique may do, but it especially requires competence to understand what constraints are present when applying given techniques. Mathematical and statistical expertise is absolutely required, but that is not sufficient. Competence in

using different forms of visualization and an ability to interpret them is also needed.

- Generating useful knowledge from acquired information – learning competences. Applying a variety of techniques and description of methods, different topologies to represent "distance" or "likelihood" are the way to enrich understanding of what is hidden within data and to allow for the capturing of knowledge. The ability to critically address the obtained information according to its correspondence to the domain of the problem is also vital. Verifying the sources and considering limitations of applied technologies, exploring suitable tools for avoiding or reducing the risks caused by misunderstanding or misinterpretation, or other instruments of critical assessment of information are necessary components of this competence.
- Building "wisdom" – competences to develop experience. Experience is developed via experimenting with obtained knowledge to prove that in a particular context the effect is what is expected within given circumstances. Wisdom corresponds to understanding the driving forces behind events, the cause-and-effect relationships or the nature of entities and processes in general. Acquiring wisdom requires competences such as abstract thinking and ability for generalization, distinguishing between major, existential factors from secondary, temporary, or specific factors.

Active Role

Active role includes competences to effectively explore data in a way to produce a meaningful resource, secondary information, that will be used by others. Several specific competences can be distinguished to address effective ability to provide information, which may reach receivers and become viral:

- Data collection. Technology allows for the collection of practically unlimited amounts of data, in all known data formats. In most cases data is recorded as it appears without a clear idea about how this data will be used further. We must consider the following: What one can learn from it? How it can be processed? What is its value? Recorded data represents facts, events, and ideas, opinions and thoughts, but often there is no clear distinction between real and imaginary. Both are important and may bring value. Additionally, whether the stored data is original or edited, or even a product of manipulation, it is still considered data. Collecting data with a clear idea about its further life is a critically important skill. In the case of "Small Data" any data item can be considered and assessed by a human; in the case of "Big Data" this will be done by robots and may lead to higher risk of misinterpretation.

- Data storing. There are two issues related to storing data: location and public-private access. Currently, the problem of ownership of data, based on where data is stored, needs clarification and discussion. Clouds offer a new highly convenient option for storing data, but who can guarantee that one's data will be actually removed from all archives of the Cloud. Who can guarantee that private data stored on Cloud will not be accessed by unauthorized users?
- Data accessing. Communication technologies have made the problem of security in accessing data as one of the most sensitive issues today. Access to data may violate certain rules or even laws of privacy. Competence in assessing the property of data from this point of view and establishing a working mechanism to guarantee proper access to data is another component of Big Data literacy.
- Data structuring. The way data is organized directly corresponds to the ways data can be processed and what available analytical techniques can be used to explore and learn from the data. Preparing data for its further usage is another important skill required today.
- Data presentation. Ability to customize output in a way to reach particular category of recipients.

This brief list of specific competences needed in dealing with data allows us to speak about "Data Literacy". Most of those competences are components of general digital literacy, but in the case of Big Data they bring new dimensions toward the needed knowledge and skills. Obtaining those specific competences is a challenge to a particular individual, to a social organization, and to the society as a whole. Big Data is characterized by the inability to explore data directly, but only via computer data processing or data analytic applications. More specifically, lacking above listed competences may result in misinforming of participants involved in either of the two roles. Risks on personal level are associated with:

Information expertise result of following barriers:

- Age and education. In many areas professional competence is accumulated through experience built on top of the education. Still the top professionals have obtained their education well before the Internet era and their competences in using Internet technologies are not obtained via systematic training. Lack of systematic training regarding acquiring and processing information available on the web may result in "white spots" in technology skills.
- Traditional education in the majority of professional areas doesn't include training on information literacy.
- Training on information literacy usually addresses only locating and accessing relevant information, but doesn't stress the skills as verifying information,

visualizing techniques, or extracting useful summaries from large sets of relevant data.

- Systematic training on information literacy is offered as an introductory university course. Dynamics of the development of technologies made the skills obtained in such training irrelevant even at the time of graduation. Developing expertise in a professional field overlaps to some extent with developing skills to deal with information, but often the person faces a difficult decision of where and how to allocate the scarce time and other resources.

Statistics expertise. Learning from Big Data requires a much deeper than usual understanding of the nature of statistics used to represent data, presented in aggregate or summary forms, when the structure of a given population of objects and relationships between objects within the population are communicate via statistical terminology.

For example, distinguishing between information provided by different measures of central tendency - mean, mode and median - is an essential expertise in obtaining information from data without being misled. The following classical case illustrates the difference: Let us assume that one applies for a job with a company with 11 employees claiming that the average salary is $100,000. After being hired, he realizes that the salary of the 10 of the employees is $10,000, and the salary of the manager is $1,000,000. The advertisement message is correct – the average (mean) salary is $100,000, but the average doesn't correctly represent the relationship within this population. For this case any of the two other central measures – median and mode – would be more informative and will represent better the structure of salaries. Existence of outliers excludes mean as an appropriate measure to represent the centrality of a given population. And the expertise needed is in two levels – firstly to understand properties, conditions, and constraints for applying the measure and second – to competences to check and proof that conditions are met.

The way of learning statistics, mostly as a mathematical discipline or as training to perform a given technique, is not productive. Also, in a great number of educational institutions statistics are not covered in the curriculum to the level it deserves. Understanding of information acquired via particular statistical techniques and conforming within the limitations and constraints of their applicability is essential. The technical side of performing the needed calculations is becoming secondary and in the computer era not even necessary. One cannot do manual statistical calculation on Big Data.

Mathematical expertise. To understand, interpret and trust nonlinear relationships is challenging. The reality is complex and rarely does the relationship between objects, events or processes follow a linear pattern. Linear modeling oversimplifies reality and may hide critically important information. On the other side, interpretation of nonlinear models may be difficult for people with limited mathematical background. This results firstly in difficulties of mapping the extracting information to the problem and secondly in trusting the discovered patterns. Even standard mathematical education often doesn't train skills to imagine complex nonlinear relationships, which is essential in developing intuition in understanding and interpreting data.

Competences effective to performing an active role in the reality of the current information-based world are more specific, but equally important. Without proper competences in providing information in proper way or format, the task to inform users is unsolvable. We have to distinguish between barriers based on individual cognitive limits from the barriers preventing organizations from addressing those problems.

Launching a data repository with a potential to store Big Data is often made by chance. Facebook is an example of this. Facebook holds a picture of generations of the globe, and it could serve as source to investigate the cultural differences based on age, gender, and nationality. Geert Hofstede (1984) may only dream of having such a resource; however, the architecture of Facebook doesn't allow for the exploration of available data in an effective manner to allow similar analysis such as the one made by Hofstede. Designers of Facebook made it without addressing this potential and now researchers have to develop special tools if they want to explore available data in a meaningful way. The Cambridge Analytics case exposes also the problem of ethical use of accumulated data and the need of appropriate regulation.

Challenges Faced by Social Entities in Current Information Reality

One of the major problems in designing data repositories is the dynamics of changes. Today we are facing changes in every facet of human life, especially in business activities. Looking at the Big Data issue from the perspective of organizing data repositories within organizations, having in mind the speed of change defines another barrier - the time horizon assumed in designing. "Bug 2000" (or Y2K) illustrates this problem. Databases designed in 70s and 80s with the available at that time technology had only 20- or 30-years long life. Data Bases designed today will prove to be inefficient in 2040ties and accumulated data will not allow comprehensive historical assessment of the process as such study will be seen reasonable then.

One aspect in the dynamics of change is dynamics of development of IT vs. age of individuals in managerial positions who are responsible for specifying the organizational needs. It is expected that in the year 2020 50% of the workforce are represented by "millenniums" - the generation who have got their first jobs in the 21st century. This is the generation who grew up with IT, Internet, Google, and Facebook. But the majority of people on managerial positions, who are responsible for initiating and specifying related to data storing and data exploring projects, are educated, trained and have acquired expertise during the previous century. The difficulties of continued training and understanding technology in a way to see the opportunities that may appear in the next five, ten or twenty years represents a major barrier. This sounds like a "Catch 22" loop - to see the opportunities provided by technology one has to learn from exploring organized data by using appropriate services, which knowledge is essential for organizing data and developing services. Fortunately, this is not a loop, but a spiral, which leads the evolution. Almost all challenges, constraints and problems related to learning from Big Data were described so nicely by Isaak Asimov in 1961 in the short story "Machine that won the war". The role of the man is critical and irreplaceable, but requires clear understanding about limitations, constraints, and potential errors.

Considering challenges faced by a man nowadays, in attempts to become informed and act rationally, the needed competences can be marked as ability to obtain, analyze, and use critically all accessible information via use of computer and communication technologies. Critical, analytical thinking is the key successful factor. Missing to apply systematically and rigorously analysis of obtained data may lead to misinforming. Also, two other sets of competences are required: technical skills for using computer and communication technologies efficiently and effectively enough, and interpersonal, soft, skills to participate in, contribute to, and benefit from a transdisciplinary team. The importance of the last set of competences is growing in parallel to the growing complexity of problems, needed synergy, combining expertise from multiple areas in a way to find an innovative out-of-box solution.

CONCLUSION

The classical proverb, presented here from its Arabian version:

"He who knows not, and knows not that he knows not, is a fool; shun him.

He who knows not, and knows that he knows not, is a student; Teach him.

He who knows, and knows not that he knows, is asleep; Wake him.

He who knows, and knows that he knows, is Wise; Follow him."

which exists as wisdom heritage in many cultural traditions, represents the attitude toward different aspects of competences. There are two parties in the case of informing via communication – providers and receivers of information – and therefore the competence of either of these two parties influences the success of informing and, in the opposite, the risk of misinforming. And the "knowledge" required has three components: knowledge on problem domain; knowledge regarding competences of other party; and knowledge regarding the process of knowledge transfer (competences regarding the usage of the communication system).

Recognized insufficient or inadequate competences or knowledge is the reason for the needs of obtaining information from external sources and justifies the execution of informing via communication. From other side, lack of competence creates many ways to misinform the receiver. Starting with unrecognized lack of adequate knowledge on the sender's side, to wrong interpretation of the obtained information caused by inadequate competences on the side of receiver. Misinforming hazard may lead to wrong decisions and wrong actions and may directly harm the receiver. As a side effect, the misinforming may also harm the reputation of the sender, as losing the image of reliable and trustful information provider. The information asymmetry between the two parties establishes circumstances to justify the need of communication but also causes the likelihood of occurring the misinforming hazard. Next chapter is dedicated to information asymmetry as causing misinforming.

The above proverb also considers confidence related to lack of competences "*He who knows not, and knows not that he knows not.*" This is a direct reference to Dunning-Kruger effect (see Chapter 5.) and shows that the likelihood of risk of misinforming when combining high confidence with low competence is too high. This also corresponds to lack of analytical competences as related to "critical thinking".

Finally, misinforming may lead to an exotic, "out-of-box", innovative solution of a problem when interpretation of provided information does not follow routine or expected ways, as assumed by the sender, but happen to be relevant and useful according to receiver's view on the problem. These positive aspects of misinforming are discussed further in Chapter 5.

REFERENCES

Asimov I. (1961). The Machine That Won the War. *The Magazine of Fantasy & Science Fiction.*

Buckland, M. (1991). Information and Information Systems. Praeger.

Christozov, D., Chukova, S., & Mateev, P. (2006). A Measure of Risk Caused by Information Asymmetry in e-Commerce. *Journal of Issues in Informing Science and Information Technology*, *3*, 147–158. doi:10.28945/879

Christozov, D., & Mateev, P. (2005). Assessment of Information Asymmetry. *Pliska Studia Mathematica Bulgarica*, *17*, 27–38.

Christozov, D., & Rasheva-Yordanova, K. (2017). Data Literacy: Developing Skills on Exploring Big Data Applications. [IJDLDC]. *International Journal of Digital Literacy and Digital Competence*, *8*(2), 14–38. doi:10.4018/IJDLDC.2017040102

Christozov, D., Rasheva-Yordanova, K., & Toleva-Stoimenova, S. (2018). *Analytical Competences in Big Data Era: Taxonomy. Proceedings of ICERi2018*, Seville, Spain. 10.21125/iceri.2018.2731

Christozov, D., & Toleva-Stoimenova, S. (2015). Big Data Literacy - a New Dimension of Digital Divide: Barriers in learning via exploring Big Data. In J. Girard, K. Berg, D. Klein, & I. G. I. Global (Eds.), *Strategic Data Based Wisdom in the Big Data Era* (pp. 156–170). doi:10.4018/978-1-4666-8122-4.ch009

Christozov, D., Toleva-Stoimenova, S., Rasheva-Yordanova, K., & Vukarski, I. (2016). Developing Big Data Competences in the Digital Era, Proceedings of "Big Data, Knowledge and Control Systems Engineering - BdKCSE'2016. Sofia.

Heller, J. (1961). *Catch-22*. Simon & Schuster.

Hofstede, G. (1984). *Culture's Consequences: International Differences in Work-Related Values* (2nd ed.). SAGE Publications.

Lotrecchiano, G. (2017). Personal communication during InSITE-2017.

Lotrecchiano, G., & Misra, S. (2017). Observational and Analytic Features for the Study of Transdisciplinary Teams. InSITE 2017: Informing Science & IT Education Conferences: Vietnam, 063-064.

Lotrecchiano, G., & Misra, S. (2019). Transdisciplinary knowledge producing teams: Toward a complex systems perspective. *Informing Science [InformingSciJ]. The International Journal of Emerging Transdiscipline*, *21*, 41–50.

Lumina Foundation. (2014). *The degree qualification profile*. Lumina Foundation. https://www.luminafoundation.org/files/resources/dqp.pdf

APPENDIX: TAXONOMY OF ANALYTICAL COMPETENCES

This taxonomy is designed to address efforts to reduce the risk of misinforming, but it is more generally applicable. To address each of categories of competencies, data, relevant to the problem, must be available and its properties known. Bur more important, the critical assessment of available information in the light of problem domain is needed to assess information validity and applicability. This is a nutshell represents analytical competencies. Following this leading principle, the categories of Analytical Competences can be classified as ability to accomplish the following activities:

A. Identify and Analyze Existence of a Problem

This category of competences addresses ability to analyze particular circumstances, to place facts into given context and identify existence and formulate the problem. These competences usually are defined as "domain" knowledge. Proper structuring or framing of the problem is critical to achieving relevant and actionable outcomes. Sometimes, analytics requires inputs via scenarios or modeling the reality caused the problem and obtaining data. Organizations need to define relevant and realistic scenarios that will drive analyses and interpretation of results.

Identify Existence of a Problem

Existence of a problem is defined by comparisons between expected outcomes and data describing the real state. Analytical skills include accepting variability in given boundaries, based on randomness of the uncontrolled factors. Understanding whether the difference between expected and achieved is based on random circumstances or not. The latest indicates existence of a problem and defines the research goal. Data Scientist has to clarify the problem and narrows the scope of the study into understandable, simple, short, and measurable goals, which might be set out in question format.

Identify What Caused the Problem

This category of competences covers ability to understand the context of appearing the problem and may allow assessing applicability of solution.

The main purpose here is to make sure that all stakeholders understand all aspects of the problem – who, what, where, when, why, and how of the problem:

- **Who**: Who is causing the problem? Who says this is a problem? Who are (not) impacted?
- **What**: What is happen if not solved? What are the symptoms? What are the impacts?
- **Where:** Where does the problem occur? Where does it have an impact?
- **When:** When does this problem occur? When did it first start occurring?
- **Why:** Why does the problem occur?
- **How:** How should this system work? How is it currently handled?

Then, the analyst has to possess competences to answer questions like the following:

- What are factors (inputs) causing the problem?
- What are the relevant variables?
- What is the acceptable variability of uncontrolled inputs?

A "cause and effect" diagram, often called a "fishbone" diagram, is used in brainstorming to identify possible causes of a problem and in sorting ideas into useful categories. It demonstrates the relationship between effects and the categories of their causes and to find the root causes.

In this stage, the variables that need to be predicted have been identified, but also the category of problem solution, whether predicting a particular value – regression, or assigning to given category – classification; and the type of learning – supervised or unsupervised; to define the scope of applicable analytical methods.

Identify Whether the Problem is Decomposable

Once the actual problem is identified the next step is to decompose the problem into smaller distinct sub-problems each with their own goals, data, computations, and actions. Often there may be many valid ways to decompose the problem, each leading to a different solution. There may be hidden dependencies or constraints that only emerge in the process of developing a solution.

This category of competences requires deep understanding of problem and interrelations between variables. The aim is to gain additional insights into the problem and also to explore independence or loose relationship which may allow solving multiple, but simpler, problems instead.

Assess Whether Factors With Impact on Problem's Solution Are Under Control

The "cause and effect" diagram also helps the analysts explore the main variables, understand which are in their control, which are measurable, etc. In addition to the cause-and-effect competences, identifying factors, which are fully under control of the decision maker from factors, which depend on environment, require understanding the limitation of available data, and impact of random forces. The independent (controllable) variables also referred to as *predictors* are used to predict the values of dependent variables.

B. Identify and Assess Information Needs, Data Quality, and Whether Data is Relevant to the Problem

A critical analysis and examination of the data itself needs to be considered. Selecting data that is used in an analysis, proper filtering of irrelevant data, ensuring high data integrity, and data element definition are core in any analytics process. This category of competences addresses ability to analyze credibility of data explored. Additionally, this category includes competences to select analytical tool (technique, method) applicable to the problem and to the properties of explored data. These competences usually are defined as "information competences".

Identify What Information is Needed

Understanding problem domain, and the context in which the problem arises, defines how to assess the relevance of data. Defining which variables influence the output is the first step in assessing whether the further analysis may bring reliable result to find a solution of the problem. Identifying which are the input variables, whether they are controllable or not, is of critical importance for the success of data analytics.

Where Relevant Information Can Be Found (Sources)?

Whether available data provides sufficient resource for building the model with acceptable level of certainty? Is it possible to enrich information base to improve the analysis?

Identifying a wider variety of data sources may increase the probability of finding hidden patterns and correlations. For example, to provide insight, it can be beneficial to identify as many types of related internal and external data sources as possible, especially when it is unclear exactly what to look for. Internal data includes policy data, insurance application documents, claim data, claim adjuster notes, incident photographs, call center agent notes and emails. In the case of external datasets, a list of possible third-party data providers, such as data markets and publicly available datasets, are compiled. Some forms of external data may be embedded within blogs or other types of content-based web sites, in which case they may need to be harvested via automated tools. Data providers from third parties, for example social network data or voluntarily contributed data bears the risk of being manipulated. For example, many spurious social media messages could be generated in order to push a statistical index derived from these data in one or another way in case it is known that the index is calculated from such data.

Ability to Access, to Retrieve, and to Structure Relevant Data

The Data Scientist has to collect sufficiently representative data in order to make sense of the problem at hand. Data can be obtained in several ways - for example by downloading it from a server, by querying a database, or by connecting to a Web API. However, even just text can come in multiple forms, sometimes, the data comes in a compressed form or in a binary format such as Microsoft Excel. This subcategory of Data Scientist's competences covers technical competences needed to obtain data and to present data in a form suitable for further processing. It includes:

- access and query many different databases and data sources (*RDBMS, NoSQL, NewSQL*),
- integrating the data into an analytics-driven data source (e.g., *OLAP, warehouse, data lake, …*)
- structuring the data in proper format as the data gathered from different has various shapes and sizes.

One of the major challenges researchers are facing is "How to integrate all the data from different sources to maximize the value of data."

Ability to Clean and to Explore the Acquired Data (Transformation Stage)

Once Data Scientist obtained the data he/she has to prepare the data from a raw form into a suitable form for data modeling. Transforming stage includes cleaning and removing any noise from the data (remove inconsistencies, dealing with missing data, etc.), normalization, aggregation and generalization. After the transformation and scaling of data duplication, i.e., removing redundancy and efficiently organizing data. This is very important in Big Data projects, which often involve terabytes of data to work with. But the trade-off between cleansing data and striving for quality data needs clear justification. Cleansing data may always result in loss of potentially useful insights.

The transforming stage is following by data exploration stage. It is like the brainstorming of data analysis. It includes analyzing the data and findings, identifying bias, patterns and dependencies among raw data in a way to allow understanding and validation of data limitations and quality. Feature engineering is an essential part of building any intelligent system. Feature engineering deals with feature selection (cutting down the features that add more noise than information) and construction (creating new features). It is an important part of cleaning data because it greatly reduces noise and the problem with dimensionality and can even address the problems with sparse data. That means the model will have an easier time navigating missing values and outliers to more efficiently learn relationships in your data.

Ability to Verify and to Assess Credibility of Obtained Information

Assessing trustfulness of data is essential to justify output of data analytics. The slogan "garbage in, garbage out" is fully applicable.

Credibility is usually used to evaluate non-numeric data. It refers to the objective and subjective components of the believability of a source or message. Credibility of data has three key factors: reliability of data sources, data normalization, and the time when the data are produced.

The data collected by these authoritative scientific bodies generally have high data authenticity and credibility because researchers in these organizations generally obey research ethics and follow good scientific practices. However sometimes Big Data are used from commercial companies or often comes from systems not directly controlled by an organization and may contain inherent biases or outright false values (for example because of bots in social media).

Ability to Assess Data Quality

There are several measures of data quality as completeness, consistency, uniqueness, integrity, conformity, accuracy, precision, timeliness, reproducibility, etc. This category covers competences to choose the right measures for given case, and skills to measure whether data satisfy quality expectations. A different set of skills and tools are often used for detecting and correcting errors and inconsistencies from a data set in order to improve its quality. A good understanding of architecture, technology, corporate culture, and other factors is often important. Besides a number of essential technical skills are also required when dealing with the data itself including parsing, standardizing, record linkage/matching, data scrubbing/cleansing, data profiling and data auditing/monitoring. These skills are often extensively used when conducting projects such as data migrations where data quality improvements need to be achieved in tight timescales.

C. Choosing and Applying Data Processing Tool

Understanding Limitations of Applied Analytical Tool

The truth is there is not a single best algorithm that is universally better in all situations –choosing the best algorithm depends on the problem type, size, available resources, etc. Moreover, machines lack common sense, so humans are still needed to supervise.

Increased capacity to process Big Data creates an inherent tendency towards include irrelevant data. On the other hand, used analytical techniques as a "black box" may mislead analysts in interpreting results in the domain context. The black box decision-making is a serious limitation as many policies execution or governance requirements need clear explanations of decisions, e.g. explain to customer why transaction was blocked.

The higher data volume increases the probability that the data files and documents may contain inherently valuable and sensitive information. In this regard, Big data analytics and purely automated processing may use personal data to make decisions affecting individuals. It can relate to privacy and security concern which lead to some ethical challenges. Sometimes during the translation of cultural clichés and stereotypes into empirically verifiable datasets, subjectivity is introduced. In some circumstances even displaying different advertisements can mean that the users of that service are being profiled in a way that perpetuates discrimination, for example on the basis of race, sex, political opinion, religion, etc. Data Scientists must have experience in dealing with such problems.

Map Obtained Data to Analytical Too: Assessment of Relevance

A critical step in Data Science is to identify an analytic technique that will produce the desired action. Whereas predictive analytics tells what will happen, prescriptive analytics suggests what to do. Prescriptive analytics can identify optimal solutions, often for the allocation of scarce resources. Organizations typically move from descriptive to predictive to prescriptive analytics. Another way of describing this progression is: what happened – why did it happen, what will happen, how can we make it happen. Things can get a little more complicated because the lines between the different types of tools can be a little fuzzy. Some business intelligence tools have data mining and predictive analytics capabilities. Some predictive analytics tools include streaming capabilities.

Lack of Adequate Competences

This is another category of technical competences – competences to apply the right tool in the right way. This category includes competences about the computer application – analytical method implemented, and characteristics of data required. In addition, how to transform raw data to suit the tool's input format. The Data Scientist may encounter a wide variety of implementation constraints. They can be conceptualized, however, in the context of five dimensions that compete for your attention: analytic complexity, speed, accuracy & precision, data size, and data complexity. Balancing these dimensions is a zero-sum game - an analytic solution cannot simultaneously exhibit all five dimensions, but instead must make trades between them. Achieving a desired analytic action often requires combining multiple analytic techniques into a holistic, end-to-end solution.

Synthesizes Solution

This category of competences addresses ability to use effectively data analytical tools. It is required specific competences in mathematics, statistics, artificial intellect, and especially efficient use of computer technologies. These competences usually are defined as "machine learning" competences.

Setting Assumptions and Checking Their Validity

Competences to define assumptions in applying analytical techniques are essential to allow beneficial interpretation and justification of obtained results. Data scientist should be able to generate hypotheses about the ways the concerned system can behave if it is changed in a specific manner. As stated by Ockham's razor the simpler is better so that less assumption is preferable. Clearly, attributes that are not in the model will have no effect on the model's predictions.

Hypothesis generation allows:

- to experiment with theories about the data;
- to take a systems-thinking approach to the problem to be solved;
- to build more sophisticated models based on prior hypotheses and understanding.

Comparing Different Applicable Courses of Action

Choosing the most informative tool for given case, requires ability to compare tools on the base of the properties of available data and data analytics objectives. The Data Scientist have to choose a machine learning algorithm or statistical methodology that suits the data, use case, and available computational resources. Many Data

Scientists choose to build and test multiple modelling methodologies to explore outputted predictions.

Modelling is where art meets science. The art comes from the a priori intuition and assumptions on the relationship between each predictor variable—i.e., the variables used to predict the outcome—and the response variable. The science comes from running quantitative analysis on the data and using a large collection of models. Model selection involves limiting the number of parameters and ultimately selecting a model that is understandable and actionable by stakeholders. Question to consider are:

- Does the model appear valid and accurate related to the launch on the dataset?
- Does the model output/behavior make sense to the domain experts?
- Do the parameter values make sense in the context of the domain?
- Is the model sufficiently accurate to meet the goal?
- Are there any tolerable or intolerable errors occurring?
- Are there enough data or we need more inputs? Are there any transformations or adjustments of the data to be performed?
- Will the kind of model chosen support the runtime environment?
- Is a different form of the model required to address the business problem?

Verifying Obtained Model

This category includes competences to apply techniques (cross validation and receiver operating characteristic (ROC) curve analysis, etc.) to verify applicability of the obtained model.

The Data Scientist can estimate how effective it is by applying it to some of the training data and comparing the prediction to the known value. Usually, the model is tested in a larger set of cases and it helps in defining the scope of circumstances where it is applicable. This part always precedes deploying or presenting the model.

D. Communicating Results

Once Data Scientist derived the intended insights from the model, he/she have to represent them in a user-friendly, re-usable and intelligible format that the different key stakeholders in the project can understand. Presenting information in such a way that people can consume it effectively is a key challenge that requires to be aware of data visualization tools, techniques and technologies used for creating images, diagrams, or animations to communicate, understand, and improve the results of Big Data analyses. Data scientists have to choose from different visualization methods depending on the machine learning model and other Data Science process flow characteristics.

Data visualization combines the fields of communication, psychology, statistics, and art, with an ultimate goal of communicating the data in a simple yet effective and visually pleasing way.

Informing Competences

Internet, and especially current stage of development marked as social networks, is highly democratic media to access and share information. It allows everyone to participate in both roles – as a user of information, and as creator and provider of information. Informing competence can viewed first as ability to become informed, but also ability to inform others. It includes two set of competences covering the two basic roles in a communication process.

The role of a sender (the active role) includes:

- ability to formulate meaning – mapping tacit to explicit knowledge.
- ability to communicate knowledge – address particular and specific receivers or groups.

The role of a receiver (the passive role):

- ability to locate and retrieve information relevant to the identified problem.
- ability to verify information.
- ability to understand and interpret information in the context of the problem's domain.
- ability to map information to the problem in a way to solve it.

For example, the two components of basic literacy - reading and writing - correspond to the passive role (reading) and active role (writing) of a literate person. These competences have many varieties such as reading particular alphabet and texts written in given language; and writing by using pen and paper or chisel and stone again by using alphabet (or hieroglyphs) and language. Computer literacy refers mostly to competences of using the instrument rather addressing the actual ability to deal with information. Digital literacy as a more general term covers all aspects of informing via the use of digitally presented data. In this context Informing Literacy is the most general umbrella term, representing all aspects of the process from exploring tools, used to convey information, till learning, or adopting information, and teaching, as well as sharing knowledge.

Chapter 3
Information Asymmetry

ABSTRACT

The chapter discusses "information asymmetry" as the critically important phenomenon for the very existence of communication. Information asymmetry is the reason the parties need to communicate to allow acquiring needed information and reducing the uncertainty in making decisions, But, from the other side extends the competences as the factor causing misinforming. The chapter presents misinforming hazards by adding the issue of asymmetric competence and double-sided asymmetry. Information asymmetry is a necessary condition for communication, but also is a factor that may cause misunderstanding.

INTRODUCTION

Failures in correct adoption of meaning provided via communication are caused by the phenomenon known as "information asymmetry". Information asymmetry is a natural reason justifying the need to acquire information from outside – via communication in a way to solve the given problem. One of the parties has information or knowledge of what the other party needs but does not possess. From other side, asymmetrical information, asymmetrical background, or asymmetrical view on the problem is necessary but also is the nutrition for the risk of misunderstanding.

The informational misbalance in the area of business was described for the first time by Kenneth J. Arrow (1963), who introduces it as "moral hazard" related to the medical industry. Later, George Akerlof (1970) used the term asymmetric information, noticing that in a market with asymmetrical information the average value of the commodity tends to go down, even for commodities with a perfect quality. Moreover, it is possible for such a market to decay to the point of nonexistence. Because of

DOI: 10.4018/978-1-6684-8800-3.ch003

information asymmetry, unscrupulous sellers can embellish the items and defraud the buyer. As a result, many buyers with a risk-averse attitude will avoid certain types of purchases or will not be willing to spend much on a given item. On the other side those who obtained the product experience unsatisfaction.

The chapter uses ideas originated in Christozov D. and Mateev P. (2005) and Christozov D., Chukova S. and Mateev P. (2006). A more complete explanation was published in Christozov D., Chukova S. and Mateev P. (2009). The approach of quantifying the information asymmetry is explored in Part 2 of the book and developed in chapter 2.1. as the difference between actual and assumed properties of a product.

The chapter is organized into the following two sections. The first one is used for defining information asymmetry, followed by the section defining this phenomenon in the context of misinforming hazards by using a simple communication process.

DEFINITION OF INFORMATION ASYMMETRY

Information asymmetry occurs when one party in a communication transaction has more or better information than the other party. The term originates in economics, addressing commercial transactions, and its impact on markets. The case was called asymmetrical information and related markets are called markets with asymmetrical information. Typically, it is the seller that knows more about the product than the buyer, however, it is possible for the reverse to be true – for the buyer to be better informed compared to the seller.

Examples, where the seller usually has better information than the buyer are numerous and include used-car salespersons, stockbrokers, real estate, and life insurance. On the other hand, there are situations where the buyer is usually better informed than the seller, e.g., in buying property insurance, when a buyer purchases insurance for a property with hidden problems.

The aim of a communication process is to allow one party – the receiver – to obtain information this party needs to solve a problem, or to reduce her/his uncertainty in making a decision regarding how to solve the problem. The other party – the sender – possesses information which may help the receiver in decreasing this uncertainty, or to become informed. Communication is meaningful if the receiver does not possess the information the sender has. Or this is the case when the information asymmetry as the necessary condition for communication exists. This is natural to any meaningful informing process – the sender provides information which the receiver doesn't have but expects and assumes that it is needed and useful to solve her or his problem.

Information Asymmetry exists in, and it justifies the need of, every communication process, but to a different degree. The objective of the informing process is to reduce uncertainty faced by receiver, based on lack of confidence or lack of certainty regarding the output of action according to given decision. By using the information passed on by the sender, the receiver expects to reach the needed level of certainty regarding the decision and to act in a way to solve the problem. If there is no such asymmetric information, which the one-side (receiver) needs but doesn't possess and the other side (sender) has and can provide, the process will not accomplish its objectives.

INFORMATION ASYMMETRY IN THE CONTEXT OF MISINFORMING

Incorrect, not as intended, interpretation of the received message, is a side effect of the informing via communication process. It may cause significant qualitative and quantitative losses to the receiver. But also, wrong selecting of meaning and not appropriate formulation of the message by the sender who misinterpret what other party needs, why, and how the receiver will interpret the information, is also result of information asymmetry. In this way, information asymmetry, in either of the two directions, may lead to misinforming and may spoil the image of sender and also receiver's trust toward sender's competence and in general. These side effects may be described as misunderstanding, misinterpretation, mis-inference, etc. and represent the misinforming hazards. The harm is basically to the receiver, but such outcome of informing process may harm the sender's reputation as well.

The two-sided information asymmetry hazard needs consideration in the case of the informing process. An oversimplified process is described in Figure 1. From one side – the sender has to understand the receiver's problem in a way to be able to identify what information among available is relevant and useful in the context of the receiver's problem. Also, to formulate the message in a way to support receiver's correct and easy understanding and adopting the meaning of provided information. And finally, to present it in a trustful way to encourage the receiver to use it. On the other side, the receiver has to understand and interpret the message in the context of her or his own problem, and to adopt the understood meaning in a way to behave according to the knowledge acquired as a result of this communication. In both cases, the corresponding party explores information based on his or her own background, bias, competences, meaning of used terminology (professional jargon, dialects), etc.

Figure 1. Risks in informing process
(Adopted from Christozov et al., 2006)

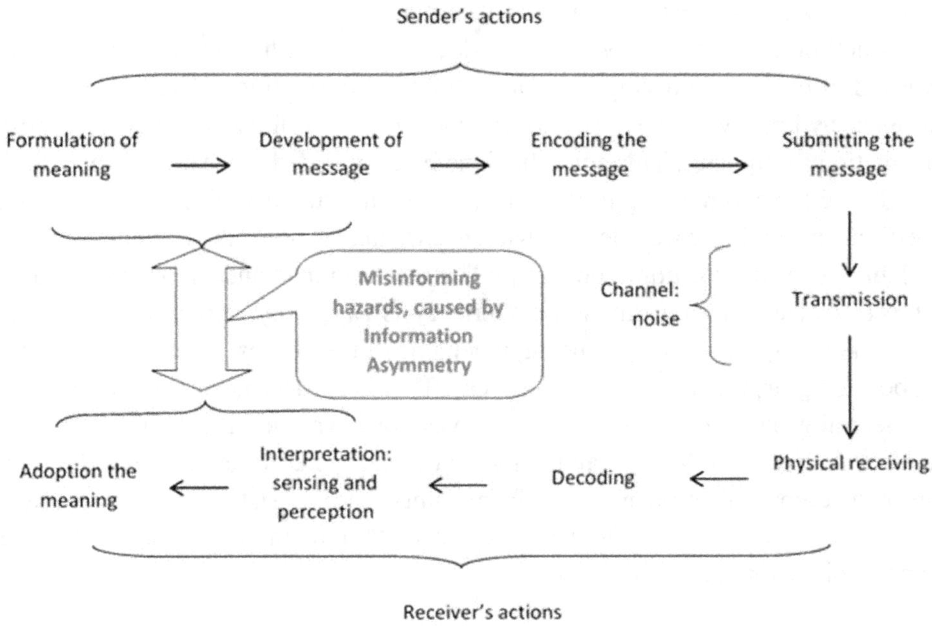

The success of communication depends on variety of factors regarding the properties of interpersonal relationship between the two parties, such as efficiency and effectiveness of the communication process, trust and confidence, content provided in the message, the form and formulation of the meaning in the message, the acceptability of provided information, and many others.

Information asymmetry, as a natural property of any communication process, may cause misunderstanding between parties and therefore may erode the trust between them as well as lead to wrong decisions. This is especially critical in indirect communication between the two parties, as in e-commerce, because the entire information is held by the message and there are no ways to clarify it beyond what was preliminary defined. Additional aspects, as circumstances, body language, environment, feedback options, etc. are not available in the case of indirect informing process.

In commerce, a customer playing the role of receiver, who is missing adequate knowledge about the product, may come up with the wrong purchase decision. From the point of view of the seller, a customer's misunderstanding about the properties of the products may result in the customer's dissatisfaction and losses in image and market positions. Often, the customer does not know exactly what s/he is buying, and the seller doesn't know completely why the customer is buying the product and how she or he is intending to use it. The two parties will benefit from overcoming the information asymmetry as well as from introducing techniques to evaluate and share the risk caused by the information asymmetry.

Reduction of losses caused by the risk associated with misinforming may be achieved either by improving the quality of the information flows between two parties or by improving the quality of the message transmitted in a way to address information asymmetry. This could be done by established mechanisms that allow considering the and reacting to feedback, maintain a rich list of Frequently Asked Questions, providing vocabulary of used terms, etc. Many of those techniques are available solely in direct communication. That is why understanding, and assessment of the risk caused by information asymmetry is especially important in indirect communication, such as e-commerce, when one of the parties (sender) is de-facto, a robot using a predefined set of answers. This is critical nowadays because of exponential grow of online commerce transactions. The boom on-line commerce has been fueled by COVID-19 and obligatory isolation. Different forms, helping in improving communication processes from point of view of risk of misinforming via implementing reasonable techniques, are needed to implement in a way to increase the probability for successful informing.

Factors, Associated With Information Asymmetry, Causing Misinforming

A formal view on Information Asymmetry requires to define what are factors for this risk. A communication process is an exchange of information between two parties – a sender and a receiver – through a given communication channel. The stages in a simple informing process are illustrated in Figure 1.

The sender sends out a message addressing the receiver's problem. The content of the message is a sign of the sender's idea of what could be useful to the receiver. The message is composed to represent the meaning as it is understood by the sender as relevant and useful. Its content, structure, form of presenting, wording, etc. are influenced by the sender's judgment regarding receiver's capability to understand and interpret the message correctly. Or the two factors applicable in composing the message – what is useful, and the receiver's ability to comprehend the message are results of information the sender has regarding the receiver and the receiver's problem.

The message is encoded to make it suitable for transmission through the communication channel and submitted to the receiver. The communication channel is another factor that may influence the success of informing, but it is out of the scope of the book. Most of the technological tools developed so far to support communication are focusing on the physical delivery and correct encoding/decoding of the message. Currently we may assume that this set of problems is resolved in communication via computer information technologies to an acceptable level.

From the receiver's side, the process also includes several stages. It starts with the physical delivery of the message followed by its decoding. The decoding is the ability of the receiver to read the message, which requires an agreement between the two parties about the language used in the message. Next step - understanding – the proper interpretation of the message is essential for the success of informing. The last phase – adoption of the information is when the receiver utilizes the obtained information in making decisions in a way to act. It depends on the success of all the previous stages in the communication process. Failure in any of them results in a failure in communication and therefore in correctly informing the receiver. Receiver's competencies to read, understand, interpret, and map the message to the problem domain are the factors that influence the success of the process.

The stage of interpretation of the content of the message is critical to whether the message informs or misinforms the receiver. The interpretation is based on receiver's expertise, perceptions, bias, etc. Success in this stage is seriously influenced by the information asymmetry defined as the difference in expertise and background of sender and receiver on the domain subject of the addressed problem.

The last stage, the adoption of the information, depends on whether the obtained information, as it is understood, is valuable to the receiver. Also, it is greatly influenced by the level of sender's credibility with the receiver. In a face-to-face communication, the trust may be revealed by many factors additional to solely the content of the message, such as whether the communication takes place in a trustful environment, what is sender's personality, sender's body language, possibilities of clarifying the meaning of the message in an easy and natural dialog, etc. The majority of these factors are irrelevant in indirect communication, and they have to be compensated by the content, the composition, and wording of the message.

From this perspective, two-sided information asymmetry is observed nowadays – sender may not understand fully, in all details and aspects, the receiver's problem in a way to provide truly relevant, useful and in the right form information; and receiver doesn't know all circumstances, sources, and data processing the receiver has accomplished in composing the message to interpret it correctly.

Some Issues

There are many issues and problems naturally arising within an indirect communication environment and as expected, reflect on the success of informing. Some of these issues are:

1. Whether the meaning of the message as sender intended to provide matches the meaning understood by the receiver?
2. What is the risk and related effects caused by wrong interpretation of the meaning of the message from a receiver's point of view as well as from sender's point of view?
3. Whether the receiver maps correctly the obtained via interpreting information knowledge to the problem domain?
4. Whether the received information via the communication process inspires sufficient trust to encourage receiver to act?
5. Weather parties recognize the existence of information asymmetry and account for the related consequences.
6. How should a communication process be modified in order to increase the chance for success?

Some of those issues are directly linked to information asymmetry, but for others the relationship is not obvious. In commerce the information asymmetry, as a natural property of any communication process, may result in misunderstanding between sellers and buyers and therefore may erode the trust between them. For example, trust related issues may cause to desert from action. It is not direct result of information asymmetry, but as Arrow and Akerlof observed, recognized information asymmetry leads to reducing the trust between parties. This is more visible in indirect communication between the two parties, as in e-commerce. In direct communication many additional factors may contribute, but the major one is the possibility for immediate feedback, clarification, and adjustment. In indirect communication, especially trading via Internet, producers need to explore techniques like Customer Related Management (CRM) to acquire more comprehensive information about customers and their needs and preferences, and what kind of problems they are facing, and what kind of works they expect to accomplish. In general, to find an answer to why they are going to buy this product.

From the customer's point of view, a lack of adequate knowledge about the product may result in wrong purchase decision. The two parties will benefit from overcoming the information asymmetry as well as from introducing techniques to evaluate and share the risk caused by the information asymmetry. An instrument used in sharing risk is via including a warranty statement into purchase contract in the form "If you are not fully satisfied money back". Warranty is typically a costly policy that needs a careful evaluation of cost-benefit outcomes. Last part of the book explores different aspects and models of warranty addressing the risks caused by misinforming.

Reducing the information asymmetry, by increasing the level of mutual understanding between the two parties may result in better informing and better decisions. Exploring the feedback, within a certain commercial activity, increases the seller's understanding about the client's expertise to correctly understand available information and, potentially, her or his ability to map the identified as reliable description of product's properties to the receiver's problems. This allows them to compose their messages in a way to target the specifics in the client's backgrounds. Market Studies define groups of customers with similar needs and interests, and allow sellers to address the group, as a whole, in an appropriate level of complexity. Customizing or personalizing the message is becoming important, even the key to success, in trading nowadays.

The misinforming risk, caused by information asymmetry, could be high enough to incur serious consequences and it is important to be studied, understood, quantified, and addressed. In commerce, a significant percentage of customers do not understand that such a risk exists. The customers confidence about her/his ability to understand correctly a certain message is often overestimated, which may lead to poor decisions and harm.

E-commerce offers great opportunities for enriching the seller-customer relationship. But, because of information asymmetry, the trust between parties often erodes. It requires development of tools to enhance mutual understanding in a way to overcome side effects caused by misinforming. Sellers/Producers aiming to promote their products by covering the risk of misinforming, usually assume a negligible impact of this risk on their business, without careful study of its magnitude. Growing customer's awareness and requirements towards product's quality, and especially to whether the product suits well to specific customer's needs, must force producers/sellers to pay special attention to this risk.

CONCLUSION

In direct, face-to-face communication, by asking and answering the right questions, the two parties may avoid misunderstanding and wrong interpretation and assessment of validity of provided information. In indirect communication, the risk of misinforming is much higher, because the designer of application must anticipate what are all the reason different categories of user to search the information. Or designers of computer information systems need to implement answers to questions users may ask in advance. This is to design the system in assuming the scope of its usage, but the actual users may use it for something else.

REFERENCES

Akerlof, G. (1970). The Market for "Lemons": Quality Uncertainty and the Market Mechanism. The Quarterly Journal of Economics, 84(3). Oxford University Press.

Arrow, K. (1963). Uncertainty and Welfare Economics of Medical Care. *The American Economic Review*, *53*(5), 942–973.

Christozov, D., Chukova, S., & Mateev, P. (2006). A Measure of Risk Caused by Information Asymmetry in e-Commerce. *Journal of Issues in Informing Science and Information Technology*, *3*, 147–158. doi:10.28945/879

Christozov, D., Chukova, S., & Mateev, P. (2009). Informing Processes, Risks, Evaluation of the Risk of Misinforming. In *Foundations of Informing Science* (pp. 323–356). ISI.

Christozov, D., & Mateev, P. (2005). Assessment of Information Asymmetry. *Pliska Studia Mathematica Bulgarica*, *17*, 27–38.

Chapter 4
The Role of Mediators in Informing Process

ABSTRACT

Chapter four addresses problems caused by informing via mediators and introduces information mediators as another risky factor for misinforming. In the cascade, two-sided asymmetry by adding mediators' subjective assumptions in a multi-steps process from the original data source toward the end-user's problem solving, are elaborated in a way to high light the factors and circumstances associated with misinforming risks. The role of the human mediators – information brokers – is discussed in the context of misinforming hazards. The issue of technology mediated informing is also addressed by emphasizing different categories of nowadays technologies. This chapter also presents and explores different topologies of communication processes according to their potential to mislead receivers. Topologies are contrasted according to their cardinality and feed-back availability.

INTRODUCTION

The components of an informing process in highly simple settings were presented in the previous chapter. They are discussed from point of view of competence' and information asymmetry of the two parties and how the asymmetry may result in misinforming. In this chapter the informing process is considered by discussing the influence made by involvement of other parties in the process – mediators.

Nowadays many ways and forms to acquire information exist. Acting is based on tacit knowledge, which is a result of:

DOI: 10.4018/978-1-6684-8800-3.ch004

- Combined information, acquired from different channels, interpreted and adopted according to attitude of receiver toward sources – how trustful are senders?
- The content and form of presentation – how well the received information correlates with existing knowledge and receiver expectations?
- The possibility to trace the path of acquiring, manipulating, changing, and updating the facts and data? And finally,
- How does newly received information correspond with the receiver background knowledge and assessment of the problem?

The first section of the chapter briefly comments different forms of delivery of information by considering two parameters – cardinality and existence of feedback – these two parameters allow to define several categories of the informing process topologies. Any of those informing forms is exposed to the risk of misinforming but in a different way. A general assumption is that existence of the feedback allows to reduce misunderstanding. Every one of the discussed topologies tries to meet the objectives to inform correctly, and this has an impact on the way information is provided to reach the end-user.

In general, it is very rare nowadays for the receiver to directly acquire information from its original source. Information mediators are playing a more and more significant role. Either human or robots may serve as mediator. The role of mediators in the informing process is associated with selecting, processing, and presenting information. Mediators serve as information brokers and the role information brokers play in creating an informing environment nowadays is discussed as well in the context of misinforming likelihood and impact. The second section is dedicated to the role of information brokers.

Nowadays we may observe two cases of mediating informing: informing via human mediators – infobrokers; and informing via technology – machinery delivered information. The later includes both observing reality via machinery tools as microscopes or telescopes with corresponding imprecisions and obtaining information via data processing by sophisticated computer software without clear understanding about executed transformations on raw data. The following section is dedicated to these two kinds of mediators: professional human mediators – information brokers; and technology mediated informing, including discussion on intelligent computer applications as artificial intelligence, machine learning and data processors, and tools used to observe reality.

The competences needed to become successfully informed, as described in the previous chapter, are extremely demanding. It is common nowadays that the end-user often does not directly access the original, raw data. Using competent mediators, who can assist in obtaining and analyzing data to instill only the true relevant information and to present it in an understandable form, is inevitable.

TOPOLOGIES OF INFORMING PROCESS: CARDINALITY AND FEEDBACK

Different processes of informing, by using different media or structures are discussed in this section. Topology is defined as the structure of the way of delivery information and variety of relationships between sender(s) and receiver(s). Topologies are described with two parameters – cardinality and availability of feedback. Cardinality represents the number of receivers who will use the same information together. This has an impact on how information is packed and presented. In general, four major cardinality ratios are considered: one-to-one (1:1); many-to-one (N:1); one-to-many (1:M); and many-to-many (N:M). The last one is possible only with the existence of feedback. The other criterion is whether the informing process allows feedback or allows clarification leading to adjustment of information. Three forms of feedback are considered: no feedback; partial feedback – feedback is allowed to only part of participants in the informing process; and total feedback.

The topology of the informing process itself also plays a role in assessing potential of misinforming hazards. It is almost impossible to consider all possible ways of acquiring information, but an attempt to consider and classify different informing topologies helps in evaluating the associated risks. A brief discussion of different topological schemas according to cardinality and feedback, illustrated with simple examples, and by pointing out the misinforming hazard potential follows.

- One-to-one without feedback.

Figure 1. One-to-one informing process without feedback

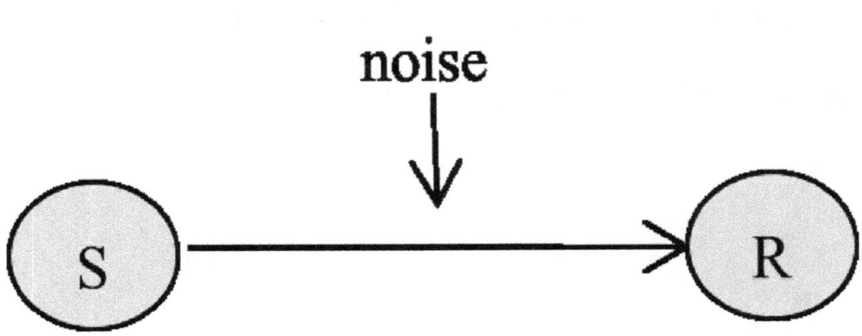

Examples could be classical letters, Christmas cards, notifications from some public institutions, or similar, when sender provides information without expecting answers. Noise may interfere with information supply – the letter can be spoiled by rain and not fully readable. The spoiled parts are subject to interpretation, based on receiver's expectations and what remains from the original text, but important information can be lost, and the result can be misinforming.

- One-to-one with feedback

Figure 2. One-to-one informing process with feedback

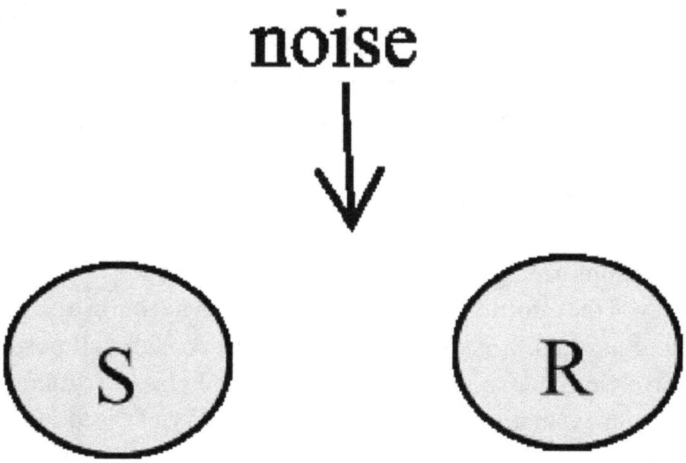

A typical example is face-to-face conversation. Also, noise negatively influences the process, but the opportunity to get feedback and to clarify the message may improve understanding of the provided information. There are additional positive factors as body language, communication environment, etc. in face-to-face communication which also contribute to mitigating the risk of misinforming.

- Many-to-one without feedback

Figure 3. Many-to-one without feedback informing process

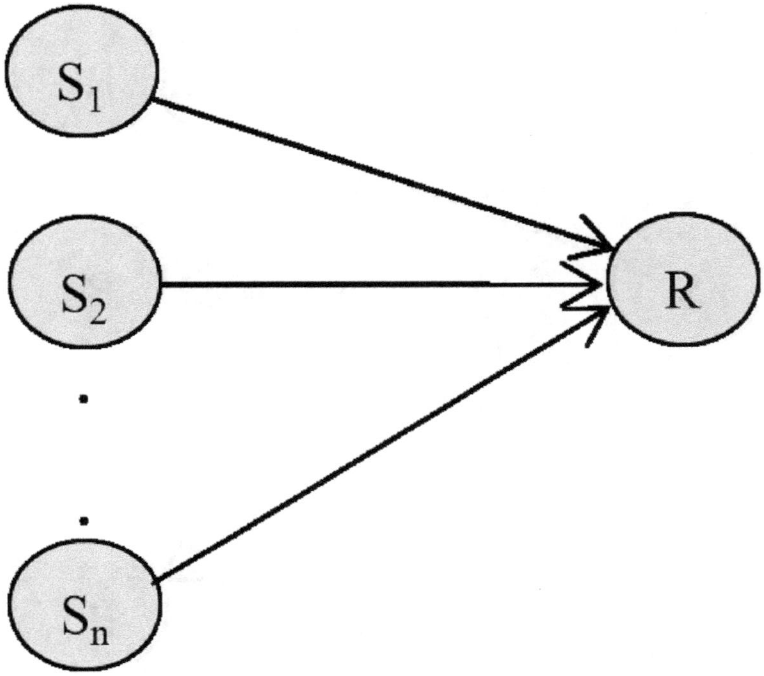

This is the case of using multiple independent sources. This case will be discussed below in more detail. An example is the flow of advertising messages for competing products. Different messages stressed different properties of the products and considering the entire set allows potential customers to build better understanding about what important properties of this kind of product are. The risk associated with information asymmetry is still valid, but it could be mitigated by the use of explanations of those properties from different points of view and by using different languages or jargons.

- Many-to-one with feedback

Availability of feedback may reduce the likelihood of misinforming in the above cases. There are two options of feedback: partial and total. In partial feedback only part of senders may answer to the *request* of receiver, and in total – all of them. "Delphi" method (see for example Sackman H., 1974) of collecting experts' opinions is an excellent example of many-to-one informing process with total feedback.

- One-to-many without feedback

Figure 4. One-to-many without feedback

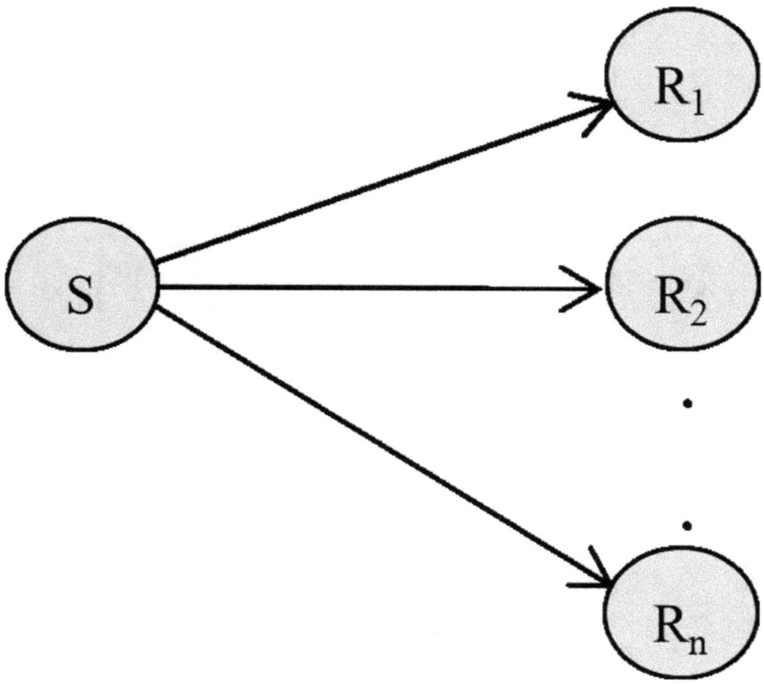

Examples are like broadcasting via public media as newspapers, radio, or TV. Receivers get the same message but there are no options for feedback.

- One-to-many with feedback

Lecturing illustrates this topology – there are opportunities for partial feedback during the lecture or total feedback via exams. Exams provide feedback of how well the meaning was communicated and understood, but this is applicable for the next lecture and next group of students or to other audience and other misinforming likelihood.

- Many-to-many

Figure 5. Model N:M

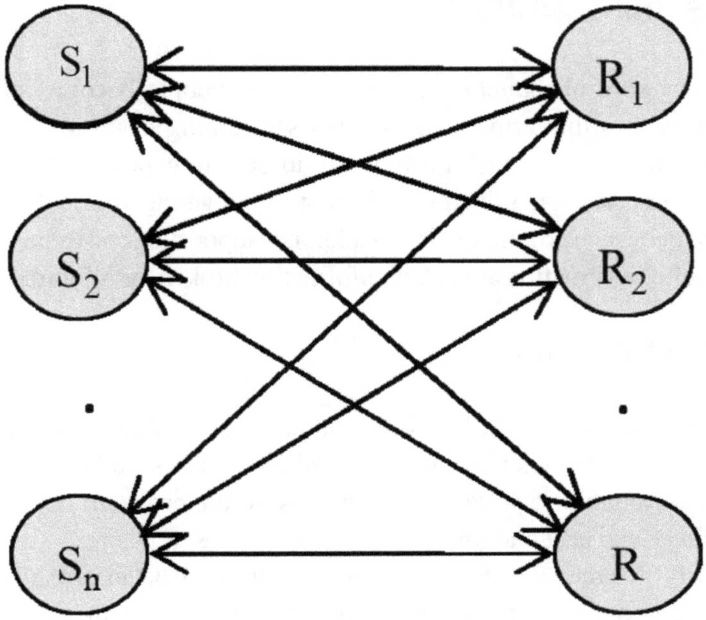

Sharing information on Internet social networks where one user receives information from multiple users and may provide information to many other users. Distribution of a message may shrink or become viral. Feedback is possible in multiple forms as comments and / or emoticons.

These topologies reflect the last stage of an informing process – how end-user acquires information that serves to make decision or act. The process is more complicated, because the providers of information in most of the cases do not create it, but received from another provider, assessing it, interpreting it, and formulating the message to provide to the next user on the sequence of this information or to serve as mediator to facilitate the process.

Attraction of the Message: The Cases Many-to-One and Many-to-Many

The informing process in the cases of many-to-one and many-to-many topologies has one initial phase – attraction. The user must be attracted to explore the provided message at the time of the initial contact – emotional impact of the visuals provided is essential.

HUMAN MEDIATORS IN INFORMING PROCESS: INFOBROKERS

Informing by "word-of-mount" describes the way people become informed for centuries. Nowadays, this term usually describes informing via informal information systems. But, nowadays also informing by information provided by a human, professional in searching, selecting, filtering, aggregating, presenting, etc. is a common practice. Such professionals – mediators – supporting end users to get access and adopt useful information are called information brokers or infobrokers in short.

Information Brokerage

The role of an infobroker is defined in relation to the six aspects of the process of access to information, as they are described by M. Buckland (1991, pp 78-79): identification, availability, price to the user, cost to the provider, cognitive access (understanding), and acceptability.

To "identify" the relevant information sources and to make information available to the users are among the essential objectives of infobrokers. In the practice of "old-style" infobrokers (infobrokers in the pre-Internet era), knowledge about information sources (*meta information*) was among the most valuable resources (Ugarchinsky B. et al., 1987) they can offer to their customers. Now, the ability to effectively search the Internet to locate the source of relevant data, and to verify credibility and trueness of accessed data, are considered even as much more valuable skills. Still, some of the most valuable information is not publicly accessible and needs competences to reach it and to make it "available" to the end-users. Efficient searching and scanning the information environments require knowledge about the information sources, channels to reach, and techniques to obtain and verify information. It also requires the ability to distinguish relevant from non-relevant, valuable from non-valuable, and trustful from not trustful information (Schoderbek, Schoderbek, Kefalas, 1990, pp. 208-210). These special competences of infobrokers made their service often unavoidable.

According to Buckland (1991), "the price to the user" can include but is not solely restricted to money: "the real price includes time, efforts, and discomfort, as well as money." Often, the role of an infobroker includes activities to reduce that price, which may increase the "cost to the provider" in its more general sense. A significant part of activities to reduce the price to the user is dedicated to improving cognitive access to information – assisting the user in the process of understanding, interpreting and exploring the true meaning of information. This may include activities as:

- Structuring of information. To relate the source (*raw*) information to the specific, problem related needs of the user: translate the original terms into the terms acceptable and understandable to the user and present information in a form suitable for further processing by the user (including easier understanding and interpreting in the context of user's problem).
- Assessment of information. Judging about its trueness, precision, relevance, and validity according to user's point of view and user's objectives. This requires clear understanding of the user's problem, circumstances, and objectives on behalf of the infobroker.
- Solving natural language related problems: Translation from foreign languages, explaining professional terminology in a way to allow user to accept the true meaning, adding dictionaries and vocabularies when needed.

The typical set of activities of one infobroker is supposed to do, can be summarized as follows:

- Searching for information
- Collecting information
- Storing information
- Classifying information
- Processing information
- Presenting information
- Disseminating (distributing) information (on request; on subscription)
- Consulting (helping clients get oriented within the information)
- Analyzing and synthesizing information.

A special category of infobrokers' activities is to produce "secondary" information in the form of analysis, summaries, or reports of performed studies. The structure of the role infobrokers played in establishing information environment is presented on Figure 6.

Figure 6. The role of infobrokers in informing environment: Conceptual structure
(Adopted from Christozov, Nikolova, 2001)

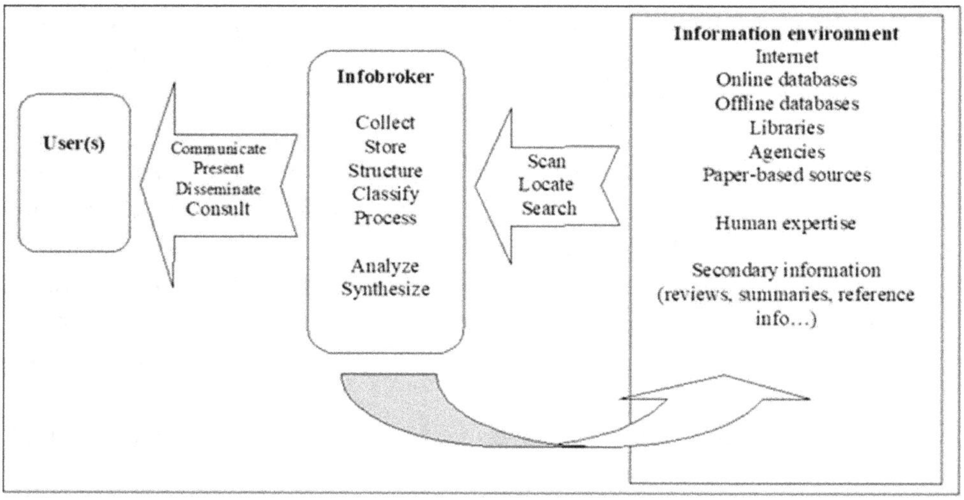

By introducing the Internet environment facilitating access to information becomes more complex. But the two major functions – to acquire information and to synthesize secondary information are vital for the role of infobrokers in building information infrastructure. Infobroker may synthesize information to serve the needs of an individual user or a group of users with identical or similar needs.

The following three types of infobrokers can be distinguished, according to the type of service provided:

- Producers of secondary information. They specialize in scanning a given sector of industry periodically on a regular basis, and provide clients with reviews (referential, analytical, etc.), statistics, summaries to inform clients about the state and changes within the scanned sector. National statistical agencies may serve as a well-known example of such infobrokers. Typical cases are rating producing agencies, accreditation agencies, or institutions scanning given segment of social or economic life to report to their subscribers the state of the sector or dynamics of change.
- Agents of a given international information service. They distribute information on given local (regional) market and scan local (regional) information sources to fill the international information funds. On a national level these agents serve to provide specific expertise, needed by global inforbrokers to assess correctly local information. Examples are local partners of credit rating agencies like Moody's, Standard & Poor (S&P) or Fitch. In

this case, the local infobroker has only one client, but this client is also an infobroker from the first category.

- "On-request" information dealers. They provide specialized informing service by request of given client. This is a typical consultancy type of service, including research of client's problem and sources of information, assessment, and analysis of obtained data, and delivering synthesized information.

In any of the above three forms of info brokerage services the risk of misinforming exists, and clients of the services could be misled.

Regarding the first type of infobrokers, the client could be informed by many concurrent sources – many-to-one informing topology. There are three possible cases when concurrent information is provided – equivalent, complement, contradicted information. Each of these cases has a different misinforming likelihood. These cases are described in more detail later.

The second form of infobroker is the case of using a chain of mediators when information passes a cascade of stages and transformation. At each stage information is adjusted according to the personal, often subjective, view of the infobroker. Misinforming is more probable if there are not well-defined standards of collecting, processing, and presenting information.

The last case – service of infobroker is as consultant, the client of infobroker also may become misinformed as a result of effect of the two-sided information asymmetry. Misunderstanding the specific circumstances of the client's problem and searching, collecting, and providing not fully relevant information have potential to mislead the client. From other side, the client may interpret wrongly provided information.

Informing via mediation also exposes the problem of trust. To adopt obtained information, and to convert it into acting knowledge, the receiver must trust that the information is correct, true, relevant, and complete. The receiver has to assess the credentials of the sender and to trust that sender possess valuable information and also, that sender provided the needed information in full, and will good will. According to Gackowski (2006) credibility of information is essential for the success of any informing process. He refers mostly to the source or provider. In case of mediated delivery, the trust must be expanded also to mediators at the entire pipeline of delivery. Trust covers both trust in human mediators and trust in used technology when applicable. Trust has special implications in concurrent sources of information.

The Case of Multiple Concurrent Sources

It is expected that information received by multiple sources enriches the picture and reduces uncertainty. Independence of providers of concurrent information is critical to ensure trust in the cases below. Independence means also that different providers are using different sources for acquired information. Also, comparing information received from multiple sources may not result only in reducing uncertainty, but could be just the opposite – the case of contradicting information increases uncertainty. To illustrate let us compare the impact of two sources in the following four cases:

1. Equivalent information: If the two independent sources provide the same information, the certainty and trust toward acquired meaning increases, but this does not add value and enriches the information used in making decision. Increases trust, but not decreases uncertainty.
2. If the two independent sources provide complementing information, the certainty and trust increases, as well as reputation of the sources, and allows better understanding of information and problem's parameters. The uncertainty is also reduced.
3. If the two independent sources provide contradicting information, both the certainty and trust decreases.
4. If the two sources are not independent, the trust to combined information decreases.

Every one of these scenarios may result in misinforming, not only the last two cases. Misinforming may happen when the origins of information are not transparent, or dependences between provides are hidden, or even the original source for all mediators is the same but it is not identifiable.

The Case of Sequence of Multiple Mediators: Sequence of Information Brokers

It is not always possible to access the original source of data. There are many reasons for that and the role of mediators, like information brokers (Christozov et al, 2008), is inevitable. But passing information via a sequence of multiple mediators gradually increases the risk caused by information asymmetry and especially increases complexity in assessing the impact of information asymmetry on the misinforming risk for the end-user. Every mediator added his or her own understanding about the problem, assessment of relevance of data, and own vision regarding composition of the content, language, structure, and format of the message. By adding more stages in creating information, the process adds more bias and options for interpretation. Also hidden mediators may are in conflict of interest with the receiver or with other infobrokers in the pipeline, which is difficult to identify. Mediators, information brokers, generate so called "Secondary information", which could be misleading if the links to origin and the way of deriving it are not transparent, clear, and trustful.

The Role of Informing by an Infobroker as Consultant

In this case, the risk of misinforming appears when the infobroker assumes the specific role of information provided without possessing the needed information or knowledge needed by the end-user, as well as clear understanding regarding the consulting process and effect of double-sided information asymmetry. Only skills to search and process raw data to compose a message are not enough for successful informing in this case. The bias of information brokers also may cause risks of approaching and searching irrelevant sources in addition to incorrect understanding of original needs.

INFORMING, DEPENDENT ON "MACHINERY" DELIVERED INFORMATION

The two different aspects of becoming informed by using machinery: informing via observing reality by using special equipment as microscopes and telescopes, and informing via obtaining information generated by computer information technologies, are elaborated in this section in the context of misinforming.

Risks in Informing by Machinery Dependent Observations

Since inventing telescopes and microscopes, human are using "machinery" in a way to obtain knowledge regarding phenomenon beyond what natural human senses allowed to observe.

Information regarding properties of natural phenomenon nowadays is obtained via heavy use of specially designed equipment. Chemical laboratory analysis of different kinds of samples widely explored technology to obtain information about the properties of a real-world phenomena. From examining soil samples in geology (Kamburova, Christozov, 1998) to COVID-19 tests, we all define our important activities based on results obtained via analysis of samples made in laboratories by using sophisticated machinery and methods. The analytical equipment includes reactor, chemical reagents, and instruction on how to perform analysis and how to interpret results produced by the reactor.

How accurate are these results and whether the applied analytical method, equipment, etc. are reliable enough to trust?

The quality of results depends on the way the samples are extracted. This could be done completely by random selecting or by random selection from subsets of the stratified population. Samples can be obtained in fully controlled experiments or just from passive observations, etc. Factors as condition of reactors that may need calibration; purity of reagents; etc. are important and must be considered. And, of course, the competence of laboratory personnel to adjust results according to actual conditions of precision and accuracy of analytical equipment and applied procedure, to correctly interpret the results. Wrong results may lead to wrong decisions and wrong behavior with harmful impact. Repeating measures is a common practice applied in a way to avoid mistakes. Proverbs like "look before you leap" represent the wisdom to look twice before deciding to do and motivate this practice.

There are several indicators regarding quality of obtained via machinery data (illustrations are provided on figures 7. and 8.):

- Accuracy is the closeness of results of observations to the true values or values accepted as being true. Data Accuracy is the element of data quality that deals with the information being exact when describing the physical characteristics of products.
- Precision is the property of measuring tool indicated that the tool would provide the same result in repeating measures.

Figure 7. Accuracy vs. precision

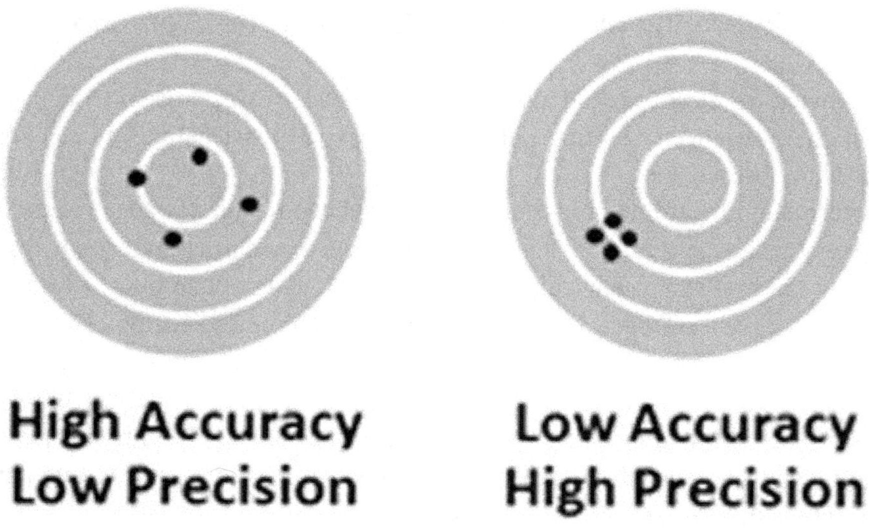

- Consistency means that data does not violate the rules for valid data. Consistence refers to the format of storing and presenting data. Whether the data values stored for an object are the correct values. To be correct, data values must be the right value and must be represented in a consistent and unambiguous form.

Figure 8. Accuracy vs. consistency

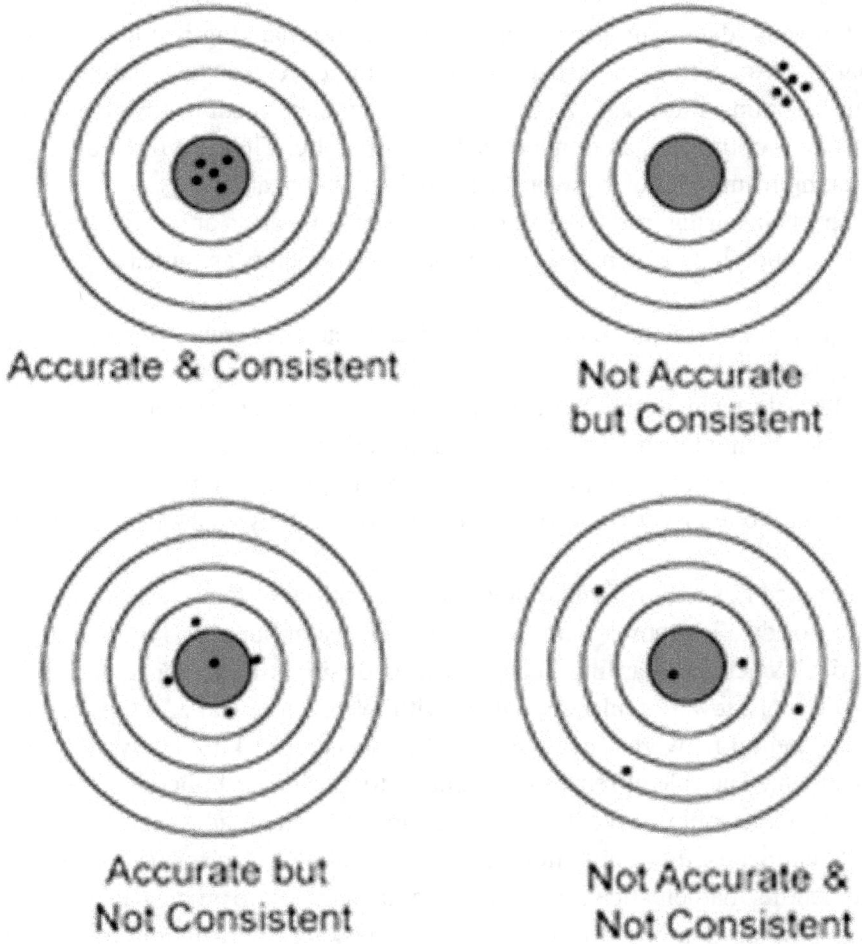

High accuracy, high precision and high consistency refers to high quality measures. Calibration of the tool is used to mitigate the risk in case it provides low accurate, but consistent results. Calibration is a technique to adjust high precision and consistent, but not accurate results obtained by the analytical equipment toward the true value. Calibration requires preliminary evaluation regarding the value of the bias in a way to define the shift of results to improve accuracy. The hazard of low consistency always creates high risk of misinforming. Wrong interpretation of results obtained via use of machinery is also a form of misinforming.

Informing via Computer Information Technologies

There are at least three sources of misinforming hazards related to use of Information Technologies: data, data processing software, and mapping results into problem domain – presentation and visualization. And, there are two ways of user's behavior toward adopting information obtained via computers leading to misinforming – over-trust – optimistic, and under-trust – pessimistic. The case of "realists" is not interesting from point of view of the misinforming hazards.

Aspects inspiring trust in IT dominated communication and use of information results of applying data analysis performed by computers are at least:

- Trust data. Whether data as captured, collected, recorded, stored, accessed is trustful.
- Trust in technology. Trust in data processing algorithms and how they are implemented in applied computer applications.
- Trust in the applicability of results to the problem domain. Trust to self-ability to interpret correctly the results produced by sophisticated software.

Roles of Information Technologies or Information Systems varies from "simple delivery of data" – known as retrieving, via Decision Support Systems, exploring Statistical Machine Learning Techniques, or Business Intelligence and Big Data Analytic tools, toward replacing human with robots, artificial intelligence or using artificial neural networks (deep learning) in decision making by avoiding human involvement. The role of retrieval systems is to mechanize collecting, storing, and accessing large volumes of data. Decision Support Systems goes further by allowing users to extract useful information by applying sophisticated software applications, implementing mathematical, statistical, or other methods to process and model data. Robots nowadays are used in places or circumstances not suitable for human for safety or other similar reason, but their use is in the process of expanding to areas usually reserved to human professionals.

Studies on the success of computer-based information services originate in the area of Information Sciences (Buckland, 1991). In a relatively narrow setting, the impact of a receiver's expertise on the success of the information services was explored. The receiver's expertise was studied by Buckland in two aspects – subject/domain expertise and expertise in using efficiently the information system providing that service. The impact of the receiver's expertise on both aspects, as defined by Buckland, is of crucial importance for the success of a user in becoming informed.

Lack of expertise in using computer information systems simply excludes those members of society from the group of users. This have been viewed even in the 1990s, but now is mutually accepted truth. This phenomenon is marked by the term "digital divide". Nowadays, competences to effective usage of computer information systems are much more complex and do not include solely technical skills. This development also extended the coverage of "digital divide" term, including understanding of data processing algorithms, validity of applied analytical techniques, and visualization.

The level of receiver's expertise in the subject area can be defined as the level of information asymmetry. As is shown in the previous chapter, information asymmetry in its different aspects is the major factor influencing misinforming. High expertise in the subject area reduces the level of information asymmetry and vice versa, but also expertise regarding the applied software and the entire information systems is critically important dimension to mitigate hazards caused by information asymmetry in case of Information Technology mediated informing.

Retrieval information systems are considered as "communication with the past" (see Mooers, 1950). Users communicate with a system, where data are already collected and stored in the databases in advance. Usually, the user has no control on data collection, and all circumstances influencing data recording. The data processing software is also developed in advance under assumptions followed by developers. And finally, results' visualization implies developers' view on what is important, relevant, and how results will be used. Computer Information Systems are designed for future usage and the design reflects the designers' expectation or assumption regarding the way the system will be used in the future.

Big Data as a Special Case in IT Mediated Informing

Since the beginning of the Computer and Communication era every organization has accumulated a huge amount of data in computer databases. Nowadays, everything about describing facts in recorded and searchable media. In the early periods, when memory was too expensive, recording of facts were carefully considered. Nowadays, practically, every value describing the facts is recorded.

There are two major trends in this process:

1. The volume of recorded data is growing.
2. The comprehension of data describing facts is growing or dimensionality of data objects is growing.

In this way, the company's computer storage has accumulated more and more data, which represents what is going on with more and more details. The third trend is the growth of diversity of the forms how data are recorded in computer storages (databases, spreadsheets, text, or multimedia files). In short, what was done in the last decades from the point of view of data and information management resulted in vast heterogeneous repositories of information. New challenges appeared to social organizations – how to benefit in full of this resource, but this is also applicable to every individual person. The complexity of solving those problems comes from:

- Data Flood: volume and availability of data today is best described by the paradox "drowning in data but striving for knowledge" (Naisbitt, 1982).
- Data heterogeneity: diversity and liberty in presenting data in today's media requires more attention on comparing, verifying, and extracting.
- Information Asymmetry: availability of data from diverse sources, imposes the problem of information asymmetry and addressing the issue of the risk of misinforming.
- IT dependency: human cognitive limits constrain the ability to explore such amounts of data without proper use of technology.
- Comprehension: dilemma between building general understanding of the process versus addressing particular fact and implications of a particular activity requires good balance of scrutiny when dealing with available data.

Natural complexity and randomness of real-life problems and availability of data reached the point marked by the term "Big Data". It exposes another set of challenges in becoming informed and added numerous new hazards, which can be marked as misinforming as well. This set ranges from hazards created by opportunity for everyone to play the role of information provider, often posting opinions as facts; to inability to cope in data in such "Volume, Variety, Velocity" and other V's describing complexity of Big Data.

One of the major challenges of Big Data Phenomenon, we all are facing today, is that the receiver of information – the user of data analytics results – practically cannot explore in full directly the source data those results are based on. To do this one need expertise and competence regarding applied analytical techniques – limitation, constraints, conditions to apply, etc. How are those techniques implemented in the software? How does the software present and visualize results? Also, the users need skills to extract applicable information needed for their specific problem by using this software. In most cases, for users, the data analytical application serves as "black box". The issue of trust is essential. Receivers may over trust results produced by the software or under trust them. In the first case this may lead to actions based mostly on confidence, not fully supported by reality and data; and, in the second case, may result in deserting from actions as suggested. In both cases the misinforming hazard occurs.

Making decisions under the pressure of globalization require using complete and comprehensive information, on time… and holistic view on real-life entity or phenomenon. "Holistic" refers to multidimensional view on properties of real entity, and it is related also to identifying which dimensions are actually relevant, and to ability to collect quality data regarding all and each of the dimensions. Or, decision makers are challenged to explore huge amounts of heterogeneous data, for short time, applying complex techniques to identify and consider all possible side effects in a way to benefit from opportunities of availability of Big Data. Using specially designed computer information systems, tools, and applications is becoming inevitable. Acquiring knowledge (learning) from data, in the case of Big Data, challenges the competence of individuals and may lead to misinforming.

Building expertise to become capable of facing and overcoming the challenges of the day is the major problem the social entities are already facing and will face on an increasing scale in the near future. In the Big Data era expertise to learn from data by using technology is becoming increasingly important. There are several aspects of learning from Big Data, related to needed competences, which need addressing by society. Those competences include:

- Knowledge regarding the nature of data and skills to trace and assess data sources.
- Knowledge of available techniques to extract valuable information from data and skills to apply them in processing particular data sets.
- Knowledge of potential risks associated with improper interpretation of data and skills to verify reliability of data and to test the validity of interpretation made.
- Social entity domain knowledge and skills to utilize what is learned from data to solve practical problems by relating the knowledge to problems.

The process of learning requires the development of "wisdom" – deep understanding of the cause and effect, which allows effective prediction and proper, rational behavior. Learning via communication requires the user to receive and understand the message, and to accept and utilize the knowledge embedded into the message. Organizations emphasizing learning via exploring accumulated data may achieve advantages of two kinds: improve efficiency and effectiveness of employees; and a reduction of the probability of lost knowledge already acquired.

Finally, the Big Data competences must address and balance both effectiveness, described as the value of the final product – the acquired knowledge; and efficiency, representing the resources as time and efforts used in data processing, learning, and applying knowledge.

What is Big Data?

Data measured with MB (as in 1960s) or data measured in PB, EB, ZB, YB (as measured today and in visible tomorrow)? To address the issue of learning via "Big Data" accumulated in organizational databases, we need to define what represents "Big Data". The three "V" definition states that *"Big Data is high volume, high velocity, and/or high variety information assets that require new forms of processing to enable enhanced decision making, insight discovery and process optimization (Laney, 2012)*." A universal definition of "Big Data" must address also the human ability to manage data of a given amount and complexity. The following definition (Christozov, Toleva-Stoimenova, 2015): "we will name an amount of data "Big Data" if it is close to the upper bound of the volume and complexity of data that a human can manage to manipulate for purpose with the aid of available information technology." helps applying the time independent approach in addressing data management issues and evolution of technologies. This definition also raises the problem of literacy with the following major aspects:

- Literacy of using technology. Technologies of data management are so rapidly growing that developing and updating the skills for effective and efficient use is a continuous job. Also, data availability and accessibility via different technologies requires diverse skills and competences.
- Literacy of exploring data to achieve better understanding of the nature of processes - literacy to transform data into information, information into knowledge and knowledge into wisdom. The impact of learning via data plays on overall performance of an organization today increases the exposure of risks associated with this process. Avoiding or leveraging those risks represents another set of important competences.
- Literacy to extract the useful patterns and relationships from data includes deep understanding of techniques, mainly mathematical, statistical, machine-learning, and their properties as applicability constraints, meaning and validity of obtained results, and impact of those patterns on behavior of the system described by the data. (For example, often a given statistical technique requires independence of variables used. In case the variables are not independent, or independence is not proved, the technique does not provide valuable results. The needed competence to solve the problems regarding how to identify these obstacles, how to proceed in such a case or how to interpret and explore results is well beyond the common statistical knowledge obtained in the school or even university).

For learning organizations, knowledge management is becoming a strategic tool to gain competitive advantages. The literacy to learn via accumulated data is strategic today by adding a new dimension in concept of digital divide of modern world.

The needed competences are composed by skills to use sophisticated computer tools, knowledge in mathematics, understanding statistics and limitations of given method, possessing deep understanding of the problem domain, as well as analytical skills, and "critical thinking", as well as competences to verify data by tracing data origin, how data is collected, stored, and processed. Hazards related to limited competences include also understanding that information is only representation of the meaning, not the meaning itself. All those assemble the "Big Data Literacy".

The process of learning from data is illustrated in Figure 9.

Figure 9. Learning from big data
(adopted from Christozov and Toleva-Stoimenova, 2015)

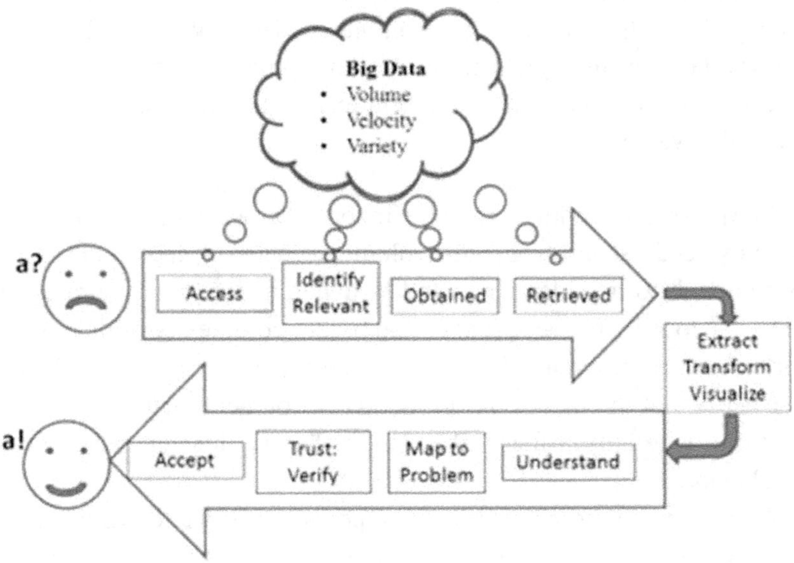

The "Big Data" challenges the human ability to learn from an amount of data significantly beyond cognitive capacity and to rely heavily on computer applications. Such competence incorporates skills to learn from data developed by all "literacies", identified so far, but needs also additional expertise – knowledge, skills, and experience accumulated in dealing with "Big Data".

When we speak about "Big Data" we understand not only the volume of available data, which we have to proceed in a way to learn something, but also its heterogeneity. The heterogeneity has multiple dimensions such as:

- Level of structure - the whole spectrum such as highly structured data stored in relational databases, to plain text, audio and video content, logs of chats, collections of e-mail messages, just to name a few examples illustrating the diversity of data everyone faces today.
- Dimensionality - the details and granularity of description of facts, events, objects result in growing of the number of dimensions - the number of properties or attributes. In historical perspective, dimensionality grow over the years with advancement of storing technologies that may lead to "missing data" phenomenon in exploring the history of a problem.
- Sources, including data created within diverse cultures, languages, professional jargons, backgrounds.
- Media used for acquiring data – from official information channels to rumors shared in cafeteria, found somewhere on the Internet, or appearing in the news on TV.
- Reliability, traceability, repeatability, reproducibility, and other attributes of data quality, which must be rationally recognized and verified.
- The available technology to access, retrieve, process, summarize and visualize data in a way to represent it within human cognitive limits by preserving its informing value.

The time pressure is another critically important aspect when discussing learning – we not only need to learn from huge volumes of heterogeneous data, but we must do it fast enough to be able to respond to dynamically changing circumstances. Resolving the conflict between higher and higher complexity of data with shorter and shorter time to comprehend it increases the dependence on smart applications. All those aspects of the current information environment influence human ability to learn from data and influence the impact the acquired knowledge has to the human behavior.

It is obvious that the complete set of competences needed to avoid misinforming in using Big Data is extremely rear. Relying on mediators to compensate one or another area of missing expertise is unavoidable but raises the likelihood of misinforming. Chapter 3.4. discusses the practice of solving complex problems by exploring cooperation and trans-discipline synergy.

MEDIATION VIA AI AND MACHINE LEARNING

The two direction of machine learning:

1. Statistical machine learning, emphasizing extracting useful knowledge, in form of a model, describing behavior of real-world phenomenon and allows users to understand cause-and-effect relationship in a way to predict and manage.
2. The so called "Deep Learning" build on the neural network approach allows building complex model to predict behavior of real-world phenomenon, without necessary explicitly explain the relationship between input data and output.

The second direction practically excludes users from the process of becoming informed and transfers this role to the computer application. This is anticipated by scientists and scient-fiction authors. The famous collection of stories by Isaak Asimov "I, the robot" was written in 1940s. The era of robots and AI and its relations with human beings became a hot topic today with launching the Chat GPT.

User-Experience

"User-experience" is a term used to define the overall experience a user receives by a service. Terms like "user-friendly" or "intuitive user interface" describe the trend toward designing interface by considering end-users preparedness to benefit in full. A misinforming hazard occurs when the end-user is not satisfied by the service and results in negative user experience with the service provider. Having positive user-experience among the top priorities in designing a information service is critical in mitigating the risk of misinforming.

In this book, misinforming is understood as the case in which the information provided is correct and useful, but it is understood and interpreted wrongly. Misinforming in the case of user experience leads to dissatisfaction to the service, the provider and information provided, and results in resistance to use further all or some of them. Understanding the fact that a given service misleads the user allows learning about how to use the service next time, or how to use other services offered by the same provider, including how to interpret provided information. Recurrent use of a service may result in adapting of both parties – users and service – to user-service interactions by reducing the likelihood of risk of misinforming. Learning is beneficial not only to the end-user, but also to the service provider. Or learning by identifying misinforming hazards is a two-sided process leading to improving the user experience.

Two issues need addressing in designing user interface to address the user-experience issues in customization of design:

1. To identify, distinguish, and set rules to classify categories of users according to whether and how they are exposed to misinforming when using the service.

2. To identify risks associated with each of these categories, and how to adjust the service for given category of end-users to overcome potential for misinforming.

Ideas regarding the role of user interface evolved in parallel with evolution of computer information systems. A brief historical overview of the development of computer information from the point of view of user-system communication demonstrates the trend and what we can expect in the near future.

Background: Historical Perspective of Users-Experience

Developing computer information systems has a relatively short history. The invention of the programming language COmmon Business Oriented Language (COBOL) in 1959 can be considered as the beginning of the era of using computers in serving business. The period of those more than 60 years can be divided in three phases:

1960-1980: This is the period of exponential progress in developing computer and related technologies. It starts with the invention of semiconductor transistors that replaced vacuum tubes in electronic computers and fast development toward miniaturization of hardware and increasing its productivity and ending with introduction of personal computers. The period is characterized by heavy needs of mediators in using services provided by computer information systems. There were needs from different categories of mediators playing different roles as data preparation, data entry, computers' operators, software engineers, etc. Stress was on computer productivity, performance, and efficacy.

1980-2000: Developing of computer connectivity in mid-70s allows reducing the role of mediators. Connections via dumb monitors were gradually replaced with smart devices and personal computers. Direct interaction between computers and end-users introduced the "user-interface" as a set of problems deserving equal attention as productivity. The user experience as a field of research was born, even not fully identified.

The limitations of the original definition of the discipline Computer Information Systems became more visible. Several authors pointed out these limitations: N. Ahitov and S. Neumann (1990); K. Loundon (1996). M. Buckland in his book Information and Information Systems (1991) presented those limitations in the form of several paradoxes. Two of them are relevant to our current study – on page 10 he wrote "Information systems are supposed to inform people, but in practice they are designed to deliver physical stuff, such as books, papers, and signals on glowing screens." and on page 173 "the expert's paradox is that greater subject expertise both increases and decreases information seeking success. The greater the subject expertise, the greater the probability of finding information (pertinent material) and the lower the probability that it would be informative (novel to the searcher)." Buckland distinguished two categories of expertise needed for success in becoming informed via information systems: subject expertise – expertise on the problem and information domain, and systems expertise – expertise on efficient use of information system's functionality.

In 1999, Eli Cohen published a paper summarizing accumulated understanding that the focus of information systems had shifted from productivity and efficacy of computer technologies applied toward effectiveness for the users in becoming informed. He introduced the term "informing science" to mark this change. According to Cohen, informing science is a trans-discipline of mutually penetrating disciplines as technical, algorithmic, economic, cognitive, etc. Considering users' experience from point of view of informing science represents the essential component of development of information services for 21st century. It emphasizes both the subject's and system's expertise by adding the notion that the system must be designed in a way that supports success in informing end-users. The terms mentioned above "user-friendly" or "intuitive" interfaces mark this new round of evolution of human-machine relationship.

After year 2000: The current development added three new aspects in user experience evolution: first the tremendous grow of impact of computer information services to every aspect of the human live makes informing via computer information systems unavoidable global phenomenon; second – social coverage – introduced with social media established a new era of connectivity and social relationship and life; and the third is the huge diversity of services implemented with the use of computer information systems, practically a whole new branch of economy appeared, known as electronic commerce that changed completely the business landscape.

The complexity of information services provided nowadays is growing and resulting in sophisticated ways to access, locate, identify, and retrieve relevant information. Design of effective user-interface, suitable for highly diverse population of potential users in a way to suit to diverse expertise, diverse needs, and diverse navigation attitudes is the key success factor for computer information systems today.

Misinforming as Risk for Building Positive User Experience

What represents "positive" users' experience? Looking on this question from point of view of subject and system expertise (M. Buckland, 1991), and informing science, the following categories can be identified:

According to subject's matter:

- The received information is useful, relevant, and allowed solving the problem.
- The received information is not relevant, not useful at all.

- The received information looks relevant and useful, but it misleads user in solving the problem.

According to finding information by using system's functionality:

- The user accessed and obtained information in an easy and pleasant way.
- The user accessed and obtained information, but this needed much more time than anticipated.
- The user denied using the system without reaching the information considered relevant.

"Positive" user experience is achieved when the information is obtained according to combined two first cases. Any other combination of subject's and system's experience can be considered as "not positive". The combination of both third cases corresponds to clearly negative user experience.

CONCLUSION

This chapter extended discussion regarding the factors and circumstances that influence the success of an Informing process. It introduces the idea of process's topology in a way to distinguish different ways one is becoming informed nowadays. Different topologies lead to different risks of becoming misinformed. The two parameters – cardinality and availability of feedback – were used for defining informing topologies.

Next two sections introduce the role of mediators in informing end-users. The risks associated with informing via human mediators – inforbrokers, and the variety of risks associated with informing via use of machinery provided information. In the latter, the stress is on information provided by computer information systems. The short historical evolution of computer information systems marks the current stage, but also allows us to see the trend in designing information services.

All cases are discussed in the light of hazards leading to misinformation.

REFERENCES

Asimov, I. (1940). *I, robot.* SFU. https://www2.cs.sfu.ca/~vaughan/teaching/415/papers/I,%20Robot%20Ch1-3.pdf

Buckland, M. (1991). Information and Information Systems. Praeger.

Christozov, D., Denchev, S., Toleva-Stoimenova, S., & Rasheva-Yordanova, K. (2008). Training Information Brokers: A Curriculum Model. *Journal of Issues in Informing Science and Information Technology*, *5*, 87–94. doi:10.28945/997

Christozov, D., & Mitreva, E. (2020). Trust in Learning from Big Data: The Two Sides of the Same Coin. *Issues in Information Systems*, *21*(1), 147–152.

Christozov, D., & Nikolova, I. (2001). Infobroker – an Emerging Profession of Informing Mediators? *Proceedings Informing Science 2001*. Information Science. (http://proceedings.informingscience.org/IS2001Proceedings/pdf/Christozov.pdf)

Christozov, D., & Toleva-Stoimenova, S. (2015). Big Data Literacy - a New Dimension of Digital Divide: Barriers in learning via exploring Big Data. In J. Girard, K. Berg, D. Klein, & I. G. I. Global (Eds.), *Strategic Data Based Wisdom in the Big Data Era* (pp. 156–170). doi:10.4018/978-1-4666-8122-4.ch009

Gackowski, Z. (2006). Quality of Informing: Credibility Provisional Model of Functional Dependencies. *2006 Informing Science and IT Education Joint Conference*, Salford, UK. 10.28945/3017

Lotrecchiano, G., & Misra, S. (2018). Transdisciplinary knowledge producing teams: Toward a complex systems perspective. *Informing Science*, *21*, 51–74. doi:10.28945/4086

Mooers, C. (1950). Information retrieval viewed as temporal signaling. *Proceedings of the international congress of mathematicians*. Information Science.

Naisbitt J. (1982). Megatrends – Ten New Directions Transforming Our Lives. *Warner Books Inc*.

Schoderbek, P., Schoderbek, C., & Kefalas, A. (1990). *Management Systems: Conceptual Considerations*. BPI IRWIN.

Ugarchinsky, B., Christozov, D., Denchev, S., Hicova, T., & Deneva, L. (1987). Information Service in Technology Transfer: Basic Sources and Channels of Technological Information. *ICTT "Informa."* Sofia.

Vinge, V. (1993). *Technological singularity*. CMU. https://frc.ri.cmu.edu/~hpm/book98/com.ch1/vinge.singularity.html

Chapter 5
Other Aspects of Misinforming

ABSTRACT

Chapter five introduces the reader to a variety of other cases, leading to misinforming as negative outcome but also the cases, when misinforming may come out with positive effect. Additional to the previous chapters there are many circumstances of our nowadays life that have potential for misinforming hazards. Some of them are briefly discussed in this chapter as emotions in making decisions; misinforming in finding out-of-box innovative solution; impact of culture; Dunning-Kruger effect; short-list paradox; and the role of standards.

INTRODUCTION

The previous chapters introduced the reader to the major factors contributing to appearance of hazards leading to misinforming. There are many other factors, circumstances, and practices that may cause misinforming. This chapter discusses some of them. In particular, factors as emotions, self-confidence, the approach in decision making, and many others play a significant role in whether one is informed or is misled. One special case is when the receiver is misinformed, interpreted wrongly the received information, but this mistake helps to find an innovative, effective, and beneficial solution. This is the rear case of positive effects caused by misinforming hazard.

The chapter is divided into following sections discussing different issues:

Section 1 chapter 1 is dedicated to factors such as emotion and fashion. The next one discusses circumstances that misinforming may lead to effective, innovative outcomes. Culture is the factor addressed in section 1 chapter 3. The relationship between competences and self-confidence is discussed in the following section in the

DOI: 10.4018/978-1-6684-8800-3.ch005

light of Dunning-Kruger effect. Also, the self-misinforming when one overestimates own competence or attractiveness is illustrated as a hiring paradox. The last section comments on the role of standards in facilitating the informing process.

APPROACHES IN DECISION MAKING: THE ROLE OF EMOTIONS

The misinforming hazard and associated risks become visible when a receiver of information makes the decision to solve a problem and the result is not satisfactory, because of wrong use of obtained information. As seen in the previous chapters this hazard can be caused by many different objective reasons. This hazard can be a result of a subjective reason as well. In too many cases, decisions are made emotionally instead of rationally via exploring available information. Over-trust to source of information, because the receiver "likes" it, the fashion of the day, or "to follow others" are typical scenarios of emotionally led decision making. The result is that our houses are full of unneeded and unused goods.

The hazards cause risks of misinforming, based on the trust, can be classified in two general categories: ungrounded trust or giving unjustified credits to received information or sender, and ungrounded trust toward own competence when reality is de-facto lack of competence to understand, assess, verify, and use correctly the received information. The first one is usually based on emotional attitude toward the source. The opposite is also possible to refuse using "good information" because receiver doesn't like the source. The second category is discussed in Chapter 2, as result of information asymmetry, in Part 2 in quantifying the value of information asymmetry. and in more detail the relationship between high confidence and low competence is presented in Section 4 in this Chapter.

In a nutshell the two categories of hazards leading to misinforming correspond to the two ways of decision-making behavior:

1. Trust corresponds to emotional based decision-making and emotional arguments in interpreting and adopting information. It corresponds to the image of the source, its credibility, and, in general, the environment of provided and received information. But also, to the personality of sender and receiver and their relations. Often, environmental factors in emotionally led decision making include fashion and "others" opinion or recommendations. Customers are purchasing obviously unneeded products simply because they are fashionable, or because "all neighbors" possess them.
2. Lack of competence in understanding correctly the information provided into the message, understanding limitation in data sources, the constraints of its

validity, the used jargon, ways of delivery, verification potential, etc. These hazards correspond mostly to rational way of decision making, or at least to attempt to address rationally the problem, and deficits in competences to apply and explore well the recognized as needed critical assessment of received information. Usage of models to describe case and to assess relevance and validity of information may mislead the decision maker in trying to behave rationally.

This section discusses emotional decision making from the point of view of the misinforming risk. A typical problem nowadays is that the receiver is informed by using only sources providing data and information that corresponds or closely correlates with the receiver's own opinion and ignoring other sources. In the current state of flooding with information, filtering of sources to explore are usually defined emotionally. A receiver may "like" information provided by a given source because she or he (1) likes the source; (2) likes the form of presenting information; or (3) likes the content of the message. The first corresponds to relationship with the provider. The second reason is related to information processing – the confidence that information is easily understood, obviously interpreted, and directly mapped to the problem, subject of decision making. The third reason is when information correlates with the receiver's expectation and confirms her or his opinion. The current marketing approach is to "attract" the potential clients by stressing on the initial contact providing visuals and other tools to establish "positive" emotional attitude toward the advertising goods. Not to support critical rational assessment of the offer.

Decision making under emotions has at least two side effects:

1. Increases the trust toward received information, without adding additional value regarding its trueness. The user increases confidence toward preferred option of information provider, without checking validity of other options, and even suitability of the "liked" one.
2. Ignoring information from sources arguing in favor about other options, not listening to others' opinion and provided evidence. Result is under trust toward alternative information. By ignoring information that contradict with her or his own opinion the receiver is de-facto jumps into the trap of misinforming.

Each of those scenarios may result in becoming misinformed and in making wrong decisions. Recognizing that decision made in this way is wrong may turn to chaotic "like-dislike" behavior. But often emotional decisions, based on intuition and like-dislike assessment about provider and information provided, are based on experience that is not fully recognized, and explicitly formulated. In many cases emotionally driven, intuitive decisions are better than decisions made in fully data driven, rational way.

The role of using models in decision making is well described by Simon H. (1965) who identifies three principal phases: intelligence, design, and choice. The second phase – design – includes practically design of two outputs. The set of alternative courses of action and a model allows us to assess them. The model sometime is not explicitly defined but usually includes selection of parameters, or variables, used to describe alternatives and assigning weights or priorities. The model defines what information in form of values for those variables are needed to find or evaluate to make rational decision. The famous statement of Box (1987) *"Essentially, all models are wrong, but some are useful"* is true in general, but also some models could be harmful and misled decision maker in searching, selecting, and assessing information to use. The principle of simplicity, known as Occam's razor states, that among competing hypotheses that predict equally well, the one with the fewest assumptions should be selected, but the law of "Requisite Variety", formulated by W. Ashby (1963) in cybernetics states that the control system (information systems) must be as complex as the controlled system. In reality, using models is the approach allowing humans to overcome the limited cognitive abilities to develop understanding about too complex phenomena, but from other side using oversimplified models may misled.

Pressure and Challenges in Decision Making as Origin for Misinforming

Rational, data-driven decision making is becoming more complex and careful assessment of data and possible outcomes usually requires time. Nowadays, in the business world in particular, the decision makers have less time to comprehend options in a way to reach the needed confidence in reached solution. Time pressure is another origin of risk of misinforming that leads to intuitive, emotional, rather rational behavior. Not having enough time to verify information, to assess its applicability, or to consider possible scenarios and alternative actions and to search additional information may lead to wrong decision and wrong action as a result of missing to acquire complete understanding of received information.

The following lists just a few of nowadays pressures and challenges faced by managers:

- Globalization of markets – the pressure to respond to global competition requires making rational, data-driven decisions. Intuition, experience, or emotion may mislead decision-makers with a much higher probability than it was in the past. The decision to follow what others have adopted is quite common, even done without careful analysis of applicability.

- Data-driven decision-making is becoming more complex because of the Big Data phenomenon. Decision makers depend on computer applications mediating learning.
- The role of trust toward the quality of obtained data, reliability of applied technology, the correctness of algorithms implemented in data analytic software, and how relevant are results to the problem is becoming critical.
- Informing, the way to build acting knowledge rely on credibility of obtained information, depends on multiple factors, divided by Z. Gackovski (2006) into primary factors, as obtaining information from multiple independent sources and possibility to trace the origin of information, and secondary factors as trust toward the source, warranty, etc.

Time pressure is becoming one of the critical factors for occurring the hazards leading to misinforming and to replace careful rational approach with intuitive, emotional one.

Importance of Emotional Attitude

Informing processes with topologies Many-to-one or Many-to-many are exposed to one preliminary step – choosing which of the potential providers or senders of information to choose, which message looks promising enough to deserve further exploring. In the information flood everyone nowadays is exposed to huge volumes of diverse messages, visuals, news, and the preliminary stage of filtering which one to pay attention to plays a highly important role.

Choosing one among many is based on emotional assessment of "likeliness" and is function of how attractive the first (often the only) contact is. In the scope of market studies, researchers investigate components of visuals used in packing products. Bearing in mind that a common person is bombarded with more than 1500 images a day, and that her/his cognitive capacity allows to recognize only few hundreds, and to memorize about tens, the attraction of the first contact is becoming crucial. Often, a nice looking, attractive wrapper gains attention, which may result in ignoring or rejecting the useful information. Choosing what information to use based on external view and attraction of the first contact may lead to misinforming.

POSITIVE ASPECTS OF MISINFORMING

So far, we have explored negative outputs of misinforming, but results of becoming misled could also be positive. The most famous example is the discovery of America by Christopher Columbus. Misinterpreting the information regarding existence of land beyond the ocean is India, he organized a mission to discover this "western path". He was so confident in his interpretation of information that he was able to justify it in front of Spanish king and to receive a grant to equip the expedition. Till the end of his days, he believed that he had discovered a Western pathway to India. We still call native American people "Indians". Information, in form of legends, about existence of a land on the western side of the ocean were spread from high North by Vikings, in Britain – about a Wales king, till western Africans. All of them had, more or less, successful expeditions reaching the cost of Americas, and some have managed to return and to share.

The study and interpretation of biblical texts launched the field of Hermeneutics. This field in the areas of humanity – in linguistics, history, law, etc. investigates interpretation as a component of social aspects of communication. Guido Sprenger (2016) explores "the productive and creative aspects of misunderstanding" and stated, "misunderstanding as a necessary and often productive aspect of communication". Other authors in this field also recognize positive aspects of misunderstanding as an essential component of interpretation.

Misunderstanding is usually the result of interpretation of information created in given circumstances and context and used in different situations. Mooers (1950) stated that the use of retrieval systems is "communication with the past" but it is also communication addressing new circumstances. Interpreting information and mapping the obtained meaning to problem domain may result in unexpected but effective innovative solutions.

One extreme example of such "modern" interpretation of past information is the image on the ancient Egyptian frieze of the Temple of Seti I in Abydos. It is considered by modern people as a helicopter and is an example of pareidolia, the tendency to perceive a pattern or meaning that isn't there.

The real explanation behind the "helicopter" is that it was re-carved. The original carving at the time of Seti I is translated as "He who repulses the nine enemies of Egypt." It was later remade by artists during the reign of Rameses II to read "He who protects Egypt and overthrows foreign countries." (see Wikipedia – helicopter).

Figure 1. The frieze with misinterpreted helicopter

Looking for innovative solutions to complex problems nowadays often requires "out-of-box" ways in considering problems' circumstances from different angles and perspectives. Often, the push for such creative thinking comes from information which contradicts the established, routine understanding and may provoke users to search for a solution in an unexpected "erethic" area. Misinforming, misunderstanding, misinterpretation may serve as a stimulus for finding innovative, "out-of-box" solutions. Also, the complexity of problems needs to be addressed in a holistic way, combining expertise from different areas of knowledge. Experts in different fields need to communicate, to share in a way to find suitable solutions. Lack of competence in interpreting messages composed by using professional jargon in the scientific field of others may result in misinterpretation. The positive effect may be reached when the wrong interpretation has a perfect meaning to the problem in receiver's field who is non-expert in the provider's field.

Paradoxical thinking is a special case of ways in addressing problems. The provided information may look like strange and contradictory to the receiver's background or expectations, but worthy enough to consider and explore instead of more simple and obvious behavior – to ignore it. Many scientific discoveries are the result of considering paradoxical information. Well known Zeno's paradox of motion, known as "Achilles and the Tortoise" or "Arrow's paradox", the paradox of dichotomy motivates development of differential calculus, limits of infinite sequences, measuring asymptotic behavior, etc. Paradoxical thinking refers to something impossible or going beyond the imaginative framework, but such exaggeration allows one to focus on finding "impossible" solution. In this way, paradoxical way to approach problems looks from one side like wrong interpretation or misunderstanding but from other forces decision maker to find an "exotic", new, innovative way for solving the problem.

Other aspect of positive role of misinforming comes with necessity of approaching problems by a trans-discipline team. Many problems nowadays can be solved only in a holistic manner, by synergy of composition of penetrated expertise coming from different scientific areas. Trans-disciplinarity requires applying methods and scientific facts of one discipline by professional in other. In such teams misinforming may play a positive role when the misinterpreted knowledge has perfect sense in the problem domain as seen by other members of the team. For more, see Chapter 3.4.

IMPACT OF ORGANIZATIONAL CULTURE: SHARING WITHIN OR BETWEEN CULTURES

Culture is one of the major factors contributed to success of informing via communication. Two aspects of culture deserve attention in the context of misinforming. Strong cultures (Gill G., 2013) support success in communication within the group and serve as barrier for communication between members of different groups. Dimensions of cultural differences, originated in Gert Hofstede's (Hofstede G., 1984) study, describe national specific properties of culture with impact on the applicable forms and means of communication.

Hofstede's measures of cultural difference shows that traditional national cultures also play a role in communication effectiveness. Here are commented the impact of low and high measures of the five dimensions on misinforming. Also, by assuming that the globalizing world evolves toward convergence of culture dominated by Anglo-Saxon influence, the impact of this change on probabilities of misinforming is discussed at the end of this section. Building organizational cultures supporting sharing is an important challenge to the business. For more see part three chapter four.

Any of the six dimensions, the original five identified by Hofstede, and the additional one mutually accepted, may play a role in misinforming:

- Individualism: Individualism is the extent to which people feel independent, as opposed to being interdependent as members of larger wholes. Higher independence may result in valuing higher the own way of interpreting and using information, ignoring others' opinion, and understanding. Often results in avoiding opportunities to check and verify the information, and correctness of its interpretation.
- Power Distance: Power Distance is the extent to which the less powerful members of organizations and institutions (like the family) accept and expect that power is distributed unequally. From point of view of the risk of misinforming, high power distance results in conformity with the principle, avoiding disagreement and providing, even reasonable, arguments.
- Masculinity: Masculinity is the extent to which the use of force is endorsed socially.

- Uncertainty Avoidance: Uncertainty avoidance deals with a society's tolerance for uncertainty and ambiguity.
- Long-term orientation: Long-term orientation deals with change.
- Indulgence: Indulgence is about the good things in life.

Two cultural changes with impact on the innovations created processes in opposite directions are visible nowadays: increased "individualism" with stress on personal achievement and rewards even in countries with original low individualism; and increasing complexity of problems and needs of trans-disciplinary, holistic, solutions need higher "collectivism". They lead to changing behavior in cooperation. The term "co-operation" (see Brandenburger A., B. Nalebuff, 1996), composed by mixing "cooperation" with "competition" describes the dilemma in developing innovations via creative contribution by different members of a heterogeneous team.

A mutually accepted assumption is that the trends of convergence of cultures, via globalization with high impact of Anglo-Saxon culture, are toward lowering Power Distance (PDI) index; higher Individualism and lower Collectivism (IDV) index, and higher Masculinity and lower Femininity (MAS) index. The changes in other dimensions are not so visible, but we may assume trends toward higher Short-term Orientation (LTO); higher Indulgence (IVR) and lower Uncertainty avoidance (UAI). Those assumptions speak about lowering readiness of sharing and motivation based on self-advancement rather than team's success. From other side, the individuals' success depends gradually more and more on the achievement of the group.

Other aspects of the progress influenced by advancement of Computer Information Technologies are marked with terms like Information Society, Fourth Industrial Revolution, Big Data, Machine Learning and Artificial Intelligence. They reflect the dependence of society and individuals on data and information, on technologies for exploring data and managed knowledge generation. The established connectivity and dependence on data and how data are processed increases the complexity. Complexity of exploring data to solve problems in an innovative way needs a multidimensional, holistic way in approaching problems. The problem-centered approach dominates successful innovation. The new round of progress and innovations, both on a local or wider level, depends on cooperation, sharing and synergy of togetherness. This represents a shift in the direction of evolution of cultures toward establishing a digital innovation paradigm in working.

Those changes have been fueled by the advancement of computer and communication technologies. The ideas and practices regarding establishing culture of sharing, while the overall trend is toward more individualism are presented in part three chapter four. The three years of isolation via Covid-19 pandemic also influenced the processes of shifting the cultures.

COMPETENCE AND CONFIDENCE: SELF-MISINFORMING

Introduction

Self-assessment of competences needed for making correct decisions is often misleading. As usual, this may go in two directions – overestimation and underestimation. The latter usually results in double check and verification of information. The first may result in the so called "Dunning-Kruger" effect.

Another aspect of self-misinforming is when one cannot correctly assess her or his position within the society or the market. Usually, it is overestimated, and the behavior of this person usually leads to dissatisfaction with the results.

These two aspects of self-misinforming – confidence heavily dominates on own competencies, and not realistic assessment of own position, attractiveness, and competitiveness are discussed in this section.

Confidence Domination on Competence: Dunning-Kruger Effect

The impact of competence on misinforming was introduced in the second chapter. The problem of low, but not recognized, competences often result in high confidence toward own knowledge. The Dunning-Kruger effect shows that the risk of misinforming when combining the high confidence with low competence, is quite high in general, but riches the extreme pick when objective competence tends to "none" and confidence to "high". Dunning-Kruger justified that this behavior is natural or typical.

Two scenarios can be distinguished in considering the relationship between confidence and competence from point of view of misinforming.

The first one literally replicates the idea behind Dunning-Kruger effect – the receiver considers himself confident enough that he or she possessed competences to fully catch the meaning provided in the message. In this scenario, misinforming leads to wrong actions and possibly to the worst outcomes.

The second one is the receiver's confidence toward the sender's competence. This is the case of over-trust toward provided information, assuming that the information is trustful, reliable, complete, and sufficient for solving the receiver's problem. Information provided is the "truth in its last instance" (sacred cow, ultimate truth). The receiver does not even attempt to assess critically the information in the message, or the meaning adopted via interpreting the message, its relevance to the problem, and whether it is useful for solving it. Misinforming leads to wrong actions. On the opposite side is "under trust" when receiver doesn't trust the competence of the sender and refuses to adopt and use information provided, even if this information is correct and relevant.

Here, the first case will be elaborated.

Some aspects of Dunning-Kruger effect have impact on misinforming:

1. Dunning-Kruger effect prevents establishing a culture of sharing. Members of a team, dominated by high confidence in their own expertise, are not willing to share and more important much less willing to listen.
2. Using IT as black-box fuel confidence in digital literacy competences and prevents investments in learning and development deeper knowledge. People, who possess skills of using an IT application developed confidence that they possess deep knowledge about the application and in general about it. This is visible the difference of generations – IT experts building their expertise in 80s or 90s are less likely to overestimate their expertise. The current user-friendly IT environment creates the filing that just skillful usage is completely enough.
3. Grade inflation, observed in many universities (Barton A., 2022) causes Dunning-Kruger effect. Grade inflation drives higher confidence of students toward their competences and prevents investments in learning and development deeper knowledge.

Self-Misinforming: The Short-List Paradox

The case of self-misinforming can also be illustrated with the widely adopted hiring procedure known as the "short list". Unrealistic expectations regarding own place in the real world, the own position on market, the own level of attractiveness, etc., which are forms of self-misinforming, may result in a failure in implementing the hiring decision.

Let us consider the following case. In a given year, 100 students complete their Ph.D. in a given discipline and move to the academic job market. In the same year 100 universities have advertised academic positions in this discipline. All 100 new doctors apply to all 100 university positions. The search committee of each of the university evaluates all those 100 applications and select a short list – the top five candidates. The top five candidates chose to go to the top five universities and the top five universities fulfil their opening. As result the remining 95 universities do not fill their positions; and the 95 candidates do not find academic job. Or perfectly suitable options remain unexplored, because of the desire to find "the best" option without considering the reality results in failure. This example shows that "short-list" procedure, assumed effective, may result in paradoxically bad outcomes.

Misunderstanding regarding what is suitable enough and not to strive to the "best" is a a form of self-misinforming.

Failures in search by following the short-list process are caused by supply-demand balance. The above example shows that the likelihood of failure in such a perfectly balanced market circumstances is significant. Theoretically, only when supply is much higher than the demand, the search process may result in success for all.

Unrealistic expectations correspond to the nature of self-assessment. The tendency is to overestimate own capability and underestimate others. Realistic approach includes altering the way to apply the short-list process by moving the major activities outside of the mainstream. In the above case, a university may initiate the search much earlier than the others and complete the search by selecting the best candidate well before the other options are even opened. Or, by starting the process later and choosing the best one among those rejected by the top universities. Either of those techniques requires clear and fair self-assessment.

This form of misinforming corresponds to Dinning-Kruger's effect discussed above, but it refers to the misinforming risk of an institution. Individuals usually apply informally the short-list technique in making purchase decisions but failures in such are not as visible.

Misinforming in assessing the supply-demand ratio or self-misinforming regarding the own attractiveness may cause the failure in selection when using a short-list kind of decision-making process.

STANDARDS AND MISINFORMING

There are many areas where misinforming is highly undesirable. In some areas people had established standards to correctly interpret data. Two such cases are discussed in this section – the evolution of numerals used to present quantities, and the standards developed in transmitting messages between computers. The first case resulted in "de-facto" standard, but the second are called standards or protocols.

Evolution of Numerals as an Example for Overcoming Misinforming in Representing Quantities

The history of evolution of numerals may serve as an example of convergence of natural differences toward mutually adopted standards avoiding misinterpretation of information regarding quantities.

Fingers, as the most natural tool to count, are used to communicate numbers from the very early stages of humans. Use of fingers resulted in launching systems with decimal numerals, but also in duodecimal numerals. The first uses fingers directly (10) and in the second the counting uses phalanges of the fingers with the thumb as a pointer. Misinterpretation among people using these two systems exists, and still reflects measuring quantities in some areas – metric, imperial, USA custom.

Several other numerals' systems emerged historically (see the excellent study of Ifrah G, 1998) to allow communicating quantities in large scales. The magic number 60, still used measuring time – as minutes in an hour, was introduced by Sumerians about 3 millennia BC, as positioning system based on 6 and 10. Roman numerals, using Latin name of numbers, are still used in marking some special quantities. But the revolution of introducing Hindu-Arabic decimal positioning numerals, with invention of zero with its two meaning – as marking no quantity, and as a place holder, gradually leads to globally accepted standard way to represent quantities. This development resulted in avoiding or minimizing the potential for misunderstanding when communicated quantities.

Representing Time

Another area of establishing standards in communication of quantities is measures of the time. Communication of chronological data (date, month, year) has a long history toward reaching standards needed to avoid misinforming. Over the centuries, data related to time, has been also subject to misinforming. Calendars (see, for example the book of David Duncan, 1998) are conventions used by a group of people to mark cycling time of the year related to rotation of the earth. The two factors used – the changes of the phases of the moon, and seasonal changes caused by the position of the earth toward the sun – have been used for millennium. Gradually, the need of predicting seasonal changes as well as TO commemorate religious events, as Easter, leads people to develop better and better calendars. There are some funny things related to calendars – the original year of the calendar, introduced by Julius Cezar, known as Julian calendar, at year 45BC is in fact minus 45 after setting the original year by the First Council of Nicaea. The current way of using it was introduced in 325 Anno Domini (AD) or Common Era (CE) (or maybe in 370 according to original chronology according to calendar of Julius Cezar). For years the chronologists used three initial years – the one of original Cezar's edict, the one assumed as the year of birth of Jesus Christ as proposed by Nicaea Council, and the also the year of the council of Nicaea. This resulted in dating one and the same event with three different years with difference of 45, 325 or 370 years. Gradually, these differences were fixed, at least in Europe. It takes several centuries to accept more precise Gregorian Calendar, which corrected the accumulated error in Julian Calendar, and still it is not used by some Christian groups. And other religious or nations have used different calendars over the years. The Gregorian calendar dominates now, because of the heritage Europe plaid in globalizing the world.

Adopting a standard calendar is a step toward reducing the misinforming possibility in communicating time of events.

Inter-Process Communication (IPC), Internet (IP), and World Wide Web Protocols Are Standards Allowing Avoiding Misinforming in Communication Between Computers

The history of establishing standards to allow communication between computers is also significant in illustrating how to address the risk of misinforming. The significant stages are to allow communication between two processes on the same machine – IPC protocol – designing of different versions end-up with merging all; next – TCP/IP – allows communication between computers with three basic services – e-mail, ftp, and remote login. This protocol is the base standard for building the connectivity infrastructure and served for building the next generation of protocol – WWW.

CONCLUSION

This chapter introduces a variety of other issues where misinforming may play a role. Without pretending for completeness that all cases, factors, circumstances, and outputs are identified and discussed, the chapter is intended to show the diversity of circumstances that may result in misinforming.

REFERENCES

Ashby, W. (1963). *Introduction to Cybernetics*. John Willey & Sons.

Barton A. (2022). Grade Inflation: What Goes Up Must Come Down. *The Harvard Crimson*.

Box, G. E. P., & Draper, N. R. (1987). *Empirical model-building and response surfaces*. John Wiley & Sons.

Brandenburger, A., & Nalebuff, B. (1996). Co-opetition: A Revolution Mindset that Combines Competition and Cooperation. Harvard business Press, Cambridge.

Duncan, D. (1998). *The Calendar: The 5000 Year Struggle To Align The Clock and the Heavens, and What Happened To The Missing Ten Days*. Fourth Estate.

Gackowski, Z. (2006). Quality of Informing: Credibility Provisional Model of Functional Dependencies. *Proceedings of the 2006 Informing Science and IT Education Joint Conference*. Informing Science Institute. 10.28945/3017

Gill, G. (2013). Culture, Complexity, and Informing: How Shared Beliefs Can Enhance Our Search for Fitness. *Informing Science*, *16*, 71–98. doi:10.28945/1778

Hofstede, G. (1984). *Culture's Consequences: International Differences in Work-Related Values* (2nd ed.). SAGE Publications.

Ifrah, G. (1998). *Universal History of Numbers: From Prehistory to the Invention of the Computer*. Harville Press.

Mooers, C. (1950). Information retrieval viewed as temporal signaling. *Proceedings of the international congress of mathematicians.* ISI.

Simon, H. A. (1965). *The Shape of Automation for Men and Management*. Harper Torchbooks.

Sprenger, G. (2016) Structured and unstructured misunderstandings: Towards an anthropological theory of misunderstanding. *Civilizations: Rue internationale d'anthropologie et de sciences humaines*, 21-38. https://journals.openedition.org/civilisations/4050

Section 1 Conclusion

This part of the book is dedicated to the phenomenon of misinformation. It attempts to define misinforming as distinguishing from other forms of communication leading to misunderstanding and wrong behavior as dis-informing. Through the entire book, under the term "misinforming" we will understand the misinterpreting, misunderstanding or in general misleading the recipient of information from correct information provided. Its major objectives are to introduce readers to possible factors, circumstances, and human endowments that may contribute to a hazard leading to misinforming.

Complete enumeration of all possible cases, circumstances, scenarios leading to misinformation is impossible and not within the objectives of this book. The first part of the book presents various aspects and factors that have impact on informing success and misinforming phenomenon. It provides the context of the misinforming hazards, and more important justifies the need to address the risk. Managing these risks by designing mitigation practices needs rational attitude and cost-benefit assessment.

The goal of this part of the book is to illustrate the phenomenon and to justify the importance of need of adequate attention to misinforming. The growing dependence on information acquired via complex paths and technologies and the complexity of problems people are facing nowadays raises the impact of those risks. Assessment of likelihood and impact of qualitative categories as "high", "low", "critical" or similar are not sufficient anymore and do not provide enough support of rational treatment and management. Developing quantified measures for the risk associated with misinforming is needed in growing scale of indirect communication and trading.

Next part of the book is proposing a way to quantify the probability of becoming misinformed and the corresponding impact. The great variety and diversity of cases and circumstances, as described here, does not allow to propose universal measures. The context in which the measures in the next part are built is borrowed from e-commerce. This is the area considered as the one that needs the most rational management of the risk of misinforming.

The third part shares ideas on how to explore quantitative measures of the misinforming risk in several business practices in a way to mitigate the risk or to reduce the harmful effect caused by misinforming.

A warranty is a special business tool to distribute the negative consequences of a hazard in a way to allow every client to assume a small portion of responsibilities caused by the risk that harms only few. The case of warranty of misinforming is the topic developed in the fourth part of the book.

Section 2

Quantitative Measures of the Risk of Misinforming

Section 2 Introduction

This section of the book is dedicated to approaches developed for building models that may allow us to evaluate the risk of misinforming. As one can see in the first section of the book there are too many circumstances and factors that may result in misinterpretation of received, otherwise correct information. To manage a risk, one needs to allocate resources and to perform activities directed to mitigate it and its outcomes in a rational, feasible, and data driven way. The one needs objective quantity measures of the risk likelihood and impact that will allow to base such activities on a reasonable cost-benefit assessment.

During the last 30, but especially in the last 20, years the business gradually is moving to on-line form of commerce. Pandemic of COVID-19 especially fueled the on-line commerce. Practically all aspects associated with the word "commerce", from trade and production to education and learning, have been heavily influenced by Information Technologies and the Internet. In a way to illustrate the proposed approach to quantify the risk caused by misinforming, the developed models here are presented in the context of a trade transaction, using "seller" and "buyer" or "producer" and "customer" instead of information "sender" and "receiver". Under these circumstances, assuming the risk of misinforming may harm finances and reputation and may lead to losses of time and opportunities.

Nowadays, any form of business requires careful assessment of risks, based on evaluation of likelihood and impact of expected hazards. Quantity measures of these two parameters are fundamental in rational managerial decision-making. The assumption applied here is that rationality dominates over emotional decision-making. This also justifies the selected relatively narrow area of circumstances to model these risks. Emotions play a significant role in making decisions, mostly as initial assessment of whether it is worthy to explore further the provided information. Attracting a client as the basic objectives of marketing activities will be discussed from risk of misinforming point of view in the next section of the book.

One approach to allow measuring the likelihood and impact of risks associated with hazards leading to misinforming is explored in this section of the book. The approach is based on evaluation of probability to make a wrong purchase decision with negative effect to customer and therefore to producer. The case of positive effect of misinforming, as described in Chapter 1.5, is not considered here.

Either of the two parameters could be specific and different for a given specific informing process with its own objectives, circumstances, and participants. By following the proposed approach, models with gradually extended complexity are proposed by adding variables that have impact on the success of the process. The second factor influencing and limiting the increasing complexity of models is the possibility to find data needed to apply the model. The complexity of considered informing processes are gradually extended by reducing or redefining associated assumptions and by adding variables. Attention is given to the possibility to collect data in a way to apply models. Examples of surveys used for collecting relevant data are presented in a way to illustrate applicability of developed methodologies. At certain point, data needed is also too complicated that do not allow collecting it in a reasonable way. Complexity of data needed also served as the upper bound for complexity of models. The cybernetic law of requisite variety is applicable here as well. Surveys used to verify the models are summarized in Appendix 2. The table below briefly illustrates the history of evolution of models and corresponding data collection initiatives:

Table 1. Stages in evolution of developed models to quantify the risk of misinforming

Year	Objectives	Type of responses	Applicability	Comments	Respondents
2001-2003	Illustrating existence of misinforming	Y/N	Easy	Not designed to allow quantifying the risk	Sophomore students in AUBG[1]MIS course
2006	Allowing basic measures	Likert scale	Easy	The survey allows evaluation of the basic measures of the risk of misinforming.	Sophomore students in OR course in Victoria University[2] First year students in IB course of SULSIT[3]
2008	Evaluation of degree of acceptance	Likert scale	Complicated	The survey was done in two stages with one week break to exclude self-plagiarism. The first one addressed degree of acceptance, and the second to assess applicability of device.	Sophomore students in OR course in Victoria University First year students in IB course of SULSIT
2008	Addressing competing messages	Likert scale	Over complicated	The survey was done in two stages with one week break. The same respondents were approached twice.	Sophomore students in OR course in Victoria University First year students in IB course of SULSIT

Notes:
1. Every survey includes the same part for assessing basic measures of the risk.
2. The last survey shows that increasing further the complexity of questionnaires to collect the needed data is not practical.
3. The third component of all surveys regarding attitude toward warranty is discussed in the Fourth Section of the book.

This section of the book is organized by following chronologically the evolutional path of developed models via increasing complexity in a way to reflect better the reality of communication between a seller and buyer. Evolution of models in most cases is done by considering additional parameters, or by extending the attributes of already used variables. The two factors mentioned above – complexity of real circumstances of appearing the misinforming hazard, and possibilities to collect data relevant to evaluation of the additional parameters or properties – are always considered in deriving next generation of models. These two aspects of modeling are discussed in every chapter in this section of the book. Additionally, the objectives in expanding models are how helpful the new versions are in making decisions about risk mitigation.

In general, all the models are developed under assumption of a business transaction, from point of view of the customer who is purchasing a product according to his assessment of its usability according to the information provided by the producer in the product's promotional message. Also, the risk of a producer composing the advertising message and exposed to unsatisfied clients was considered, but as a secondary hazard – as an aggregated result of the risks individual clients are exposed to.

The evolution of the models' complexity is presented in the chapters of this section of book in the following way:

First chapter – Nascency – presents the original circumstances leaded to identify the problem and to initiate research on how to measure likelihood of the risk of misinforming. These circumstances have completely different objectives and the construction of the initial model to quantify the risk of misinform was developed to illustrate the needs for paying attention to users in design of interface in a computer application. The aim was to expose that users could be misled by information acquired in information system and the importance of carefully designed user interface to avoid misinforming.

The title of the next chapter is Basic measures of risk of misinforming. It presents the foundations of the approach explored throughout the book – the probabilistic model regarding the risk of wrong purchase decision. It defines the basic parameters that need evaluation in a way to measure the risk of misinforming. In comparison with the initial model, described in the first chapter, the properties of the parameters are extended substantially.

The third chapter – Assessment of the degree of acceptance – provides a way to allow measuring one of the important parameters proposed in the previous chapter. Degree of acceptance is subjective measure of whether the provided information describes a product that meets buyer's expectation.

The further two chapters describe models to address specific cases of misinforming as the case of multiple competing messages, and the dynamics of reduction the misunderstanding in a process of learning during a given trial period. The latter case links this section of the book with the fourth one, which is dedicated to warranty of misinforming as a business practice that allows risk-free trial periods.

The Conclusion in this section of the book will serve as reference by summarizing assumptions, the used symbols and notations with their definitions used throughout all the chapters and models in this section of the book. The chapter refers to Appendix 1 and Appendix 2 at the end of the book, where are listed all symbols used throughout the book with their definitions; and forms to executed surveys.

ENDNOTES

1 AUBG: American University in Bulgaria, Blagoevgrad, Bulgaria

2 Victoria University of Wellington, Wellington, New Zealand

3 State University of Library Studies and Information Technologies, Sofia, Bulgaria

Chapter 6
Nascency

ABSTRACT

This chapter describes how the research for developing quantitative measures for misinforming originated. The original circumstances lead to identify that the problem of misinforming exists and deserves quantified measuring, and to initiate research on how to measure the likelihood of the risk of misinforming. These circumstances have completely different objectives and the construction of the initial model to quantify the risk of misinform was developed to illustrate the needs for paying attention to users in designing interface in a computer application. The aim was to expose that users could be misled by information acquired in information system and the importance of carefully designed user interface to avoid misinforming. The original idea was to illustrate for a potential information systems designer the importance of considering the end-users' background and the way they adopt information.

INTRODUCTION

This chapter describes the circumstances led to identify that the hazards leading to misinforming deserve attention and evaluation. As a result of the initially observed problem, the natural addresses of quantitative measures of the misinforming risk were identified as well.

Also, the early assumptions regarding what is the range of models needed to cover, at least in an over simplified way, the scope of the problem to show their applicability. Works reported on the next chapters of this part of the book were identified as needed in this original case.

Initially the research on the identified problem has started by sharing these finding to forums with colleagues with high range of relevant professional experience

DOI: 10.4018/978-1-6684-8800-3.ch006

(Christozov & Mateev, 2003; and Christozov7 Mateev, 2005). Additionally, solid research on potentially relevant literature were performed. The result of these activities was that no relevant publications were found. The area, recognized as relevant, of application of such measures – the warranty presented by the slogan "if you are not fully satisfied – money back", used for years – also have not shown publications addressing measuring the cost of this promotional policy.

ORIGINAL CASE

I identified the problem of the needs of measuring probability of risk of misinforming for the first time during teaching a class of Information Systems in 2001. One of the objectives of this lecture was to demonstrate to students how important is to consider recipients' or end-users' background and the manner to deal with data when designing computer systems interface. The use of users' professional jargon, and to have in mind the way how they will interpret information and how they will map received information to the problems they are facing. To convince students that misunderstanding is quite likely I offered students an assignment. The purpose was to contrast the information provided from the sender to receiver within a problem domain. The sender describes a product as its technical parameters and the receiver describes the needs in terms of usage of the product. To illustrate this issue of designing Information Systems I provided to students an advertisement describing personal computers (PC) and a list of reasons to use it that they may need. Major activities for accomplishment with the use of the PC they are considering justifying purchasing of a PC. Practically, the majority of students in their sophomore year faced the problem to purchase PC and they were well prepared to respond regarding what they want to do with this device. I picked one advertisement for a PC from a newspaper and modified its description a bit in the following way: increased the power of CPU, added more primary and secondary memory, replaced the colored with a black-and-white (BW) monitor, practically remove the network capability. This description is presented in Figure 1. Keep in mind that this PC configuration was typical in the year 2001.

Figure 1. Configuration of a PC

ASUS A7V333/RA sA, VIA KT333, 266, ATA 133, RAID, 3DDR, AGP 4x, USB 2.0, IEE 1394, ATX AMD XP PALOMINO 2100PR/1.75 GHz DDRAM 512 MB DDR, PC 333MHz, SAMSUNG 80 GB MAXSTOR / 7200 / ATA 133/2MB PCI ATI 1MB 17'' SAMSUNG 753S 1280x1024/65Hz 1024x768/85 Hz BW keyboard, mouse, midi tower case

Additionally, I listed a set of typical activities a PC was used at that time:

- Develop and edit text. Word Processing.
- Make complex and even sophisticated computations.
- Use of e-mail
- Access to Internet, searching.
- Organize personal data.
- Play games.
- Watch movies and listen to music.

The PC, as described above, allows one to easily accomplish some of these activities, some – not so well, but others – not at all. Students were asked to define what they are going to do with the PC, and whether the proposed one suits their needs, if the price is attractive.

Answers of students (about 50 in two sections of the course) are shown on Table 1. (see Christozov, Mateev, 2003):

Table 1. Answers of the students

Application	Needs	Assessed ability of the system	The system allows	Risk of wrong decision
Word Processing	100	100	YES	0
Computation	30	70	YES	30%
e-mail	100	80	NO	80%
Internet	100	70	NO	70%
Personal data	90	80	YES	20%
Games	70	80	NO	80%
Movies	10	50	NO	50%

Rough evaluation shows that about 40% of students will make wrong decisions in purchasing this device to accomplish what they need. Some of the problems comes from description and mostly by missing detail explanation of the of the PC properties (e.g., BW means black-and-white), but mostly because of the bias, wrong assumptions, and inability to interpret provided information in the context of their problems.

The way to evaluate the probability of risk was over simplified – I simply counted how many students want to do something with the PC that the PC doesn't allow to do – the average of the percentages of the right-most column. This too simple case allows only "yes/no" capability of a product to satisfy client's needs, and regarding computer capability.

The description of the PC provided was fully correct and complete, but it results in misleading 40% of readers – potential customers. This result shocked me, and I realize that the problem of evaluating risk of misinforming deserves attention. At the emerging times when world faces dominated by indirect communication and becoming informed via IT, it appeared as a valuable research topic.

Another reason for justifying the importance of measuring the probability was the widely used practice to advertise products with the statement "If you are not fully satisfied – money back". In the above case more than 40% of customers will claim their money back and the cost for producer advertising via a misleading message will be too, and unexpectedly, high. Practically, the above promotional statement serves as a warranty contract, but the warranty that covers the risk of becoming misinformed. Without proper evaluation of probability and impact of this risk, such offer could result in a financial disaster, or wrongly designed advertisement message, without proper quantitative evaluation of consequences represents significant risk also to the producers and sellers.

Finally, it was clear that the way to calculate the likelihood of the risk is too simple and to make it useful it needs further refinement.

LESSON LEARNED AND IDENTIFIED ASPECTS OF THE PROBLEM

The process, and different circumstances leading to misinforming risk, associated with, creating, transmitting, interpreting, and adopting information is presented in Part 1. In the simplest case there are two parties – sender and receiver. The receiver has a problem to solve but has not complete information to make rational or informed decision regarding how to solve it. The sender has information or knowledge which may be helpful to the receiver in solving the problem. The communication process includes activities of both parties. The sender, producer or seller, sends a message composed in a way to provide the needed information, according to sender's understanding what receiver is needed and how receiver will understand the information. The risk of misinforming happens when receiver does not correctly understand the message, does not correctly interpret it, and does not correctly relate it to the own problems. Or the receiver does not trust that received information is correct and does not adopt it; or does not correctly apply it in a way to solve the problems. The two parties participate in this process according to their own background, knowledge, and bias. Their behavior is highly influenced by personal attitude toward risks and toward the other party in the process, and the general attitude toward life – optimism or positivism Vs. pessimism or negativism. The phenomenon of information asymmetry, as described in Part 1, is applicable and influences the success of communication.

In terms of business transactions this could be spelled out as the following – a potential client has some work to accomplish with a product of given type, for example to do word processing the client needs a personal computer, to do this. The problem is what are the parameters of the product that suits in the best way, or it is good enough, for accomplishing the work.

For simplicity, in explaining the ideas for how to quantify this risk, the viewpoint of the receiver of information as a client facing purchasing a product based on information provided as advertisements is used as the context of all further presentations. But also, a generalization of the measures of risk for the case of multiple receivers is made, which is assumed to represent the misinforming from the viewpoint of the sender, producer or seller of the product who need to calculate the cost of misunderstanding of the created message.

The earliest try to evaluate the risk of misinforming described above shows that this risk is high enough to deserve careful assessing, measuring, and managing. To manage a risk in a rational, data driven manner the likelihood and impact of those hazards must be quantified. The immediate assessment of the identified problem pointed out two research areas – the area of information theory and information systems; and the area of quality control and warranty analysis. The assumption that the studies in warranty analysis have paid already attention to this kind of problems looked natural, because for years a statement like "if you are not fully satisfied, money back" was used to promote sells. Unfortunately, it shows that this technique was explored solely in marketing and was not investigated as risk sharing as a kind of warranty at that time. Also, information theory had not addressed the issue. Those findings encourage us to investigate the problem and to propose models and techniques to evaluate the risk of misinforming. Later, with raising the e-commerce and on-line trade the issue of not satisfied client become visible and even appeared in the regulation of those kind sells. Or evaluation of risk of misinforming made in the context of business transactions looks practical.

The following topologies of informing processes as marketing cases deserve attention:

- Risk of client making purchase decision by exploring a single message describing one product: one-to-one (1:1).
- Risk of producer advertising one product to many potential clients: one-to-many (1:M).
- Risk of client in case of choosing among competing products, described by competing messages: many-to-one (M:1).
- Real market case where many products are offered to many clients: many-to-many (M:N).

The risk for the parties involved in a business transaction – seller and buyer – need evaluation, nevertheless the role for offering actions for mitigation of this risk lays solely on seller. Evaluation of the seller's risk is an aggregation function of individual buyers' risks.

Additionally, the dynamics of learning deserve attention. What happens during the time a client is using the product? How the parameters of the misinforming risk changed via learning process that reduces information asymmetry?

As seen in the previous part, hazards leading to misinforming may have many origins. The real problem is that they appear naturally in a communication process and may prevent correctly inform receivers. Difficulties in quantifying those risks are because hazards are results of failures in communication between parties involved. Neither of the two parties have full control on the process and therefore ability to evaluate the likelihood and impact of such risks. The bias of either of the parties does not allow it to assume full responsibility for the success or failure of the process. The existence of information asymmetry between parties is both the necessary condition for the need of communication and major reason causing misinforming.

Fundamental assumption is that the customer makes rational decisions, based on acquired knowledge via information provided by the producer or seller solely in the message. The measures of the risk of misinforming developed here do not address problems related to trust, emotional decision making, or decisions based on fashion. Identifying factors influencing creation of acting knowledge, under those assumptions, is the most essential component in proposed approach and developed models.

Those models are developed in a simple business transaction with five actions in mind:

- Informative – the stage where the two parties are identified and met.

- Negotiations and contracting – the stage of defining the parameters of the deal and setting agreement.
- Delivery – the stage of executing the agreement.
- Payment – the stage of completing the deal.
- Reporting – the stage of informing the public entities, as tax agency.

In these five stages, the first one is when the misinforming hazard may occur. At this stage, the producer or seller provides information regarding the properties of the product and the client who received it assesses whether that the product will serve well in accomplishing needed activities. The problems in quantifying the two parameters of misinforming risk exposure are based on subjectivity in the interpretation and the acceptance of the message sent by the seller. One and the same message may correctly inform some clients and misinform others. The misinforming could be of different degrees and consequences for an individual receiver within a given group, and the impact may vary also to the entirely different groups of customers. Grouping customers to address with the same message is also a legitimate problem addressed in next Part of the book.

Additional difficulty in developing models for measuring the risks of misinforming is caused by the complexity of the message. A portion of the message regarding some of the properties of the product may inform clients correctly, but another part of the same message may misinform them regarding other properties.

For the receiver, the risk of misinforming is very personal. On the other hand, as in commercial activities, the seller is also influenced by own failures in informing clients. The seller's risk is associated with the composition and the content of the message and how this message meets clients' objectives. The risk is measured by the portion of misinformed clients and by the nature of the incorrect actions caused by misinterpreting the message.

To evaluate the risk of misinforming for a group of receivers, we have to consider each, and every personal reaction caused by the message, i.e., the individual's risk, and to aggregate these risks over the whole group. The attitude of an individual receiver towards the message will allow to divide the group of receivers into subgroups (clusters). The study the risk of these subgroups allows to obtain a better insight on the nature of the failures, causes and effects in the informing process.

One other significant aspect of the informing process is whether a receiver realizes that there is possibility to misinterpret the obtained information and can become misled. Or whether they are prepared to consider the hazard of misinforming as existing real risk. In most of the surveys presented in this part of the book, this aspect is assessed by offering to respondents three different types of warranties:

- Classical warranty – warranty of malfunctioning shares the risk of misfunctioning of the product as it is designed for.
- Warranty of misinforming – covers the risk of clients who have purchased a not suitable to their need product, and
- Mixed warranty policy – combining coverage of the two kinds of risks.

Respondents who choose only the first option are those who definitely ignore the possibility that they may interpret the message wrongly. Clients who are over-confident in their competences.

A successful informing process as considered here is based on the structural, hierarchical definition made in the first part of the book. This definition is applicable in designing models to quantify the parameters of this risk. In brief, according to this definition an informing process is successful if four different activities are successful. All models in this part of the book assumed that the first two levels are passed successfully, and even the third on – related to the trust – have not led to ignoring the message.

To summarize, the informing process includes two parties:

- Receiver, or buyer, who is facing to do a set of works and expects that by using a product of given type these works will be accomplished in an effective and efficient way. The problem of the receiver is defined in terms of work she or he needs to do.
- The sender, or seller, is the one providing information, in the form of an advertisement, describing the product, which is potentially suitable to meet the receiver's expectations. The message, composed by the seller, describes the technical parameters of the product.

The informing process, on the side of receiver, is to map technical properties of the product, as described by the seller, into set of works and to decide whether a product with given properties will suit well in accomplishing each and all these works.

Misinforming is the case when the buyer misinterprets the properties of the product by either purchasing a product with technical properties that is not capable to do a given work from the set effectively or in expected efficiency ("not fully satisfied"); or when the buyer decided not to purchase the product which otherwise is suitable for accomplishing all expected works in full.

CONCLUSION

This part of the book represents the evolution of understanding of how to measure and quantify the risk of misinforming. This chapter explains how the research problem was born by an attempt to illustrate a common-sense issue and defines the overall circumstances to address in developing the quantitative measures. Practically, existence of misinforming in commerce was recognized for years, but appearing of the e-commerce and the in-direct trade raised its importance, validity, and the range of influenced cases significantly.

The problem addressed was defined as participants in the process – Seller and Buyer; content of informing message – properties of the product as described by the Seller; objectives of informing process – assessing the suitability of the product for accomplishing works as expected by the Buyer. The attributes of the problem and the variables used in describing the proposed models are defined more fully in the next chapter.

REFERENCES

Christozov, D., & Mateev, P. (2003). *Warranty as a Factor for e-Commerce Success*. Informing Science and IT Education Conference, Pori, Finland. http://InSITE.nu

Christozov, D., & Mateev, P. (2005). Assessment of Information Asymmetry. *Pliska Studia Mathematica Bulgarica*, *17*, 27–38.

Chapter 7
Basic Measures of Risk of Misinforming

ABSTRACT

This chapter introduces the adopted approach in modeling likelihood and impact of the risk of misinformation. The approach presented here is explored throughout the book and it serves as a foundation to all models developed further. This chapter introduces the variables and parameters in developing a probabilistic model regarding the risk of wrong purchase decision. It defines the parameters that need evaluation in a way to measure the risk of misinformation and proposes a way to collect data. In comparison with the initial model described in the first chapter, the properties of the parameters are extended substantially.

INTRODUCTION

The objective of this part of the book is to develop quantitative measures, models, and data gathering, to allow assessing the risk of misinforming. The basic properties of the approach developed to address the problem of misinforming hazard, and ideas leading to build measures to quantify the probability and impact of the risk of misinforming, as well as definitions of the variables used, are defined in this chapter. In next sections we will elaborate the basic ideas evolved to address the evaluation of the risk of misinforming and explored throughout the chapters in this and next parts of the book.

The variables used in the model developed to measure the risk are defined in the context of an informing process, including only two participating parties – Seller and Buyer. A business case – purchasing by the Buyer a product offered by the

DOI: 10.4018/978-1-6684-8800-3.ch007

Seller in a way to fulfil identified by the Buyer needs, to accomplish a set of works, as described in the previous chapter will be used as a context in defining variables used in building models.

Complete set of variables used a cross the book, notations, symbols, definitions, and assumptions are given in the Appendix 1, which can be used as reference.

BASIC MODEL

Assume that there is a set of Buyers $B=\{b_j\}, j=1,2,\ldots,N$, where b_j represents the jth buyer. There is also a set of products by $D=\{d_i\}$, $i=1,2,\ldots,M$, potentially suitable for accomplishing the set of K_j works, activities or tasks $A_j=\{a_{kj}\}$, $k=1,2,\ldots,K_j$, the buyer b_j needs to do by using a product from the set D.

Let the Buyer b_j (the indices could be avoided to simplify the formulae, when assuming a single customer or when using indices will not add to understand the meaning of given formula) needs to do a set of works and to find a suitable tool to accomplish them. To do this the customer has to be able to accomplish a set of k works, activities, or tasks, let us mark this set as $A=\{a_k\}$, by using a product $d \in D$. Some of these works may help in solving different problems needed by the customer as well.

For example, a customer b is looking for a PC to watch movies or to listen to music on-line. For both of those activities b needs Internet access, a sound system, and for watching movies b also needs a high-quality screen. Quality access to the Internet is common property to almost all activities b faces and wants to accomplish with the use of this PC. If b needs only to listen to music, she or he needs high quality sound system but may accept lower quality for the screen. Or to obtain a PC that will satisfy all needs of b, the PC must meet the highest requirements for quality to all the works related to all the problems that b wants to solve by using the product.

Subsequently, we will refer to this customer as a customer with set $\{A\}$. The elements $\{a\}$ of A are assumed disjoined and are called works or activities.

$$\{A\} = \{a_k, k=1,\ldots,K\},$$

where K is a positive finite integer.

For the above example, the customer is looking to buy a PC. He wants to do word processing, to use the Internet, and many other works with this PC. Or the set $\{A\}$ is {word processing, use of Internet, making calculations, listening to music, play games, etc.}.

Also, let assume that by applying certain methods, devices or services, the activity a_k from $\{A\}$ can be accomplished and the problem can be assessed as solved. We will call these methods, devices, or services products, which the Buyer needs to acquire or purchase. Moreover, there is a set of products $D=\{d_i\}$, $i=1,\ldots,M$, available on the market, appropriate for accomplishing the works faced by Buyer b or the set $\{A\}$ of activities.

For different customers, who have the same set of works $\{a\}$ to do, the complexity and importance of corresponding properties of product varies and, subsequently, the suitability of the products, available for accomplishing them, also varies. We assume that for each work $\{a\}$ from the set, and for given customer b with the set $\{a\}$ of activities, exists specific threshold or the level of acceptance q, $0 <= q <=1$ – the minimal quality that makes the product suitable for accomplishing this work by this Buyer. Level of acceptance is the minimal quality or minimal level of performance related to a given property of the product. This level (value) is pre-set by the customer in assessing the suitability of a product. The threshold of acceptance for given property of the product is the lowest level, set by the customer, of product's performance still acceptable for accomplishing all works from the set $\{a\}$ that need the given property. In that way the level of acceptance is the maximal requirement among the minimal for all the works sharing or needed the same property.

If a product d satisfies thresholds for all works from the set $\{a\}$, the customer problem of finding suitable product will be solved, and the product d is acceptable for b. The threshold of acceptance represents the customer's opinion on what is a suitable product. And whether it can be considered as a possible solution to accomplish works in $\{a\}$. The value of q is independent of the set of products D and it is property solely to the customer's needs and priorities. Different customers may have different sets of thresholds for the product's properties for the same activities they are looking to do with this product. For a given buyer the acceptance level for different activities could be different, but to make a decision for purchasing the product must satisfy the all of them and the threshold for this customer is the highest one.

The set of works $A=\{a\}$ can be considered as a sample space of all possible outcomes for the customer b. Let $P=P(a)$ denotes a probability distribution on $\{a\}$, induced by the customer with set $A=\{a\}$. This probability distribution is subjective and represents the importance of works in $\{a\}$ to this customer.

The probability of the case when a given product is suitable for a customer with set of activities $A=\{a\}$ is denote "success" and marked by S.

Let mark with $P(S|a)$ the probability that the customer can accomplish work $a \in A$ without applying any product. For example, the customer can do text editing without using computers. Then, based of the total probability rule, the probability that the customer will successfully solve the problem, or accomplished all the works in the set $\{A\}$, without applying any product is

$$P(S)=\sum_{a\in A}P(S|a)P(a) \tag{1}$$

Further, let us apply the product $d\in D$ for $a\in A$. Now, the probability of success is $P(S|a,d)$, which is a measure of the suitability of the product d to accomplish work a. The product d is suitable for accomplishing a if and only if

$$P(S|a)<P(S|a,d), \tag{2}$$

i.e., the probability to do work a with applying product d is higher than the probability of accomplish the same work without applying any product. The difference represents effect of using the product d to accomplish work a. For example, editing text with a word processing tool on a PC is more efficient than on paper or without computers. Let us assume that this inequality holds for product d and at least one of the works a, $a\in A$. Otherwise, the product d is completely irrelevant to the needs of the customer with set of works $A=\{a\}$.

The suitability of product d for a customer with set $\{A\}$ can be measured with the probability of success when applying this product to all works $a\in A$, i.e.,

$$p=P(S|d)=\sum_{a\in A}P(S|a,d)P(a). \tag{3}$$

Therefore, if a satisfactory estimation for the aforementioned probability is available it can be used to measure the suitability of product d for set $\{a\}$, and therefore for the customer b.

The information asymmetry is due to a mismatch between the seller's and the buyer's estimations of the suitability of product d with respect to a set $\{A\}$. The seller is familiar with the product and its suitability to execute a specific works with specific complexity with given level of performance, whereas the seller is better informed on the suitability of the product related to known problems and level of performance for all works in $A=\{a\}$, measured by the probability $P(S|a,d)$, the product is designed for.

The customer b is the only one who knows his/her own set of problems/works $A_b=\{a_b\}$ and related distribution $P(a_b)$. Therefore, a customer b is identified by the pair $\{(A,P),q\}$, the set of problems with associated works she or he needs to accomplish, the measure of the importance of the works, and the threshold of acceptance for every work from the set $A_b=\{a_b\}$. The triple $\{(A,P),q,d\}$ describes how a product d meets customer's needs q in accomplishing works a from given pair (A,P).

Any message from the seller to the customer aims to enrich the customer's information about the product, which will reflect on the value of $P(S|a,d)$.

A customer makes his/her purchase decision based on the estimation of

$$\hat{p}\,(\mathrm{d}) \text{ of } p(d)=P(S|d), \qquad (4)$$

where p is given by (1). The estimation $\hat{p}$ summarizes the customer's understanding regarding the suitability of the product to solve problems in his/her set $A=\{a\}$ The difference between $\hat{p}(d)$ and *p*(*d*) is the difference between subjective assessment of the product's property and its objective value, and it is the measure of information asymmetry. In general, there are three categories of customers, optimists with $\hat{p} > p$, pessimists with $\hat{p} < p$ and realists with $\hat{p} = p$ (or competent customers)

The case of having probability of assessment equal to actual value $\hat{p} = p$ is negligible because it refers to exact equality of these two real numbers. More practical is to refer to a Buyer as realist for those of them to whom the difference is small enough $|\hat{p} - p| < \varepsilon$, where ε is a very small positive value. The group of realists deserve attention, but in this case, we cannot speak about the existence of information asymmetry and risk of misinforming. This category of customers is not the subject of this study.

The purchase decision is a discrete "yes-no" value, depends on the comparison between q and $\hat{p}$. If $q < \hat{p}$, then the purchase decision should be positive, i.e., customer's subjective estimation for the suitability of the product is greater than the threshold of acceptance and the product is assessed as suitable. If $q > \hat{p}$, the purchase decision should be negative, because customer's estimation of the suitability of the product is less than the threshold of acceptance and customer's assessment is that the product is not suitable for solving problems defined by $\{a\}$.

There are six possible scenarios, caused by the information asymmetry and subjectivity of interpreting information describing properties of the product, and corresponding success in informing (correct decision) or misinforming (wrong decision):

1. $p < \hat{p} < q$ - the product is not suitable, the customer's estimation of the suitability of the product is **optimistic** and **below the threshold of acceptance,** thus the decision is **negative** and **correct**.
2. $p < q < \hat{p}$- the product is not suitable, the customer's estimation of the suitability of the product is **optimistic** and **above the threshold of acceptance,** thus the decision is **positive** and **wrong**.

3. $q < p < \hat{p}$ - the product is suitable, the customer's estimation of the suitability of the product is **optimistic** and **above the threshold of acceptance**, thus the decision is **positive** and **correct**.
4. $\hat{p} < p < q$ - the product is not suitable, the customer's estimation of the suitability of the product is **pessimistic** and **below the threshold of acceptance,** thus the decision is again **negative** and **correct.**
5. $\hat{p} < q < p$ - the product is suitable, the customer's estimation of the suitability of the product is **pessimistic** and **below the threshold of acceptance**, thus the decision is **negative** and **wrong**.
6. $q < \hat{p} < p$ - the product is suitable, the customer's estimation of the suitability of the product is **pessimistic** and **above the threshold of acceptance**, thus the decision is **positive** and **correct**.

The three parameters q, $\hat{p}$, and p are acceptance threshold, subjective assessment of the product suitability, based on individual's interpretation of provided information, and objective suitability of the product to accomplish given work in a way suitable to this customer's need.

The first three cases define the customer as an optimist ($\hat{p} > p$) and the last three – as a pessimist ($\hat{p} < p$). In each of these two categories exists one case of wrong decision or misinforming. For optimists, the wrong decision is in case 2 – the product is not suitable, but the purchase decision is positive. This case of misinforming leads to direct harm to the customer. For pessimists, the wrong decision is in case 5 – the product is suitable, but the purchase decision is negative. This is the case of missed opportunity.

MEASURING THE RISK OF MISINFORMING

A measure of the risk of misinforming r is a function with three variables – probability of wrong decision (r_{ij}), level of misunderstanding or information asymmetry $\left(\hat{p}_{ij} - p_i\right)$, and Buyer's need ($n_{ij}$) or Buyer's weight for importance of the works. Let us consider first the risk r_{ij} of a wrong decision related to one activity a_i and needed by one buyer b_j. Further, this measure will be extended to the entire set of activities $A_j=\{a_{ij}\}$ for one buyer, say $r_j = r_{b_j}$. Later it will be generalized to measure the risk R of the entire group of buyers.

The measure of risk of misinforming will be extended further gradually from one-to-one, many-to-one, and one-to-many cases to many-to-many. The first two cases address the customer's risk and the latter two – the risk of producer. The complexity of the models to measure these risks is extended by adding variables. Potential and ways for collecting data is the key criteria for adding variables.

The Risk of a Wrong Decision of a Single Buyer b_j With Respect to a Single Work a_{ij}

To measure the risk of a wrong decision of a single buyer b_j with respect to a single activity a_{ij} the two possible outcomes for the buyer's purchase decision regarding the product *d*, are "YES", positive, decision is to purchase the product, or "NO" negative, decision is not to purchase the product.

The buyer b_j will make a positive decision if for all $a_{ij} \in A_j$, such that $n_{ij}>0$, the work is in "to do" list of the Buyer, and $q_{ij}>0$, not all products on the market are suitable, the inequality $\widehat{p}_{ij} \geq q_{ij}$ holds and negative decision is when the opposite inequality $\widehat{p}_{ij} < q_{ij}$ is valid for at least one activity a_{ij} recognized as needed ($n_{ij}>0$).

The correctness of this decision depends also on the relationship between p_i, the actual ability of *d* to accomplish work a_{ij}, $\widehat{p}_{ij}$ – the estimated by the Buyer ability of *d* to perform acceptable in accomplishing a_{ij}, q_{ij} – the degree of acceptance, and n_{ij} – the need to do the activity a_{ij}. The above six possible combinations between p_i, $\widehat{p}_{ij}$ and q_{ij} allow to identify whether buyer's decision to buy the product is wrong or correct with respect to a single activity a_{ij}.

The following notation indicates the correctness/incorrectness of the buyer's purchase decision with respect to a_{ij}:

$$r_{ij} = \begin{cases} 1 & \textit{the decision is wrong} \\ 0 & \textit{the decision is correct} \end{cases} \tag{5}$$

The six cases are:

1. $p_i < \widehat{p}_{ij} < q_{ij}$: decision is **negative** and **correct** and $r_{ij}=0$;
2. $p_i < q_{ij} < \widehat{p}_{ij}$: decision is **positive** and **wrong,** and $r_{ij}=1$;
3. $q_{ij} < p_i < \widehat{p}_{ij}$: decision is **positive** and **correct,** and $r_{ij}=0$;
4. $\widehat{p}_{ij} < p_i < q_{ij}$: decision is **negative** and **correct,** and $r_{ij}=0$;
5. $\widehat{p}_{ij} < q_{ij} < p_i$: decision is **negative** and **wrong,** and $r_{ij}=1$;
6. $q_{ij} < \widehat{p}_{ij} < p_i$: decision is **positive** and **correct,** and $r_{ij}=0$.

The quantity measure of misinforming is represented by the distance between p_i and $\widehat{p}_{ij}$, but the risk is materialized, only if the purchasing decision is wrong, i.e., only if r_{ij} =1. Also, the customer experiences the negative effect of this risk only in the case of a positive purchase decision.

Two forms of the risk of misunderstanding measures are proposed. The first one is the measure of the adjusted risk, represented by the triple: $n_{ij,} r_{ij}, abs\left(\widehat{p}_{ij} - p_i\right)$. This measure accounts for the weight of need for the work that will be satisfied/unsatisfied, adjusted for the level of misinforming (information asymmetry). The second measure of the misinforming risk, so called unadjusted risk, is represented only by the pair of variables – n_{ij} and r_{ij}. It is based on the weight of need of the work that will be satisfied/unsatisfied under right/wrong purchase decision with respect to a_{ij}. The unadjusted risk does not consider the level of information asymmetry. It is difficult to evaluate this variable in the majority of real-life cases. The impact of wrong decision is a function of importance of the activity (need) for the customer.

The Risk of Misinforming of a Single Buyer b_j for the Entire Set of Activities $A=\{a_{ij}\}$

The set of all categories of works, assumed relevant for accomplishing with a product from *D*, is marked with A^*. It is not necessary that all these categories are relevant to the scopa of usage of every buyer, but for the unneeded activities from a given category the need is set to zero.

The overall adjusted risk for the buyer b_j is

$$r_j^a = \frac{1}{\sum_i n_{ij}} \sum_{i=1}^{k} n_{ij} r_{ij} abs\left(\widehat{p}_{ij} - p_i\right) \tag{2.2.6}$$

where the summation is over all categories of activities $A=\{a_{ij}\}$ relevant to b_j. The overall unadjusted risk for the buyer b_j is equal to

$$r_j^u = \frac{1}{\sum_i n_{ij}} \sum_{i=1}^{k} n_{ij} r_{ij}, \tag{2.2.7}$$

where, again, the summation is over $A*$.

In Table 1 are summarized all components needed for further modeling of the risk of misinforming.

Basic Measures of Risk of Misinforming

Table 1. Summary of variables used in modeling the risk of misinforming

Category of activities Client	A^*_1 $\{p_1\}$	A^*_2 $\{p_2\}$	...	A^*_K $\{p_K\}$
b_1	$\{a_{11}, n_{11}, q_{11}, \hat{p}_{11}, r_{11}\}$	$\{a_{21}, n_{21}, q_{21}, \hat{p}_{21}, r_{21}\}$	...	$\{a_{K1}, n_{K1}, q_{K1}, \hat{p}_{K1}, r_{K1}\}$
b_2	$\{a_{12}, n_{12}, q_{12}, \hat{p}_{12}, r_{12}\}$	$\{a_{22}, n_{22}, q_{22}, \hat{p}_{22}, r_{22}\}$	...	$\{a_{K2}, n_{K2}, q_{K2}, \hat{p}_{K2}, r_{K2}\}$
...	...	...	...	...
b_N	$\{a_{1N}, n_{1N}, q_{1N}, \hat{p}_{1N}, r_{1N}\}$	$\{a_{2N}, n_{2N}, q_{2N}, \hat{p}_{2N}, r_{2N}\}$	...	$\{a_{KN}, n_{KN}, q_{KN}, \hat{p}_{KN}, r_{KN}\}$

The Risk of Misunderstanding of the Group of Buyers

From Seller's point of view, the risk is the aggregation of the individual risks for the members of the group $B=\{b_j\}$, $j=1,2,\ldots,n$ (seller's risk). To assess the risk potential related to the provided message, it is appropriate to measure the risk of misinforming, separately to the categories of works as well as in general. Depending on the available information about $\hat{p}_{ij}$, n_{ij} and q_{ij}, three possible measures of the risk of misinforming from seller's point of view can be defined (see Table 2):

Table 2. Measures of seller's risk (risk associated with the group of buyers)

Measure	For *i*-category of works (A_i^*)	General
Simple:	$R_i^s = \frac{1}{n}\sum_{j=1}^{n} r_{ij}$	$R^s = \frac{1}{kn}\sum_{i=1}^{k}\sum_{j=1}^{n} r_{ij}$
Unadjusted:	$R_i^u = \frac{1}{\sum_j n_{ij}}\sum_{j=1}^{n} n_{ij} r_{ij}$	$R^u = \frac{1}{k}\sum_{i=1}^{k}\frac{1}{\sum_j n_{ij}}\sum_{j=1}^{n} n_{ij} r_{ij}$
Adjusted:	$R_i^a = \frac{1}{\sum_j n_{ij}}\sum_{j=1}^{n} n_{ij} r_{ij} abs(\hat{p}_{ij} - p_i)$	$R^a = \frac{1}{k}\sum_{i=1}^{k}\frac{1}{\sum_j n_{ij}}\sum_{j=1}^{n} n_{ij} r_{ij} abs(\hat{p}_{ij} - p_i)$

ε-Definition of Clustering the Group of Buyers

This definition allows us to distinguish between the three categories of buyers: optimists, pessimists, and realists.

Definition. For a given positive number ε, we say that the buyer b*j* is an ε-optimist if $\sum_{i=1}^{k} n_{ij}\left(\hat{p}-p\right) > \varepsilon$, or he is an ε-pessimist if $\sum_{i=1}^{k} n_{ij}\left(\hat{p}-p\right) < -\varepsilon$ or he is an ε-realist if $-\varepsilon < \sum_{i=1}^{k} n_{ij}\left(\hat{p}-p\right) < \varepsilon$.

EMPIRICAL SURVEYS: DATA COLLECTION TO ALLOW EVALUATION OF THE RISK

The objective of the original survey (2001-2003) was to show students that it is possible to misinterpret otherwise correct information. It was not designed to allow quantifying the risk of misinforming, just to show that such risk exists. This survey shows that misinforming problem is significant and deserves investigation and especially deserves management and measuring quantities associated with this risk. Measures were done just on a Yes/No scale. The measures developed in this chapter needed a completely different form of questionnaire to collect data in a way to illustrate the above models.

To illustrate the ideas above, a survey was conducted, and data needed to evaluate the risk caused by information asymmetry collected in a way to incorporate the impact on the choice of the product warranty. Details were published in Christozov, Chukova &Mateev, (2006). The paper presented the models described above and discussed the survey and the design of the questionnaire. The collecting data necessary for the evaluation of the risk of misinforming have not allowed to assess this risk at a reasonable level of precision. Moreover, the relationship between warranty and risk was left, despite that this attribute indicate self-assessment of respondents' competences and confidence in made decision. Also, variation of purchase decisions, not simply Yes/No, but including the trade-off options were recognized as critically important to gain measures of the risk, relevant to real situation.

2006 Survey

A new survey was needed to extend the original approach, as presented in the previous chapter, to evaluate the above measures. It was designed by using Likert scales. The survey was conducted in 2006 (see Appendix 2). The context of the survey again was to evaluate the risk of misinforming in selling/buying a personal computer but deserted from Yes/No decisions. In this survey we introduce also offering of three forms of warranty to check clients' attitude toward possibility to become misinformed. Whether the customer assumes the possibility to become misinformed and explores the risk mitigation option. In later surveys using warranty as a tool to assess clients' self-confidence regarding their competence is further developed and will be presented and discussed later. Part four is solely dedicated to warranty of misinforming.

The general idea of this survey, as of the original one, was that seller and buyer have different perspectives when looking on the product. Usually, the information provided by the seller, regarding the configuration of the system is presented in the following form:

Pentium IV/1.6C GHz
Intel 440 - LX Power Pro ATX
256MB DDR RAM
1.44 MB FDD
30GB HDD QUANTUM
16MB SGRAM VGA card AGP
15'' Color HANSOL 0.28, LR
N.I. (1024x768), CPU CONTROL

On the other hand, usually, the buyer is looking for information, regarding the capabilities of the systems to allow effective execution of activities from the set $\{A\}$:

- develop and edit text;
- perform high precision computations;
- use of e-mail;
- easy access to the Internet;
- organize a personal data;
- play games;
- watch movies.

The buyer, while making his/her purchase decision, need to understand, interpret, and map to the set of activities the following components from the seller's message:

- What is the meaning of ATX, AGP, etc.?
- Whether this configuration is suitable for the level of complexity of my works, weather it fits to Buyer's needs in terms of software compatibility and computing capabilities?
- Whether s/he needs all the listed components of the system? and so on.

In the original survey the Target group was a group of sixty students (35 responded), mostly sophomores. They were offered to purchase a personal computer (PC). We assume that these students have a good understanding of their needs regarding the usage of a personal computer, because they are facing purchasing computers but have limited knowledge regarding hardware. In the 2006 survey the respondents in the target group had a similar profile.

The message: the target group was approached with an offer to buy a PC, with powerful computational capabilities, designed to serve professional scientists. It had no communication devices; no color graphics, and the sound capabilities were highly limited. Again, it was borrowed from a real advertisement, but changed accordingly. The offer was presented in the following form:

ASUS A7V333/RA sA, VIA KT333,266,ATA 133,RAID,
3DDR,AGP 4x, USB 2.0, IEE 1394, ATX
AMD XP PALOMINO 2100PR/1.75 GHz
DDRAM 512 MB DDR, PC 333MHz, SAMSUNG
80 GB MAXSTOR / 7200 / ATA 133/2MB
PCI ATI 1MB
17'' SAMSUNG 753S 1280x1024/65Hz 1024x768/85 Hz BW
keyboard, mouse, midi tower case

The offered PC were designed to allow word processing and complex computations, but not for the heavy use of the Internet and even e-mailing, did not have any capabilities for multimedia, playing games, watching movies, etc. The price was realistic, but highly attractive. The students were asked to evaluate whether the given PC satisfies their needs, according to the following list of applications:

- word processing,
- complex computations,
- management of personal data,
- Internet,
- e-mail,
- games,
- music,
- movies.

Assumptions and Default Values for the Model Parameters

The assumption is that the features of the PC, described in the survey, as evaluated by the producer or the values of p_i's for different activities are:

- Using word processing 1.00
- Using spreadsheets, (e.g. Excel) 1.00
- Using e-mail 0.60
- Surfing Internet 0.40
- Solving complicated problems 1.00
- Playing Games 0.20
- Watching movies 0.20
- Listening to Music 0.20

The estimation of the degree of acceptance q_{ij} is discussed in the next chapter, in this study it is set to q_{ij}=0.05 for all activities and all buyers. Moreover, in order to distinguish between optimists, pessimists and realists, we fixed ε =0.05.

The students had to provide two answers for every item of this list, firstly, whether they need the given application and, secondly, whether the given PC allows for such an application. The answers were provided in Linkert scale. Table 3. provides a summary of results.

Table 3. Summary of results of 2006 survey

Application	Needs		Assessed ability		Actual ability	Wrong decision
1	2		3		4	5
$A=\{a\}$	#	$P(a)$	#	$\hat{p}$	p	$abs(p-\hat{p})$
Word Processing	33	0.143	27	0.77	1.00	**0.23**
Complex Computations	10	0.043	19	0.54	1.00	**0.44**
e-mail	35	0.152	25	0.71	0	**0.71**
Internet	35	0.152	25	0.71	0	**0.71**
Maintain Personal data	33	0.143	27	0.77	1.00	**0.23**
Play Games	22	0.095	21	0.60	0	**0.60**
Movies	28	0.121	21	0.60	0	**0.60**
Music	35	0.152	20	0.57	0	**0.57**
Overall Risk:						**0.51**

The column "Applications" represents the set of activities $\{A\}$. The column "Needs" consists of subjectively defined needs, which are proportional to the estimates of the probabilities $P(a)$. The third column shows the subjective estimate of product's suitability (expressed by $\hat{p}$) with respect to the tasks as seen by the customers. The fourth column consists of $p=P(S|a,d)$, the objective ability of the product to solve the task. The last column shows the share of customers who may make wrong decision, based on misunderstanding the ability of the product to accomplish the given work. It is computed using the approach discussed above (see equations six in chapter two of part two).

In this case p is either 1 or 0 and the threshold for the level of acceptance q does not play any role, because if we consider a particular work a_i, we have the following options:

1) if $p=0$, the product is totally unsuitable, then both q and $\hat{p}$ are greater or equal than p and any positive purchase decision is wrong.
2) if $p=1$, the product is absolutely suitable, possesses the highest possible quality, and both q and $\hat{p}$ are less or equal than p, and any negative purchase decision is wrong.

Comments on the Results of 2006 Survey

The risk caused by misunderstanding is calculated as follows: The risk of a wrong decision caused by the information asymmetry is equal to $r = abs\left(p - \hat{p}\right)$ and depends on p - the objective suitability of the product, described by the seller in the message (seller's information), and on $\hat{p}$ – the suitability of the product as the buyer understands and interprets the message (buyer's information). For the i-task (w_i) the measure of its risk caused by information asymmetry is either $r = \left(p - \hat{p}\right)$ if $p=1$ and the product is suitable, but purchase decision is negative, or $r = \left(\hat{p} - p\right)$ if $p=0$ the product is unsuitable, but purchase decision is positive.

The overall risk of a wrong decision due to misinforming is evaluated by the weighted average of the information asymmetries of the tasks, where the weights set to be equal to the corresponding "needs" $P(w)$, i.e., $R = \sum P(a_i)r_i$.

The overall risk of misinforming turned out to be relatively high for this particular case. This could be due to number of reasons such as a low level of expertise of the buyers (students) regarding computer hardware, weather the proposed PC configurations suits the software applications, lack of easy to read and informative description of the components of the computer system, and many others.

Degrees of Misinforming for the Group

One of the main difficulties in quantifying the risk of misinforming is that the risk is subjective, i.e., one and the same message containing information on the product of interest, may convey correct information to some customers and misinform others. This misinformation can have different degrees and consequences for an individual Buyer within a given group of customers. Thus, on the one hand, in order to evaluate the risk of a group of customers, we need to take into account each individual reaction to the message, and the risk of the group will be the aggregated result of these individual reactions. On the other hand, stratifying the group into subgroups and investigating the risk on subgroup level could gain an additional insight regarding the value of risk likelihood.

The message describing the product may inform some of the customers correctly regarding several properties or features of the product, as well as abilities of the product to support accomplishing a particular activity or category of works, and at the same time, it can misinform the same customer regarding some other features or activities. The model aims to allow measuring the risk of misinforming at the individual activity level.

The issue of assessing whether the client understands the existence of risk of misinforming is of special importance. Whether a customer recognizes the potential of becoming misinformed also needs to be evaluated and included into models. Here this is done by including customers' response toward the type of warranty – recognition of misinforming risk results in giving higher priority to the warranty of misinforming and vice versa. Part four is dedicated to different aspects of warranty policies, emphasizing the warranty of misinforming. Here we will use reaction toward warranty statement, which is provided as an addition to product description, as indication of client's self-assessment about own competence to assess applicability of the product and existence of risk to become misinformed.

To assess whether the respondent is aware of the existence of misinforming hazard information regarding the preferred product warranty was requested. Three options of warranty policies as listed earlier were offered. Respondents were divided into two groups – the first one was given to choose between two out of the three options and the second sample – all three options.

The three warranty options are:

- W1: pure malfunctioning warranty – if the product fails to perform as stated during a given period of time (three years) it can be replaced or repaired for free.

- W2: pure misinforming warranty – if the product does not satisfy the customer's expectation for a given period (3 months) it can be returned, and money reimbursed.
- W3: mixed warranty policy – there are two periods. First one (one month) to return the product if the customer is not satisfied by its properties (misinforming warranty). And the second one (one year) to replace or repair the product for free if it fails to perform as stated.

Choosing one of the last two options means that customer recognizes that risk of becoming misled by the message describing the product exists when mapping information to his or her problem domain. Choosing the second option – pure misinforming warranty – represents a higher level of uncertainty regarding suitability of the product as well as doubt about own competence in assessing the product suitability.

It seems that the best strategy for any buyer is to purchase the PC with the second type of warranty and after three months, i.e., when the warranty expires, and the PC proves to be suitable for his/her needs, to replace it with a new one with three years free replacement warranty. At the same time, to examine whether the computer is suitable for performing a particular set of activities, quite a lot of effort and time must be invested. For example, several software packages have been installed and tested, compatibility between different software applications has been adjusted, the computer must be tuned up to achieve its best performance, etc. Therefore, in our opinion, it is not reasonable to give up all this time and effort and start all over again with a new computer in return of only three months extra warranty of malfunctioning. Additionally, knowing that electronic devices usually show high burn-out failures rate – failures in early stages of their life – also supported the idea that it is not feasible to replace a device that passed this early stage and perform well.

Three months trial period, which is the second type of warranty, seems a reasonably long period of time to allow the customer to test almost all features of the product that he/she is interested in. For the third warranty option, often one month is not sufficiently long to comprehensively examine the suitability of the product.

The survey was conducted on two independent groups of respondents. The first one was given the choice of the first two types of warranty, while the second group had to choose from all three. This was done to observe the effect of the third, mixed, warranty policy on the consumers' choice.

Summary of Responses Based on Warranty Options

Measures for the Buyers' risk are shown on Table 4, and the Seller's risk on Table 5.

Table 4. Results of 2006 survey of Buyers' risk contrasted according to the selected warranty option

	Survey 1 – two forms of warranty			Survey 2 – three forms of warranty		
Category	#	$\frac{1}{n}\sum_{j=1}^{n} r_j^a$	$\frac{1}{n}\sum_{j=1}^{n} r_j^u$	#	$\frac{1}{n}\sum_{j=1}^{n} r_j^a$	$\frac{1}{n}\sum_{j=1}^{n} r_j^u$
Overall	118	0.256	0.464	54	0.296	0.492
Optimists	77	0.284	0.484	38	0.337	0.541
Pessimists	16	0.249	0.433	4	0.311	0.421
Realists	25	0.177	0.422	12	0.159	0.361
Warranty 3 months	13	0.224	0.465	1	0.535	0.774
Warranty 3 years	105	0.260	0.463	34	0.303	0.498
Warranty 1 month + 1 year				19	0.269	0.466

Table 5. The three measures of seller's risk according to 2006 survey's data

	Survey 1: Two warranty options	Survey 2: Three warranty options
$R^s=$	0.463	0.488
$R^u=$	0.450	0.488
$R^a=$	0.252	0.298

Interpretation

As expected, the analysis of the two surveys led to essentially equivalent results, because the surveys were conducted on two samples taken from one and the same population, namely, first-year students in non-technologically oriented majors. Despite that, surveys show that students do not admit the existence of high risk of misinforming. This increases the likelihood of becoming misinformed and "not satisfied" clients by the time of making purchasing decision.

CONCLUSION

The proposed methodology allows to measure the likelihood of the risk of misinforming and show that this risk is significant. Also, the impact of the risk to customer was discussed briefly according to the type of wrong decision – optimists purchased a product that is not suitable for their needs; and pessimists do not purchase a perfectly suitable product.

The designed survey and obtained results demonstrated that it is possible to collect objective data essential to measure the risk. The values of some of the essential parameters, as degree of acceptance and actual capability of the products, were assigned according to the bias of survey organizers. Assessment of degree of acceptance had proved challenging and complicated as one can see in the next chapter. The actual capability of the product is a subject of the producer's expertise regarding how customers expect to use the product.

All surveys conducted later (see Appendix 2) included the way for collecting data originated in the survey presented in this chapter, designed to evaluate the basic measures of the risk of misinforming. Additional objectives were targeted as evaluation of degree of acceptance (see next Chapter) and misinforming in the case of competing products (Chapter 2.4) as well.

REFERENCES

Christozov, D., Chukova, S., & Mateev, P. (2006). A Measure of Risk Caused by Information Asymmetry in e-Commerce. *Journal of Issues in Informing Science and Information Technology*, *3*, 147–158. doi:10.28945/879

Christozov, D., Chukova, S., & Mateev, P. (2009). Informing Processes, Risks, Evaluation of the Risk of Misinforming. In *Foundations of Informing Science* (pp. 323–356). ISI.

Chapter 8
Assessing Degree of Acceptance

ABSTRACT

This chapter extends the methodology developed for quantifying the risk of misinformation by adding an approach to measure the degree of acceptance. Assessment of this parameter of the model developed in the previous chapter is essential for practical use of the approach and modeling developed. Degree of acceptance is subjective measure of whether the provided information describes a product that meets buyer's expectation. It represents how the buyer interprets the provided description of the product. This measure is essential for a buyer's purchase decision.

INTRODUCTION

Evaluation of the risk of misinforming likelihood, as presented in the previous chapter, requires knowing the subjectively assumed minimal degree of product's quality that makes the product acceptable for considering as candidate for purchasing. Degree of acceptance is another subjective parameter that needs measuring. The real challenge is how to collect relevant data. This chapter stresses survey design and data processing.

The survey, conducted in 2008 (see Appendix 2), is the one designed to collect data regarding degree of acceptance and is explored in this chapter. It is an updated version of the survey conducted in 2006 and presented in the previous chapter. This survey was designed in three parts. In the first part the respondent is offered a five-level Likert scale to answer the questions related to her/his needs to do a particular

DOI: 10.4018/978-1-6684-8800-3.ch008

work, as in the previous surveys – to use a computer application, and to estimate the suitability of the product to allow effective accomplishment of this work. The second part addresses the issue of evaluation of the degree of acceptance – what is acceptable to accomplish an activity, and the third part was designed to allow evaluation of the risk of misinforming in competing messages (see the next chapter). For more details you can look at Christozov, Chukova & Mateev (2006, 2007, 2008, 2009).

GENERAL NOTES

In the previous section we introduced one approach to quantify the risk of misinforming. One of the parameters of the model is "Degree of acceptance" - q_{ij}. To illustrate the approach used to evaluate the risk likelihood by the collected in Survey 2006 data, the constant 0.5 for the degree of acceptance for all clients and all product's properties was used. This chapter addresses the issue of how to collect data that allows us to evaluate this parameter.

Assessing what is acceptable performance as recognized by the customer is difficult for the cases of optimists and pessimists. One category underestimate what properties are needed, and the other overestimates them. From other side, these two categories of customers are the most interesting from the point of view of evaluating the risk of misinforming. It is a mutually agreed assumption that pessimists tend to set the degree of acceptance too high, and optimists – too low in comparison with their subjective assessment of the properties and suitability of the product. If a customer is pessimist and assess that a hard disk with 500GB capacity will be fully enough, more likely he or she will report acceptable level of the disk capacity at 750GB or even 1.0TB.

In this chapter an approach for evaluating the degree of acceptance of the product with respect to subjective expectations of individuals and related to activities they consider needed is proposed. The approach is presented, as well as data collection and data processing, in the context of one-to-one informing process as part of a business trading transaction. Adding procedure to evaluate the "degree of acceptance" completes techniques for evaluation of all relevant variables for the methodology to measure the likelihood of the risk of misinforming for this the simplest case of informing process.

DEGREE OF IMPACT OF THE RISK OF MISINFORMING

The degree of acceptance is related to the importance, needs, of given categories of activities to the customer. The assumption is obvious – for the one customer who doesn't need to do something in a given category of activities, every product will look acceptable for every work in this category. And the opposite is also true, if one needs and very often uses a product to execute given work, he or she will accept a product with high quality of the relevant properties needed for effective and efficient performance in accomplishing this work.

One of the main difficulties in quantifying the risk of misinforming is that the risk is subjective, i.e., one and the same message containing information on the product of interest, may convey correct information to some customers and misinform others. This misinformation can have different degrees and consequences for the individual customers within a given. A message describing the product may inform a customer correctly regarding several properties or features of the product, as well as abilities of the product to perform well in accomplishing particular work or a category of activities in given circumstances. And at the same time, it may misinform the same customer regarding some other features related to other works. The proposed model aims to allow measuring the risk of misinforming at the activity level. In order to simplify the model, we will model only the risk of misinforming between a single producer/seller to a group of customers/buyers regarding a single product.

Assume that with respect to each of activities a_{ij}, buyer b_j has a degree of acceptance regarding the product's d_i attribute C_l. Note that C_l, a property of the product, is one of the advertised physical or technical properties as capacity of the hard disk, or frequency of CPU. Let denote this degree of acceptance by q_{ijl}. And let this is a number between *0* and *1*, i.e., $0 \leq q_{ijl} \leq 1$. This degree of acceptance q_{ijl} defines the buyer's minimal quality required for the attribute C_l in order to accept the product d_i as suitable to executing activity a_{ij}.

On the other hand, the importance of each of the attributes of the product with respect to ability of the customer to accomplish for particular category of works can be measured and expressed in terms of weights, say w_{il}. The weight is a measure of C_l for performance of the product in executing activity $a_{i.}$ These weights are independent from buyer's opinion and are objective property of the product as designed. For example, let the product $d_i \in D$ is a personal computer (PC) and the attributes of interest are the CPU, RAM, HDD, VRAM, and the Ethernet, i.e., $C = \{C_1$=CPU, C_2=RAM, C_3=HDD, C_4=VRAM, C_5=Ethernet$\}$, with $L = 5$. Further, for the work' category "word-processing", we can assign weights of importance to each of the attributes of the product. These weights are assumed to be objective and known in advance by the producer. Table 1. provides an example for the weights of importance in the context of the PC example. The weights are given on a five-level scale. In this case, weights are assigned by developers of the survey and reflect the performance of the PC as presented in the survey.

Table 1. Importance of basic technical properties of the PC to category of activities, related to 2008 survey

Category of activities	Weights: importance of property for activity				
	CPU	RAM	HDD	VRAM	Ethernet
Word-procesing	4	2	2	1	0
Use Excel	4	2	2	1	0
e-mailing	2	2	1	0	4
Use Internet	2	2	1	2	4
Complex math	4	4	4	0	0
Play Games	4	4	4	4	2
Watch Movies	3	3	3	4	2
Listen Music	2	2	2	2	2

Evaluation of the degree of acceptance $\hat{q}_{ij}$ of the buyer b_j for the product $d_i \in D$ with respect to activity a_{ij} can be computed as follows:

$$\hat{q}_{ij} = \sum_{l=1}^{L} q_{ijl} w_{il} / \sum_{l=1}^{L} w_{il}, \tag{1}$$

for all activities a_{ij} the buyer b_j intends, or has a "need", to accomplish with the product $d_i \in D$. If every product is acceptable for given activity than $\hat{q}_{ij} = 0$, whereas if $\hat{q}_{ij} = 1$, the buyer has very high-quality requirements on $d_i \in D$ regarding this particular work a_{ij}.

THE NEED OF A BUYER TO ACCOMPLISH AN ACTIVITY

Assume, that the need of the buyer b_j to execute for a work from category A^*_i is n_{ij}, where $0 \leq n_{ij} \leq 1$. If $n_{ij}=0$, this means that the buyer b_j does not need to do works from A^*_i, while $n_{ij}=1$ means that b_j definitely needs to do activities from category A^*_i and this is one of the major reasons for the purchase a product from this kind. It is reasonable to assume that if $n_{ij}=0$, then $q_{ij}=0$, i.e., if the buyer b_j does not need to do a_{ij}, then every product is acceptable with respect to a_{ij}.

Therefore, the buyer b_j can be described through the set of the triples:

$b_j = (a_{ij}, q_{ij}, n_{ij}) | \; a_{ij} \in A^*_i, i=1,2,\ldots,k; 0 \leq n_{ij}, q_{ij} \leq 1).$

It is naturally to assume that for b_j, $j=1,2,\ldots,n$, all activities in A^* are presented in his description, but for some of them the corresponding need is equal to zero.

2008 SURVEY

To illustrate the ideas described above, a survey (see Appendix 2) was designed to collect information needed to evaluate the risk caused by information asymmetry that allows to measure the degree of acceptance as well. The survey also allows us to analyze the impact of the choice of the type of product warranty. The survey consists of two parts. The first part addresses the needs and the minimal properties of the products – assessment of the degree of acceptance by the attributes/components of the product, while the second part is a repetition of the 2006 survey. The second part of the survey included two forms to collect data about the warranty preferences. The two parts of the survey were given to the same group of respondents – students in the same class – on two different days with one week's distance. Firstly, the respondents were asked to fill in Form 1, which addresses the degree of acceptance q_{ij} and how often they need to do the given activity n_{ij}. The latter, the frequency of usage is considered as a measure for the needs. This was done to avoid a direct comparison between the acceptance level for different properties of the product with actual values of the same property as offered in advertisement and what later respondents were asked to evaluate. In this way the assessment of acceptable quality is to some extent independent of the property of the offered product. After one week, the second part of the survey was given out. It is divided into two forms and the third form was in two versions given to two subgroups. It replicated the previous survey. Evaluation of the risk of misinforming in the three forms uses the averages of the degree of acceptance, because it was impossible to map the respondent who filled the first form with the one who completed the second. This doesn't look problematic, because of the homogeneity of the group of respondents.

The survey was conducted on two independent groups of respondents. The first part of the survey (Figure 1.) to evaluate the need and degree of acceptance was identical for both groups. The number of respondents of the two groups was 53 and 10 (number of students in the two sections of the same class). The second part was divided into two forms according to warranty options. The first form of the second part of the survey offers a choice of two warranty policies: one for malfunctioning (for three years repairing or replacement) and one for misunderstanding (three months for trial), whereas the second form of the second part of the survey offered three warranty options by extends the list of choices with an additional one (one year for repairing and one month for trial), a mixture between the two policies offered in the first form of the second part of the survey. Each of the groups of respondents was given only one of the forms of the second part of the survey. The responses for Form 1 for both groups were collected in one dataset, while the data from the second part of the survey for the two groups were considered separately. The two forms of this survey are given in Appendix 2. of the book.

Figure 1. The form for collecting data regarding minimal requirement and frequency of using an activity

Form 1: Please, select the minimal configuration of the PC to meet your needs for using it for:
a) Using word processing

PC property	Low 0	1	2	3	High 4
CPU	0,35 GHz	1 GHz	1.6 GHz	2.4 GHz	4.8 GHz
RAM	256 MB	512 MB	1 GB	2 GB	4 GB
HDD	20 GB	40 GB	80 GB	120 GB	240 GB
VRam	16 MB	64 MB	256 MB	512 MB	1 GB
Ethernet	56 Kbs	10 Mbs	100 Mbs	1 Gbs	10 Gbs

How often you use PC for word processing	Low never	yearly	monthly	weekly	High daily
	0	1	2	3	4

The following assumptions and default values for the model parameters were used in evaluating risk of misinforming. The objective values – p_i's – about the features of the PC, described in the survey, as evaluated by the producer (the survey designers) are presented in Table 2.:

Table 2. Actual capability of the PC with given configuration to accomplish specified activities

Category of activity A^*		p_i
a_1	Using word processing	1.00
a_2	Using spreadsheets, (e.g. Excel)	1.00
a_3	Using e-mail	0.60
a_4	Surfing Internet	0.40
a_5	Solving complicated problems	1.00
a_6	Playing Games	0.20
a_7	Watching movies	0.20
a_8	Listening to Music	0.20

This PC is perfectly suitable for word processing, using spread sheets and performing complex mathematical computations and only partially suitable for the rest of activities.

The average value of the degree of acceptance of the PC with respect to each activity is given in Table 3. These values were computed according to formulae 1. and using the weights shown in Table 2 and the average of responses from the survey by following the approach described above and form for each category of work as the one in Figure 1.

Table 3. Degree of acceptance by type of work

Word	Excel	e-mail	Internet	Complex	Game	Movies	Music
0.324	0.280	0.369	0.449	0.392	0.478	0.428	0.377

Further, in the assessment of the risk of misinforming, these values of the degree of acceptance of the product with respect to the category of activity as given in Table 4. are used in computing the measure of the likelihood of the risk. In previous chapter the degree of acceptance was assumed as q=0.5. In this study, the values shown in Table 3 were used. These values are aggregated for the entire group. They still do not take into account separately the degree of acceptance of every individual buyer. The means are for the group of respondents, but the actual degree of acceptance is personal. Those group measures can be used by the seller to customize the message, describing the product, in a way to reduce the misinforming risk.

Summary of Results of 2008 Survey

In the following tables are presented the rest of the results acquired in the 2008 surveys:

Table 4. Buyers' risk (2008 survey)

	Two forms of warranty			Three forms of warranty		
Category	#	$\frac{1}{n}\sum_{j=1}^{n} r_j^a$	$\frac{1}{n}\sum_{j=1}^{n} r_j^u$	#	$\frac{1}{n}\sum_{j=1}^{n} r_j^a$	$\frac{1}{n}\sum_{j=1}^{n} r_j^u$
Overall	10	0.203	0.425	53	0.213	0.438
Optimists	8	0.234	0.477	23	0.265	0.515
Pessimists	1	0.075	0.188	8	0.098	0.203
Realists	1	0.083	0.250	22	0.200	0.443
Warranty 3 months	2	0.191	0.420	4	0.242	0.496
Warranty 3 years	8	0.206	0.427	22	0.207	0.441
Warranty 1 month + 1 year				27	0.213	0.427

Table 5. Buyers' risk (2008 survey)

	Two forms of warranty	Three forms of warranty
R^s=	0.450	0.431
R^u=	0.450	0.432
R^a=	0.220	0.222

DISCUSSION

The estimated degrees of acceptance, shown in Table 3., are lower than the assumed in the previous chapter value of $q_{ij}=q=0.5$ for $i=1,2,\ldots,n$, and $i=1,2,\ldots,k_j$. The clients expect a PC with higher quality for multimedia – 0.478, 0.428 and 0.377 respectively, but the offered PC allows only 0.2 for these categories of activities. The lower degrees of acceptance, as evaluated, influence the assessed level of the risk of misinforming. As expected, and confirmed by our analysis, it led to lower risks. For example, 0.213 vs. 0.296 for the overall adjusted buyers' risk and 0.438 vs. 0.492 for overall unadjusted buyers' risk in the case of three forms of warranty. This effect was expected, because a lower degree of acceptance means, roughly speaking, lower requirements towards the quality of the product, which of course, leads to a smaller number of wrong purchase decisions and respectively lower risk of misinforming.

The risk for the seller appears to be high enough to deserve attention. For this level of risk, because of the domination of optimists, the seller has to offer a better explanation of the product's properties emphasizing the lower quality in the area of multimedia, and to recommend warranty coverage of the third type. Also, it is clear that only a small proportion of respondents recognize their inability to judge properly the qualities of the product.

CONCLUSION

A way to evaluate the degree of acceptance is proposed. It illustrates that it is possible to collect data that will allow us to evaluate the likelihood of the misinforming risk in needed precision. The example describes how to use degree of acceptance but uses the aggregated for the entire group value of this parameter. On other side, the complexity of survey and practically inability to map individual's value of degree of acceptance to individual's decision makes the proposed approach only partially useful. As more homogenous the group of respondents is the more relevant and useful the proposed approach is.

Two approaches are applied to define subgroups. The first one is by splitting the group regarding purchase attitude as optimists, pessimists, and realists. The second is by self-assessment of competence to correctly understand the received information by choosing the form of warranty. Also, a-priori, the group of respondents is considering homogeneous by-default. Respondents in both universities, where the survey was offered, are students on a junior level studying subjects related to the use of computers but not technically experienced.

The growing complexity of needed information and the corresponding surveys challenges further development of models. Such complexity prevents us from collecting reliable information with acceptable accuracy. Despite this challenge, even in the relatively imprecise evaluation of the measure of misinforming risk likelihood, the information obtained may serve to improve communication with customers and to adopt reasonable and feasible policies to mitigate the risk.

In the next chapter the complexity of the model is extended even further to address the case of multiple competing messages. Also, the period of using the product is associated with learning about its properties and what is needed to accomplish expected activities. Chapter 2.5. is dedicated to dynamics of learning and adjusting expectations, needs, and what quality of the products is acceptable as function of product' adopting period. This includes adjustment of both parameters – degree of acceptance and personal assessment of the product's quality.

REFERENCES

Christozov, D., Chukova, S., & Mateev, P. (2006). A Measure of Risk Caused by Information Asymmetry in e-Commerce. *Journal of Issues in Informing Science and Information Technology*, *3*, 147–158. doi:10.28945/879

Christozov, D., Chukova, S., & Mateev, P. (2007). On the Relationship between Warranty and the Risk of Information Asymmetry. *Journal of Issues in Informing Science and Information Technology*, *4*, 235–249. doi:10.28945/946

Christozov, D., Chukova, S., & Mateev, P. (2008). Warranty and the Risk of Misinforming: Evaluation of the Degree of Acceptance. *Journal of Issues in Informing Science and Information Technology*, *5*, 667–677. doi:10.28945/1035

Christozov, D., Chukova, S., & Mateev, P. (2009). Informing Processes, Risks, Evaluation of the Risk of Misinforming. In *Foundations of Informing Science* (pp. 323–356). ISI.

Chapter 9
The Risk of Misinforming for Competing Messages

ABSTRACT

This chapter makes a next step toward developing the model for evaluating the risk of misinforming in more realistic settings. The market case, described by 1:N topology, explored in the first chapters of this part of the book, is valid only in a monopoly dominated trading environment. The market is described typically with M:N communication topology. This chapter extends the model to the case of 2:N – the case of assessment of risk of wrong purchase decision when there are two competing products. As above the stress is on the design of a survey that may reveal clients' attitude.

INTRODUCTION

This chapter extends previous studies on quantifying the risk of misinforming by introducing models, which allow measuring the likelihood of the risk of misinforming in case of competing messages. The example, as in the previous chapters, is to make a decision for purchasing a product, but in this section the objectives of the Buyer are not only to buy or not to buy (Yes/No decision) but also to choose among some competing products. The Buyer's options are to not purchase any of the offered products, to purchase product 1, or to purchase product 2. The objectives are to evaluate the risk of misinforming in more realistic settings. The marketplace is a place where messages, describing different products suitable for accomplishing one and the same set of clients' works, are competing. It may appear also that one of the products is better for a given subset of activities and the other – for the other subset.

DOI: 10.4018/978-1-6684-8800-3.ch009

The previous chapters addressed the evaluation of the risk of misinforming in two cases – the risk of misinforming in offering a single product to a single buyer ("one-to-one") – the case of individual Buyer; as well as the risk of misinforming in offering a single product to many buyers ("one-to-many") – the case of Seller. In this section, these models are expanded by proposing models to cover the cases of "many-to-one" – the risk of individual Buyer; and "many-to-many" – the risk of Sellers on a real competing market.

First, for simplicity, in the first section, the case of offering two competing products to one and the same group of buyers is considered ("two-to-one" topology). The model is later generalized to *n* competing products ("many-to-one"). These models are better representation of the real market situation, where purchasing decisions are made based on assessment and comparison of different offers and selecting the one, which satisfies in the best way the buyer's needs as the buyer assesses it. In the later section, the case many-to-many is discussed. For further details one can refer to Christozov, Chukova & Mateev P. (2008, 2009).

THE CASE OF TWO COMPETING MESSAGES: TWO-TO-ONE

The "two-to-one" topology is the simplest case for competing messages, describing two competing products. In this case, the client b_j receives two competing messages ${}^1D$ and ${}^2D$ from two competing sources of information, describing two competing products ${}^1d$ and ${}^2d$ and s/he has to choose which of the knowledge, acquired only by one of them, is suitable to solve her/his problem or to ignore both. In the business transaction context, the client purchases only one of the two products or does not purchase them at all. The case of two complementing messages is not discussed here, nevertheless that in reality the information describing one of the products can be used in assessing suitability of others.

The probability space describing this case extends the decision options described in Chapter 2.2. The client has the following options in making her/his decision:

1. choose ${}^1D$: this message is useful, the client b_j solves her/his problem a_{ij}, the decision is correct, and the risk is ${}^1r_{ij}=0$.
2. choose ${}^1D$: this message is not useful, the client b_j doesn't solve her/his problem a_{ij}, the decision is wrong, and the risk is ${}^1r_{ij}=1$.
3. choose ${}^2D$: this message is useful, the client b_j solves her/his problem a_{ij}, the decision is correct, and the risk is ${}^2r_{ij}=0$.
4. choose ${}^2D$: this message is not useful, the client b_j doesn't solve her/his problem a_{ij}, the decision is correct, and the risk ${}^2r_{ij}=1$

5. ignore both messages, but ${}^1D$ is useful and client b_j could have solved his problem a_{ij} if s/he has used the information from this message, while the message ${}^2D$ doesn't bring any useful information. The decision is wrong, the risks are ${}^1r_{ij}=1$, and ${}^2r_{ij}=0$.
6. ignore both messages, but ${}^1D$ is useful and the client b_j could have solved his/her problem a_{ij} if s/he has used the information from this message; the message ${}^2D$ also contains useful information. The decision is wrong, and the risks are ${}^1r_{ij}=2$, and ${}^2r_{ij}=1$.
7. ignore both messages, but ${}^2D$ is useful and client b_j could have solved his/her problem a_{ij} if s/he has used the information from this message, while the message ${}^1D$ doesn't bring any useful information. The decision is wrong, and the risks are ${}^1r_{ij}=0$ and ${}^2r_{ij}=1$.
8. ignore both messages, and both messages do not bring any useful information. The decision is correct, and the risks are ${}^1r_{ij}=0$ and ${}^2r_{ij}=0$.

In all of these cases, the client b_j interprets each of the two messages independently according to her/his need and level of acceptance for a given activity and according to her/his own assessment of how useful and relevant the information received is.

Now, we have ${}^1p_i$ and ${}^2p_i$ as the objective probabilities that each of the two products is capable to accomplish effectively and efficiently the category of activities A^*_i. Also, we have $\widehat{{}^1p_{ij}}$ and $\widehat{{}^2p_{ij}}$ the subjective probabilities, as assessed by the client b_j, regarding the capabilities of each of the two products to serve her/him in accomplishing her/his specific work $a_{ij}\in A^*_i$. Regarding the work a_{ij}, the client b_j has level of acceptance q_{ij} and need n_{ij}, which are the same as above and are using in evaluating both products. In general, number of inequalities between objective probability p, subjective probability $\hat{p}$, and degree of acceptance q are 12. In this framework, there are totally 96 different cases to consider in order to identify the risks ${}^1r_{ij}$ and ${}^2r_{ij}$, compared to only 6 cases for a single message as given in the Chapter 2.2. By assume that the client chooses to use the information from the message with higher $\widehat{{}^*p_{ij}}$, i.e., if $\widehat{{}^1p_{ij}} > \widehat{{}^1p_{ij}}$ the client chooses to use ${}^1D$ and vice versa the total number of possible decision cases grow further. The risk of a wrong decision is zero if the chosen option is correct and the product is satisfying the client's expectations. Nevertheless, the alternative option could be also correct, or even better.

The risks for the three models in this case, by following the way introduced above, are:

$$r_j^s = \frac{1}{I}\sum_{i=1}^{I} \max({}^1r_{ij}, {}^2r_{ij}), \tag{1}$$

$$r_j^n = \frac{1}{\sum_i n_{ij}}\sum_{i=1}^{I} n_{ij} \max({}^1r_{ij}, {}^2r_{ij}), \tag{2}$$

$$r_j^a = \frac{1}{\sum_i n_{ij}}\sum_{i=1}^{I} n_{ij} \max({}^mr_{ij}, {}^mr_{ij}) \max_{\widehat{{}^m p_{ij}}}(abs(\widehat{{}^m p_{ij}} - {}^m p_i)), \quad m = 1,2 \ . \tag{3}$$

Note that in the above formulae the maximal risk for any activity is used. In this way the measure is the upper bound of the actual risk.

By following the above approach, the formula for the risk in exploring both messages can be done by aggregating the individual risks to the group of receivers (clients) – the two-to-many case. The aggregated risk for a given category of tasks and the overall risk – on the whole set of categories of tasks can be defined as analogues of the simplest case, developed in the previous section:

A simple model: the risks regarding A^*_i:

$${}^kR_i^s = \frac{1}{J}\sum_{j=1}^{J} {}^kr_{ij}, k = 1,2. \tag{4}$$

A simple model: the overall risk:

$${}^kR^s = \frac{1}{IJ}\sum_{j=1}^{J}(\sum_{i=1}^{I} {}^kr_{ij}), k = 1,2. \tag{5}$$

A model accounting for the needs: the risks regarding A^*_i:

$${}^kR_i^n = \frac{1}{J}\sum_{j=1}^{J} n_{ij}\, {}^kr_{ij}, k = 1,2. \tag{6}$$

A model accounting for the needs: the overall risks:

$$^{k}R^{n} = \frac{1}{J}\sum_{j=1}^{J}\left(\frac{1}{\sum_{i} n_{ij}}\sum_{i=1}^{I} n_{ij}\,{}^{k}r_{ij}\right), k = 1,2. \quad (7)$$

A model, accounting for the needs and the degree of information asymmetry: the risk regarding A^{*}_{i}:

$$^{k}R_{i}^{a} = \frac{1}{\sum_{j} n_{ij}}\sum_{j=1}^{J} n_{ij}\,{}^{k}r_{ij}\,(abs(\widehat{^{k}p}_{ij} - {}^{k}p_{i})), \quad k = 1,2. \quad (8)$$

A model, accounting for the needs and degree of information asymmetry, the overall risk:

$$^{k}R^{a} = \frac{1}{I}\sum_{i=1}^{I}\left(\frac{1}{\sum_{j} n_{ij}}\sum_{j=1}^{J} n_{ij}\,{}^{k}r_{ij}(abs(\widehat{^{k}p}_{ij} - {}^{k}p_{i}))\right), \quad k = 1,2. \quad (9)$$

2008 SURVEY: DISCUSSION

The 2008 survey (see Appendix 2) follows and extends the approach presented earlier by including a third part asking respondents to choose between the two PCs. The respondents were divided into two groups placed in two different market situations – the first one is assumed that they make their purchase decision in a marketplace with direct comparison between products (as in a supermarket); the second places respondents to make individual purchase decisions for each of the products independently, which is more likely the case of purchasing through internet.

The respondents – first year students in disciplines related to Information Technologies, but not technical in nature – were split into two groups. The first group was offered two steps of the questionnaire and the second group – the three. The first phase follows exactly the approach described in the previous chapters for collecting data about the respondents needs and degree of acceptance.

Second phase, for the first group, who were required to directly compare the two PC's configurations (see Figure 1). In principle, the first PC is designed mostly for scientific usage and the second one allows more entertainment. The respondents have to compare directly the two PCs by filling in the form (Figure 2.) and specify which of the two they will purchase. Additionally, they have to specify, which of the three warranty policies, as in the previous studies they will prefer.

Figure 1. The PCs configurations

PC 1
AMD 64: AMD Athlon 64 4800+ Quad Core
Hardware

- 107S 17" Flat Screen Beige or Black
- PowerColour X300SE 64MB PCI Express Video Card
- 2 GB DDR 400 RAM
- Seagate 500 GB Serial ATA Hard Drive
- Samsung Internal IDE 52/24/52 CDRW
- 3.5" Floppy Drive
- 56 kbps V92 PCI Fax Modem
- Integrated 10/100 Network Card
- Microsoft 101 Keyboard
- Microsoft Optical Wheel Mouse

Software

- Microsoft Windows XP Professional
- Open Office ver. 2
- AVG Antivirus

PC 2
AMD 64: AMD Athlon 64 4800
Hardware

- 107S 21" Flat Screen
- PowerColour X300SE 512MB PCI Express Video Card
- 2 GB DDR 400 RAM
- Seagate 160GB Serial ATA Hard Drive
- Samsung Internal IDE 52/24/52 DVDRW
- 256 kbps V92 PCI Fax Modem
- Integrated 100/1000 Network Card
- Microsoft Multimedia Keyboard
- Microsoft Optical Wheel Mouse

Software

- Microsoft Windows XP Home
- MS Office Professional
- AVG Antivirus

The second group of respondents were approached twice in one week distance to evaluate the level any of the above two PCs satisfies their needs.

The results about needs coincide with the previous surveys, because the populations of respondents were similar. Results about the risk of misinforming in its three forms, was significantly lower for the group, which directly compared the two PCs (see Table 1.), which also was expected.

Figure 2. Form for direct comparison of the two PCs

Applicatione	**Degree to which the given PC satisfies your needs**					**Degree to which the given PC satisfies your needs**				
	low				**High**	**Low**				**High**
	0	1	2	3	4	0	1	2	3	4
Word processing										
Spreadsheets, (Excel)										
e-mail										
Internet										
Complex computational problems										
Games										
Movies										
Music										

Measures of the risk of misinforming are summarize in Table 1.

The major problem in this survey was how to match the two or even the three responses. Initially we didn't want to ask respondents to identify themselves, because of their status. But the model requires mapping the needs with preferences and such identification becomes unavoidable. After receiving the results, we realize that only a small percentage of respondents participated in each of the three phases of the survey - literally twelve out of 53 in the group of two phases and seven out of 46 in the group of three phases. This makes the achieved results highly unreliable. This problem in collecting data seems unavoidable and definitely affects applicability of the proposed model.

Table 1. Aggregated risks of the two groups of respondents

	Direct comparison	Sequential comparison
$R^s=$	0.350	0.441
$R^n=$	0.336	0.442
$R^a=$	0.120	0.232

MANY COMPETING MESSAGES (MANY-TO-ONE): GENERALIZATION

The above formulas can be easily expanded for the case of *N* competing messages (products) by the following formulae:

The formulae for individual's (Buyer's) risks:

$$r_j^s = \frac{1}{I}\sum\nolimits_{i=1}^{I} \max_{m=1,2,\ldots N}\left({}^m r_{ij}\right), \tag{10}$$

$$r_j^n = \frac{1}{\sum_i n_{ij}}\sum\nolimits_{i=1}^{I} n_{ij} \max_{m=1,2,\ldots,N}\left({}^m r_{ij}\right), \tag{11}$$

$$r_j^a = \frac{1}{\sum_i n_{ij}}\sum\nolimits_{i=1}^{I} n_{ij} \max_{m=1,2,\ldots,N}\left({}^m r_{ij}\right) \max_{\widehat{{}^m p_{ij}}}(abs(\widehat{{}^m p_{ij}} - {}^m p_i)),\ m=1,2\,. \tag{12}$$

The formulae for the risks of the sender regarding A^*_i:

$$^mR_i^s = \frac{1}{J}\sum_{j=1}^{J} {^m r_{ij}}, m = 1,2,\ldots,N, \tag{13}$$

$$^mR_i^n = \frac{1}{J}\sum_{j=1}^{J} n_{ij}\, {^m r_{ij}}, m = 1,2,\ldots,N, \tag{14}$$

$$^mR_i^a = \frac{1}{\sum_j n_{ij}}\sum_{j=1}^{J} n_{ij}\, {^m r_{ij}} (abs(\widehat{^m p_{ij}} - {^m p_i}), m = 1,2,\ldots,N. \tag{15}$$

The overall (Sellers') risks:

$$^mR^s = \frac{1}{IJ}\sum_{j=1}^{J} (\sum_{i=1}^{I} {^m r_{ij}}), m = 1,2,\ldots N, \tag{16}$$

$$^mR^n = \frac{1}{I}\sum_{i=1}^{I} (\frac{1}{\sum_j n_{ij}}\sum_{j=1}^{J} n_{ij}\, {^m r_{ij}}), m = 1,2,\ldots,N, \tag{17}$$

$$^mR^a = \frac{1}{I}\sum_{i=1}^{I} (\frac{1}{\sum_j n_{ij}}\sum_{j=1}^{J} n_{ij}\, {^m r_{ij}} (abs(\widehat{^m p_{ij}} - {^m p_i}))), m = 1,2,\ldots,N. \tag{18}$$

Many Competing Messages (Many-to-One and Many-to-Many): Discussion

In this study the model to quantify the risk of misinforming is expanded to many-to-many topology, which is reflecting much closer the real market situation. An experiment designed to illustrate how it is possible to collect data needed to apply the above models for two competing products was conducted and illustrates how these models can be used, but the way of collecting data is over complicated. The way to data collection to make the developed model applicable needs to be revised significantly. By exploring data accumulated in CRM systems (see Part 3) a producer may acquire the needed data to apply such measures. A Seller using CRM practically doesn't offer the true competitive products.

CONCLUSION

Trying to model market situations, the measures of misinforming likelihood become more and more complex. In case of two-to-one the probability decision space includes more than 96 options; in case 3:1 this number grows to more than 198 if comparison between options is considered as well. Even in the simple case of two-to-one the probability space grows significantly compared with the case of one-to-one. In the real market cases (many-to-many) the proposed measures are obviously not applicable. In practice, such an evaluation is needed and could be performed by one producer, or one seller and the models developed in the previous chapter may serve well enough.

This size of the decision space requires corresponding variety of data with sufficient size of respondents that will allow a representative to the group measures Such amount of relevant data that is needed to collect in an empirical study doesn't allow further developing the ideas of increasing complexity of the models and clustering the population of respondents.

The problem of data gathering also doesn't allow building practical recommendations about how the results can be interpreted to serve management practice, for example in defining warranty policy or customizing the advertising messages. This places the task for more careful design of the empirical study and data collection as an open problem.

Despite those limitations and concerns, the developed approach may serve for developing general understanding regarding the potential for misinforming hazards and associated risks for a given group. The complications associated in evaluation the likelihood of the misinforming risk in case of multiple competing products is not relevant to a single Seller. Next part of the book addresses different scenarios when the models developed here can provide benefits to improve communication with clients.

REFERENCES

Christozov, D., Chukova, S., & Mateev, P. (2008). Warranty and the Risk of Misinforming: Evaluation of the Degree of Acceptance. *Journal of Issues in Informing Science and Information Technology*, *5*, 667–677. doi:10.28945/1035

Christozov, D., Chukova, S., & Mateev, P. (2009). The risk of misinforming for competing messages. *Journal of Issues in Informing Science and Information Technology*, *6*, 351–364. doi:10.28945/1064

Chapter 10
Assessment of Risk of Misinforming:
Dynamic Measures

ABSTRACT

This chapter discusses some ideas regarding how to model the changes of the value of misinforming after the wrong purchase decision is made. How the likelihood and impact of the risk changes as a result of adoption of the newly acquired product during the initial period of using it. Changes in assessment of a product's suitability are considered for the two categories of users – optimists and pessimists. The role of encouraging pessimists to purchase the product by providing incentives in the form of warranty that offer free trial period may serve as a bridge to the fourth part of the book.

INTRODUCTION

In the previous chapters we presented models which allow us to evaluate the risk of misinforming in a static scenario – at the time of making decision. In a business trade case this is the time of making the decision to purchase or not, or which product to choose in the case of competing options. Usually, the act of purchasing initiates the process of adopting the product. Adoption is learning weather and how the buyer (at that time owner) will be able to accomplish all works she or he intended to do with the product. Additionally, during this lengthy period, the buyer learns also what else can be done with the product, what additional or better properties of the product will give more benefits, and for what the product is not suitable at all or only partially.

DOI: 10.4018/978-1-6684-8800-3.ch010

The learning process is a process of decreasing misinforming. In this chapter we will discuss the case of how the risk of misinforming changes during accumulation of experience in using the information – exploring product's capability. Or the learning dynamics and progress as related to the level of misinforming.

During the period of using a product, the knowledge regarding its properties and suitability of the product to accomplish needed activities increases as well as the skills for efficient use of the product. Usually, the change is toward increasing understanding in the two aspects of utilizing the product. First is the knowledge regarding the product's properties and what the new owner can do by using the product, what are constraints, and what are extra options. The second is increasing the more general understanding of what kind of relevant activities can be executed with a product in this category. This results in adjustment of the set of relevant problems, works and activities. Also this experience redefines the needs, degrees of acceptance, and in general redefining the conditions leading to justify the acquiring of the product. This process is defined also by the updates of assessment of the risk of becoming misinformed. In general, learning increases competences and results in decreasing the misinforming risk's exposure.

This chapter addresses the evolution of the risk of wrong purchase decision over the period of adoption of the new product. The offered warranty of misinforming may play a significant role in this process by offering a risk-free trial period that may encourage pessimists to purchase the product and to try it. Part 4 is dedicated to warranty, including discussion about launching warranty policy to enhance learning in product adoption process.

SETTING THE STAGE

Let us assume that a customer b_j purchased a new product d, e.g., a new personal computer (PC). The purchase is made in order to address some particular, recognized before the time of purchasing, b_j needs to solve for a particular set of problems by using the product d. For example, in the case of purchasing a PC, these problems or works are to develop text documents, to perform simple or complex calculations, to send and receive e-mails, to browse Internet, to play games, or to listen music and watch movies. The PC has characteristics (technical properties), such as CPU's speed, memory's capacity, etc., which allow the customer to accomplish her or his work.

There are two stages in the adoption (acceptance) of the new product. The first one is to select the product, to make the purchase decision, and to acquire the product. The second one is to utilize the product. The second stage is related to the initial period of product usage when the buyer discovers whether and how the product satisfies expectations and meets the initially recognized needs, but also what else can be done with product not considered as a reason to buy it at the time of purchasing.

Over the period of learning, the risk that the product will not satisfy the customer's needs evolves as well. On one hand, the customer learns how the product properties relate to her/his needs, but on the other hand, the client learns what the product could offer, and based on this new information, extends/modifies the set of relevant works and related needs. The case, that the buyer realized that the product is good enough for originally identified works but need a better device from the same category of products to allow accomplishing the newly identified options for usage.

The objective of this chapter is modelling the dynamics of the change of buyer's attitude toward the new product at the time of its adoption.

Trial Period as Related to Warranty

The two types of pure warranties, the warranty of malfunctioning $W_R(t^R)$ and warranty of misinforming $W_I(t^I)$, have one main parameter of interest – their warranty period, t^R and t^I, respectively. During this warranty period – the time warranty claims against a faulty product are legitimate. Here, by "time" we mean any measure of the warranty coverage, not necessarily the calendar time. For example, in automobile industry, the warranty coverage is identified not only by the vehicle's age, but accounts also for the accumulated mileage, i.e., "time" could by the age of the vehicle, or it could be the accumulated mileage. A mixed warranty policy $W_p=\{t^R,t^I\}$ accounts for both types of warranties and it is identified by the two ordered time periods, t^R and t^I. During a time period of length t^R after the product sale all warranty claims against the product performance are legitimate and during t^I all warranty claims against the product suitability are legitimate. With $\mu i_{j,}$ $0\leq$ $\mu ij_{\leq}$ $\mu ij_{\leq I}$.0, we denote the importance of the warranty of misinforming for client bj w_ith respect to activity aij. $_W$hen the warranty of misinforming is included into purchasing deal, the buyer is given a period tI t^o a risk-free trial.

THE NATURE OF DYNAMIC MEASURES

The proposed dynamic measures assume a limited trial period, usually associated with warranty coverage tI· Or dynamics of learning will cover changes of the value of the risk of misinforming over the warranty periods tR and tI· It is a free trial in case of tI>0 and dependences on the coverage of the misinforming risk is natural. This period de facto provides risk-free learning opportunities in respect to both: product's properties $\widehat{p}_{ij}$ and customer's level of acceptance q_{ij}. We assume that the degree of relative importance of the warranty of misinforming μi_j for client bj with respect to work ai_j is known. Dynamic measures are justified by the fact that while using the product the client accumulates knowledge about the features and suitability of the product to accomplish her/his activities with this product, or subjective probability regarding the product's properties is approaching the true values:

$$\hat{p}_{ij} = \hat{p}_{ij}(t) \underset{t\to\infty}{\rightarrow} p_i \,. \tag{1}$$

Other aspects influencing the time dependency of the risk of misinforming relate to client's learning regarding needs – what the client can do with this product and what she or he assumes as important. By using the product, the client learns not only whether the product is suitable for her/his initial needs but also whether it is able to help in accomplishing newly identify needs that could be addressed by this category of products. Obviously, this time dependent learning could affect the levels of product acceptance q_{ij}, i.e., $q_{ij}=q_{ij}(t)$ as well.

The third parameter, which characterizes the client b_j is her/his set of activities $A_j=\{a_{ij}\}$ and the needs n_{ij} to accomplish them in an efficient way. The assumption is that this parameter will not change during the trial period and therefore will not be influenced by the dynamics of learning and the changes of the misinforming risk $n_{ij}(t)=n_{ij}$ allows to model learning progress with reasonable complexity. This assumption is not always true. The buyer may identify a completely new area of useful implementation of the acquired product (see Section 2.5.3. for an example).

Figures 1 and 2 illustrate the relationship of the two learning curves: learning about the product's property – how $\hat{p}_{ij}(t)$ changes over time; and learning regarding $q_{ij}(t)$ for the two categories of clients – optimists and pessimists. The positive purchase decision is represented that initially for both categories of customers, the $\hat{p}_{ij}(0) > \hat{q}_{ij}(0)$. The optimists overestimate initially the product quality that is why the learning curve $\hat{p}_{ij}(t)$ decreases in time. The pessimists initially underestimate the product quality, therefore for them the curve $\hat{p}_{ij}(t)$ is increasing. For pessimists the two curves may intersect if the learning regarding $\hat{p}_{ij}(t)$ decreases slower in time than the learning regarding $q_{ij}(t)$. Here, we consider only the cases when the level of acceptance $q_{ij}(t)$ increases in time. In case the buyer is a pessimist, the level of acceptance may also decrease with learning, the pessimist sets initially too high the acceptance level, the two-learning curves will not intersect, and the trial period will not change the level of misinforming. In the optimist case and decreasing level of acceptance the situation is similar, but symmetrical, with the case of pessimists and increasing level of acceptance – the two curves may intersect if the learning regarding $\widehat{p}_{ij}(t)$ decreases faster than the learning regarding $q_{ij}(t)$.

Figure 1. Dynamics of learning in case of optimist customers
(Adopted from Christozov et al., 2011)

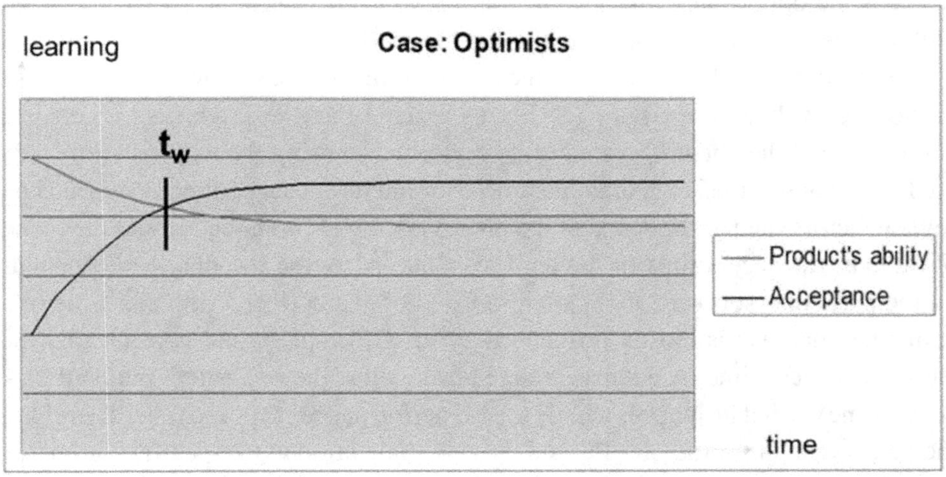

Figure 2. Dynamics of learning in case of pessimist customers
(Adopted from Christozov et al., 2011)

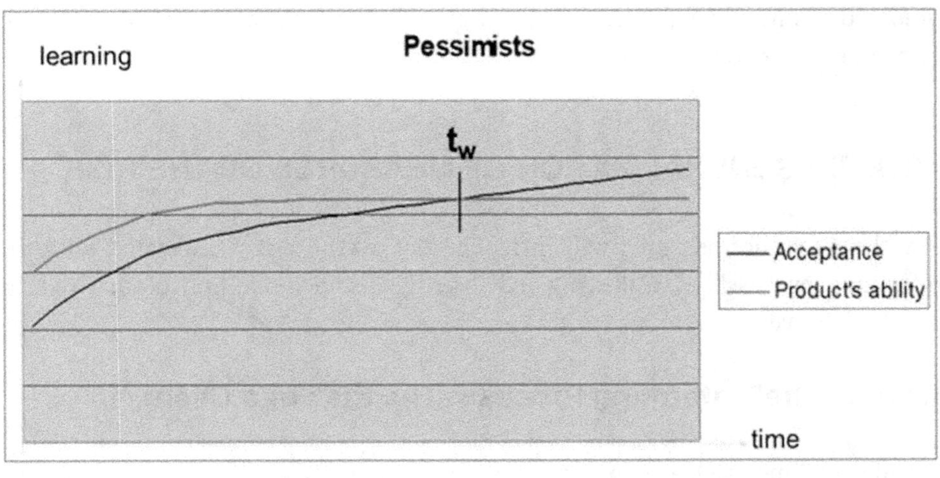

If the two learning curves intersect, which means that the product's quality becomes under the level of acceptance, the customer will realize that she/he has made a wrong purchase decision regarding the product. Therefore, the claim of customer's unsatisfaction depends on the coverage provided by the warranty of misinforming and the warranty periods play significant role in quantifying the risk of misinforming $r_{ij}(t) = r_{ij}(p_i, \hat{p}_{ij}(t), q_{ij}(t) \mid t \leq t^I)$. An unsatisfied customer, who has the opportunity provided by warranty of misinforming to be reimbursed will not keep a negative attitude regarding the producer.

To illustrate the above ideas and the proposed measures, we provide an example on how to evaluate the risks $r_{ij}(t)$. Let us assume that the product is a personal computer, and the client b_j evaluates its performance using the response time, i.e., the PC response time is the main parameter of interest. This parameter depends on several factors such as the speed of the processor, the PC architecture and the speed of the bus, the access time of the hard disk, etc. Also, the response time depends on the particular software application in use. For example, the response time of a computational task is mostly influenced by the CPU speed, and not much by the hard disk access time. A database related task is just the opposite – the hard disk access time is what influences mostly the PC performance/response time. Therefore, the actual response time of a PC is a user or application/work specific parameter. Usually, the seller provides information on the technical parameters of the product, but not the subjective, user-related performance parameters. It is well known that in the process of using the product, the user learns whether the PC performance meets her/his specific needs. Also, during this learning period, the user might face the need to explore the product in a larger scale problem than initially intended. This additional requirement will affect (increase) the level of needed performance compared to initially expected, and subsequently increase the requirement toward the degree of acceptance.

DYNAMIC GENERALIZATION OF MEASURES OF THE RISK

How the dynamic measures will influence the overall risks associated with the "informing process" by following the three levels in modelling of this risk as presented above.

"One-to-One" Informing Process: The Risk of a Client

Considering time as a learning parameter, several models will be defined to evaluate the overall risk, regarding all works a_{ij}, a client b_j is exposed to do, as a function of the time. When purchasing the decision is based on received information regarding the features of the product $d\in D$ and according to her/his understanding of this information. The difference in these models is associated with different information components available in evaluation of the risk: the needs – n_{ij}; the risk of a wrong decision regarding a given task – r_{ij} and the degree of information asymmetry – ia_{ij}. Including different components, according to what data is available, we may construct the following three measures:

- A simple model - only data regarding the probability of wrong decisions r_{ij} is used. It is not difficult to collect such data – in commercial activities; one must count only the claims of the unsatisfied clients:

$$r_j^s(t) = \frac{\sum_{i=1}^{k} r_{ij}(t)\left(\mu_{ij}t^I + \left(1-\mu_{ij}\right)t^R\right)}{\sum_{i=1}^{k} \mu_{ij}t^I + \left(1-\mu_{ij}\right)t^R}. \tag{2}$$

If all decisions are wrong and corresponding degrees of misinforming importance μi_j are equal to 1, then, as expected, $r_j^s = 1$.

- Model accounting for the client's needs. We assume that if a client b_j doesn't need to solve tasks from given category A^*_i then n_{ij}=0, and she doesn't need to know and interpret the message regarding these tasks. In general, it is easy to see that there is a simple relationship between the level of needs and the risk of misinforming, i.e., the higher the need of a client to solve for a given task is, the higher corresponding risk of misinforming is:

$$r_j^n(t) = \frac{\sum_{i=1}^{k} n_{ij}(t)\, r_{ij}(t)\left(\mu_{ij}t^I + \left(1-\mu_{ij}\right)t^R\right)}{\sum_{i=1}^{k} n_{ij}(t)\left(\mu_{ij}t^I + \left(1-\mu_{ij}\right)t^R\right)}. \tag{3}$$

- Model accounting for the needs and for the degree of information asymmetry. In this model, we collect and use feedback data on the third component, the degree of error in understanding the message. The measure of the risk in this case is the most complex, but the most precise:

$$r_j^a(t) = \frac{\sum_{i=1}^{k} n_{ij}(t) r_{ij}(t) ia_{ij} \left(\mu_{ij} t^I + (1 - \mu_{ij}) t^R \right)}{\sum_{i=1}^{k} n_{ij}(t) \left(\mu_{ij} t^I + (1 - \mu_{ij}) t^R \right)} \tag{4}$$

"One-to-Many" Informing Process

In defining these risks from the seller's viewpoint, we generalize the above formula for a whole group of clients. This risk is a measure of the informing quality of the message that is sent out to clients. It measures the quality of the message, i.e., how the content or meaning the sender intends to convey to the clients is described and presented in the message. In this case, we also consider three models accounting for the three information components:

- A simple model:

$$R^s(t) = \frac{\sum_{j=1}^{J} \sum_{i=1}^{k} r_{ij}(t) \left(\mu_{ij}^a t^I + (1 - \mu_{ij}^a) t^R \right)}{\sum_{j=1}^{J} \sum_{i=1}^{k} \left(\mu_{ij}^a t^I + (1 - \mu_{ij}^a) t^R \right)} \tag{5}$$

- A model accounting for the clients' needs:

$$R^n(t) = \frac{\sum_{j=1}^{J} \sum_{i=1}^{k} r_{ij}(t) n_{ij}(t) \left(\mu_{ij}^a t^I + (1 - \mu_{ij}^a) t^R \right)}{\sum_{j=1}^{J} \sum_{i=1}^{k} n_{ij}(t) \left(\mu_{ij}^a t^I + (1 - \mu_{ij}^a) t^R \right)} \tag{6}$$

- A model accounting for the needs and degree of information asymmetry:

$$R^a(t) = \frac{\sum_{j=1}^{J} \sum_{i=1}^{k} r_{ij}(t) n_{ij}(t) ia_{ij} \left(\mu_{ij}^a t^I + (1 - \mu_{ij}^a) t^R \right)}{\sum_{j=1}^{J} \sum_{i=1}^{k} n_{ij}(t) \left(\mu_{ij}^a t^I + (1 - \mu_{ij}^a) t^R \right)} \tag{7}$$

AN ILLUSTRATIVE EXAMPLE

Next, in Table 2.5.1, we illustrate the dynamics of the risk of misinforming on a PC case with a fixed period of $t^R = 1$ year of warranty of malfunctioning and four different misinforming warranty periods, such as t^l= {0 months, 3 months, 6 months, 9 months}.

Let $\hat{p}_j(t) = \min(\hat{p}_{ij}(t))$ is the expected product performance for all tasks for client b_j and $q_j(t)$= $\max(q_{ij}(t))$ is the threshold of the level of acceptance for the same client.

Initially, at the time of the purchase, $t=t_0=0$, $\hat{p}_j(t_0) = 1.0$. This is so, because at that time, the client believes that the product is suitable for all of his tasks, i.e., $\hat{p}_{ij}(t_0) = 1$, for $i=1,\ldots,k$, and $\hat{p}_j(t_0) = \min(\hat{p}_{ij}(t_0)) = 1$. Let us assume that for the set of tasks of client b_j, the actual performance of this PC is $p_j=0.7<p_j(t_0)$, or b_j is an optimist. Also, let us assume that for client b_j the level of acceptance for her/his initial need for the PC performance is $q_j(t_0)=0.75$ and 5 months are needed to fully understand the capability of the product. Let us assume also that the learning curve for the actually needed performance follows an increasing function. The dynamics of this data is presented in Table 2.5.1. The presented data regarding the initial parameters of the risk are drawn from the survey conducted in 2010. This survey repeated the one in 2008 for a new sample of respondents.

Table 1. Dissatisfaction risks in a learning process

Time (months)	$\hat{p}_j(t)$	$q_j(t)$	Risk when t^l=0	Risk when t^l=3	Risk when t^l=6	Risk when t^l=12
0	1.00	0.750	0	0	0	0
1	0.90	0.770	0	0	0	0
2	0.82	0.780	0	0	0	0
3	0.75	0.785	1	**0***	**0***	**0***
4	0.72	0.790	1	1	**0***	**0***
5	0.70	0.800	1	1	**0***	**0***
6	0.70	0.805	1	1	**0***	**0***
7	0.70	0.810	1	1	1	**0***
8	0.70	0.813	1	1	1	**0***
9	0.70	0.815	1	1	1	**0***

(Adopted from Christozov et al., 2011)

* The dissatisfaction risk is zero, because the client is protected by the warranty of misinforming and can return the product for full reimbursement.

To illustrate the behavior of risks of misinforming over the time, we will make an additional assumption that for b_j the ratio of importance of the two warranties is set to μ=0.3. Also, for simplicity, we assume that the group of tasks is composed of only one task. Under these settings, the risks for b*j* are presented at Table 2. The values of the other two risk measures are obtained by multiplying the values in Table 2. by the needs or by the needs and coefficient of information asymmetry.

Table 2. Dynamics of misinforming risk as a function of time and warranty coverage

Time t	r_{ij}				$r_j^s(t)=\frac{\sum_{i=1}^{k} r_{ij}(t)(\mu_{ij}t^I+(1-\mu_{ij})t^R}{\sum_{i=1}^{k}\mu_{ij}t^I+(1-\mu_{ij})t^R}$			
					t^I			
	0	**3**	**6**	**9**	**0**	**3**	**6**	**9**
0	0	0	0	0	1.00	0.44	0.28	0.21
1	0	0	0	0	1.00	0.44	0.28	0.21
2	0	0	0	0	1.00	0.44	0.28	0.21
3	1	**0**	**0**	**0**	1.00	0.44	0.28	0.21
4	1	1	**0**	**0**	1.00	1.00	0.28	0.21
5	1	1	**0**	**0**	1.00	1.00	0.28	0.21
6	1	1	**0**	**0**	1.00	1.00	0.28	0.21
7	1	1	1	**0**	1.00	1.00	1.00	0.21
8	1	1	1	**0**	1.00	1.00	1.00	0.21
9	1	1	1	**0**	1.00	1.00	1.00	0.21

(Adopted from Christozov et al., 2011)

AN EXAMPLE, ILLUSTRATING THAT THE SET OF ACTIVITIES ARE ALSO SUBJECT TO UPDATING

Let us assume that the buyer needs to buy a smartphone. The activities motivated the purchasing are "making calls" and "sending/receiving SMS". The property considered is the size of the screen. And let the price is a function of the diagonal of the screen – larger screen, more expensive phone. The buyer optimizes the purchasing by price and assumes the 2" screen will fully satisfy the needs to do the two activities. Later, s/he realizes that there is an easy-to-use application for navigation, and this additional activity "GPS Navigation" is highly useful, but the screen with 2 inches diameter is too small to be useful.

The buyer learns what additionally can do with a smartphone (a product from the same category) and what are the technical properties (five inches screen) are needed to make use of this additional activity. The original degree of acceptance is updated. In this or similar cases, the warranty of misinforming may help in easy and relatively cheap replacement the product with one of the same categories but on higher level.

CONCLUSION

An approach to quantify the dynamics of risk of misinforming over the learning period during the adoption of a new product is proposed in this chapter. The proposed measures may help in better understanding the process of adoption with respect to buyer's satisfaction and the risks associated with dissatisfaction. The misinforming warranty coverage is considered as a tool to encourage learning and to facilitate adoption by reducing the risk of uncertainty and potential dissatisfaction.

On Part 4 the learning dynamics in the adoption process is discussed as function of warranty. Further incorporation of these ideas into measuring the quality of warranty policies will provide a better insight into the seller/buyer relationship and on instruments used to facilitate and support successful communication between them.

An open issue is how to collect data regarding the learning evolution during the adoption process of a new product. The illustration presented in this chapter uses simulation of the process of growing learning with initial values drawn from a survey.

REFERENCES

Christozov, D., Chukova, S., & Mateev, P. (2009). On two types of warranties: Warranty of malfunctioning and warranty of misinforming. *Asia-Pacific Journal of Operational Research*, *26*(3), 399–420. doi:10.1142/S0217595909002274

Christozov, D., Chukova, S., & Mateev, P. (2009). The risk of misinforming for competing messages. *Journal of Issues in Informing Science and Information Technology*, *6*, 351–364. doi:10.28945/1064

Christozov, D., Chukova, S., & Mateev, P. (2011). Assessment of Risk of Misinforming: Dynamic Measures. *Interdisciplinary Journal of Information, Knowledge, and Management*, *6*, 163–176. doi:10.28945/1374

Christozov, D., Chukova, S., & Mateev, P. (2013). The role of Warranty of Misinforming in New Product Adoption. *Journal of Issues in Informing Science and Information Technology*, *10*, 111–120. doi:10.28945/1799

Section 2 Conclusion

The importance of misinforming nowadays was justified in Part 1. Facing increasing dependency on indirectly received information increases the effect caused by the hazard of becoming misled. To address and manage it in a way to reduce, mitigate, avoid, but also explore outcomes of misinforming, evaluation of probability and impact is definitely justifiable. Using quantitative measures allows us to address these issues rationally and to make data driven decisions. This part of the book presented one approach about how likelihood of risk of misinforming can be quantified in different, business oriented, scenarios. Complexity and difficulties to quantify this risk comes from the nature of its appearance – misinforming is naturally a failure of communication process, it is based on two-sided information asymmetry, and natural insufficient competences in interpreting obtained information. In every chapter, the difficulties of applying practically the proposed models from point of view of acquiring relevant data to allow evaluation of misinforming measures is discussed. Examples of surveys used to collect needed data are designed and may serve to illustrate these difficulties. Complexity of relevant data needed and complexity of acquiring data limits the complexity of models as well.

The models developed in Part 2 of the book and used in the next two parts describe several sets of objects and concepts, marked with appropriate symbols. The models of the risk of misinforming are developed with the assumption of a context of a single business transaction. Or there is a producer or seller who is selling a product that can satisfy the needs of a customer or buyer to accomplish a known set of tasks, to solve problems, or to execute activities, etc. The buyer is looking for the product on the set of similar, competing products on the given market, which may satisfy in the best way his or her needs. Different customers may need products with different qualities, properties, characteristics, because their needs are different.

Appendix 1 summarizes the symbols and definitions of the variables, formulae developed, and indices used throughout the book.

Appendix 2 summarizes the surveys used to illustrate the models and the ways for data collection.

Section 3

Management of and Management With Misinforming

Section 3 Introduction

This section of the book is dedicated to business practices addressing the misinforming phenomenon. Some of those practices use directly misinforming and measures discussed so far, and some others are developed for solving problems considering misinforming as a background, environmental issue. In all these cases the objectives are to make better decisions and in general to improve the rationality of management. How and why the measures presented in the previous section may help in achieving these objectives.

Several typical business problems are elaborated from the light of misinforming as misinforming is a real phenomenon which nowadays increases its impact on overall business and not only activities. What is needed to have trusted data in making managerial decisions? What to do to avoid wrong interpretation that may result in wrong decisions and cause harm? In general, how to reduce the risk associated with misinforming? The role of the advertising component of the trade is to inform and attract potential customers to purchase the advertised product.

Misinforming hazard happens as a failure of communication process between parties. To investigate risks associated with these hazards we need to understand how information obtained by receiver, in a way to reduce uncertainty in making decisions, is transformed into actable knowledge, and is leading to conduct actions in a way to solve the receiver's problem. Uncertainty is natural in even the simplest cases in real life. For example, crossing an empty street on a walkway in a green traffic light looks highly certain decision, but it always may happen that a crazy driver may decide to test what is the maximal speed of his or her car at the same time and on the same street. Green light, and of course knowledge regarding traffic regulations – knowledge regarding what "green light" means; and real time data – observation of specific traffic conditions on the street; are information used in making this decision. Car driven by a crazy driver around the corner represents the unknown component of the whole picture. A decision is made based on available information, what is known, and when this information is assessed as sufficient by the decision maker, or it reaches the acceptable level of confidence and certainty. This leads the receiver to make decisions and to act (crossing the street). Risk of becoming misinformed that causes making wrong and harmful decision has two origins – the first is the natural uncertainty existing in any circumstances as described in the above example; and the second is based on failures in considering this hazard, which can be avoided by adopting relevant measures in the process of communication.

The last three decades, since the World Wide Web (WWW) have been introduced, changed completely the way of how people communicate and learn, and consequently, the risks of being misled changed in nature, likelihood, and impact. The magnitude, likelihood and therefore the exposure of such risks are increased recently by overwhelming dependence on achievement of Computer Information Technologies, growing volume, and complexity of data, as well as the pressure of becoming informed on time. Business practices nowadays are heavily influenced by computer and communication technologies, global connectivity, and indirect communication via a variety of computer applications. Nowadays, communication is cheaper and faster as never before, but also growing dependence on technology assisted communication increases possibility to misinterpret information and the likelihood of becoming misinformed. The origin and circumstances of the misinforming hazards are discussed in the first section of the book. Rational decision-making needs balancing of pros and cons and quantitative measures to evaluate the potential ways of action. The second section of the book introduces one approach to evaluate relatively comprehensively the factors caused and the properties of the risk of misinforming.

Throughout the chapters in this section of the book different techniques to manage a given social system are discussed by having in mind that the phenomenon of misinforming exists, and it is a valuable factor influencing business activities nowadays. Issues like how to manage collecting, capturing, and exploring data to highlight the exposure of misinforming risk are discussed and ideas how to do are presented as well. Rational managerial decisions are based on careful assessment of their impact on the various aspects of the business and need to be done in a quantitative manner. From this perspective, quantitative measured of the misinforming risk may serve as a toll allowing improving the management in general. What to do and how to explore the quantitative measures of misinforming risks in a way to improve communication between different parties and to increase probability for success are the objectives of this section of the book.

Producers, suppliers, or sellers are on one of the sides of the business world. They may explore quantitative measures of the risks associated with misinforming in two ways. The first way is to use those measures to address the market and to manage communication with potential clients by providing adequate messages. The second is to use the quantitative measures of the misinforming risk in applying different practices to mitigate such risks to avoid causing unsatisfaction among clients. The first is managing with understanding of the risks, their exposure and potential effects caused by hazards leading to these risks. This aspect is management with considering existence of misinforming and managing with misinforming or under the circumstances of existence of misinforming hazard. The second aspect is to implement activities to mitigate the risks caused by hazards leading to misinforming. This includes managerial activities directed to reduce misinforming but also to explore misinforming in acquiring some benefits. Or managing the misinforming. In some cases, misinforming may provide opportunities, and by missing to explore them also represents losses.

The chapters in this section of the book address both those sides of management. Management of business activities under understanding that the risk of misinforming exists and exploring this understanding in managing relationship with clients. The other aspect is building managerial policies in a way to mitigate this risk – management with misinforming and management of misinforming.

Next section of the book – Warranty of Misinforming – is dedicated to widely used business practice of sharing the risk. How may warranty integrate these two aspects of management by extending the current practice in a way also to address the risk of misinforming? The fourth section of the book explores the two types of warranty – warranty of malfunctioning and warranty of misinforming – in more detail. The chapters of this section of the book explore warranty only in considering these two aspects – as an indicator for self-confidence in data interpretation; and as a possible reaction to specific circumstances.

The following issues are elaborated in this section as separate chapters:

Chapter 3.1. explores the problem of market segmentation from the point of view of misinforming. To reduce the negative outcomes of wrong purchase decisions, customers often need additional information. The cost of providing such additional details in reducing the risk of wrong decision caused by misinforming allows a justifiable way to split the population of potential clients into categories. This represents market segmentation based on the ability of potential customers to interpret provided information.

Next Chapter 3.2. discusses the way of using the developed measures in customizing or personalizing messages that can be incorporated in an application of the Customer Relationship Management (CRM) techniques. Avoiding mediators from one side reduces this risk, but from other by increasing diversity of recipients may create communication problems.

The third Chapter 3.3 is dedicated to the informing of users via computer applications. The role of user interface in informing may allow users to get full benefit of computer-generated output. An idea how to develop user-customized interface by considering the risk of misinforming is presented and discussed. In this chapter the misinforming hazard is also considered from its positive role when it provides opportunity for the user to learn. The role of interface in computer's accessed and delivered information is not only a tool to deliver information filtered by its origin and results of data processing, but also it may serve as tool to guide user in learning about the property of data domain, data processing techniques, and validity of results. The well-designed user interface of a computer application can lead to better understand and interpret results of data processing by adding explanations and guidelines to overcome lack of competences and to reduce the risk of becoming mislead by provided information. This is especially important in applications dealing with Big Data when the user can consider only secondary and aggregated information, produced by using sometime quite sophisticated analytical algorithms.

Chapter 3.4. discusses other business practice addressed the opportunity for collective data interpretation and the synergy of cooperation. Transdisciplinarity is the way to avoid misinforming in facing a complex multidimensional problem. The chapter also emphasizes the new business practice – philanthropy of data – which is a form of public-private collaboration that allows sharing of private data, expertise, and infrastructure with public entities to avoid misinforming in case of exploring Big Data and other informing services for the benefit of entire society.

Chapter 3.5. discusses techniques to mitigate the risk of misinforming and serves as link to the next section of the book. It introduces the reader to different techniques used in mitigating various categories of misinforming hazards. Techniques used with the following objectives are included:

1. Techniques to reduce probability for rejecting useful information by enhancing trust.
2. Techniques to reduce the likelihood of misinterpretation by providing tools to allow verification.

3. Techniques allowing traceability in both breadth and depth of the way the message is created, as well as the role of visualization in indirect, via computer applications, communication.

Throughout of entire section, the following different aspects of misinforming hazards are considered:

1. Risks for receivers and risk for senders of information – risks for clients and risks for sellers.
2. Risk for different categories of human behavior as pessimists, optimists, and realists.
3. Selling and marketing: composing and customizing the advertisement message.

The previous section addresses mostly the impact of misinforming to the receiver of information in the context of a trade deal, assuming that the risk of sender is summary of risk for individual receivers. This section emphasizes dominantly the risk, behavior, and way of actions of the senders of information, again in the business context of seller-client business relations.

Chapter 11
Market-Segmentation Based on Level of Reduction of Risk of Misinforming via Adjusting Information

ABSTRACT

This chapter explores the problem of market segmentation from the point of view of misinforming. To reduce the negative outcomes of wrong purchase decisions, customers often need additional information. The cost of providing such additional details in reducing the risk of wrong decision caused by misinforming allows a justifiable way to split the population of potential clients into categories. This represents market segmentation based on the ability of potential customers to interpret provided information.

INTRODUCTION

This chapter proposes an approach for market segmentation based on how information is used and on reduction of misinforming risk according to different categories of human behavior as optimists, realists, and pessimists. The technique presented in the chapter is developed and published originally in Christozov D., Chukova S. & Mateev P. (2012).

The measures for quantifying the risk of misinforming developed in the previous part of the book are explored in the way to use them in market studies. The goal is to develop an approach allowing us to identify different clusters in the market of

DOI: 10.4018/978-1-6684-8800-3.ch011

potential clients having a similar way to use the information provided. The proposed segmentation is based on the "cost" of the additional information an individual customer needs for the revision of her/his purchase decision, so that her/his initially wrong purchase decision is appropriately corrected.

The fundamental assumption is that the ability to make a conscious and realistic purchase decision is critical for the success of a market activities of both parties Producers and Sellars. Market segmentation, based on the specific information needs of the targeted group, and reducing the likelihood for clients in the group to make wrong purchase decision is essential for the success of marketing. The wrong purchase decision has a negative effect on the customer and can lead to a significant loss incurred by the seller as well. These losses could be of two types – based on missed sales or due to creating an unsatisfied customer. If the product is covered by a warranty of misinforming, an unsatisfied customer could cause direct financial losses to the Seller by making a legitimate warranty claim. This concept was introduced in Christozov, Chukova, Mateev (2006) and elaborated in the fourth part of the book. The "positive" and "negative" wrong purchase decisions were identified in Chapter 6 as well. The "positive" wrong purchase decision will generate conditions for legitimate warranty claim, whereas the "negative" wrong purchase decision will lead to a missed sale. Both risks are caused by the misunderstanding or misinterpretation of the message provided by the seller to the customers.

The risk of a wrong purchase decision is two-fold – to buy something that is not perfectly suitable or not to buy something which is perfectly suitable for a given customer. Additionally added or adjusted information may reduce either of those risks. If the cost of this additional information is calculated, then a marketing segmentation based on grouping customers by using this cost to define distance can be developed. This is the cost paid for adjusting buyer's purchase decision regarding the buyer's needed to accomplish activities with the product, over possible informing scenarios. Further, the cost for providing this additional information is used to define the distance between clients. This distance serves to identify clusters on population of buyers, and to identify market segments, or groups of customers with similar information needs. In general, this segmentation will allow us to define how to approach buyers in the given cluster, what information to provide, in a way to reduce or even minimize the probability of wrong purchase decisions and reduce the number of unsatisfied clients.

Producer's cost of wrong decisions made by customers, as a result of the misinforming hazard, also has two sides. The first one includes direct losses. Missed sales by pessimists may remain unnoticed but claims from unsatisfied optimists, claiming reimbursement as direct compensation, are usually recorded. The second source of losses comes from the generated bad image. Negative opinion shared by unsatisfied optimistic customers may spread widely and erose the image of the producer. The scope of this negative effect is usually unpredictable. Reduction of these losses is a natural problem the producer's management faces and needs to solve. Approaching all customers with the same message is the easier and cheaper, but not the most effective, way to encourage potential customers to consider purchasing the product.

This chapter explores the cost of providing additional information with the intention to reduce customers' misinforming. The different needs for such information are associated with different costs to provide it and allow us to identify and separate different categories of customers. This cost is a simplified criterion but still allows us to cluster the population of potential customers.

Providing the appropriate specific information to a given group of potential customers in the right format by using the right language and using the right channels regarding the product is the natural objective in market segmentation. How to explore the quantity measures of the risk of misinforming to use in market studies to allow identifying clusters in the market? Here, a market cluster is considered as a group of potential customers, with similar background and similar behavior in adopting information.

The proposed segmentation is based on the "cost" of the additional information a particular customer needs for the revision and further adjusting of her/his purchase decision, so that her/his initially wrong purchase decision is appropriately corrected. The risk for a wrong purchase decision has two forms – to buy something that is not perfectly suitable or not to buy something which is suitable. Additional information that allows adjusting or changing the decision may reduce either of those risks. The cost of this additional information is calculated as the minimal cost for adjusting purchase decision regarding the buyer's objectives over all possible informing scenarios. Further, the cost for additional information is used to define the distance between clients and this distance serves to identify market segments, i.e., clusters of clients with similar information needs.

Warranty preferences are used here as the source of information that allows distinguishing categories of customers' attitude or behavior. Warranty covers two types of risks – the risk of malfunctioning of a product quantified by evaluation of product's reliability, and the risk of misunderstanding about the features and qualities of the product, and its suitability for supporting the accomplishing of works the customer needs. This suitability is assessed by the customer at the time of deciding whether to buy the product or not. Offering the two warranty contracts and choosing one of them highlights the customer's attitude and self-assessment regarding his or her own competences in making this decision. Customers confident in their competences are expected to prefer choosing the warranty covering malfunctioning, and those who do not trust too much on their own expertise in making decision will prefer to choose the warranty of misinforming or mixed warranty contract (for more see Part 4, Chapter 4.2.).

Information provided by the Seller informs different clients differently, because the level of competences in interpreting the message, or information asymmetry between sender and receiver of information, is different for different customers and personal. Some customers are informed correctly regarding all properties of the product, but the same information may mislead others. Market segmentation allows sellers to approach different categories of potential buyers by using different message, so that they can address them with advertising messages, or messages with the product description, in the most appropriate and beneficial to customers in given group way. The proposed approach for segmentation of the population of potential customers is based on how they understand the seller's message. The level of needed additional adjusting information for reducing their risk of making wrong purchase decision, or the risk of misinforming, is used to separate groups.

BACKGROUND AND METHODOLOGY

The methodology developed to address the market segmentation based on the information needed to be added in a way to reduce the risk of misinforming, is based on the measures developed in the previous part of the book. Additionally, segmentation uses the ideas behind maximizing the well-known measure "information gain". See, for example Chapter 8 of Han, Kamber & Pei (2011). The objective of information gain is to improve the communication process by identifying the most informative components of the message. The general assumption behind proposed techniques is that maximization of information gain minimizes the risk of misinforming. The distance between clusters of customers regarding the given product is based on the information needed to minimize the risk of misinforming and the seller's losses caused by the misinforming hazard.

A natural question aiming to address this misunderstanding is: what the content of this additional message provided by the Seller to the customer must be to allow that her/his understanding about the real properties and applicability of the product is appropriately adjusted toward correct decision. Also, what is the Seller's cost for providing such a message. A particular customer must be provided with specific additional information, which reflects her/his specific product needs and level of acceptance (see Part 2 of the book). It is obvious that if a given customer needs to accomplish multiple works with the same product, the message to adjust her/his decision must address the needs and minimal requirements for every separate activity. In other words, for a given customer, the seller has to provide an additional message addressing every needed work, and in this way the cost of this additional message is composed as the sum of costs for adjusting the message for every distinct need. In this way a customer can be identified by a vector of costs for the message that will adjust her/his understanding regarding the product. This cost is called here as "Information Adjusting Cost. Two customers, who need the same or very similar adjusting information, can be considered as belonging to one and the same "market niche" or cluster. The additional information needed to ensure a correct purchase decision can be used to define a distance between customers, and further to use this distance for clustering the customers' population. In that way, the market segmentation is made by the degree of success in correctly informing the customers in the given group by the same message.

Notations used further were developed in Part 2 and explained in Appendix 1.

OPTIMIZATION PROBLEM: MINIMIZING INFORMATION ADJUSTING COST

Next component of the methodology is to formulate an optimization problem via the introduced Information Adjusting Cost. Distance between customers is defined further as a function of the Information Adjusting Cost. Ideas regarding how to use this distance to structure the market via distinguishing clusters of clients with similar information needs is discussed in this section.

To formulate the optimization problem related to the risk of misinforming the related "costs" must be minimized. An appropriate measure of the cost is introduced under the condition of limited resources. The idea is to find the minimal cost of formulating and transmitted additional information to adjust customer's decision.

As elaborated in Part 2, there are two types of risks leading to wrong purchase decisions:

$p_i < q_{ij} < \hat{p}_{ij}$ - the product is not suitable to accomplish activity a_{ij}, the buyer's estimation of the suitability of the product is **optimistic** and **above the threshold of acceptance,** thus the decision is **positive** and **wrong,** and r_{ij}=1. This is the case with the potential to file a warranty claim (*wc*). In case warranty of misinforming is not contracted it may create a certain number of dissatisfied customers and affect the overall market reputation of the seller. Denote this type of risk by r_{ij}^{wc} .

$\hat{p}_{ij} < q_{ij} < p_i$ - the product is suitable to solve for task a_{ij}, the buyer's estimation of the suitability of the product is **pessimistic** and **below the threshold of acceptance,** thus the decision is **negative** and **wrong,** and r_{ij}=1. This is the case of a missed sale (*ms*), which leads to a reduced profit for the seller. Denote this type of risk by r_{ij}^{ms} .

It is easy to notice that the risk of misinforming is non-zero only if

$$q_{ij} \in \left(\min\left(p_i, \hat{p}_{ij}\right), \max\left(p_i, \hat{p}_{ij}\right)\right)$$

i.e., q_{ij} is between p_i and $\hat{p}_{ij}$. Let the preference of the seller regarding which of the two types of risks r_{ij}^{wc} or r_{ij}^{ms} to minimize is given by (τ,1−τ), where 0≤ τ ≤1. Therefore, the objective function of the optimization problem related to the customer bj $c_o$uld be formulated as follows:

$$\min Z = \tau R_j^{ms} + (1-\tau) R_j^{wc}$$

where $R_j^{ms} = \sum_{i=1}^{k} r_{ij}^{ms}$ and $R_j^{wc} = \sum_{i=1}^{k} r_{ij}^{wc}$.

Let us assume that the risks (r_{ij}^{wc}, r_{ij}^{ms}) are zero whenever $p_i < q_{ij} \le \hat{p}_{ij}$ or $\hat{p}_{ij} \le q_{ij} < p_i$, or the risk is zero if the acceptance level q_{ij} is equal to the probability $\hat{p}_{ij}$.

Next, let us define the possible constraints for the above optimization problem. Assume that q_{ij} and p_i are known whereas $\hat{p}_{ij}$ is uncertain, i.e., it is a random variable with known probability distribution $\hat{P}_{ij}$. We assume that $\hat{P}_{ij}$ has a standard beta distribution with parameters (αi$_{j,}$$\beta$ij$_{)}$, i.e., $\hat{P}_{ij} \sim Beta\left(\alpha_{ij}, \beta_{ij}\right)$ and the reported (observed) value $\hat{p}_{ij}$ is the mode of this distribution.

Why beta distribution is suitable to serve in this case?

The Beta distribution is a continuous probability distribution defined on [0,1]. For more details on the standard beta distribution see Owen C. B., (2008). The probability density function (*pdf*) of this distribution is defined by

$$f_{\hat{p}}(x) = \frac{x^{\alpha-1}(1-x)^{\beta-1}}{B(\alpha,\beta)} \text{ for } x \text{ in } [0,1]; \text{ where } B(\alpha,\beta) = \int_0^1 x^{\alpha}(1-x)^{\beta-1}dx.$$

The mean value of $\hat{P}: Beta(\alpha,\beta)$ is equal to $\mu = \frac{\alpha}{\alpha+\beta}$, its mode is given by $\hat{p} = \frac{\alpha-1}{(\alpha+\beta-2)}$ and the variance by $\sigma^2 = \frac{\alpha\beta}{(\alpha+\beta)^2(\alpha+\beta+1)}$.

Both parameters of beta distribution α and β are shape parameters. It is well known that the *pdf* of Beta distribution is unimodal and strongly skewed to the right if $\alpha>1$, $\beta>1$ and $\alpha\leq\beta$. Further, if we keep α fixed and increase the value of β it makes the density more picked. The distribution gets less skewed and the mode approaches 0.5 as α and β approach each other. The distribution is symmetric around 0.5 if $\alpha=\beta$. If $\alpha=\beta=1$ then the beta distribution becomes the well-known uniform distribution over [0, 1]. In the case of left skewed pdf, if we keep β fixed and increase the value of α it makes the density more picked. The pdf is right skewed if the values of α and β were switched. If P is Beta(α,β), then $Q=1-P$ is Beta(β,α).

Beta distribution is very flexible because its two positive shape parameters α and β are frequently used to estimate an unknown proportion parameter p, which is between 0 and 1. Increasing the parameter α is equivalent to evidence of positive behavior, because the mean value and mode are moving to right. The opposite case – increasing parameter β – leads to decreasing the mean value and mode, which corresponds to negative behavior. In both cases the variance is decreasing. So, the two parameters of the beta distribution may be used to weigh all pros and cons regarding the values of the proportion parameter p.

In case of modeling misinforming, the information asymmetry, represented as $ia_{ij} = \left|p_{ij} - \hat{p}_{ij}\right|$ are define as the distance between α and β. The case $p_{ij} > \hat{p}_{ij}$ corresponds to pessimistic judgement and depending on the subjective value of qij – the acceptable level of quality of the product, the purchase decision is negative and wrong. The case $p_{ij} < \hat{p}_{ij}$ corresponds to optimistic behavior leading to positive and wrong purchase decision. Misunderstanding may differ in assessing applicability of the product for accomplishing different activities and parameters of beta distribution also differ.

More information about the standard beta distribution with parameters (αij,βij), including the probability density function, mean value μij and variance σij one can find in Wikipedia. Therefore, for the specific activity aij of bj the triple $\left(\hat{p}_{ij}, q_{ij}, p_i\right)$ represents the level of informing induced by the sellers' message regarding the features of product $p\epsilon D$. Assume that for a customer bj it is true that $(r_{ij}^{wc}, r_{ij}^{ms}) \neq (0, 0)$. The seller could provide additional information to the buyer bj, so that the buyer's risks $(r_{ij}^{wc}, r_{ij}^{ms}) = (0, 0)$. For providing this additional information the seller will incur certain cost but will benefit from the reduction of the risk of misinforming of bj with respect of activity aij. Assume that the effect of the information obtained by the additional message is measured by the shift of the initial Beta(αij,βij) distribution to $Beta\left(\tilde{\alpha}_{ij}, \tilde{\beta}_{ij}\right)$ with adjusted parameters. This transformation preserves the variance of the initial distribution and assures that the mode of the new beta distribution

$Beta\left(\tilde{\alpha}_{ij},\tilde{\beta}_{ij}\right)$ is equal to qij, i.e., assures that the corresponding risk of misinforming becomes zero. How bad the initial message was, measured by Beta(αij,βij) is illustrated on Figure 1. and is estimated by the "cost", which meaning is the absolute value of the difference between the mean values of the initial beta distribution μij and the mean value $\tilde{\mu}_{ij}$ of the transformed beta distribution, see Figure 2, by the new message, normalized by the common standard deviation σij of these two distributions.

Figure 1. Initial beta distribution

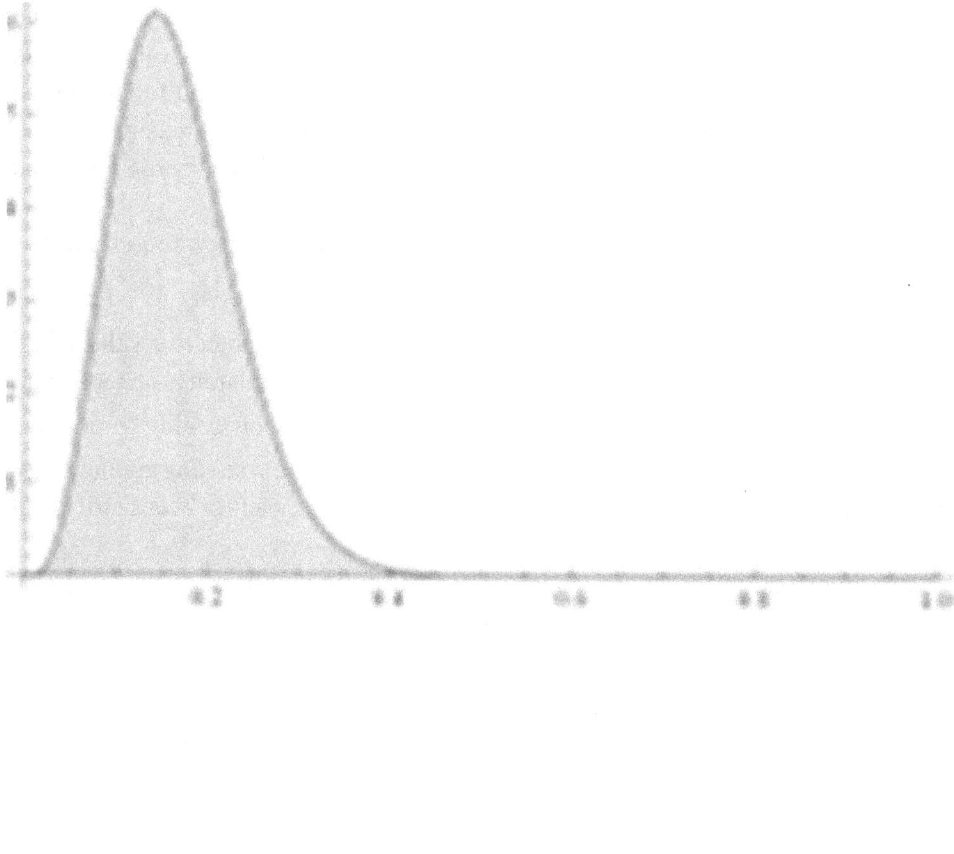

Figure 2. Initial and induced beta distributions

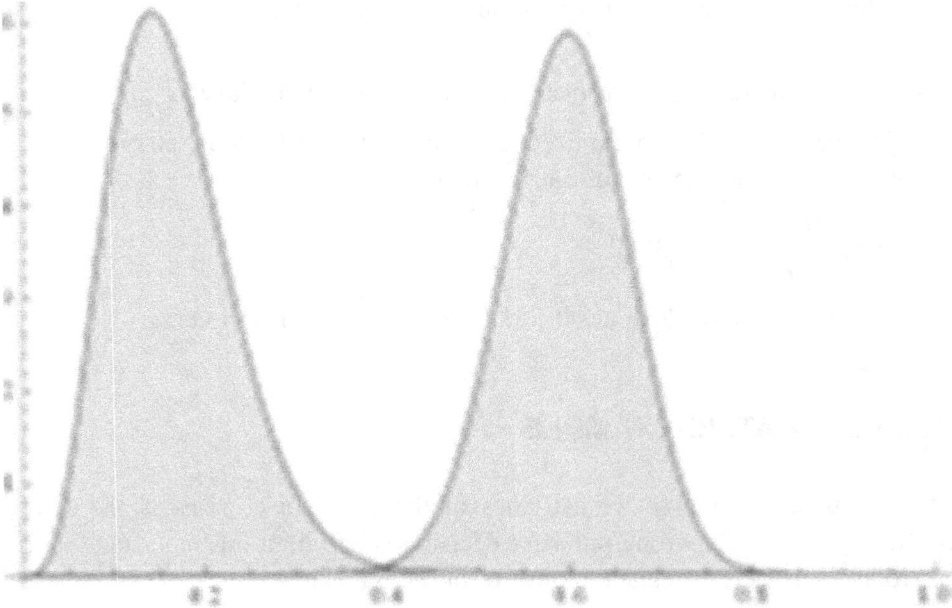

The last component to formulate the optimization problem is to identify the "best" new message for bj, given limited sel$_l$er's resources is to address the entire set of works of bj is expecting to ac$_c$omplish, not only for the one aij, as it was explor$_{ed}$ above.

Let vij, 0≤ vij ≤1, i=1, $_{....}$ kj be $_{th}$e importance from seller's viewpoint, in addressing with the new message to adjust understanding related to the ith task of the cust^{om}er bj. Due to marketing or competitive reasons the seller may have preferences in investing her/his resources in a specific subset of works relevant to the product. To formulate the optimization problem, the vij parameters are a_{ss}umed to be known. Therefore, the optimization problem can be defined as follows:

$$\min Z = \tau R_j^{ms} + \left(1-\tau\right) R_j^{wc} \quad (1)$$

$$\text{subject to: } \sum\nolimits_{i=1}^{k} v_{ij} \frac{\left|\mu_{ij} - \tilde{\mu}_{ij}\right|}{\sigma_{ij}} \le C \qquad (2)$$

where $R_j^{ms} = \sum\nolimits_{i=1}^{k} r_{ij}^{ms}$, $R_j^{wc} = \sum\nolimits_{i=1}^{k} r_{ij}^{wc}$, and C is a known constant, which represents the limited resources of the seller.

Solving this optimization problem raises two questions:

- What type of solution for this optimization problem are we looking for?
- What is the meaning of this solution? How to interpret it?

We need to identify a transformation form Beta(αij,βij) to $Beta\left(\tilde{\alpha}_{ij}, \tilde{\beta}_{ij}\right)$, s$_o$that the objective function Z is minimized, and the "cost" constraint is satisfied.

Let us also denote the cost of transformation for a given activity as

$$c_{ij} = v_{ij} \frac{\left|\mu_{ij} - \tilde{\mu}_{ij}\right|}{\sigma_{ij}}. \quad (3)$$

The example below illustrates the ideas presented in this chapter.

AN ILLUSTRATIVE EXAMPLE

Let us assume that the set of activities of the buyer bj co$_n$sists of six items: Aj={a_1j,a_{2j},...$_{,a}$6j}. $_T$he wrong purchase decision is based on misunderstanding of the product's properties related to three of the activities:

- $a_{1j} : \widehat{p}_{1j} < q_{1j} < p_1$ – the decision is negative
- $a_{3j} : p_3 < q_{3j} < \widehat{p}_{3j}$. – the decision is positive
- $a_{4j} : \widehat{p}_{4j} < q_{4j} < p_4$ – the decision is negative.

Therefore, we have risks for these activities as the following: $r_{1j}^{ms} = r_{3j}^{wc} = r_{4j}^{ms} = 1$.

In addition, it is known that the acceptance levels are q_{1j}=0.6; q_{3j}=0.55, q_{4j}=0.65; and let p_1=0.7, p_3=0.3, p_4=0.8.

Also, let us assume that that the initial beta distributions are as the follow:

- $\widehat{P}_{1j} : Beta(5,25)$, larger β parameter corresponds to right skewed shape (negative mistake).
- $\widehat{P}_{3j} : Beta(23,7)$, smaller β parameter corresponds to left skewed shape (positive mistake).
- $\widehat{P}_{4j} : Beta(3,12)$, larger β parameter corresponds to right skewed shape (negative mistake).

This leads to the following values for $\widehat{p}_{1j} = 0.142857$, $\widehat{p}_{3j} = 0.7857$ and $\widehat{p}_{4j} = 0.153846$.

For the remaining three activities risks for wrong decision are zero: $(r_{ij}^{wc}, r_{ij}^{ms})$ = (0, 0), $i = 2,5,6$.

Next, let us assume that the seller assigned the following values for the parameters of the model:

v_{1j}=0.2, v_{3j}=0.4, v_{4j}=0.7, and α=0.7, C=1.5.

What does this particular set of model's parameters reveal?

The value of $\alpha = 0.7$ suggests that for the seller the major concern is to minimize the losses due to missed sales, i.e., the seller places higher priority on reducing the risk of the missed sales compared to the risk of receiving a warranty claim. This is a realistic expectation because customers naturally resist recognizing that they are making mistake, because of lack of competence at the time of purchasing. Moreover, the values of v_{ij}, show that the seller places the highest importance in eliminating the misinforming related to activity a_{4j}, whereas he is least concern with the risk associated with a_{1j}. The value C=1.5 represents the upper bound of the resource (or the "cost") the seller is allowed or willing to invest in the new message aiming to reduce the risk of misinforming.

The optimization problem formulated above can be written as the following:

$$minZ = 0.7R_j^{ms} + 0.3R_j^{wc},$$

$$\text{subject to: } \sum_{i=1,3,4} v_{ij} \frac{|\mu_{ij} - \tilde{\mu}_i|}{\sigma_{ij}} \le \frac{3}{2}$$

The solution of the problem:

- For activity a_{1j}, given as that $\hat{p}_{1j} \le q_{1j} < p_1 \Rightarrow 0.142857 \le 0.6 < 0.7$, with risk $r_{1j}^{ms} = 1$ is for wrong negative decision. We need to find a transformation, preserving the standard deviation, of the initial *Beta*(5,25) with mode equal to $\hat{p}_{1j} = 0.142857$ to a new *Beta*(α,β) with mode equal to q1$j_{=0}$.6. By using MATHEMATICA software package is possible to find such transformation. For task a1j $_t$he new beta distribution with the required properties is Be*ta(3*1.4405, 21.2936) and the "cost" of this transformation is

$$c_{1j} = v_{1j} \frac{\left|\mu_{1j} - \tilde{\mu}_{1j}\right|}{\sigma_{1j}} = 6.41729.$$

- For activity a_{3j}, given as $p_3 < q_{3j} \leq \widehat{p}_{3j} \Rightarrow 0.3 < 0.55 \leq 0.7857$, with risk $r_{3j}^{wc} = 1$ for wrong positive decision. The transformation is from initial *Beta*(23,7), with mode equal to $\widehat{p}_{3j} = 0.7857$, to *Beta*(*α*,*β*) with mode equal to q*3j*$_{=0}$.55. Again, by using MATHEMATICA the new beta distribution for a3*j*$_w$ith the required properties is Be*ta(*22.9616, 18.9685) and the "cost" of this transformation is

$$c_{3j} = v_{3j} \frac{\left|\mu_{3j} - \tilde{\mu}_{3j}\right|}{\sigma_{3j}} = 0.28836.$$

- For activity a_{4j} with $\widehat{p}_{4j} \leq q_{4j} < p_4 \Rightarrow 0.153846 \leq 0.65 < 0.8$, the risk $r_{4j}^{ms} = 1$ is for wrong negative decision. The transformation is from initial *Beta*(3,12), with mode equal to $\widehat{p}_{4j} = 0.153846$, to a new *Beta*(*α*,*β*) with mode equal to q4*j*$_{=0}$.65. Again, by using MATHEMATICA the new beta distribution for a4*j*$_w$ith the required properties is Be*ta(1*4.0898, 8.04836) and the "cost" of this transformation is

$$c_{4j} = v_{4j} \frac{\left|\mu_{4j} - \tilde{\mu}_{4j}\right|}{\sigma_{4j}} = 4.36449.$$

We have evaluated the "costs" of the transformations related to each one of the tasks of interest. Next, we consider all possible transformations scenarios and select the "best" one that satisfies the resource constraint and leads to the smallest value of the objective function. Table 1. summarizes those findings.

Table 1. Cost of all informing scenarios

# Scenario	Number of Transformations	Activity 1	Activity 3	Activity 4	Cost of the Scenario	Constraints Satisfied?
1	3	yes	yes	yes	5.49404	No
2	2	yes	yes	no	2.4389	No
3	2	yes	no	yes	4.3406	No
4	2	no	yes	yes	4.20858	No
5	1	no	no	yes	3.05514	No
6	1	no	yes	no	1.15344	Yes
7	1	yes	no	no	1.28546	Yes

It is easy to conclude from data in Table 1. that only the last two scenarios satisfy the constraints of the optimization problem. A decision on which of these two scenarios to use in formulating the new message is based on computing the value of the objective function over each of these scenarios. We have for scenario 6, $Z_6=0.7x2+0.3x0=1.4$ and for scenario 7, $Z_7=0.7x1+0.3x1=1$. Thus, the minimum value of the objective function is reached over scenario 7, and therefore the new message should be designed so that it targets only activity a_{1j} of the buyer b_j.

DEFINITION OF DISTANCE BASED ON INFORMATION ADJUSTING

An approach for computing the optimal cost for composing an adjusting message for a single independent potential buyer was outlined above. The problem of the Seller is to minimize the total cost. To do this, it is important for the Seller to identify groups of buyers, which can be targeted simultaneously with one and the same adjusting message. This will allow multiplication of benefits by reusing efforts. This is a typical cluster analysis problem where the essential part is to define distance between any two objects $dist\left(b_{j_1}, b_{j_2}\right)$, belonging to the studied population (the set of all buyers B).

Let us assume that the risks of wrong purchase decision for buyer b_j with respect of her/his set of activities are $r\left(b_j\right)=\left\{r_{1j}, r_{2j}, \ldots, r_{kj}\right\}$ which is a binary vector, composed only by zeros and ones. The buyer needs additional information addressing the properties of the product $d \in D$, which are essential for the description of the performance of the product $d \in D$ regarding activities considered needed by b_j which have risk of wrong purchase decision equal to one. The initial message correctly informed the buyer regarding the properties of the product relevant to the activities with risk of wrong purchase decision equal to zero. This adjusted message leads to reducing the risk of wrong decision. This additional information must address only the properties of product $d \in D$ that have impact on performance of activities with non-zero risk needed by buyer b_j. The adjusting message must address the buyers' specific information needs. Natural segmentation of the market is to group buyers who have similar information needs to avoid wrong purchase decisions. The needed adjusting information may serve as a distance between buyers. Two possible definitions for the "distance" between two buyers are:

Activity-based distance: the distance or similarity is based on the set of activities that need adjusting information. It is to compare the two binary vectors $\left\{r_{1j}, r_{2j}, \ldots, r_{kj}\right\}, j-1,2$. If the adjusting message addresses product's properties relevant only to the risky activities, these vectors $\{r_{1j}, r_{2j}, \ldots, r_{kj}\}$ are asymmetric. Risks equal to one are important, and those equal to zero can be ignored. The distance can be defined by counting differences only for the activities with risk one. This distance doesn't reflect the type of wrong decision – positive or negative.

Cost-based distance: in composing the adjusting message the "cost" for developing it is taken into account as well. This measure of distance uses the vectors $\left\{c_{1j}, c_{2j}, \ldots, c_{kj}\right\}$ which includes continuous values. The "costs" of the transformation needed to convert non-zero risks tasks into zero risk tasks are calculated according to the formulae (3) above. The Minkowski distance $dist\left(b_{j_1}, b_{j_2}\right)$ between buyers b_{j_1} and b_{j_2} based on the corresponding cost is given by the formula:

$$dist\left(b_{j_1}, b_{j_2}\right) = \sqrt[h]{\sum_{i=1}^{k} \left|c_{ij_1} - c_{ij_2}\right|^h} \tag{4}$$

Any of the values of h in this formula is suitable. If in the above formula $h = 1$, we have Manhattan distance, and if $h = 2$ – Euclidean distance; and when $h \to \infty$ we get, the so called, Chebyshev's distance. The last is defined as following:

$$dist\left(b_{j_1}, b_{j_2}\right) = \lim_{h \to \infty} \left(\sum_{i=1}^{k} \left|c_{ij_1} - c_{ij_2}\right|^h\right)^{\frac{1}{h}} = \max_{i=1}^{k} \left|c_{ij_1} - c_{ij_2}\right|.$$

Any of these cases for calculating distances could be used in clustering the population of buyers. It seems that Chebyshev's distance is the simplest to apply and reflects well enough the ideas of optimizing the effect of the adjusting message under given cost-constraints. The cost-based distance will identify buyers with the smallest maximal cost distance over all their activities. These buyers could be grouped together in a cluster that could be targeted by one and the same appropriately designed adjusting message. These clusters will form the market segments based on the risk of misinforming.

CONCLUSION

The presented approach to structure the market by segmentation based on information needed by customers to make accurate risk-free purchase decision. Providing the necessary information in the correct format to the targeted group of customers is the natural objective of market segmentations. The proposed segmentation aims to reduce the risk of misinforming leading to two categories of losses – losses due to missed sales/purchases and losses due to customer dissatisfaction. These risks may have monetary implications for both parties - the sellers as well as the buyers.

The two approaches to define distance between potential buyers, based on the process of adjusting the message on the properties of the product, are presented. The first addresses only the content of the message for different groups of buyers. The second one is based on minimizing the cost of the adjusting message. Either of these approaches can be used for further clustering of the market. Their applicability depends on the available information regarding buyers' attitude and developed measures. The first is suitable for the simplest case as on Chapter 2.1.

In the next Chapter are presented another idea for customizing messages, exploring opportunities provided by Customers-Relationship-Management (CRM) applications.

REFERENCES

Christozov, D., Chukova, S., & Mateev, P. (2006). A Measure of Risk Caused by Information Asymmetry in e-Commerce. *Journal of Issues in Informing Science and Information Technology*, *3*, 147–158. doi:10.28945/879

Christozov, D., Chukova, S., & Mateev, P. (2012). Market Segmentation Based on Risk of Misinforming Reduction. *Journal of Issues in Informing Science and Information Technology*, *9*, 253–265. doi:10.28945/1620

Han, K. Pei (2011). Data Mining: Concepts and Techniques, (3rd ed.). Morgan Kaufmann Publishers.

Owen, C. B. (2008). *Parameter Estimation for the Beta Distribution*. [MSc thesis, Brigham Young University, Utah, USA].

Chapter 12
Measures of Risk of Misinforming in Personalizing the Message in Applying CRM

ABSTRACT

This chapter discusses the way of using the developed in part two measures in customizing or personalizing messages that can be incorporated in an application of the customer relationship management (CRM). CRM is a special managerial technique dedicated to establishing direct relationships with end-customers. Avoiding mediators from one side reduces the risk of misinforming, but from other side, by increasing the diversity of recipients and amount of separate recipients, may create additional communication problems associated with need of big data processing.

INTRODUCTION

In the previous chapter an approach about how to use the quantity measures of the risk of misinforming in a way to divide the population of potential clients into groups with similar expertise and attitude was proposed. The proposed approach explored the needed additional adjusted information to correct clients' wrong purchase decisions. The issue of how to compose the initial advertising message to potential customers is the objective of this chapter.

The approach and technique presented here follows the ideas developed and published in Christozov D., Chukova S. & Mateev P. (2015). They are applicable only if the Producer, or Seller, possesses historical information about clients' preferences. The technology enabled Customers Relationship Management (CRM)

DOI: 10.4018/978-1-6684-8800-3.ch012

allows to capture, collect, and store such information. CRM is an application that allows avoiding mediators in relationship and communication with clients and allows Producer to hold the history of relationship with every individual client. As it was discussed in the first part of the book mediators, especially in a sequence of cascade information delivery, are one of the important factors contributing to the misinforming hazard. The classical business products delivery process goes from producer of the product to wholesalers and further to retailers and finally to reaching the end-users. The wholesalers and retailers play the role of mediators between producers and end-users within this process, who aggregate and summarize the feedback data.

This chapter presents an approach for customizing the messages provided to individual clients via a CRM application. The essential component of the message is the form of warranty contract offered to clients within the message. The conditions of the warranty of misinforming within informing component of CRM issues extends the offer to address the client's personality as attitude toward innovation, as well as expertise in the product's domain. Warranty complements the offering by providing more favorable and encouraging conditions to customers. In this function, warranty message serves as a promotional tool. Its role as a risk sharing tool is elaborated in detail in the next part of the book. Customization or personalization of warranty parameters as the component of the advertising message aim to mitigate the risk of misinforming.

Customer-centered management is an established practice allowing a company to relate directly to their customers by addressing them as independent individuals in a way to avoid mediators. The initial practice in the beginning of industrial era, presented by Ford's famous statement that "A customer can have a car painted any color he wants as long as it's black" is passed and forgotten. Even though this stamen was not said to be a serious business strategy, Ford's Model T was painted only in black for pure economic reasons. Now customization, reflection to personal preferences is the way to market success. CRM as a tool to implement such practice allows additionally to maintain customers' profiles, history of relationship with customer, and can use the first-hand information regarding customer's activities, preferences, and expectations. Nowadays Information Technologies (IT) allows us to do it at an acceptable price. In contrast, the established way of trading via extensive use of mediators – wholesalers and retailers – leads to cascade aggregation of feedback provided by individual clients. This allows producers to use only secondary, aggregated by mediators, information regarding clients' needs and does not allow addressing the specific needs and preferences of the individual client.

The current IT allows building information services, known as CRM, that allow to avoid mediators. It is marked with the term "disintermediation" (see Wikipedia) and is one of their advantages that allow producers to collect the first-hand information related to end-user's attitude during the process of purchasing, acquiring, and utilizing the newly obtained product. This kind of service allows companies to customize their products to reflect the needs of any individual customer who receives personally targeted service.

But, regardless of those opportunities, the usual advertising practice nowadays continues to address all customers with the same unified message. Additional to customizing the product, generating customized message based on client's profile including personalized warranty conditions may encourages clients to explore new products and may result in higher sales and easy adoption of the new products.

Customization of the message can be made according to the two parameters: customer attitude toward purchasing; and customer expertise toward product domain. These two characteristics are explored in this chapter in building models allowing customization of the initial message.

BACKGROUND

The product warranty, offered by the seller/producer, could provide coverage for two types of hazards that the customer may encounter while purchasing and acquiring a new product. The first one is related to the malfunctioning of the product, i.e., the product does not function according to its specifications. In this case, the product is repaired or replaced with no charge to the customer. This warranty is called "warranty of malfunctioning". The second issue is related to the customer's satisfaction, or to what extent the product meets the customer's expectations in accomplishing works intended to be done better with the use of the product. In other words, to what extent, at the time of the purchase, the customer has been correctly informed regarding the product capability to allow customer to accomplish works as expected. This warranty is called "warranty of misinforming". If the customer is not "fully satisfied", the warranty of misinforming allows for the return of the product and full reimbursement. The warranty of misinforming provides an opportunity for the customer to explore and learn more about the properties and features of the product without incurring a risk or significant cost. Part 4 is dedicated to the concept of the two types of warranties and adequate warranty policies. Here, reaction toward warranty is used as a source of information to assess customer attitude and expertise and to formulate the initial advertising message or to serve as a promotional tool. Chapter 4.1. discusses the warranty as a business practice aiming at the sharing risks.

Let us define the following problem: how the measures of the risk of misinforming and customers' attitude toward the messages describing product $d \in D$ can be utilized in formulation a customized message by using a CRM. The two issues - exploring customers' expertise related to the product domain, measured by the value of the information asymmetry $ia_{ij} = abs\left(p_i - \hat{p}_{ij}\right)$ and customers' attitude toward purchasing products under uncertainty are in the focus in formulating the message. Based on their purchase attitude the customers are classified as

(1) optimists – they are incline to overestimate the product's quality $\sum_{i=1}^{k} n_{ij}\left(\hat{p}_{ij} - p_i\right) > \varepsilon$,
(2) pessimists – inclined to underestimate product quality $\sum_{i=1}^{k} n_{ij}\left(\hat{p}_{ij} - p_i\right) < -\varepsilon$ and
(3) realists – they access relatively (within acceptable limits) correctly the product quality $-\varepsilon < \sum_{i=1}^{k} n_{ij}\left(\hat{p} - p\right) < \varepsilon$ (see section two, chapter two).

The optimists tend to purchase the product even when it is not entirely suitable for their needs; the pessimists are very cautious and often do not purchase a product that may otherwise fully meet their needs. Notations are developed in Part 2 and presented in Appendix 1.

Combining approaches and ideas explored by the three areas of research: data analytics, CRM and informing science, which are currently fast developing, allows viewing the problem of serving customers in a new light:

- Developing of Data analytics field in the last twenty years pass through two stages - early results explore historical data to allow better understanding of processes and driving forces; recently the focus moved to support real-time solutions. In this chapter these two concepts are combined by exploring historical data to define customer profiles and use it in customizing the message content. The real-time problem is still open. The message is composed according to historical records accumulated for the individual clients. Assessing the progress trend in client's attitude represents interesting research problems but without availability of relevant data it is not practical.
- CRM evolved dramatically in the last decades by combining opportunities provided by information technologies to customize products offered to individual customers. The boom of on-line purchasing caused by COVID-19 pandemic fuel advancement of relevant technologies and scaling the usage of direct trading. Using CRM and direct trading resulted in better understanding of customers' behavior that allows us to go one step further by customizing also the messages used to approach different groups, or even any individual customer. In mass production it is practical to address a group of customers with the same unified message.

- The development of informing science foster studies on the multidimensional aspects of the way of acquiring information. One aspect of these studies is elaborating the concept of misinforming and risks associated with effectiveness of conveying messages and factors affecting these risks. Exploring models developed so far allows for customers' portfolio classification with emphasis on their purchase behavior - attitude and expertise, assigning quantity measures on these, and exploring warranty as a tool to address the risk of misinforming. Clustering, described in the previous chapter, allows assigning a customer in a group with other customers with similar needs for additional information to reach required certainty in purchasing.
- The models exploring the aggregated measures of attitude and expertise developed in the second part of the book, do not allow to distinguish between realist-expert (R/E) and realist-nonexpert (R/NE) customers. Developing further metrics, based on the analysis of customers' response to any of the components of the message, and exploring useful relationships between these responses, requires further attention and study under a given specific context and circumstances.

The explored down simulation techniques demonstrated that the proposed approach may be feasible. Access to real-life data is essential to demonstrate the practicality of the proposed approach; real data regarding a real product, real market, and clients' population in a CRM is needed.

MEASURES FOR CUSTOMERS' ASSESSING ATTITUDE AND DOMAIN EXPERTISE.

Let us assume that there is one-to-one correspondence between a property or a characteristic $\{c_l^d, l = 1,2,\ldots,L^d\}$ of the product $d \in D$ and a category of activities $A_k = \left\{a_k^p\right\}$ customers are looking to accomplish by using the product $d \in D$. Also, let us assume that each property of $d \in D$ is described by $\{c_l^d\}$ which can be considered as a separate part of the seller's message. Let us assume that the property corresponds to the activity as one-to-one. To simplify notations, we will use a single notation a_i to denote each of the above: the product characteristics, the customer category of works, and the related part of the seller's message. Thus, the expertise and attitude of a customer towards the product is measured by how s/he interprets the product's quality associated to her or his needed work as described in the related part of the message.

Measure of Attitude

The three categories of customers' attitudes while making purchase decisions used here are: optimists, realists, and pessimists. They are distinguished according to whether customers are willing to overestimate, estimate correctly, or underestimate product's properties as related to their needs and as interpreted the description provided. In general, those three categories are not clearly distinguishable and using the proposed ε-definition is difficult to implement in practice. Instead, we can measure customers' attitude by the difference between the actual value of product's properties and the value as it is assessed by the customer, based on her interpretation of the seller's message. The customer attitude is measured by the weighted sum across all the works the client is intended to do with the product, where the weights are equal to the customer's needs (or customer's utility):

$$C_j^A = \frac{1}{\sum_{i=1}^{k} n_{ij}} \sum_{i=1}^{k} n_{ij} \left(\widehat{p}_{ij} - p_i \right),$$

where n_{ij} is the need of customer b_j in using property a_i; p_i is the actual value of the property a_i, measured as the probability that the product d allows the customer to accomplish the work a_i as expected; $\widehat{p}_{ij}$ is the customer b_j's assessment of the probability that the product is capable to serve as expected related to property a_i based on the provided message (see Chapter 2.1). A negative value of C_j^A refers to the class of pessimists, a positive value - to the class of optimists. Values of C_j^A that is close to zero describes a customer-realist, i.e., a customer with realistic assessment of the properties of the product.

The proposed measure suffers from the typical aggregation problem when "optimistic" attitude toward one property is compensated by "pessimistic" attitude toward another. Weighted by needs aggregation, assumes that attitude toward the most needed properties dominate the overall attitude.

Another possible approach of constructing a measure of customer's attitude is instead of a scalar measure C_j^A of customer attitude, to use $C_j^{A*} = \left\{ \left(\widehat{p}_{1j} - p_1 \right), \left(\widehat{p}_{2j} - p_2 \right), \ldots, \left(\widehat{p}_{kj} - p_k \right) \right\}$, which is a vector of dimension k measuring the customer attitudes toward each of the product's properties described in the message separately. Therefore, there are two possible approaches to measure the customer's attitude – an "aggregated" approach or a "distributed" approach.

Measure of Expertise

In building a model regarding the customer expertise, it is expressed mainly by $\hat{p}_{ij}$ – how the customer b_j estimate the product suitability for accomplishing the work related to property a_i based on the provided message. So, there are two viewpoints regarding the properties of product d – the true suitability p_i of the product regarding activity a_i and estimated by customer b_j suitability $\hat{p}_{ij}$ of the product regarding a_i. Based on these two viewpoints regarding the suitability of the product, we may construct appropriately two probability distributions and use the Kullback - Leibler (see Kullback and Leibler (1951)) divergence (KL divergence) between these two distributions to measure the customers' level of expertise.

Let us denote the probability that customer b_j has to do work a_i as $\frac{n_{ij}}{n_{.j}}$, where $n_{.j} = \sum_{i=1}^{k_j} n_{ij}$ or n_j is the total need for all tasks customer b_j needs to accomplish with d. Then, the probability that work a_i has to be done by customer b_j and s/he will be able to do it with d is

$$p(i \mid j) = P_{ij} = p_i \frac{n_{ij}}{n_{.j}} \geq 0 .$$

We can apply this idea to the entire set of activities that a product $d \in D$ is designed for, having in mind that a particular customer b_j doesn't need to do some of those works and for them corresponding need n_{ij}=0 and also the related probability can be considered as zero. Therefore $\sum_{i=1}^{k} P_{ij} \leq 1$, and it is equal to 1 if and only if p_i=1, for all i. Let us denote by $P_{oj} = 1 - \sum_{i=1}^{k} P_{ij} \leq 1$ the complemented probability and then $P_j = \{P_{0j}, P_{1j}, \ldots, P_{kl}\}$ represents the "true" probability distribution characterizing the suitability of d regarding the categories of activities adjusted to the customer b_j needs. If we use $\hat{p}_{ij}$ instead of p_i, we can construct the "estimated" probability distribution characterizing the suitability of d regarding the categories of tasks adjusted to the customer b_j needs

$$\widehat{P}_j = \left\{ \widehat{P}_{0j}, \widehat{P}_{1j}, \ldots, \widehat{P}_{kj} \right\} .$$

Then the measure of expertise of customer b_j is given by

$$C_j^E = \sum_{i=1}^{k} P_{ij} \log \frac{P_{ij}}{\widehat{P}_{ij}}.$$

CLUSTERING OF CUSTOMERS

Distance

The measures of attitude and expertise from the customer's profile are used to define the distance between customers. To illustrate the proposed approach, the two aggregated measures – the one of of attitude and the measure of expertise will be used. In this way, every customer can be represented as a point in a two-dimensional XY-plane as shown in Figure 1, where coordinates are customers' measures for attitude and expertise. Four categories of customers, which can be naturally distinguished, are: Realist-expert (R/E); Pessimist-nonexpert (P/NE), Optimist-nonexperts (O/NE), and customers with rational behavior who are not experts (R/NE) those who overestimate some of the properties of the product and underestimate other.

The goal is to form clusters (groups) of customers based on their purchase attitude and domain expertise related to the product offered. These clusters are used to design a specific message conveying the offer, customized to address the specifics of the group.

The aggregated measure of purchasing attitude allows us to assign to a customer b_j a value of x_j, such that

$$x_j = \frac{1}{\sum_{i=1}^{k} n_{ij}} \sum_{i=1}^{k} n_{ij} \left(\widehat{p}_{ij} - p_i \right),$$

which varies within the interval $\left[\min_i \left(\widehat{p}_{ij} - p_i \right), \max_i \left(\widehat{p}_{ij} - p_i \right) \right]$.

To measure the domain expertise of b_j customer we use the Kullback-Leibler (KL) divergence as follows:

$$y_j = \sum_{i=1}^{k} P_{ij} \log \frac{P_{ij}}{\widehat{P}_{ij}}.$$

Therefore, for each customer b_j, using the above two factors, is assigned a point $B_j=(x_j,y_j)$ on the XY-plane. The group of customers are represented as a set of points on the two-dimensional XY-plane. For example, the points representing customers who were classified as realists should be located somewhere close to the origin (according to the attitude) and their y_i value (domain expertise) should be also close to zero. The main idea is that customers with similar expertise and similar purchase attitude must be addressed by similar message describing the product, i.e., this is the notion of "close" points and adjust the message to reduce the risk of misinforming as much as possible for these "close" points.

Figure 1. Clustering population of customers in attitude/expertise plane

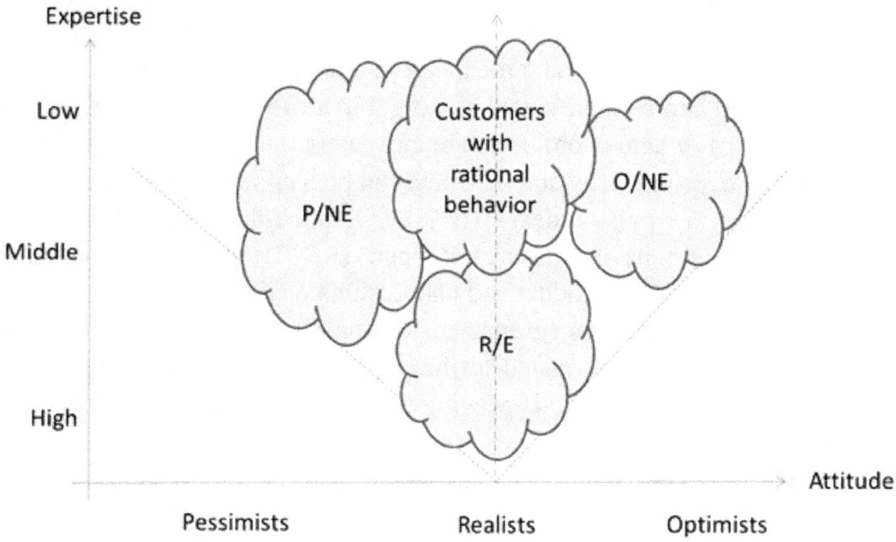

By applying these ideas, the points representing the customer population may look like the upper parts of Figures 3.2.2 and 3.2.3. where two populations with 15 000 customers with 5 (left column) and 15 (right column) activities are generated. By applying clustering algorithm (k-means) based on the Euclidean distance between two customers b_{j_1} and b_{j_2}, i.e.,

$$d_{j_1 j_2} = \sqrt{\left(x_{j_1} - x_{j_2}\right)^2 + \left(y_{j_1} - y_{j_2}\right)^2},$$

the corresponding clusters can be identified (5 and 7 clusters). The bottom part of the figures shows the clusters separated within these populations. For customers in a given cluster, the producer may apply the most appropriate message addressing the levels of expertise and the attitude of a typical member of the group.

Figure 2. 15 000 customers with 5 (left column) and 15 (right column) activities with 5 clusters

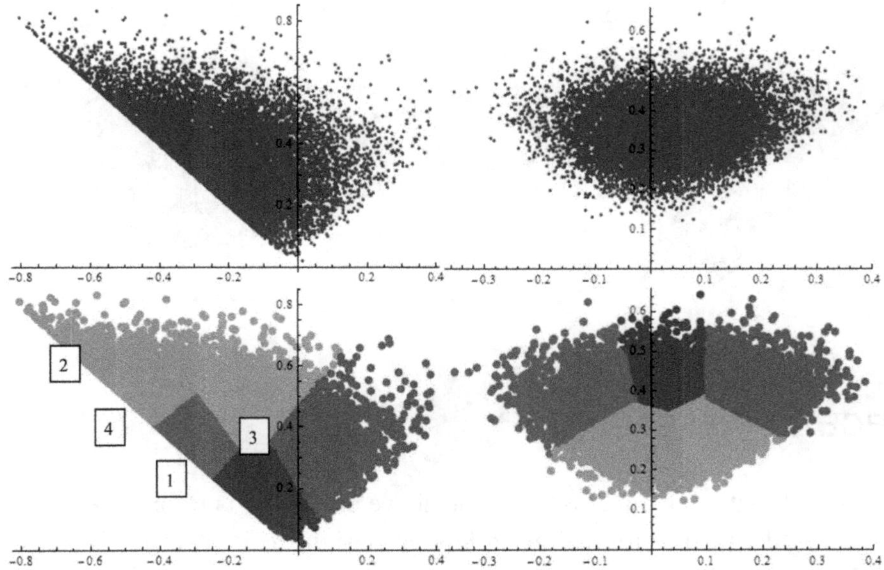

Figure 3. 15 000 customers with 5 (left column) and 15 (right column) activities with 7 clusters

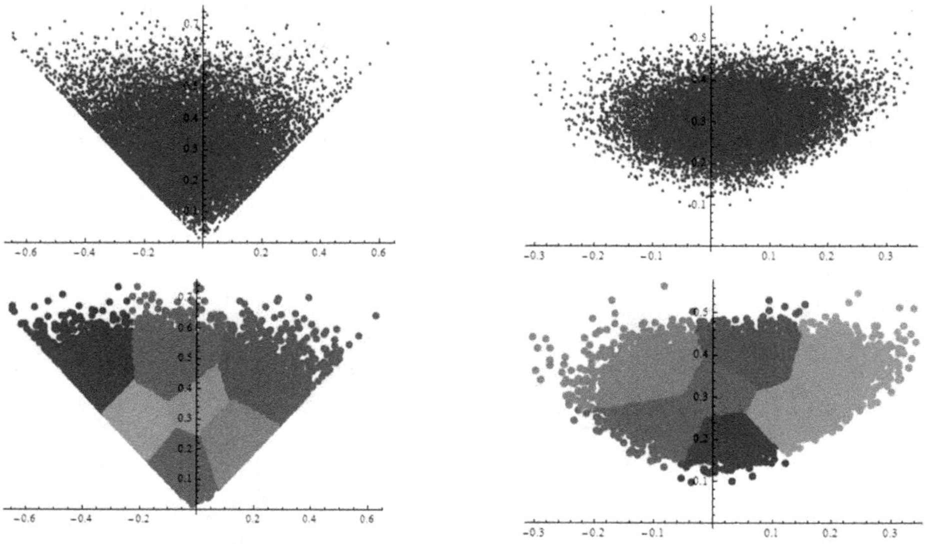

TARGETED MESSAGING

Let us recall that the main reason for the above clustering is to provide the seller with some additional information on how to design the content of the message describing its product *d* aiming to reduce the risk of misinforming for a particular group of customers. The recommendations are focused on warranty component of the message, by assuming that the description of technical properties of the product, addressing domain of its applicability, is done correctly and comprehensively. In Table 1 are outlined some suggestions on how to compose the message for the case represented by the lower left picture in Figure 2.

Table 1. Recommendation for customizing messages for clusters of customers as on left column on Figure 2

Cluster	Recommendation in designing the message
1 R/E	For the group of realists with low level of information asymmetry, the one located around the origin of the two scales, the design of the current message provides adequate information for their correct purchase decision making regarding product *d* and no adjustment of the message is needed. So, for the purposes of this study, this group of customers is well addressed and could be excluded from further discussion.
2 P/NE	To the customers in this group (pessimists with low expertise), the seller must offer the highest possible warranty of misinforming to allow trial purchasing and to give sufficient training opportunity.
3 O/NE	To the customers in this group (optimists with low expertise), the seller must offer the highest possible warranty of misinforming to allow opportunity to avoid dissatisfaction.
4 P/E	Customers in the violet group possess relatively high expertise, but pessimistic attitude. For them the message must include more technical details regarding the product, and good balance between warranty of misinforming and warranty of malfunctioning.

Note: even though for groups 2 (P/NE) and 3 (O/NE) the recommendation is to offer the highest warranty of misinforming, the message may vary to stress the different purposes of the offer. Pessimists need encouragement to try, and the optimists need to be warned about the possibility that product may not suit to them perfectly.

In general, the following categories of customers can be distinguished, related to the composition of a customized message (see Table 2.):

Table 2. Recommendation for customizing the message for different categories of customers

Category of customers	Recommendation in designing the message
Realists, Experts (R/E) Customers with realistic behavior (R/NE)	The way expertise and attitude as defined here, doesn't allow distinguishing these two groups, because in the case R/NE pessimistic attitude compensates optimistic attitude for some of the product's properties. The R/E group of customers is well addressed by the current message. The R/NE group is a significant part of the population, the aggregate measure of attitude is not applicable. This group represents those of the customers who are not experts, but don't clearly demonstrate pessimist's or optimist's behavior. Customers in this group follow a rational approach, trying not to overestimate or underestimate their expectation of the product. To attract such customers the two types of warranties must be well balanced.
Optimists, experts (O/E)	Those are customers who overestimate the quality/features of the product and the decision to buy the product could be incorrect. They will realize that the product is not suitable for their purposes and need time to eventually return it. This group should be provided with a relatively short warranty of misinforming and the associated expected warranty cost could be relatively high compared to the same cost for the other customer groups. In order to reduce the risk of misinforming, the message related to product *d* should be modified to use a suitable for product *d* professional terminology describing the detailed specifications and functionalities of the product. The role of the warranty of misinforming for this group is protective and will be a seller's tool in neutralizing any customer dissatisfaction.
Optimists, non-experts (O/NE)	These customers overestimate the quality/features of the product and their decision to buy the product could be incorrect. They will realize that the product is not suitable for their purposes and need longer (compared to O/E) time to eventually return it. This group should be provided with a relatively longer warranty of misinforming and the associated expected warranty cost could be relatively high compared to the same cost for the other customer groups. In order to reduce the risk of misinforming, the message related to product *d* should be modified to use non- professional terminology describing the usability of the product, avoiding "scary" technical terminology. The role of the warranty of misinforming for this group is also protective and will be seller's tool in neutralizing any customer dissatisfaction due to an incorrect purchase decision.
Pessimists, experts (P/E)	Customers who underestimate the quality/features of the product and therefore their decision not to buy the product could be incorrect. This group should be provided with a relatively long warranty of misinforming and the associated expected warranty cost could be relatively low compared to the same cost for the other customer groups. In order to reduce the risk of misinforming, the message related to product *d* should be modified to include all technical specifications, usability/features and comparison with other similar products available on the marketplace, all given in suitable technical terms. The role of the warranty of misinforming for this group is promotional and will be a seller's tool to promote its product and stimulate the sales volume.
Pessimists, non-experts (P/NE)	Customers who underestimate the quality/features of the product and their decision not to buy the product could be incorrect. This group should be provided with a relatively long warranty of misinforming and the associated expected warranty cost could be relatively low compared to the same cost for the other customer groups. In order to reduce the risk of misinforming, the message related to product $d \in D$ should be modified so that technical terminology is avoided but clearly identifying the usability of the product $d \in D$ and its advantages in comparison with other similar products available on the marketplace. The role of the warranty of misinforming for this group is promotional and will be seller's tool to promote its product and stimulate the sales volume.

CONCLUSION

This chapter proposes another way to define clusters of customers. The objectives now are to provide adequate customized message to promote positive purchase decisions to customers with different expertise and attitude. The approach explores the measures of the risk of misinforming, which are based on historical data accumulated by the CRM, used to create the customer's profile, and to cluster/group customers according to their ability to utilize information regarding the product. The proposed methodology may allow customers to learn about the product's properties and how to use it. The composition of the product's personal promotional message used by the sellers to reach individual customer and to facilitate his or her purchase decision is of high importance due to the growing competition in the marketplace as well as the increasing product complexity. Both of those aspects, well visible nowadays, require support for learning. This is the role that the warranty of misinforming could play. The role of warranty as a learning supporting instrument is explored further in several scenarios in the fourth part of the book. Here it is limited to the promotional role only. Also, the cost associated with the warranty of misinforming could have an impact on the producer/customer relationship and needs consideration when offering.

Applying customizing messages to approach different categories of potential customers from Customer-centered management point of view is important and could benefit both parties involved in the process – producer and customer. Customers will receive information regarding the product in an easy to understand, interpret and assess form, which will increase the certainty of their purchase decision. This will prevent the optimists from buying a non-suitable product and will encourage the pessimists to buy and try a potentially suitable product. As a result, the producers will benefit by increasing the overall number of correct purchase decisions, which will reduce the number of unsatisfied customers and related warranty costs. Additionally, trust and loyalty of customers who are receiving an advertised message visually developed to them may increase.

From this point of view, message customization via exploring appropriate models related to the risk of misinforming is a win-win strategy in building CRM systems. The availability of data related to the customer preferences, stored appropriately for computer-based processing, will allow not only to define different groups, as presented in this chapter, but also to map every customer to the most suitable cluster and even to prepare an individually personalized message.

In this chapter we presented an approach that explores some of the measures of the risk of misinforming, which are based on historical data in the customers' profiles and uses these measures to cluster/group customers according to their ability to utilize information regarding a product. Another aspect of facilitating customers' purchase decision is related to the role that the warranty of misinforming could play. Also, the cost associated with the warranty of misinforming could have a strong impact on the producer/customer relationship inferring the trust between them.

REFERENCES

Bella, A., Ferri, C., Hernández-Orallo, J., & Ramírez-Quintana, M. J. (2009). Negotiation with price-dependent probability models. *CEUR Workshop Proceedings*, *635*, 9–20.

Brandenburger, A., & Nalebuff, B. (1996). Co-opetition: A Revolution Mindset that Combines Competition and Cooperation. Harvard business Press, Cambridge.

Christozov, D., Chukova, S., & Mateev, P. (2006). A Measure of Risk Caused by Information Asymmetry in e-Commerce. *Journal of Issues in Informing Science and Information Technology*, *3*, 147–158. doi:10.28945/879

Christozov, D., Chukova, S., & Mateev, P. (2007). On the Relationship between Warranty and the Risk of Information Asymmetry. *Journal of Issues in Informing Science and Information Technology*, *4*, 235–249. doi:10.28945/946

Christozov, D., Chukova, S., & Mateev, P. (2009). The risk of misinforming for competing messages. *Journal of Issues in Informing Science and Information Technology*, *6*, 351–364. doi:10.28945/1064

Christozov, D., Chukova, S., & Mateev, P. (2011). Assessment of Risk of Misinforming: Dynamic Measures. *Interdisciplinary Journal of Information, Knowledge, and Management*, *6*, 163–176. doi:10.28945/1374

Christozov, D., Chukova, S., & Mateev, P. (2014). Warranty of Misinforming: An Overview. *Issues in Informing Science and Information Technology*, *11*, 31–46. doi:10.28945/1978

Christozov, D., Chukova, S., & Mateev, P. (2015). Risk of Misinforming and Message Customization in Customer Related Management. *Issues in Informing Science and Information Technology*, *12*, 47–61.

González Díaz, V., Barberá Martínez, L., Gómez Fernández, J. F., & Crespo Márquez, A. (2012). The management of a warranty assistances program: A suggestion as reference framework. *Advances in Safety, Reliability and Risk Management, Proceedings of the European Safety and Reliability Conference*. Research Gate.

González-Prida, V., Gómez, J., Barberá, L., & Crespo, A. (2012). The customer relationship in the warranty management of distribution network service providers, *11th International Probabilistic Safety Assessment and Management Conference and the Annual European Safety and Reliability Conference, ESREL*. Research Gate.

Hseih, C.-T., Lai, F., & Shi, W. (2006). Information orientation and its impact on information asymmetry and e-business adoption: Evidence from China's international trading industry. *Industrial Management & Data Systems*, *106*(6), 825–840. doi:10.1108/02635570610671506

Huang, Y.-S., Lin, Y.-J., & Ho, J.-W. (2013). A study on negative binomial inspection for imperfect production systems. *Computers & Industrial Engineering*, *65*(4), 605–613. doi:10.1016/j.cie.2013.05.017

Kullback, S., & Leibler, R. A. (1951). On Information and Sufficiency. *Annals of Mathematical Statistics*, *22*(1), 79–86. doi:10.1214/aoms/1177729694

Niazi, M., & Hussain, A. (2009). Agent-Based Tools for Modeling and Simulation of Self- Organization in Peer-to-Peer, Ad-Hoc and Other Complex Networks. *IEEE Communications Magazine*, *47*(3), 166–173. doi:10.1109/MCOM.2009.4804403

Slovac, P. (1993). Perceived Risk, Trust, and Democracy. *Risk Analysis*, *13*(6), 675–682. doi:10.1111/j.1539-6924.1993.tb01329.x

White, M., & Eiser, R. (2005). Information Specificity and Hazard Risk Potential as Moderators of Trust Asymmetry. *Risk Analysis*, *25*(5), 1187–1198. https://en.wikipedia.org/wiki/Disintermediation. doi:10.1111/j.1539-6924.2005.00659.x PMID:16297224

Wilensky, U. (1999). *NetLOGO*. Northwestern University, Evanston.

Wilensky, U. (2002). *Netlogo PD N*. Person Iterated.

Chapter 13
Computer Providing Data, Services, and Analytics:
The Role of User Interface

ABSTRACT

This chapter is dedicated to informing users via computer applications. The role of user interface in informing may allow users to get full benefit of computer-generated output. An idea how to develop user-customized interface by considering the risk of misinforming is presented and discussed. In this chapter the misinforming hazard is also considered from its positive role when it provides opportunity for the user to learn. The role of interface in computer's accessed and delivered information is not only a tool to deliver information filtered by its origin and results of data processing, but also it may serve as tool to guide user in learning about the property of data domain, data processing techniques, and validity of results. The well-designed user interface of a computer application can lead to better understand and interpret results of data processing by adding explanations and guidelines to overcome lack of competences and to reduce the risk of becoming mislead by provided information.

INTRODUCTION

This chapter addresses the issue of misinforming from the point of view of communication of a user with computer delivered information – the role of interface and user-experience with the computer application; and the opportunities provided by nowadays Information Technologies to support users in assessing and interpreting data. The latter is especially important in informing by "Big Data" analytical that

DOI: 10.4018/978-1-6684-8800-3.ch013

requires additional competences (see Christozov D. & Toleva-Stoimenova S.,2015) going well-beyond data domain, but also needed competences in statistics, data processing algorithms, validity of applying mechanically an algorithm to data with specific structure, format, scales, etc.

The problem of composing the advertising message was discussed in the previous two chapters under assumption that the potential clients are already attracted by the product and the objectives of information provided were to help them to make a rational informed purchase decision by reducing the risk of becoming misinformed.

In on-line commerce, the first problem the seller must solve is how to attract clients and to encourage them to pay attention to the messages and to consider the advertised product as a potential solution for their needs. This stage relay mostly on the emotional impact of the visual component of the message and its attractiveness. The visual load nowadays is extremely stressful, and the visual noise has significant impact on how to perceive information. Some authors (see for example Kim D. 2010 or Kyvykaite R. et al. 2009) argue that an average individual is exposed to more than 1500 images a day, less than 70 of them captured her or his attention, and only 5 to 10 are attractive enough and lead to be memorized. Designing visuals often over emphasized attractiveness on the expense of informativeness, especially in e-commerce information systems designed for advertising products.

Designing interface that balances between attraction and avoiding misinforming is addressed throughout the chapter. The ideas for user-interface design model follow the one proposed in Christozov D. & Mitreva E. (2020), which emphasizes the trust in information generated by data analytics. The trust aspect in designing interface is essential to complement attractiveness of an advertisement.

Building an application in a way to support reaching confidence and trust is based on the way how the user acquires, understands, and interprets obtained information. Additional component is that the user must “like” the way data is presented. In the case of Big Data information is presented in the form of summary statistics, aggregations, and especially important – visually as diagrams, charts, maps, etc. In the case of e-commerce, the application attracting potential clients by illustrating the usage of the product and use of visuals are highly used. Balance between “exact” quantitative characteristics and qualitative visual presentation marks the good design. Overestimation of one of these aspects may lead to either negative attitude – the potential customer doesn’t like and is not attracted by the offer; or positive but wrong purchase decision – decision made emotionally; the presentation is highly attractive, but its technical properties are hidden that leads to post-purchasing unsatisfaction.

MISINFORMING AND TRUST IN THE CASE OF ADVERTISING IN E-COMMERCE

Attraction of the Message: The Cases Many-to-One, One-to-Many, and Many-to-Many

The informing process in the cases of one-to-many and many-to-many topologies has one initial phase – attraction. The user must be attracted to explore the provided message. The initial contact with the system must generate an emotional impact on the user by the visuals provided. Pictures and graphics are essential, not data provided in textual form. Attraction doesn't seem so important in other topologies. In any case when the receiver has options to choose, attraction plays the key role. It includes two stages – first to grab attention, otherwise the receiver will ignore the message even without considering it; and second to allow immediate mapping to the user's needs – to preserve the attention in a way to decide whether to continue considering the message. These two steps must not expect any efforts on behalf of the users.

Overemphasizing the attraction is beyond these first stages is contra-productive from point of view of misinforming risk. Making the decision solely by emotions increases the risk of making mistakes. Without addressing attraction, the message will become unnoticed, relying only on attraction, the message will lead to mistake. Good balance is the key for sustainable user interface that pays attention to long-term positive user-experience.

Rich vs. Reach Advertising

Advertising on the Internet has two properties: it can "reach" a wide audience and provide "rich" information. This is a significant advantage compared with other advertising media, which emphasize one or the other aspect.

To design an application to meet the "reach" aspect, the interface must be highly attractive, and visuals must capture the attention of the user. There are some additional components to design the website in a way to appear on top of the search results by different browsers, especially google. Visuals usually demonstrate how the product can be used to accomplish different categories of work or activities that a potential client may need. This component of design usually stresses emotional acceptance of the message. The potential clients are expected to "like" the web page and to wish to go further in understanding the applicability of the advertised product.

The "rich" part of the advertisement message is to allow potential clients to obtain more detailed information regarding the properties of the product. The design of this part usually follows the old pattern of presenting technical information by using technical jargon, assuming domain competence of users. This leads to problems described throughout the book.

Trust to Obtained Information

Trust is a key aspect of transforming information into acting knowledge. Trust is acquired by a combination of source, presentation, and content of information. There are many other factors (see Gackowski, Z., 2006) that influence trust, but here we will focus on the last two. Inspiring trust is the essential objective of user-interface. Trust has different forms, including trust to the service provider; trust to quality of data used in building the presented output; and trust for self-competences to understand, interpret, and use correctly the obtained information or acquired service. In all those cases, the user-interface may play significant role in inspiring trust or in inspiring uncertainty.

THE CASE OF INTERFACE IN ON-LINE SERVICES

Detecting and Addressing Misinforming Outcomes in Designing Sustainable IS Applications

Sustainable user experience by a computer application faces the following challenges:

1. Becoming misinformed as a user by a service leads to long-term dissatisfaction regarding the service and often resistance to using it.
2. Understanding the fact of misinforming results in learning about how to use the service the next time, or how to use other services from the same category.
3. Recurrent use of a service may result in adaptations of user-service interactions in ways that reduce the risk of misinforming. This form of learning may serve not only the given user, but also to service providers. Or learning by misinforming outcomes could be a two-sided process.

The solution, which is in the focus of this chapter, is to build an intelligent, adaptive, user interface customized according to specific category of users. The following three issues need to be considered:

1. What are user categories relevant to misinforming.
2. What are the risks associated with each category.
3. How to assign/classify a specific user to a specific category.

Additionally, ideas about implementing adjustment and customization of user interfaces per user category are shared and discussed.

Undesired User's Behavior: Risks and Learning

To illustrate the presented ideas, I assume to investigate user experience in the following circumstances: there is an on-line application that provides a given category of services. For example, a converter of pdf files to MS Word file, with a demo trial for free.

To make the discussion easier, let us use the following three categories representing three outcomes:

0. Successful and satisfactory trial. Competent users.

This is a desired and not interesting case. Users are happy with the results of the free trial and are ready to pay for the application.

1. Unsuccessful trial. Incompetent, naïve, inexperienced users.

Users are unable to complete navigation in a way to do what they desire. This is the case of unsuitable user interface to the users' competences. The users are able to get the service or information they want. They couldn't get to the point where they can download and use the demo version.

2. Successful but unsatisfactory trial.

Users manage to navigate the interface and get the trial but decide not to use the service because they are disappointed and not satisfied. There are two sub-categories here:

2.1. Quality obstacles. Optimists.

The conversion of the pdf file was not satisfactory. For example, there are some formulas that are not readable in the converted file.

2.2. Trust issue. Pessimists.

Users don't trust the application or conditions to accept the service. For example, the application asks for sensitive information in advance, as credit card details, to allow free trial.

Log-files accumulate data about the users' communication and navigation paths with the application and may allow to classify the behavior of users in categories "1" and "2.2". The log-files do not hold data that could allow to distinguish between users' behavior in categories "0" and "2.1".

How to identify that a new user belongs to one or another category?

This can be achieved by monitoring the navigation paths of users and comparing the steps that users perform.

Sustainable Users' Experience: Categories "0" and "1"

Sustainable user experience in case of avoiding misinforming can be achieved by support building experience – learning – allowing the competence of users in category "1" to grow to the level in category "0". The key word to achieve users' satisfaction is "balance". Providing too much support and guidance to experienced users (category "0") is boring and user attitude toward the application could be relatively negative. On the other hand, inexperienced users may benefit from guidance and support. The interface must allow both approaches – short-cuts navigation, and slow, step-by-step path with explanations and guidelines.

Optimists and Pessimists Users: Category "2"

This category refers to users who are competent to perform expected operations and get the service.

The first case "2.1" is the case of misinformed, optimist users – they used the service and were not satisfied. During the time of working with application, they missed understanding in sufficient details what the application can do for them. Their dissatisfaction results in not purchasing our application and spreading negative opinion regarding the application.

The second case "2.2" is the category of misinformed, pessimist users – they decided not to use the service, without trying. They missed a potential benefit from using it and are dissatisfied with the application, but they are not likely to share negative opinions. Most likely, they refuse to use the service, because they were not able to establish sufficient trust.

The important aspect of misinforming is the damage to the IS image created by dissatisfied users (category "2.1") – mostly optimists.

User Experience: How to Mitigate Risks?

The following cases summarize the above considerations:

1. Competent users – the user interface must allow such users to do their job in easier and fast ways: short cuts, site maps, indexes, visual tabs, etc. are only a few options to do this. Following long paths by clicking on multiple pages to reach the needed service is the origin of unsatisfaction and bad user experience.
2. Incompetent, naïve, inexperienced users – the user interface needs to provide a well-organized guide, training tool, to support learning and to avoid misinterpretation, and mis-action. Good design may lead to the creation of a satisfied and later competent user.
3. Optimists – to mitigate the risk of post-action spreading of negative opinion regarding the application, the IS needs to design and use some forms of follow-up support. This may include customization, adjustment, improving parameters, as well as providing Q&A sessions to help improve experiences. FAQ is a good form, but it needs frequent update. Forums are another form allowing sharing of experience, but they need to be monitored by a competent expert from the provider site. Issues raised by users must be addressed by improving the application or by explaining ways that prevent usage leading to unsatisfaction.
4. Pessimists – by studying where exactly users decide to stop using the service, specific points can be identified where various mechanisms to encourage users can be used. For the above example, allow free trial at least once without collecting sensitive data. Or maybe try an online service (SaaS), without downloading.

THE CASE OF BIG DATA APPLICATION INTERFACE.

Producing confident knowledge, leading to acting (active knowledge), or building an informative application, requires that the user trusts the information obtained via the data processing computer application. The source data and the data processing application is considered often as a black box, which results in different users' attitude toward confidence in applying it. The two extreme kinds of users' acceptance and consequently attaining knowledge are:

- Over trust: the user believes that once the information is produced by computer application it is correct, valid, and trustful.
- Under trust: because the user cannot observe the entire story from data generation, storing and processing, toward generating results, the information produced is doubtful and cannot automatically result in action.

Both extremes are risky from the point of view of the success of the application to inform the user. Optimists, over-trusting obtained information, will act according to it without critically assessing whether it is true or applicable to the problem domain. Pessimists, under trusting, may not act even if obtained information is useful, because they are unable to trace how it is created and are not ready to adopt it.

Reaching confidence in decision-making is becoming more and more critical for business, but also in every aspect of human life today. To make a decision, one needs to reach the level of confidence that this decision is correct and solves the problem. There are two general approaches in reaching confidence:

- Rational – by using known quantified measures, reflecting the state of the problem domain and build solely on available data; and
- Emotional – by using one's intuition and subjective, often qualitative, feeling regarding the correctness of decision and confidence toward invoked actions.

In practice, the two are usually combined. Even in rationally oriented decision-makers reaching 100% confidence is almost impossible to achieve and some component of emotion is needed to make an effective decision; as well, an emotion-based decision-maker needs some pieces of evidence to justify their decision, as well as their intuition" is built on past experience.

There are at least three aspects of inspiring trust to machinery delivered analytics results:

- Trust about data and data quality.
- Trust toward applied technology – algorithms and computer applications.
- Trust regarding the relevance of obtained results to the domain and applicability in solving the problem.

Designing User Interface (UI) in a way to support building trust toward obtained knowledge is a challenging task. It is not solely designing "intuitive, user-friendly" interface. Such requirements address only how to explore application in an efficient way to obtained results, but do not provide support of how to use the results, and especially to support building trust that the obtained results are meaningful and useful in solving user's problem. This problem was identified by M. Buckland (see section "Variety of Task Complexity", Buckland M. 1991, page 171) more than thirty years ago.

The conceptual model of User Interface presented here tries to support enhancing trust. A model of UI architecture based on a three-level hierarchy is proposed. The model requires generating specific user's profiles by exploring application logs and accessing other relevant logs, which captures information for all of the requests of the users, then based on that profile customize the interface. The UI, as generated by the method, shows only the information that the user is interested in in a way the user may capture it. When it comes to Big Data it is quite a challenge to visualize it, because the human perception cannot process too much data (Agrawal, Kadadi, Xiangfeng, & Adres, 2015). The model considers the user's interest and competency and provides analytical results in a way to avoid being overwhelmed by the amount of data or by the complexity of analytical techniques. When needed a meaningful explanation is provided, as well as a tool to trace the origin of raw data.

Figure 1. Customization of UI based on user's profiling

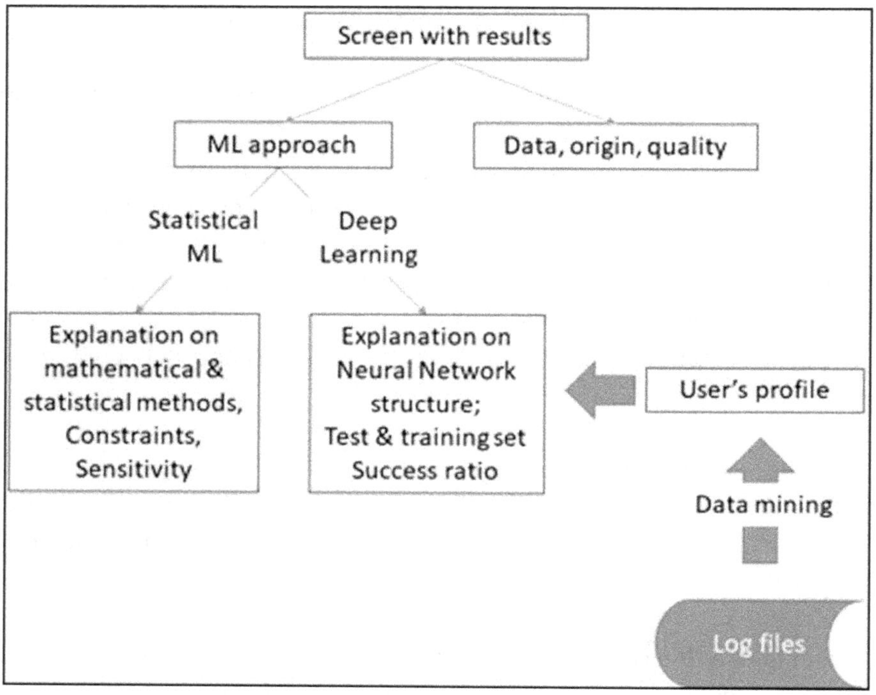

The proposed architecture can be divided in:

1. Cleaning and processing logs.
2. Forming user profiles based on:
    a. Interests - a user might be interested in more detailed information about the actual algorithm that was used or just some explanation why this was the best approach that was used.

   b. Competencies – a user might be interested in a simple explanation just because they cannot understand the theory behind the actual method.
3. Defining three levels of complexity for the details for the explanation of the mathematical and statistical methods:
   a. Beginner – simple explanations on the methods used with more visualization and less mathematical details – this level can be used by either people that are not interested in the more complex details or don't have the competency to comprehend the details.
   b. Intermediate – additional details, but still with less mathematical and statistical formulas.
   c. Advanced – this level will provide the most details – visual, mathematical and statistical information.
4. The model will offer at some extend customization of the complexity of the information that is shown.

Use of Log-Files in Classifying Users: Behavior Patterns

Illustration of using log-files to identify and customize user-interface are illustrated in Tables 1., 2., and 3.

Table 1. Log-files indications to classify users

Competence	Indicative pattern
Competent users	Fast, direct navigation toward the page offering the service
Incompetent users	Chaotic navigation, existence of loops
Behavior	Indicative pattern
Realists (satisfied)	Returning users (identified by IP address)
Optimists (misinformed)	Not-returning users (single session)
Pessimists (mistrusted)	Deserted users (in the middle of navigation)

Table 2. Impact of behavior

Category	Behavior
Realists – competent	Satisfied, returning, learning
Realists – Incompetent	
Optimists – competent	Unsatisfied, never returning, misinformed
Optimists – Incompetent	
Pessimists – competent	Deserted, mistrusting, misinformed
Pessimists – Incompetent	

Table 3. User-interface scenarios

Scenarios	Suitable for user's category
Short-cuts for fast and efficient usage	Competent realists
Free-trial option, without asking for sensitive data	Competent pessimists Incompetent pessimists
Careful, step-by-step guiding navigation	Incompetent realists Incompetent optimists Incompetent pessimists
Warning about side-effect, limitations, constraints.	Competent optimists Incompetent optimists Competent pessimists
Identifying the point when the users deserted. Update the interface accordingly.	Competent pessimists Incompetent pessimists

Discussion

The architecture that are proposing formally can be divided in:

1. Cleaning and processing logs.
2. Forming user profiles based on:
    a. Interests – a user might be interested in more detailed information about the actual algorithm that was used or just some explanation why this was the best approach that was used.
    b. Competencies – a user might be interested in a simple explanation just because they cannot understand the theory behind the actual method.
3. Defining three levels of complexity for the details to do the explanation of the mathematical and statistical methods:

   a. Beginner – simple explanations on the methods used with more visualization and less mathematical details – this level can be used by either people that are not interested in the more complex details or don't have the competency to comprehend the details.
   b. Intermediate – additional details, but still with less mathematical and statistical formulas.
   c. Advanced – this level will provide the most details – visual, mathematical and statistical information.
4. The model will offer at some extend customization of the complexity of the information that is shown.

For the first two parts of the model, we could use web usage mining process – the process of extracting useful information from web pages – from logs, content or hyperlinks (Rathi & Vishwavidyalaya, 2019). The web logs can provide information about the interests of the users based on the time they spent on a particular part of the explanation of the method. But before we could be able to form the profiles of the user, the data from the web logs must be cleaned. Cleaning the data before using it will make the process of extracting user profiles more effective because around 30% - 40% of the data that is captured in the access logs is meaningful, the rest is as a result of robot requests (Marsden, n.d.) and unsuccessful requests (Manchanda, 2018). After cleaning the data, the preprocessing in the WUM includes session and user identification (Mehra & Thakur, 2018). The user behavior identification can be done using different methods like:

- The amount of time a user spent on a certain part of the explanation of the method might tell us their interests – if a user spent a little to no time on something we could either conclude they are not interested in this part or they considered it too complex for their competency. Either way, this means that the UI architecture could adapt and show only the parts that the user is interested in.
- Using path profiles to predict future user behavior (Mobasher, Dai, Luo, Sun, & Zhu, 2000).
- Clustering user sessions (Mobasher et al., 2000).

The web logs processing might give information for the user profile, but further granularity might be needed (identifications of the user sessions) to obtain the knowledge for the interests of the user.

Using just the created user profiles sometimes is not reliable enough, because the interests and the competencies of the user might change, or they would like to manual configure what information to be visible. Because of that the architecture includes also customizations using two methods:

- Offering three levels of competencies – beginner, intermediate or advanced for the user to choose from. Depending on the level different details will be shown – from just simple details for the method used if the first level is used to details about the statistics and mathematics used to mine the data.
- Offering a way to even further customization of what the UI will show – overriding the predefined three levels that were previously mentioned.

Two of the aspects in the architecture were the forming of the user profiles and creating the three levels of hierarchy, however visualization of the data is an essential tool in understanding data, because dealing with large amounts of data can lead to chaos (Syed Fiaz, Asha, Sumathi, & Syed Navaz, 2016), thus making handling big data not only an advantage, but a challenge. The proper interpreting and visualizing the data can help both a layman and a research trust in big data, but the proper visualization and tools should be used (Keahey, 2013).

Two approaches that could be used for the visualization are:

- Building samples of data (Syed Fiaz et al., 2016) with which to analyze the data.
- Creating template charts and graphs to display the data ("Shield UI," n.d.).

CONCLUSION

In this chapter is offered a simple conceptual model of User Interface architecture, which incorporates intelligent use of accumulated in the applications' log file data. Customizing the interface based on user's competences and history of using it is expected to increase (1) user's awareness regarding application, data, and especially constraints, limitation, and applicability; and (2) to enhance the trust toward provided analytical results and confidence in making decisions based on those results.

The presented conceptual model is used to design a prototype of an intelligent back-end tool for customizing user interface for complex data analytic applications. The prototype is under construction for a cloud-based e-commerce web site. It is designed to serve decision makers on tactical or strategic managerial level. The accumulated experience in applying the prototype will serve in adjusting the concept in designing customizable user interface.

REFERENCES

Agrawal, R., Kadadi, A., Xiangfeng, D., & Adres, F. (2015). Challenges and Opportunities with Big Data Visualization. *7th International Conference on Management of computational and collective IntElligence in Digital EcoSystems (MEDES)*, (pp. 169–173). ACM. 10.1145/2857218.2857256

Buckland, M. (1991). *Information and Information Systems*. Praeger.

Christozov, D., & Mitreva, E. (2020). Trust in Learning from Big Data: The Two Sides of the Same Coin. *Issues in Information Systems*, *21*(1), 147–152.

Christozov, D., & Toleva-Stoimenova, S. (2015). Big Data Literacy - a New Dimension of Digital Divide: Barriers in learning via exploring Big Data. In J. Girard, K. Berg, D. Klein, & I. G. I. Global (Eds.), *Strategic Data Based Wisdom in the Big Data Era*. doi:10.4018/978-1-4666-8122-4.ch009

Gackowski, Z. (2006). Quality of Informing: Credibility Provisional Model of Functional Dependencies. *Proceedings of the 2006 InSITE Conference*. ISI. 10.28945/3017

Keahey, T. A. (2013). Using visualization to understand big data. *IBM Business Analytics Advanced Visualisation*, 16. IBM.

Kim, D. (2010). The interactive effects of colors on visual attention and working memory: in case of images for tourists attraction, *International CHRIE conference*. University of Massachusetts. https://scholarworks.umass.edu/cgi/viewcontent.cgi?article=1487&context=refereed

Kyvykaite, R., Dovaliene, A., & Navickiene, L. (2009). Impact of package elements on consumer's purchase decision, *Ekomomika ir vadyba*. file:///C:/Users/dgc/Downloads/9405-Article%20Text-30522-1-10-20150210.pdf

Manchanda, M. (2018). Web Usage Mining: Dynamic Methodology to Preprocessing Web Logs. *Helix*, *8*(5), 3810–3815. doi:10.29042/2018-3810-3815

Marsden, S. (n.d.). *How Do Search Engine Crawlers Work?* DeepCrawl. https://www.deepcrawl.com/knowledge/technical-seo-library/search-engine-crawling/

Mehra, J., & Thakur, R. S. (2018). An Effective method for Web Log Preprocessing and Page Access Frequency using Web Usage Mining. *International Journal of Applied Engineering Research: IJAER*, *13*(2), 1227–1232. http://www.ripublication.com

Mobasher, B., Dai, H., Luo, T., Sun, Y., & Zhu, J. (2000). Combining Web Usage and Content Mining for More Effective Personalization. Lecture Notes in Computer Science (Including Subseries Lecture Notes in Artificial Intelligence and Lecture Notes in Bioinformatics), 1875, 165–176. doi:10.1007/3-540-44463-7_15

Rathi, P., & Vishwavidyalaya, G. K. (2019). An Efficient Algorithm for Data Pre-Processing and Personalization in Web. *International Journal of Computer Sciences and Engineering Open Access An Efficient Algorithm for Data Pre-Processing and Personalization in Web Usage Mining*, *7*(May), 160–164. Advance online publication. doi:10.26438/ijcse/v7i5.160164

Syed Fiaz, A. S., Asha, N., Sumathi, D., & Syed Navaz, A. S. (2016). Visualization: Enhancing big data more adaptable and valuable. *International Journal of Applied Engineering Research: IJAER*, *11*(4), 2801–2804.

Chapter 14
Cooperative Way of Problem Solving to Avoid Misinforming:
Trans-Discipline and Data Philanthropy

ABSTRACT

This chapter discusses two other business practices addressing cooperative efforts in problem solving. The first one refers to a transdisciplinary approach in solving complex, multidimensional problems by exploring the opportunity for collective data interpretation and the synergy of cooperation. The second one discusses the cooperation of public and private entities to solve problems for the benefit of society. This is a new business practice – philanthropy of data – which is a form of public-private collaboration that allows sharing of data, expertise, and infrastructure possession of a private entity with the public institution to solve problems of society that need resources the public entity doesn't possess. This is especially true in avoiding misinformation in the case of exploring big data and other informing services for the benefit of entire society. Nowadays, a lot of private companies collect and store huge amounts of data, which can be reused for public goods.

INTRODUCTION

The first part of this chapter discusses the trans-discipline way to find an innovative, holistic solution of a complex problem. Trans-disciplinarity is the way to avoid misinforming that may lead to undesired side-effects in implanting solutions that emphasize only one of the sides of a problem. The complex multidimensional problem usually needs a holistic solution with emphasis on all possible consequences. Trans-

DOI: 10.4018/978-1-6684-8800-3.ch014

disciplinarity is the next round of evolution in approaching complex problems that need expertise developed in many scientific or engineering areas.

The next section is dedicated to evolution of forms of cooperation in data assessment, interpretation, and mapping to the users' problem. Different forms of cooperation as inter-, multi-, and trans-discipline are discussed from point of view of mitigating the misinforming risks.

The complexity of problems users is facing nowadays originates from the nature of the problem. Nowadays reasonable solution of a problem requires variety of competences; uses a vast amount of potentially relevant data satisfying the 3Vs of Big Data phenomenon; needed special equipment and data processing software; and must account for potential side-effects. The advancement of science in all areas leads to accumulation of a vast amount of facts, models, approaches, methodologies developed in different scientific fields with different objectives. Multi- or inter-disciplinary forms of cooperation, widely adopted in the last centuries, do not allow the needed penetration of knowledge to solve real-life complex problems. Trans-disciplinary is the form of cooperation that exploring learning by adoption of knowledge instead of delegation.

Some problems faced by modern societies need cooperative efforts going beyond forming a trans-disciplinary team – the cooperation of different entities with their resources and accumulated expertise. The phenomenon of "Data Philanthropy" which emerged recently offers a form of cooperation between private and public entities. One specific aspect of data philanthropy is its role to overcome the misinforming problem by providing not only data and results but also expertise, methodology, and equipment to process and interpret data for public good.

MISINFORMING AND COOPERATION: TRANS-DISCIPLINARITY

Evolution of Cooperation in Solving Scientific Problems

Generation of new knowledge is always associated with solving problems, where essential is to understand different aspects associated with circumstances, nature, and the origin of the appearance of the problem. This understanding is combined with the existing knowledge to generate a solution to the problem. Complexity of problems, the number of factors, amount and diversity of analyzed data, and rules needed to investigate the problem, as well as constrained human cognitive capacity, leads to a narrow discipline analysis as the way to solve problems. Accumulated over the years scientific knowledge also impacts human ability to comprehend the entire set of factors influencing the problem. The cartoon of Figure 1. illustrates the results of analysis of a complex problem from a narrow uni-disciplined perspective.

Figure 1. Uni-discipline approach in generating knowledge

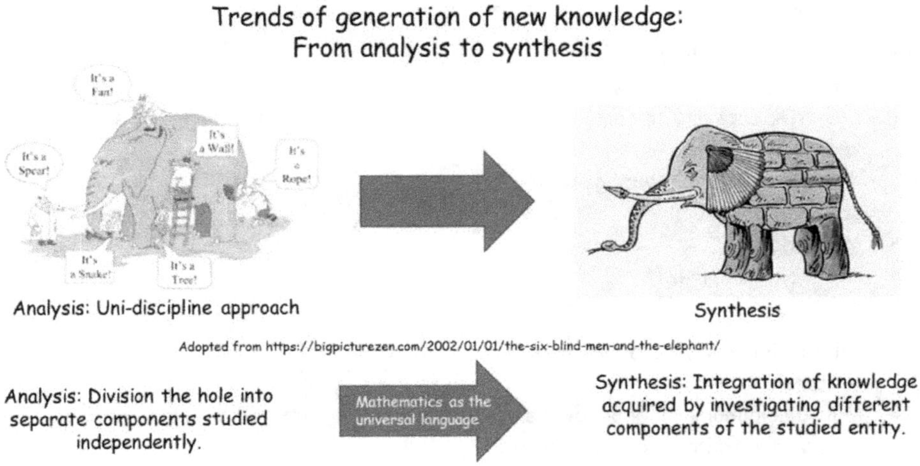

During the Renaissance some of those limitations did not exist, especially the amount of scientific results, and this allows comprehension of existing knowledge by so called “encyclopedists”. With the progress of sciences and the accumulation of vast amounts of knowledge this kind of scientist disappeared. But the need for a holistic view on problems remains valuable and even its impact on the success of the proposed solution increased. This resulted in the growing need for cooperation from experts with different backgrounds. The forms of cooperations are marked with “Multi”, “Inter” and recently “Trans” disciplines. Attempt to define and contrast different approaches originated in the “Seminar on Interdisciplinarity in Universities, 1970, Paris” (see Apostel L., 1972). Figure 2. illustrated different forms of cooperation and listed some of the factors influencing the type of cooperation to choose.

Figure 2. Factors influencing cooperation and illustration of the forms of cooperation

Factors

- The nature of the problem.
- Amount of needed knowledge.
  - Cognitive capacity to comprehend knowledge.
  - Available tools to investigate observations.
- Methodology.
- Available equipment.

- Uni-disciplinarity - independent research.
- Multidisciplinary - independence of research with integration of results.
- Interdisciplinarity - research on border "grey" areas. Preserving independence but requires communication and mutual understanding.
- Trans-disciplinarity - research, requires holistic approach with mutual penetration of different disciplines - adoption of approaches, methodologies, knowledge of "other" discipline.

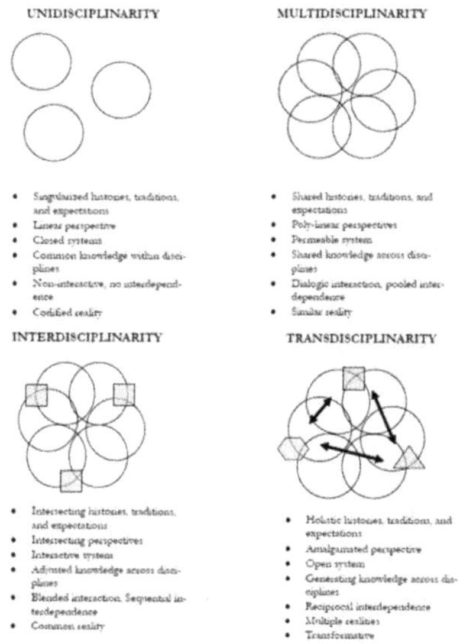

Figure 1. Complexity Perspectives of Cross-Disciplinary Knowledge Economies (adapted from Lotrecchiano, 2011).

Transition from Renaissance toward the nowadays science as it was established by development in 18, 19 and 20 centuries is marked by exponential grow of amount of knowledge in every area of science and vast advancement of tools used in scientific research and innovations. From microscopes and telescopes, statistical data analysis, mathematics, to satellites and nuclear cyclotrons. Advancement of science resulted in innovations in production with major steps marked as "industrial revolutions". At the same time the cognitive capacity of the human remained practically the same. Naturally, analytical approach in research dominated. In the middle of 20th century scientists started to understand that analytical approach constraints the "out-of-box" creativity. The invention of electronic computer offered a tool to overcome cognitive limitations and 4th industrial revolution marks this stage of development.

Gradually, understanding of the need of trans-discipline approach for innovation is adopted for different areas of research. New scientific fields appear as trans-disciplines. (See E. Cohen, 1999, introducing Informing Science as a trans-discipline, or D. Christozov et al (2019) pointing that Data Science holds all properties of a trans-discipline). Arise II report (see Arrise II, 2014) recommended trans-disciplinary training in some natural science areas. And recently, ACM proposed to move education on computing toward trans-discipline, by recognizing that nowadays computing become much more than a single narrow discipline or a set of well-defined scientific disciplines.

Building an organizational environment supporting trans-disciplinary way to solve the problems results in finding holistic solutions, avoiding undesired side-effects, and secondary problems, and avoiding the misinforming hazards. Practically, such an environment is associated with domination of culture of sharing within the organization.

Trans-Disciplinarity as a Component of Organizational Culture

The Hofstede's (see Hofstede G., 197x) fundamental research, identifying nationally defined cultural dimensions, in 1970s is usually used as the framework of organizational culture discussions. The advancement of computer and communication technologies allows from one side globalization of markets and convergence of cultures, but from the other side this progress increases the need of holistic view on problems, considering the whole set of diverse and complicated aspects of the sequence from identifying the problem and its origin via the ways of observing the circumstances, and capturing evidence toward the step of building solutions. Big Data, Machine Learning, Artificial Intelligence are just a few names describing this change, address predominantly the technologies allowing to perform complex investigation. But human contribution is still the key success factor. The cultural aspects in building environment of knowledge sharing and cooperation needed to achieve synergy in innovations in a digital, relying on Big Data economy, is essential.

Organizational culture is an important component of successful management nowadays. Hofstede's research identifies dimensions, still in use, to assess and distinguish cultures of different counties. This research was done under specific conditions, literally survey employees in the same company serving in different countries and grow by different national cultures. This allowed Hofstede to instill national specific to the cultures of employees' behavior within organization. The study was done in the 1970's well before the current state of globalization and convergence of cultures.

Considering trans-discipline form of cooperation from point of view of Hofstede's cultural dimensions, the following conclusions are obvious as influencing building trans-disciplines' environment:

- Power Distance:

Impact of "power distance" on culture of sharing is not dominant, but a low distance usually aids freedom of communication and sharing.

- Individualism Vs. Collectivism:

Organizations dominated by "individualism" is less likely to build culture supporting trans-discipline cooperation. High level "collectivism" provides supporting environment for developing trans-discipline teams and behavior.

- Masculinity Vs. Femininity:

The comfortable atmosphere typical for organizations with dominating "femininity" is positive in building trans-discipline attitude among employees.

- Uncertainty Avoidance:

Uncertainty avoidance restricts initiatives for trying and considering "exotic" option. This is contra-productive in searching for innovative solutions.

- Long Vs. Short Term Orientation:

Long-term orientation usually allows employees to search for effective solutions even in case of not immediate return. Such an attitude may encourage considering others' viewpoint.

- Indulgence Vs. Restraint:

Indulgence refers to tolerance toward mistakes and encouraged trials. Considering and trying a solution proposed by others is a typical form of cooperation within a trans-discipline team.

MISINFORMING AND DATA PHILANTHROPY

The Philanthropy as a Social Phenomenon

The term "philanthropy" is associated with donating money or other material objects, services or aids from a private entity for public good. The terms philanthropy and charity, or corporate giving are distinguished mostly by the objectives in donating. In "charity" the resource is provided to directly solve the problem of beneficiary, as direct gift for a surgery of the needed. In "philanthropy" the gift to solve a social problem, as purchasing equipment for the hospital which will be used for all who needed. In Wikipedia philanthropy is defined as "Philanthropy is a form of altruism that consists of "private initiatives, for the public good, focusing on quality of life".

Some authors find positive correlation between philanthropy and company's success (Brammar and Millington, 2008), others find that philanthropy contradicts the objectives of private for-profit entities (Friedman, 2007). According to Wang there is an optimal norm for philanthropy (Wang et al, 2011). In any case, philanthropy plays a positive role in building the image of the donor company and its effect is more than purely financial.

Data Philanthropy

Data generated, captured, and recorded by a private entity is a company resource. Also, the knowledge, experience, and data processing technologies are among the resources a company invested in developing to implement its strategy and to gain competitive advantages. Providing these resources for public good is a form of philanthropy – philanthropy of data. There are some specifics which distinguished it from the classical forms of philanthropy:

- According to M. Buckland, 1992, information or data is a commodity, but as different from any other commodity, the owner can sell it unlimited and to continue owns it. In this respect, the data philanthropy differs from donating financial or material goods.
- Investing in maintaining data sets is done to solve the company's own problems. But those data can serve to help in solving problems of society outside of the scope of the company's business scope. Providing it for such a purpose may not impact on the company's competitive status.
- Providing data and expertise and technology for data processing may improve the overall environment where the company operates and add a secondary benefit to the company. Also, the company data analytics experts helping in solving problems of society may increase their competences in exploring the same data for different purposes.

Those specifics of data philanthropy motivate the willingness and practice of sharing. This is especially important in the Big Data era, when gaining benefit from exploring data requires much more than sole access, but also technology and professional expertise. Creation and development of such expert resources requires investment in humans and in expertise for data driven management. Both are often beyond the capacity of every company. Those who can benefit from such investment gain competitive advantages.

The following three examples illustrate how the society can benefit from privately own data resources:

- The logistic problems identified in delivery humanitarian help to people in Haiti after the earthquake in 2010 were resolved to some extend with use of the data and its bar-code identification system provided by United Parcel Service (UPS) to United Nations. Later, UPS with United Nations Office for Project Services developed software for reaction in catastrophic events – Trackpad – for management of humanitarian aids supply (see IPS 2014).
- Master Card created the Center for Inclusive Growth in 2014 to help the entire development of financial services in developing countries. Data Philanthropy is the basic component of this program. The center provides grants in the form of data for non-for-profit, state-owned, or even other entities together with expert analysis and interpretation. Projects vary from evaluation of economic impact of a given project to assessment of specific program. In Kenya Master Card contributed to non-cash payments in a country with not developed credit infrastructure (see Anzilotti E., 2017).
- United Nation Global Pulse (UNGP) Data for Climate Action Innovation Challenge. UNGP is a United Nations initiative in the field of Big Data. The mission of the initiative is to speed up discovery, development, and adoption of innovation for sustainable development. One of the first is "Data for Climate Action Innovation Challenge" (see UNGP).

A summary of comparison of the three examples, allows defining the basic characteristics of Data Philanthropy: donors' motivation, and donation forms.

Donors' motivation:

- Image and social responsibility.
- Establishing regulations in the market of Big Data services.
- Developing of own capacity.

Forms of donations:

- Providing access to data sets.
- Providing data analytics technologies.
- Providing access to professional expertise.

Social Impact:

- Big Data is a new round in "digital divide" phenomenon – access to Big Data expertise is a form to reduce social division.

Success factors:

- Data Philanthropy improves public managerial effectiveness land efficiency.
- Two-sided partnership.

Nevertheless, that the objectives of Data Philanthropy initiatives are not mitigating the risk of misinforming, the outcomes of such private-public partnership are reducing its likelihood.

CONCLUSION

Cooperation and sharing knowledge considering different interpretation is mutually adopted way to address the hazards of misinforming. The chapter introduces cooperation in two forms – cooperation within a team appointed to find solution of a complex, multidimensional problem; and between organizations – private and public.

Trans-disciplinarity requires culture of sharing and excludes effects typically named for the authors who first described the phenomenon of over confidence combined with low competence – "Dunning-Kruger" effect. Trans-disciplinarity also need organizational culture defined in Hofstede's dimensions as {high collectivism, low masculinity, low uncertainty avoidance, long-term orientation, and high indulgence}.

Data philanthropy, as a new form of private-public cooperation, emerged under the circumstances established by advancement of IT. This allowed a private company to generate, own and maintain huge amounts of data, and to build expertise and technologies to explore it. Usually, such a company uses the data for its narrow needs but the potential in learning from accumulated data can offer much more benefit to society.

REFERENCES

Anzilotti, E. (2017). *How Mastercard's "Data Philanthropy" Program is Tackling the Global Financial Information Gap.* Fast Company. (https://www.fastcompany.com/40457902/how-mastercards-data-philanthropy-program-is-tackling-the-global-financial-information-gap)

Apostel, L. (1972). *Seminar on Interdisciplinarity in Universities.* Lib. https://lib.ugent.be/catalog/rug01:000175104

Brammar, S., & Millington, A. (2008). Does it pay to be different? An analysis of the relationship between corporate social and financial performance. *Strategic Management Journal, 29*(12), 1325–1343. doi:10.1002mj.714

Brandenburger, A., & Nalebuff, B. (1996). Co-opetition: A Revolution Mindset that Combines Competition and Cooperation, Harvard business Press, Cambridge.

Buckland, M. (1991). *Information and Information Systems*. PRAEGER.

Christozov, D., Rasheva-Yordanova, K., & Toleva-Stoimenova, S. (2019). Challenges in Designing Curriculum for Trans-Disciplinary Education: On Cases of Designing Concentration on Informing Science and Master Program on Data Science. *Informing Science, 22*, 19–30. doi:10.28945/4300

Christozov D., Reeves-Ellington R. (1995). *Measures for Culture's Influence in Managerial Area*. SDA'95, Varna, Bulgaria.

Freedman, M. (2016). *Using Data as a Force for good* (TED talk). TED. (https://splvers.ups.com/what-if-2016/Using-Data-as-force-for-good-ted-ups-video)

Friedman, M. (2007). *The social responsibility of Business is to increase its profit, Corporate Ethics and Corporate Governance*. Springer.

Hofstede, G. (1984). Culture's Consequences: International Differences in Work-Related Values. *Sage (Atlanta, Ga.)*, 1984.

Lotrecchiano, G., & Misra, S. (2018). Transdisciplinary Knowledge Producing Teams: Toward a Complex Systems Perspective. *Informing Science, 21*, 2028. doi:10.28945/4086

Orlitzky, M., Schmidt, F. L., & Rynes, S. L. (2003). Corporate Social and Financial Performance: A Meta-Analysis. *Organization Studies, 24*(3), 403–441. doi:10.1177/0170840603024003910

UPS. (2014). *Before, During and After: Disaster Preparedness and Recovery*. UPS. https://www.ups.com/assets/resources/media/en_US/UPS_disaster.pdf

Wang, H., & Qian, C. (2011). Corporate Philanthropy and Corporate Financial Performance: The Role of Stakeholders Response and Political Access. *Academy of Management Journal, 54*(6), 1159–1181. https://www.gartner.com/it-glossary/big-data/ https://en.wikipedia.org/wiki/Data_philanthropy. doi:10.5465/amj.2009.0548

Chapter 15
How to Mitigate the Risk of Misinforming in Case of Mistrust?

ABSTRACT

This chapter discusses techniques to mitigate the risk of misinforming and serves as link to the next part of the book. It introduces the reader to different techniques used in mitigating various categories of misinforming hazards. The objectives of discussed business practices are to enhance the trust toward providers and received information. Techniques used in the following circumstances are included: 1) Techniques to reduce probability for rejecting useful information, and 2) Techniques to allow verification of received information. Traceability of information is essential to enhance trust by verifying origin and quality of raw data, and transparency and adequacy of applied data processing to build the outcomes. Techniques allowing traceability in both breadth and depth of the way the message is created. The role of visualization in indirect, via computer applications, communication is essential in verification in big data circumstances.

INTRODUCTION

Two ideas about using measures of misinforming risks to classify potential clients and to customize the approach to induvial one in the context of marketing circumstances were shared in the first two chapters of this part of the book. This chapter is dedicated to other issues related to managing risks caused by misinforming or mitigating the two aspects of risks – likelihood and impact. Several cases leading to hazards that

DOI: 10.4018/978-1-6684-8800-3.ch015

may result in misinforming and to harm receiver of information are discussed from point of view of mitigation the associated risks. The issue of data collection and data analyzing practices is regarding as needed special attention and design.

Nowadays the exposure of the risk of misinforming is a subject of increased likelihood, based on growing use of indirect communication conducted via IT, and also of increasing impact. This is a result of raising the volume and importance of information obtained through indirect communication. The recent pandemic of COVID-19 speed-up the process of transforming direct communication, including exploring techniques such as body-language, and obtaining immediate feedback to clarify the message, to indirect communication via use of computer technologies. In direct communication trust and correct understanding and correct interpreting are supported by factors outside of the content of the message itself, as opposite to indirect communication when message content, wording, jargon, format, etc. are the only properties to verify it ant to mitigate the risk of misinforming. COVID-19 highlighted one additional problem – reliability of laboratory tests to inform users regarding particular property of investigated phenomenon.

The chapter is organized in a way to discuss several issues associated with hazards leading to misinforming and ideas regarding the ways to mitigate the associated risk and caused harms. Answers to the following questions are needed to react adequately.

What are origins of the misinforming hazard? What causes the risk? In what circumstances this risk will occur?

What are factors influencing (contributing to it happening – likelihood) misinforming?

What is the magnitude of the harm (exposure) caused by misinforming risks?

How to identify, prevent and/or mitigate the misinforming risks in the informing process?

Different scenarios leading to misinforming, as well as factors contributing to the origin of misinforming are presented in Part 1 of the book. Here all cases are illustrated by considering a simple one-to-one informing process (see Figure 1.) to allow discussion on considered cases. The cases of misinforming and corresponding mitigation techniques considered in this chapter are:

- Emphasizing the trust:
  - Trusted-third Party.
  - Informing via use of mediators. Mediators as two-sided information brokers.
  - Block-chain technology as a tool addressing the trust problem by replacing costly mediators, with potential conflict of interests.
- Emphasizing the competencies:
  - Traceability in "machinery" delivered information.

- Role of AI and Big Data.

are presented and discussed. They are discussed regarding likelihood and impact as well as techniques used to mitigate the associated risks. In all these cases, some ideas, approaches, and techniques to mitigate the risks of misinforming are discussed.

TECHNIQUES EMPHASIZING TRUST

As seen in the first two parts of the book, trust toward received information is one of the important factors that play a role in becoming informed but also misinformed. Either of the two extremes – over trust and under trust – may lead to misinforming. There are several business practices adopted by societies to address the trust problem.

Trusted Third Party

"Trusted Third Party" is a common technique to guarantee that provided information in a framework of communication between two parties is trustworthy. The third party is an independent agent, which role is verifying that the information provided is true. This practice is commonly used on many occasions and for many and diverse purposes. Most common of its usage is the role of the public notary, used to verify deals between the two parties, by verifying that the two parties agree about conditions in the deal. Also, the established banking systems play the role of "Trusted Third Party" to guarantee transfer of money.

The entire philosophy of ISO 9000 standards is based on issuing certificates of quality by a "Trusted Third Party" to ensure the public that information provided regarding product or service quality is correct as well as the way of theirs's production is sound, meets standards, and follows "good practices". The role of Accreditation or Certification Agencies in education, as another example of "Trusted Third Party", in verifying quality provided by a higher education institution is to ensure public (potential students, parents, but also donor and financing agencies), that information provided by the institution in advertising its services is correct, and the training provided by the institution meets standards.

Use of information brokers (see Chapter 4.) also explores the idea of "Trusted Third Party". In this case the end user relies on (trusts the) competence of the broker to find needed information, to select what is relevant, to verify it, but also to present the acquired and identified as useful information in an acceptable, understandable way.

Usually, "Trusted Third Party" is used to address potential risks of misinforming by enhancing both trust and lack of competences. Conditions of "Trusted Third Party" agent to play its role are that it must be independent, competent, and to provide clear and transparent justification of the provided service and regarding the compensation for the service. Often, the use of Trusted Third Party is exposed to secondary risks if it does not meet the above conditions. It may have hidden conflict of interest; use hidden fees that can make the service overpriced; or not possess expected expertise and competence.

Reducing Conflicts Caused by Misinforming: The Role of Mediators

Mediators, used to settle conflicts, are also a form of two-sided information brokers, adopting the role of a "Trusted Third Party" toward both sides in the conflict in a way to convey and interpret information from one of the parties to the other to achieve mutual understanding.

Conflicts often are based on misunderstanding the other's viewpoint, misinterpreting the other's objectives, and mistrusting the other. Often the role of mediator is "to translate" the message of one of the parties to the "language" of the other.

Many cases moved to the courts could be resolved by mediators translating the claims of one of the parties to the other and vice versa. Saving money, time efforts, and broken relationships.

Successful mediators inspired trust in either of the parties. The process of mediation is interactive in nature and follows several, potentially repeating, stages:

1. Building a trustful atmosphere in mediation is the first and the most important step in the process of resolving conflicts.
2. It follows by educated parties regarding the role of mediator,
3. The actual process includes:
    a. Investigating the origin of the conflict as seen by either of the parties.
    b. Analysis of circumstances, side-effects, and different outcomes' scenarios.
    c. Identifying and understanding the objectives and expectations of either of the parties.
    d. Analysis of obtained information.
    e. Synthesis of potential solution.
    f. Presented the solution to both parties with clear pointed positive and negative aspects to either of parties and justifying the overall benefit.
    g. If the proposed solution is not accepted: (1) consider arguments for rejecting solution; (2) repeat the process for deeper understanding the conflict; (3) adjust solution to react to rejection arguments.

The trust of either of the parties that the mediator is independent is essential to allow sharing the correct and fair information.

Blockchain and Crypto Currency

In many cases, transferring the role of "Trusted Third Party" from a human to computer technology may mitigate some of the above secondary risks. Computer applications may serve better as independent agents than a human. For example, block-chain technology resolves over-pricing of bank transactions by introducing "crypto-currency" and excluding banks as a Trusted Third Party in this process while ensuring transparent, reliable and trustful financial transactions.

"Blockchain is a distributed ledger that provides a way for information to be recorded and shared by a community. In this community, each member maintains his or her own copy of the information and all members must validate any updates collectively. The information could represent transactions, contracts, assets, identities, or practically anything else that can be described in digital form. Entries are permanent, transparent, and searchable, which makes it possible for community members to view transaction histories in their entirety. Each update is a new "block" added to the end of the "chain." A protocol manages how new edits or entries are initiated, validated, recorded, and distributed. With blockchain, cryptology replaces third-party intermediaries as the keeper of trust, with all Blockchain participants running complex algorithms to certify the integrity of the whole." (see Piscini et al., 2016).

From point of view of misinforming hazards, blockchain technology provides easy way to trace the origin of information, and, because it is not possible to alter data, original wording cannot be altered by mediators, serving to convey information from its source toward the end users correctly.

TECHNIQUES EMPHASIZING COMPETENCES

Lack or not adequate competences are essential and critical factors causing misinforming. This issue was explored in Part 1, Chapter 2., of the book. Two aspects of competences were distinguished (see Buckland M., 1991) – the competences in the problem domain allows customer to realistically assess the properties of the offered products or services; and competences in the information systems delivering information to the customer – these competences allow to gain the best service in a way to correctly assess the received information. The latter category of competences is considered here.

Techniques Emphasizing Critical Assessment of "Machinery" Delivered Data

Dependence on machinery delivered data in making decisions has been growing in the last decades and recently reached a stage of dominance. Two phenomena and two sets of techniques are closely related to this way of acquiring data.

The first one is the Big Data phenomenon. Hazards with Big Data leading to misinforming are numerous, including difficulty or even impossibility to verify data; and acquiring information presented in data by solely viewing secondary information – summaries or statistics, but not original raw data. From other side this stage of current development is characterized by rich data available, and easiness to access and process huge volumes of heterogeneous data. One have access to data, but the human limited cognitive capacity allow to observe only aggregated summaries. The trust toward results is challenged by two issues – whether these summaries represent correctly the important properties of the real world objects the data comes from; and whether some important, but miner details are lost in presented only aggregated views.

Possessing all necessary competences for learning from Big Data is obviously extremely rare. It includes understanding regarding data and circumstances about data collection and data storing Also, it requires possessing sufficient knowledge on data processing techniques, mathematics behind them as well as to judge whether given technique is applicable to the given set of data, whether all required properties of data to guarantee correct and reliable result obtained via applying technique are on place. Last, but not least, competence in the problem domain is needed to interpret results of data analysis in a beneficial way correctly.

The risk of over relying on software application may result to a secondary risk. This secondary risk is related to "over trust" to machinery delivered data by considering these applications as a trustful "black box".

Developing intelligent, customizable interface is essential in a way to mitigate the risk of misinterpreting information, but also to support trust toward results produced by Big Data analytics. (see Christozov, Mitreva, 2020 and Chapter 3.). Interface that will allow to view application as "white box" that allows to make transparent the way results are produced. Development of interface to Big Data Analytic tools need to consider categories of users according to variety of expected competences. The typical architecture of such interface is multitiered. Interface that allows fast and easy access to results for competent users and to provide well-developed help with explanation regarding data collected, and data processed in producing the results.

Rapid development of sophisticated data analytics tools also answered these challenges and can be used as attempts to allow mitigation of the risks of misinforming. Areas of application development marked as Data Mining, Data Warehouses,

Business Intelligence, Data Analytics, etc. represent efforts to reduce the exposure of the risks in making misinformed decisions and allow users to understand how and why results are received.

The other Machine Learning approach, known as Deep Learning, relies on artificial neural networks, and practically transfers the needed competence to the computer application. Over relying on or over trusting such an application is a natural way that a user could be misled.

Other form to avoid misinforming in the case of Big Data analytical application is to allow transdisciplinary explanation of the results. To avoid misinforming cooperation, synergy of a trans-discipline teams is essential. Practically positive use of Artificial Intelligent (AI) tools is to complement user's competences. Learning always requires investment, usually time, but also money and harms by made mistakes. AI may reduce those costs.

Self-recognized lack of adequate competences leads to reduced confidence in making decisions based on received information. Non confidence has two potential risks – to make decision and act with probability to make mistake and to assume the consequences but to learn from the made mistakes; or not to make decision, not to act and not learning.

Bias (as Statistical Category) in Machinery Obtained Data

Since the Renaissance science have developed and used more and more sophisticated equipment to observe and study the real world. Two measures – Repeatability and Reproducibility – are used to justify correctness of machinery obtained data. This is the case when data is achieved by applying laboratory tests on physical objects like soil samples in geology or blood sample in medicine. The sample is analyzed by a reactor, by using reagents, and by applying given methodology or algorithm, describing how to perform analysis and how to interpret results.

Repeatability refers to laboratory tests that produce the same (or statistically close enough) results by repeating the test on different fragments of the same material sample. To illustrate, let assume that a test guarantees 70% precision. The second attempt, if coincide with the first one, will increase precision to 90%, the third – to 97%, etc. Repeatability refers to stability of the results obtained by a triple {reactor, reagent, methodology}, not exactly that the obtained result corresponds to the true value. The shift of results (statistical bias) is the difference between obtained results and the true value (unknown). Calibration is the technique used to adjust obtained results in a way to correspond to the real, true value. Calibration needs to evaluate "the shift" and to apply identified correction (caliber) to obtained results in a way to adjust them toward the true value. Calibration can be done in two general ways – by applying the test to samples with known value (etalons) or by comparing results obtained by the test with results of the same sample obtained by applying other techniques (reproducibility). For comparing the two approaches see Kamburova, Christozov, 1998. Etalon-based calibration is more reliable and provides better results, but at a much higher price. Producing samples of etalons is very expensive.

Reproducibility refers to obtaining the same results by applying different analytical techniques. Different reactors, reagents, or methodologies. One technique will support results obtained by another and the overall trust toward its correctness will increase. This directly corresponds to the trust of receiving the same information from two truly independent sources.

Another aspect of risk in using information produced by a sequence of mediators is the adjustment and aggregation of original raw data. Eliminating mediators (see Chapter 2.) from one side allows to acquire complete data with all details, but from other side results in accumulating large volume of data holding all attributes of the Big Data. The probability of misinforming increases by every passed mediator in a cascade data delivery. Details of reality in messages representing information melt away. In a classical trade process, products go on the way:

producer→wholesaler→retailer

and feedback information is provided on its path back by generalizing it on every step – retailers summarize information acquired by end users, eliminating opinion of small, unimportant, groups, the wholesalers further discriminate opinions of underrepresented group. In this way the producer receives only summarized and generalized feedback, excluding all minor details.

Customer Relationship Systems (CRM), discussed in Chapter 2, is a technology, or Information System, designed to avoid mediators. By using CRM producers receive complete and detailed feedback regarding the product or service, including all nuances of end-users' opinions. Processing collected data in a CRM is a typical case of Big Data processing.

The Role of Traceability of Information

Traceability includes the two aspects of how results of data processing were produced – the original data used, and the data processing procedures applied.

A clear description of how original data is created, captured, stored sometime is essential to interpret results correctly. The following two examples can illustrate these challenges:

Let us consider data collected from auto vehicles claims. For producer's cost-management, the relationship between cost to cover claims and the age of the vehicle is essential. Age is measured as time, but also as mileage. The garage, where vehicle's maintenance is accomplished reports the claim, and usually data about the labor and replaced spare parts is provided correctly, but the data regarding milage is different and mechanics often do not bother to check the speedometer and to enter the true value of accumulated miles. Knowing this may explain the relatively large number of claims with "one-digit" mileage. Such data do not show that vehicles are breaking almost immediately after purchased.

The other example is the case of "hidden witnesses". The data represents only one fragment of real objects and data for other is missing. In this case interpretation of conclusions must reflect the missed data and must not extend to cover the entire population.

Traceability must also cover the steps in data processing. Aggregation of data is implemented by reducing numerosity or the size of the explored sample; and, by reducing dimensionality or the number of variables describing the real objects. Knowing how these two operations are executed may reveal the origin of unexpected anomalies and improve understanding and correct interpretation.

TECHNIQUES TO TRANSFER RISK

Transferring risk is a common practice in risk management. It is used to find an external source to compensate for the negative outcome in the case when the hazard happened. The standard technique used in such cases is a warranty contract used in commerce. The two categories of warranty contracts, warranty of malfunctioning and warranty of misinforming are discussed in more detail in the next part of the book. Making a decision without reaching the needed level of confidence, as not having sufficient time to explore all possible options and to consider all side effects, is quite often nowadays. This form of risk mitigation allows transferring the risk, which means to get compensation in case of acting according to wrong decision made by using received information, which is not complete, not well understood, or misinterpreted. The slogan "if you are not fully satisfied – money back" describes this form of warranty – buy now, but if you make a wrong purchase decision you will not be harmed (at least financially).

CONCLUSION

Several ideas regarding misinforming risk and corresponding mitigation techniques are presented. The great variety of misinforming risk origins, cases and circumstances doesn't allow to make this review comprehensive.

The chapter explores two major categories of misinforming hazard origins: information credibility or trust toward obtained information; and competences in its correct understanding, assessing, and use.

Practices as trusted third party, appointment of mediators, traceability, or calibration of measuring equipment are widely used to increase the trust toward information by acquiring mutual understanding for origin of data, performed data processing operations, and ability to interpret anomalies or unexpected results.

Understanding that the risk associated with the misinforming hazard exists is the first step in deciding to adopt a technique to mitigate it. Next comes the criteria which technique is the most suitable to given circumstances, and objectives in using information. Often, just acknowledging that this risk exists and it is probable is sufficient to avoid the negative consequences.

REFERENCES

Agrawal, R., Kadadi, A., Xiangfeng, D., & Adres, F. (2015). Challenges and Opportunities with Big Data Visualization. *7th International Conference on Management of computational and collective IntElligence in Digital EcoSystems (MEDES)*, (pp. 169–173). ACM. 10.1145/2857218.2857256

Buckland, M. (1991). *Information and Information Systems*. Praeger.

Christozov, D., & Mitreva, E. (2020). Trust in Learning from Big Data: The Two Sides of the Same Coin. *Issues in Information Systems*, *21*(1), 147–152.

Christozov, D., & Toleva-Stoimenova, S. (2015). Big Data Literacy - a New Dimension of Digital Divide: Barriers in learning via exploring Big Data. In J. Girard, K. Berg, D. Klein, & I. G. I. Global (Eds.), *Strategic Data Based Wisdom in the Big Data Era*. doi:10.4018/978-1-4666-8122-4.ch009

Gackowski, Z. (2006). Quality of Informing: Credibility Provisional Model of Functional Dependencies. *Proceedings of the 2006 InSITE Conference*. ACM. 10.28945/3017

Kamburova, E., & Christozov, D. (1998). Assessment of and comparison between Bulgarian and International standards for quality control of evaluation of the element composition of geological samples. Sofia.

Piscini, E., Guastella, J., Rozman, A., & Nassim, T. (2016). *Blockchain: Democratized trust. Distributed ledgers and the future of value*. Deloitte University Press.

Section 3 Conclusion

The role of this Part of the book is to discuss business issues which are important in addressing hazards of misinforming. Several communication scenarios were presented and discussed, together with associated hazards that may result in misinforming. Different business practices were considered from the point of view of misinforming.

There are many ways an individual may become informed and therefore misinformed. Understanding the origin of those risks helps to define mitigation techniques and assess their effectiveness. Also, the natural likelihood of misinforming phenomenon may serve to build better relationships between different parties in a business process. Of course, the list of scenarios presented here is far from complete but may illustrate what may go wrong.

Different origins of misinforming risks are discussed in Part 1 of the book. Some of them have a direct impact on business activities and for others this relationship is not obvious. In general, the misinforming risk is discussed from the point of view of receiver of information, but also as implication to information provider. Elaboration those issues in a business context is natural because harm caused by misinforming is measurable but factors for appearing are difficult to identify and quantify. The previous part of the book presented a way to do this. Next part of the book is dedicated to one specific way to explore the misinforming hazard – the warranty of misinforming.

Section 4

Warranty of Misinforming

Section 4 Introduction

The current market is becoming more and more complex and complicated. Globalization, widely available and easy access to information and growing the volume of indirect sells increases, from one-side, self-confidence of clients regarding capability to make informed rational purchase decisions, but, from other side, increases the possibility for misunderstanding and wrong decisions. Wrong purchase decisions are associated with significant costs for both parties.

Market regulations are another way to guarantee clients' rights and to reduce the harm caused by mistakes in purchase decisions. This regulation is offered in the form of a warranty – warranty of misinforming – allowing the client to return a product if the later does not satisfied client's expectation. This form of warranty added to the "classical" warranty defended client if the product fails – warranty of malfunctioning.

This section of the book is dedicated to warranty as business practice of sharing and transferring market risks. Two types of risks and two types of warranties – warranty of malfunctioning and warranty of misinforming – are elaborated as leading to composition of united warranty policy addressing the two risks. Several aspects of such policy are discussed as market segmentation based on reducing the risk of becoming misinformed; assessment of quality of warranty policy; using warranty of misinforming to provide opportunities to tune client's expectations; and support learning and product utilization.

The chapters in this section of the book are as following: the first chapter introduces the concept of sharing the risk by offering warranty coverage, defines the two types of risks and the two types of warranty contracts, emphasizing the warranty of misinforming. The second chapter introduces criteria and practice to assess quality of warranty policy in case it is composed by mixing the two types of warranties contracts or by covering only one of the types of risks – pure Vs. mixed warranty policy. The third chapter addresses a positive side effect of applying warranty of misinforming – by allowing cost-free replacement of the product, the warranty may serve as an option to utilize more fully the potential of given category of products. The fourth chapter discusses the learning process supported by warranty of misinforming.

Chapter 16
The Concept of Sharing Risks:
Warranty

ABSTRACT

This chapter introduces the readers with the concept of sharing risk. A warranty contract is mutually adopted for the distribution of the negative outcome of a malfunctioning product affecting few among the entire population of the product's users. The warranty as a business practice has legal aspects, as the warranty is a form of contract, and also uses mathematical modeling based on evaluation of the probability of malfunctioning of the product over its lifetime. Misinforming added a new aspect on the risk in acquiring new products – the risk that the product doesn't behave as assumed by the client at the time of purchasing. The warranty of misinforming is a form to mitigate the risk of unsatisfaction by sharing the cost among the clients' population.

INTRODUCTION

Risk sharing is a technique to mitigate negative outcomes result of occurring the hazard covered by the warranty contract. The cost is spread to all customers, with the assumption that the hazard will happen to only a few of them. The warranty is an adopted policy to share the cost of risk of failure of a product purchased by some of the customers among all who had obtained the same product. In this way the share of the cost is included in the product's price and paid by every one of the customers. The assessment of likelihood of hazard and the cost to cover the damage it creates, is essential to define the warranty parameters, including the share of the product price dedicated to covering warranty claims.

DOI: 10.4018/978-1-6684-8800-3.ch016

This chapter addresses warranties offered to cover the two types of risks associated with the two types of hazards, the risk of malfunctioning of a product and the risk of misinforming. The probability for the first one is quantified by the product's reliability. This is the risk of malfunctioning of the product during a given period. The second risk is a function of success or failure that may occur during communication when a customer decides whether to buy or not the product. This is the risk of misinforming. Both are subject to warranty contracts. This chapter introduces the relationship between the two risks and product warranty contracts from the customer's and producer's viewpoint. The purposes, legalities and types of warranties are briefly presented, followed by a summary of mathematical models and concepts for quantifying the financial implications of warranties of malfunctioning. Part 2 of the book is dedicated to models and approaches to quantify the risk of misinforming and is not detailed here. The policy to define product warranty to address these risks is becoming important and represents a complex managerial problem, especially in indirect sells.

The success of a business deal, involving two parties, a seller, and a buyer, depends on various factors, which can be divided into two major groups. The first group consists of factors, which are properties of the environment in which the seller-buyer relationship takes place, such as IT, logistic, financial infrastructures, government regulations, etc. The second group consists of factors, which are properties of the interpersonal relationship between the two parties, such as efficiency and effectiveness of the communication process, trust and confidence, content, and acceptance of the exchanged messages, etc.

A product's warranty, as a risk sharing mechanism, affects the business transactions in two aspects: firstly, by providing a legal frame of the deal, and secondly, by enhancing the trust between the parties. The two sources of risk that warranty covers are:

- the risk of malfunctioning of the product and
- the risk of making a wrong purchase decision while buying the product caused by misinterpreting or misunderstanding the usability of the product as described in the advertising message.

The first type of warranty is well represented by the slogan "if the product fails – free of charge repair or replacement", whereas the second type of warranty is summarized by "if not fully satisfied – money back guaranteed". The risk of malfunctioning of the product and related warranty modeling is well represented in the literature. At the same time, recently, due to the increased volume of indirect commerce, the impact of the risk of misinforming on the business transactions has been extensively considered, including developing and launching regulations. This chapter considers warranty from this broader perspective, emerging from e-commerce, by using models, approaches, and algorithms to quantify the risk of misinforming, developed in Part 2, to design appropriate warranty policies. This chapter follows closely the ideas presented in Christozov D., Chukova S. & Mateev P. (2009).

OVERVIEW OF THE CONCEPT OF WARRANTY[1]

The warranty is a contract that commits the manufacturer or the seller to stand behind their product. It is a statement about the functionality of the product and the commitment of the warrantor to correct problems when the product fails. A product warranty is an agreement offered by a warrantor to a buyer to replace or repair a faulty item, or to reimburse the buyer partially or fully in the event of a failure. Warranties are widespread and serve many purposes, including protection for producers, sellers, and consumers. They are used as signals of quality and as elements of marketing strategies. A general treatment of warranty analysis is given by Blischke and Murthy (1993, 1996), Chukova, Dimitrov and Rykov (1993), Murthy and Djamaludin, (2002) and Karim and Suzuki (2004). From the buyer's point of view, the main role of a warranty is to provide protection. Specifically, the warranty assures the buyer that a faulty item will either be repaired or replaced at no cost or at a reduced cost. In addition, the warranty as a signal of quality has an informational impact on the buyers.

From the producer's point of view the warranty also provides protection. A warranty agreement may and often does specify the use and conditions of use for which the product is intended and provide for limited coverage or no coverage at all in the event of misuse of the product. A second important role of warranty for the seller is promotional. As buyers often infer a more reliable product when a longer warranty is offered, this has been used as an effective advertising tool. In addition, a warranty has become an instrument, similar to product performance and price, used in competition with other manufacturers in the marketplace.

Even though warranties are so commonly used, the accurate pricing of warranties in many situations remains an unsolved problem. This may seem surprising since the fulfilment of warranty claims may cost companies large amounts of money. Underestimating true warranty costs results in losses for a company, overestimating them results in uncompetitive product prices.

Warranties and Legalities

Most of the studies of warranties treat them from the producer's or customer's point of view. In what follows, we elaborate on warranties from the decision-maker's point of view. There are two main types of warranties recognized by the lawmakers, implied and express warranties. The implied warranties are unspoken, unwritten promises, created by the decision-makers. There are two types of implied warranties, an implied warranty of merchantability and an implied warranty of fitness for a particular purpose. The implied warranty of merchantability assures us that the goods will do what they are supposed to do. The implied warranty of fitness for a particular purpose is a promise of the seller, which he makes when the customer relies on his advice that a product can be used for some specific purpose. Implied warranties are promises about the condition of products at the time they are sold, but they do not guarantee that a product will last for any specific length of time. Generally, there is no specified duration for implied warranties, and they can be disclaimed, which means the entire product risk falls on the buyer. The implied warranty cannot be waived if the product is covered by a written warranty.

Figure 1. summarizes the forms of warranty contracts from a legal point of view. Expressed warranties, unlike implied warranties, are an explicit offer to the customers during a sales transaction. They are statements, the warrantor makes, about the product or about the commitment to remedy the faults and malfunctions of the product. Express warranties can be given in the form of advertising claims, certificates and others and can be made either orally or in writing. Only written warranties are recognized by the law. In addition, the express warranty is "full" if it does not limit the duration of the implied warranties, i.e., the warranty is available to anyone who owns the product and there are no restrictions for receiving the warranty service. Otherwise, the warranty is called a "limited" warranty.

Figure 1. Types of warranties from legalities point of view
(Reproduced with permission from Christozov D., Chukova S. & Mateev P., 2009).

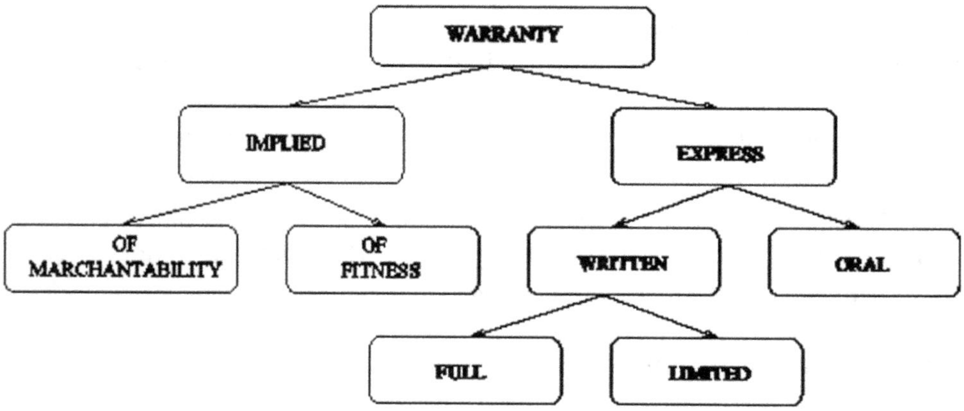

The main legal document in the USA related to warranty legalities is the Magnuson-Moss Warranty Act, 1975. Usually, the express warranty is given in written form, that is why sometimes it is called a written warranty. Figure 1. summarizes the warranties from the legal point of view.

Mathematical Modelling in Warranties

The study of warranties through mathematical models and methods is a recent, very active area of research. The common warranty parameters of interest are the expected total warranty cost and the warranty cost per unit of time over the warranty period, as well as over the life cycle of the product. These quantities summarize the financial risk or burden carried by buyers, sellers, and decision makers. Their values are assessed by using analytical or approximation models, often in combination with solving an optimization problem. Due to the complexity of the models, it is almost always necessary to resort to numerical methods since analytical solutions exist only for the simplest cases.

In order to provide structure to the analysis of warranties, it is necessary to identify some of its specific features. Figure 2. presents a classification of mathematical models for warranty. The aim is to give the reader an idea about the complexity involved, and, also, to highlight the reason why so many important problems in warranty cost analysis are still unsolved. We call the specific warranty agreement between a buyer and a seller a warranty contract. Firstly, we elaborate on the classification levels preceding the warranty contract as they reflect the reliability framework of the modeling. It follows by a discussion on the sub-levels that identify the essence of the modeling warranties. Moving from the top to the bottom of Figure 2, we identify five classification levels preceding the warranty contract and elaborate on the meaning of each of them.

Level 1. An item/product could be either repairable or non-repairable. While a failure of a non-repairable item requires replacement (or a complete repair), a repair could resolve the claim for repairable items. Complex items (or systems) form a separate group, because they can consist of repairable as well as non-repairable components.

Level 2. The second level of classification is relevant only for complex items. It is related to the structure and the interaction between the components of the system, which may need to be modeled, and the existence of partial warranty, i.e., pre-assigned warranty for some of the subsystems of the complex item, but not for the entire item.

Level 3. The third level addresses the "degree of repair", which describes how good the repaired product is compared to the newly purchased one. To what extent does the requirement restore item' resources. The post-failure repairs (see Pham and Wang 1996) could be complete, minimal, imperfect, worse and worst. The type of repair applied to rectify a claim depends on the warranty contract, related costs, assigned warranty maintenance, reliability, and safety requirements of the product. Also, the existence of an extended warranty or any additional agreements may influence the degree of the repair. Mathematically the degree of repair can be modeled through different characteristics of the lifetime distribution of the item, such as, the mean total time to failure, the failure rate function, or the cumulative distribution function (Chukova, Arnold and Wang 2004). Introducing parameters related to the age of the item before and after the repair leads to, so called, age-dependent repair models (Dimitrov, Chukova and Khalil 2004).

Level 4. At this level the models are divided into two groups according to whether the warranty applies to a single item or many items, which are warranted as a group. The latter reflects on the distribution of the warranty reserves and leads to variety of models for these reserves (Kulkarni, Shau-shiang Ja, Amit Mitra, and Jayprakash Patankar, (2002)).

Level 5. The warranty contract itself is a set of sub-levels, which identifies the rules and conditions of the warranty agreement and specifies the guidelines regarding the warranty remedies.

The choice of the warranty contract depends on the goals and the "point of view" of the modeling. Again, moving from the top to the bottom of Figure 2., after the warranty contract, four sub-levels are identified:

Level 5.1 reflects the "point of view" of the modeling. The "best" warranty from consumers' point of view may differ substantially from the "best" warranty for warrantors' point of view (interested in profit, sustainability, indemnity, public image, etc.) or the one from public decision makers' point of view (concerned with public health and safety, regulation of competition, etc.). The most common type of modeling is associated with the warrantors' point of view.

Level 5.2. The form of reimbursement of the customer due to the failure of a warranted item is an important characteristic of the warranty. The most common forms are a lump-sum rebate (e.g., "money-back guarantee"); a free repair of the failed item; a repair provided at reduced cost to the buyer or some combination of the preceding terms.

Level 5.3. The warranty can be one-dimensional or multidimensional. Nowadays, the most common type of warranty is identified by a single variable or parameter. Usually, it is specified as "time", such as the time since the purchase, the time since the first use of the product, or the time in use. It may also be specified as the number of uses, e.g., number of take-off/landing cycles of an aircraft, or other measure of usage – accumulated milage of a motor vehicle. A warranty, which is specified by a single warranty parameter is said to be a one-dimensional warranty. Warranty with higher dimensionality, where two or more warranty parameters are involved, results in significant additional complexity to warranty cost analysis. The most common two-dimensional warranty is the one based on both the age and usage of the product. In Figure 4.1.2., we depict only one dimensional and two-dimensional warranty. Lately, the two-dimensional warranty has attracted the attention of many warranty experts because it is a typical warranty coverage offered in the automotive industry.

Level 5.4. Under the one-dimensional scenario, the warranty coverage over warranty period of length ***W***, can be defined as nonrenewing or renewing coverage. Under a nonrenewing warranty items are repaired until the total service time of the original and all repaired items is no more than ***W***, whereas under a renewing warranty for all repaired items the warranty starts anew. The warranty expires when the lifetime of the item, the original one or its repaired version, exceeds ***W***. A combination of the preceding terms is called a combined warranty. In two-dimensional case, the warranty depends on the shape of the two-dimensional region, where the warranty parameters are well defined.

Figure 2. Classification of mathematical models in warranty studies
(Reproduced with permission from Christozov D., Chukova S. & Mateev P., 2009).

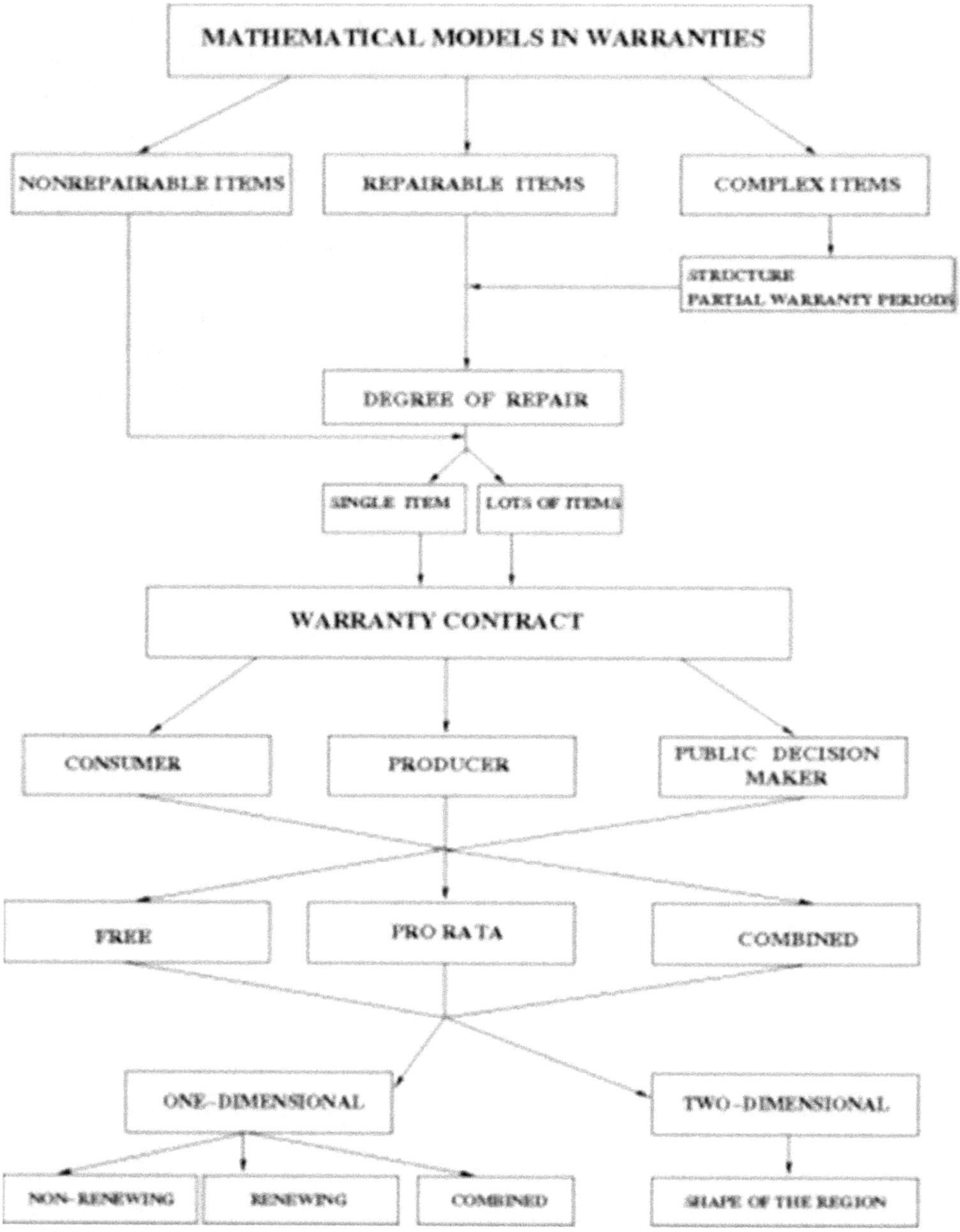

WARRANTY OF MISINFORMING

The risk of misinforming is discussed in detail in the first two parts of the book, including ideas for quantifying the risk and data collection and processing.

To develop a measure of the risk of misinforming in purchase decision making, the following factors (see Figure 3.) have to be taken into account:

1. The parameters related to information asymmetry (the likelihood of the occurrence of misunderstanding):
    a. The sender, while formulating the information message regarding the product, is not aware of the receiver's background/expertise and the problem he faces. For example, the sender is not aware of the tasks the receiver intends to perform, his needs in executing these tasks and the resources available for solving the problem.
    b. The receiver does not know well the relevance of the received information, its reliability, trustfulness, and value.
2. Factors reducing the risk of misinforming such as:
    a. opportunity to clarify the message – the existence of feedback.
    b. the trustfulness of the environment where the message was transmitted, e.g., buying goods from a shop in a mall compared to buying goods from a stall on the street.
    c. risk sharing mechanism – e.g., product warranty.
3. Factors affecting the level (as an impact on receiver) of the risk of misinforming:
    a. client's needs in executing a particular task using the product – a low level of needs results in a low impact of the misinforming on the receiver and therefore to a low-risk exposure.
    b. the acceptance level of the product – a low acceptance level means that almost every solution is acceptable, e.g., there are no strict requirements for the suitability of the product for the client's needs, and therefore related misinforming has a low impact on the client and his purchase decision making.

In practice, quite often the receiver is not aware that he may misinterpret the received message and should consider options for controlling/reducing this risk.

Figure 3. Risk of misinforming map
Note: Notations developed in Part 2 are used in this chapter with the same meaning (see Appendix 1).

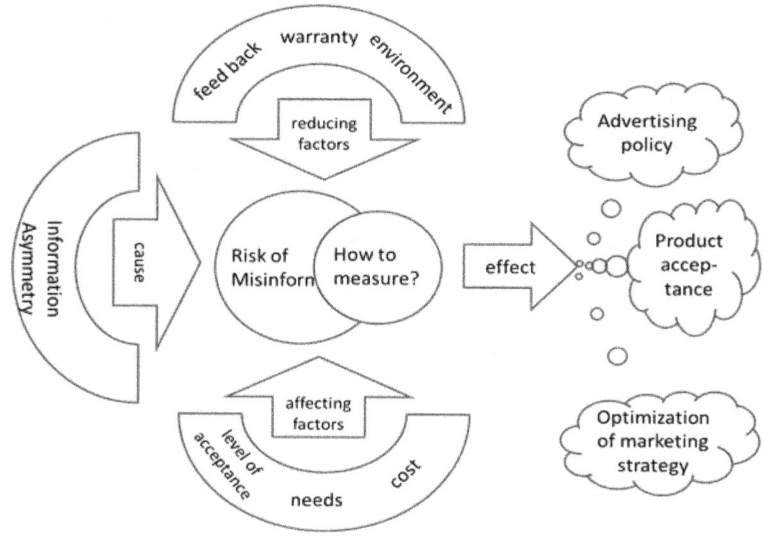

To discuss warranty contracts in case of misinforming, let us recall in brief the circumstances of misinforming hazards as presented in the first two chapters. It occurs within the communication process, representing an exchange of information between two parties, a sender and a receiver, through a given communication channel (see Figure 1.). The sender sends out a message addressing the receiver. The content of the message is a sign of the sender's idea of what is useful to the receiver. The message is composed to convey certain information, as the sender understands it. Its structure is influenced by the sender's judgment on the receiver's capability to understand and interpret the message correctly. The message is encoded to make it suitable for transmission through the communication channel and submitted to the receiver.

From the receiver's viewpoint, the process also includes several stages. It starts with the physical delivery of the message followed by a decoding. The proper interpretation of the message is essential for the success of the communication process. The last phase of the communication process from the receiver's point of view is the adoption of the information contained in the message. The communication process is successful if the receiver utilizes the obtained information in making decisions. Most of the technological tools developed to support communication are focusing on the physical delivery and correct decoding of information. The stage of the interpretation of the content of the message is critical to whether the message informs or misinforms the receiver. The interpretation is based on receiver's expertise, perceptions, bias, etc. The success in this stage is influenced by the information asymmetry, which is defined as the difference in expertise of the sender and receiver on the subject matter of the message. Also, it is greatly influenced by the level of sender's credibility with the receiver. In a face-to-face communication, the trust may be revealed by many factors additional to the content of the message, such as whether the communication takes place in a trustful environment, what is sender's personality, sender's body language, possibilities of clarifying the meaning of the message in an easy and natural dialog, etc. In indirect communication, the majority of these factors are absent, and they have to be compensated by the structure and the content of the message. This property of indirect communication increases the likelihood of misunderstanding and therefore the risk of misinforming is becoming dominant.

An approach and corresponding models for quantifying the exposure of the risks associated with misinforming hazards are developed in Part 2 of the book.

RELATIONSHIP BETWEEN RISK AND WARRANTY

The two aspects of the relationship between the risk of misinforming and warranty are discussed further. Firstly, how the risk of misinforming, caused by information asymmetry is affected by the product warranty offered by the seller. Secondly, the type of information the risk of misinforming provides to the seller that can be utilized for improving his marketing policy. Onwards we assume that:

1. The seller and the buyer are negatively affected by a wrong purchase decision. For a buyer, any wrong purchase decision results in financial and emotional disadvantages. On the other hand, for a seller, a wrong purchase decision is also strongly undesirable, because unsatisfied customers have a negative impact on the producer's reputation and generate mistrust toward him. A disappointed customer may harm the seller's reputation much more strongly than a number of satisfied customers can contribute to its improvement.
2. In Chapter 2 were distinguished three categories of customers:
    a. Optimists are customers who overestimate the capabilities of the product. They buy the product even if the product is not suitable to their needs and requirements.
    b. Pessimists are customers who underestimate the capabilities of the product. These customers do not buy the product, even if it is suitable for their needs and requirements.
    c. Realists are customers, who estimate the capabilities of the product correctly and buy only if it suits their needs and requirements.

The harm to the seller's reputation caused by an optimists' wrong purchase decision is higher than that caused by the pessimists' wrong purchase decision. In the later, the harm is simply the loss of one sale, whereas in the former, the harm comes from spreading negative information about the product, which can have a long-term negative impact on the producer's reputation.

3. The seller identifies two thresholds for the values of the risk, say R_l (low risk) and R_h (high risk), which divide the risk into three categories.

    1. Let $0 \leq R \leq R_l$. This is the category of low risk, i.e., the risk of misinforming is such that only a few customers end up making a wrong purchase decision due to misinforming hazard. The risk is so small that the harm caused by this hazard is acceptable for both parties involved in the sales/purchase process. Hence, the message with the description of the product, used to market the product, is adequate and serves well to attract and convey correct information to the majority of the customers.
    2. Let $R_h \leq R \leq 1$. This is the category of high risk. The risk of misinforming is such that too large number of the customers are unsatisfied with their purchase decision, i.e., the impact of the information asymmetry is very high. Therefore, the description of the product for marketing purposes is not adequate at all and misleads many of the customers.
    3. Let $R_l \leq R \leq R_h$. This is the category of moderate risk. The risk of misinforming reflects the existence of two groups of customers. The description of the product is suitable for and informs well one of the groups, but it is unsuitable for the other group of customers and misinforms them. It is obvious that to clarify the features of the product, a revision of the message with the description of the product should be made, such that it targets most of the potential customers appropriately. Here the measures of the risk for different categories of activities may serve to update only the parts of the message, which are mostly misinterpreted.

A survey, aiming to identify the various works customers intend to do by using the product, can provide useful information in deciding what is the most suitable warranty policy for this product. Of course, the current description of the product, used for advertising and marketing purposes, significantly influences this decision. We consider the following three types of warranty contracts:

1. If the product fails within the first three years after the sale, it is replaced or repaired free of charge to the buyer.

2. If the buyer is not fully satisfied with the product within the first three months after the sale, s/he is fully reimbursed.
3. If the buyer is not fully satisfied with the product within the first month after the sale, s/he is fully reimbursed and afterwards the product is covered by a one-year free repair/replacement warranty.

Next, we discuss how to identify which of the above warranties is the most appropriate for customers with different risk levels. We distinguish the following cases:

1. If the level of risk is low, the customers make well-informed purchase decisions. As a result, the first type of warranty is the most appropriate for this type of customer.
2. If the level of risk is high, the second type of warranty seems to be the best, because it will encourage the customers to examine the features of the product for certain period of time and decide whether to keep the product or to inquire full reimbursement. This warranty policy is especially useful in case of pessimists group dominates.
3. If the level of risk is moderate, the ratio of the number of pessimists to the number of optimists, within the group of buyers, determines the choice of the best warranty. If the optimists are the dominating group, the mixed policy, i.e., the third warranty option, is the best choice, because as much as optimists are open for challenges, they need the option of getting a full refund in case that the product is not suitable for their needs. If the group of pessimists dominates, the second warranty option is the best.

CONCLUSION

The risk caused by Information Asymmetry could be high enough to lead to serious business disadvantages and it is important to be studied more systematically. A significant percentage of buyers do not understand the risk caused by the information asymmetry. Sellers, offering warranties to cover this risk, are doing that basically to promote their product, assuming negligible impact on their business. E-commerce offers great opportunities to enrich the seller-customer relationship, but indirect communication requires to emphasize on the trust between them and to develop tools to enhance understanding and overcoming the information asymmetry. The learning aspect of warranty, covering the risk of misinforming is underestimated as well. On one hand, the warranty provides the seller with feedback on the sensitivity of the buyers towards this risk, and, on the other hand, provides the customers with the opportunity to experiment and learn more about the product.

Studying the risks of misinforming is still in a very early stage, but the results obtained so far show that this risk exists, and it is significant especially in indirect trading, which became very popular during the last decade. In addition, designing an appropriate warranty policy, as an instrument to enhance the trust between parties, requires cost-benefit analyses based on quantified assessment of the risk of misinforming. In this study, the proposed approach to quantify the risk caused by information asymmetry is mostly practical and it needs further improvement. One of the main directions for our future work will be to update the design of the survey in order to address the estimation of the buyer's degree of acceptance.

REFERENCES

Blischke, W., & Murthy, D. N. P. (1993). *Warranty Cost Analysis*. Marcel Dekker.

Blischke, W., & Murthy, D. N. P. (1996). Product Warranty Handbook, Marcel Dekker
Chang-Tseh Hseih, Fujun Lai, and Weihua Shi, (2006), Information orientation and its impact on information asymmetry and e-business adoption: Evidence from China's international trading industry. *Industrial Management & Data Systems*, *106*(6), 825–840.

Christozov, D. (1999). Evaluation of the Quality of an Option Compare to Its Alternatives, in Polis, Dontchev, Kall, Lasiecka, Olbrot Systems Modelling and Optimization. *Proceedings of the 18th IFIP TC7 Conference (Research Notes in Mathematics Series)*. CRC Press.

Christozov, D., Chukova, S., & Mateev, P. (2006). A Measure of Risk Caused by Information Asymmetry in e-Commerce. *Journal of Issues in Informing Science and Information Technology*, *3*, 147–158. doi:10.28945/879

Christozov, D., Chukova, S., & Mateev, P. (2009). On two types of warranties: Warranty of malfunctioning and warranty of misinforming. *Asia-Pacific Journal of Operational Research*, *26*(3), 399–420. doi:10.1142/S0217595909002274

Christozov, D., & Mateev, P. (2005). Assessment of Information Asymmetry. *Pliska Studia Mathematica Bulgarica*, *17*, 27–38.

Chukova, S., Arnold, R., & Wang, D. (2004). Warranty Analysis: An Approach to modelling Imperfect Repairs. *International Journal of Production Economics*, *89*(1), 57–68. doi:10.1016/S0925-5273(03)00200-7

Chukova, S., Dimitrov, B., & Rykov, V. (1993). Warranty Analysis. A survey. *Journal of Soviet Mathematics*, *67*(6), 3486–3508. doi:10.1007/BF01096273

Dimitrov, B., Chukova, S., & Khalil, Z. (2004). Warranty Costs: An Age - Dependent Failure/Repair Model. *Naval Research Logistics*, *51*(7), 959–976. doi:10.1002/nav.20037

Karim, R., & Suzuki, K. (2004), Analysis of warranty claim data: A literature review. In *Proceedings of the 2004 Asian International Workshop on Advanced Reliability Modeling*. World Scientific. 10.1142/9789812702685_0030

Kulkarni, V., & Shau-shiang, J. (2002). Warranty Reserves for Non-stationary Sales Processes. *Naval Research Logistics*, *49*(5), 499–513. doi:10.1002/nav.10023

Magnuson-Moss Warranty and Federal Trade Commission Improvement Act of 1975, Pub. Law No 93 – 637 (15 U.S.C. 2301)

Murthy, P. D., & Djamaludin, I. (2002). New product warranty: A literature review. *International Journal of Production Economics*, *79*(2), 236–260.

Pham, H., & Wang, H. (1996). Imperfect maintenance. *European Journal of Operational Research*, *94*(3), 425–439. doi:10.1016/S0377-2217(96)00099-9

Slovac, P. (1993). Perceived Risk, Trust, and Democracy. *Risk Analysis*, *13*(6), 675–682. doi:10.1111/j.1539-6924.1993.tb01329.x

U.S. Code Collection. (n.d.). Cornell University. http://www.law.cornell.edu/uscode/html/uscode15/usc_ sup_01_15_10_50.htm

White, M., & Eiser, R. (2005). Information Specificity and Hazard Risk Potential as Moderators of Trust Asymmetry. *Risk Analysis*, *25*(5), 1187–1198. doi:10.1111/j.1539-6924.2005.00659.x PMID:16297224

ENDNOTE

1 Warranty covering the risk of product's failure is well developed in literature and the concept of warranty is presented here from point of view of warranty of malfunctioning. Prof. S. Chukova is the major contributor in writing the paper this section is based on.

Chapter 17
Assessment of Quality of Warranty Policy

ABSTRACT

The two forms of warranty contracts, introduced in the previous chapter, increase the complexity of decisions the producers need to make in offering risk-sharing contracts. The considered risk is composite and requires assessment of parameters to offer a meaningful and feasible warranty contract. The chapter introduces the structure of composite warranty policy and by referring to the measures introduced in the second part of the book proposes a possible way to target clients by combining the two forms of warranty. The proposed measure of policy's "quality" allows to build a rational solution.

INTRODUCTION

Let us recall that product warranty is used by the manufacturers/vendors as a mechanism to share the risks associated with the uncertainty of the product performance with their customers. Nowadays warranty is one of the product's attributes and it is used also as a competing tool on the marketplace. Appropriately assigned product warranty could significantly stimulate the sale process and positively impact the producer's profit. At the same time, the warranty servicing cost should be considered, because if it is high enough, warranty coverage could lead to considerable losses.

The "quality" of a warranty policy is an integral measure, based on the balance between the two types of warranty – the warranty of malfunctioning and warranty of misinforming – as discussed in the previous section. This measure is represented in terms of the length of the warranty coverage, which is the main one-dimensional

DOI: 10.4018/978-1-6684-8800-3.ch017

warranty parameter. The period of coverage is the time the client is allowed to file a claim and to get compensation. A possible approach what represents the "best" quality warranty policy is discussed as well as how to choose one in different contexts.

The parameters of the two warranty contracts are "times". Here, by "time" we mean any measure of the warranty coverage, not necessarily the calendar time. For example, in the automobile industry, the warranty coverage is identified not only by the vehicle's age, but accounts also for the accumulated mileage, i.e., "time" could by the age of the vehicle, or it could be the accumulated mileage:

- warranty of malfunctioning – it is related to product's failure to perform the functions as specified in its description for a predetermined (warranty) period of time t^R=[0,t^R], which usually starts right after the sale. The length (size) of the warranty period is usually closely related to reliability and quality of the product.
- warranty of misinforming – it is related to a failure in the communication process during the course of the product sale, which leads to customers being misinformed regarding the product's features and scope of usage. The warranty of misinforming shares the risk of misinforming for a period of time t^M=[0,t^M], during which the customers are protected against misinforming, i.e., during this period they can return the product for full reimbursement.

Quantifying the risks of malfunctioning of the products is relatively well studied; see the previous chapter. It uses models, based on information obtained from reliability tests, quality control or other activities carried out by the producer to study product's performance measures and the accuracy of this assessment is entirely under the control of the producer and the assigned warranty parameter fully reflect the objectives of the warrantor. The producer may assess with needed precision the expected probability of the product to fail, as well as the cost associated with every type of failures. In this way, the producer may calculate the expected warranty cost and how this cost will be spread over the period of warranty coverage.

On the other hand, measuring the risk of misinforming is related to failures in communication processes. It is not under the control of either of the two parties involved in the communication and its evaluation requires different approaches and techniques for collecting and processing data. The primary data source for evaluating the risk of misinforming is the customer's feedback on their satisfaction with the performance and suitability of the product. Part 2 is dedicated to present approaches to evaluate the likelihood of misinforming.

This chapter explores findings made and published in Christozov D., Chukova S. & Mateev P. (2010).

WARRANTY POLICY: DEFINITIONS AND MEASURES

The two types of warranty, the warranty of malfunctioning and warranty of misinforming, have one main parameter of interest – the warranty coverage period. During this period of time, a warranty claim against a faulty product is legitimate. Warranty contract that covers only one of those risks is a "pure" in comparison to the contracts that cover both – "mixed warranty policy". Here are extended notations, presented in Part 2 to define the warranty policy.

Definition 1. A warranty policy, $W_p=\{W_R(t^R);W_M(t^M)\}$, is called a mixed warranty policy, if it accounts for the two types of warranties: $W_R(t^R)$ - the warranty of malfunctioning over $t^R=[0,t^R]$ and $W_M(t^M)$ – the warranty of misinforming over $t^M=[0,t^M]$.

The mixed warranty W_p is identified by two ordered time periods, t^R and t^M, and we will use interchangeably to the notation in definition 1, the notation $W_p=\{t^R,t^M\}$. This definition is an attempt to put together the ideas of warranty of malfunctioning and warranty of misinforming and propose a uniform mechanism for risk sharing for both types of uncertainties – uncertainties related to malfunctioning as well as uncertainties related to unsuitability of product as intended by the buyer – misinforming.

How to compare different warranty strategies?
How to choose between "pure" and "mixed" policy?
How to choose the "best" parameters of warranty contract?

To answer these questions, one needs to define a measure – "quality of warranty policy" from producers' as well as from client's viewpoints. Usually, the term "quality" is used to define the complete set of properties pertinent to a given object. From a business point of view, the term quality also represents a measure of excellence. Here, the quality of a mixed warranty policy is defined as well as criteria to assess the "level of excellence" of warranty policy – what represents high quality warranty policy – from producer's as well as from client's viewpoint.

Definition 2. From producer's point of view, the quality, as a measure of excellence, of a mixed warranty policy W_p, is identified by the expected warranty servicing cost and by the level of client's acceptance and satisfaction of the product.

Definition 3. From producer's point of view, a mixed warranty policy W_p is of high (optimal) quality, if it minimizes the expected warranty servicing cost and it maximizes the level of product acceptance by the clients.

These definitions address the two major roles of a warranty from the seller's point of view – sharing with the customers the uncertainties of the product performance and promoting the product on the marketplace. Offering no warranty on malfunctioning will reduce the expected warranty cost to zero and will lead to a lower sale price, but at the same time will place the entire risk of malfunctioning or dissatisfaction on the customer. Maximizing the level of acceptance of the product by allowing warranty returns for unlimited time is also an unjustified policy from the producer's point of view, because it could lead to substantial financial losses. A high-quality warranty policy provides a balance between these two extremes. The balance is based on the evaluation of the two risks – the risk of malfunctioning and the risk of misunderstanding.

Definition 4. From client's point of view, the quality of a mixed warranty policy W_p, is identified by the "balanced" value of the "warranty parameter" that provides the best support for the client's correct purchase decision and the level of uncertainty it allows in supporting client's correct purchase decision.

Definition 4. From client's point of view, a mixed warranty policy W_p is of high (optimal) quality, if the "balanced" value of the "warranty parameter" is maximal and the level of uncertainty it allows in supporting client's correct purchase decision is minimal.

Selection of the warranty periods t^R and t^M from producers' point of view is regarding by the proportion of optimists in the clients' group, the level of their risk of misinforming, and the level of corresponding information asymmetry (see Part 2). The second warranty parameter t^R represents the warranty coverage related to malfunctioning of the product. Selection of its "best" value is based on the evaluation of the lengths of the following three (well-known in product reliability studies) sub-periods within the product's lifetime – the period of decreasing failure rate, the period of a normal performance and the period of increasing failure rate because of aging. The warranty period t^R has to cover the period of decreasing failure rate and expire before the beginning of the increasing failure rate period. Due to the fact that the promotional strength of the warranty policy is proportional to the length of t^R, the aim is to maximize t^R.

Discussion

There are several important reasons for the manufacturer to cover his products with a warranty of misinforming along, of course, with the usual warranty of malfunctioning. For example:

- It is well known that even only one dissatisfied client has a much higher negative impact on the producers' reputation compared the positive impact coming from many satisfied clients. For example, usually while selecting a product, say from Amazon.com, one reads carefully all negative reviews, so we become aware of the drawbacks of the product. Often one strong, well-written negative review could affect our purchase decision. It is reassuring for the clients to see that the product is covered by warranty of misinforming in case that they have picked the "wrong" for their need product. This warranty conveys the manufacturer willingness to share with the client the risk of "wrong" purchase decision and reinforces his firm standing by the strength and quality of his product.
- The warranty of misinforming has a positive impact on the sales process. It stimulates purchases of the product by clients that are uncertain in their ability to read the information message related to the product. Also, it contributes for a positive purchase decision of clients that are not entirely sure what they need the product for, i.e., they have not completely identified the set of their works $A_j=\{a_{ij}\}$, $i=1,2,\ldots,I_j$.
- The finite warranty period t^M of the warranty of misinforming protects the manufacturer from unreasonable claims related to products used for a long time. It provides a reasonable time to explore the features of the product and eliminates client dissatisfaction due to a possible misunderstanding of product capabilities but prevents the misuse of warranty for unjustified free replacement or returns of the product for unlimited time period.

QUALITY COMPARISON BETWEEN THE MIXED AND PURE WARRANTIES (CLIENT'S VIEWPOINT)

When making a purchase decision, the client usually trades off between the following two warranty-related arguments:

- Is the product life cycle long enough? This question is linked to the reliability of the product. The warranty of malfunctioning provides a message related to this question – the longer the warranty of malfunctioning is, the longer the product will preserve its value to the user. Such a message supports decisions regarding the expectation of long enough usage of the product.
- Is the product suitable for my needs? This question is related to the level of informing during the sale process. The warranty of misinforming encourages clients to examine the product with reduced risk of making a wrong purchase decision.

Let us denote, from client's b_j point of view, the measure of importance of the two warranty parameters by $V_b(q^b,m^b)$, where $0\leq q^b \leq 1$ is the measure of importance for the reliability parameter and $0\leq m^b \leq 1$ is the measure of importance for the parameter of misinforming. Let assume also that

$$q^b + m^b = 1, \quad (1)$$

i.e., we assume that only these two parameters will influence the client's purchase decision. Another way of looking at (1) is to say that we have imposed a probability distribution on the two warranty parameters.

One possible way of quantifying the quality of a warranty policy $W_p=\{t^R,t^M\}$ is by assessing how the warranty parameters t^R and t^M support the clients in making a correct purchase decision. An incorrect purchase decision is also unfavorable to the producer/seller, i.e., it increases the warranty servicing cost. This assumption is reasonable because, firstly, the client may not be "fully satisfied" and seek reimbursement and secondly, s/he may use the product for solving problems the product is not suitable for, which may result in misuse and failure of the product.

Let us denote the set of the warranty parameters by $w:=(t^R,t^M)$. So, we have a discrete random variable w, which represents the "warranty parameter" with a set of possible values $w:=(t^R,t^M)$ and distribution $V_b(q^b,m^b)$.

The following interpretation of the expected value $E(w)$ and the standard deviation of $\sigma(w)$ is possible:

- the expected value $E(w)=t^M.q^b+t^R.m^b$ represents the "balanced" value of the "warranty parameter" that provides the best support for the client's correct purchase decision. From client's point of view, the "balanced" value $E(w)$ integrates fully the importance of the two warranty aspects – malfunctioning and misinforming. Moreover, increasing the value of the balanced warranty parameter increases the quality of the warranty policy.
- the standard deviation $Var(w)=(t^M-E(w))^2.q^b+(t^R-E(w))^2.m^b$ represents the possible error (or deviation) from the best "balanced" value of the warranty parameter. We interpret this deviation as a measure of uncertainty allowed by the policy in supporting the client's correct purchase decision. Decreasing the value of this uncertainty increases the quality of the warranty policy.

Therefore, in comparing warranty policies, we may assess their quality by comparing their balanced warranty parameters and the measures of uncertainty they allow in supporting a client's correct purchase decision. From the client's viewpoint, the warranty strategy with the largest balanced warranty parameter and the smallest measure of uncertainty is the one with the highest quality. Sometime, in order to identify the best quality warranty policy, a compromise between these two criteria is needed.

Let us compare the expectation of w for the three cases – the two pure warranty strategies and the mixed one. We will obtain:

- For the pure warranty of malfunctioning, $W_p=\{1,0\}$, we compute that the expected value is

$E(w) = 1x0.5 + 0x0.5 = 0.5$,

or the warranty policy supports about 50% on average the correct decision of the clients. The variance is equal to

$$Var(w) = \frac{(1.0-0.5)^2 + (0.0-0.5)^2}{2} = 0.25;$$

- For the pure warranty of misinforming, $W_p=\{0,1\}$, the expected value is

$E(w) = 0x0.5 + 1x0.5 = 0.5$

or the warranty policy supports about 50% on average the correct decision of the clients. The variance is equal to

$$Var(w) = \frac{(0.0-0.5)^2 + (1.0-0.5)^2}{2} = 0.25;$$

- For the mixed warranty $W_p=\{0.5,0.5\}$, the expected value is equal to

$E(w) = 0.5x0.5 + 0.5x0.5 = 0.5$,

or the warranty policy supports also about 50% on average the correct decision of the clients. In this case the variance is equal to

$$Var(w) = \frac{(0.5-0.5)^2 + (0.5-0.5)^2}{2} = 0.0$$

but the uncertainty of the decisions is equal to zero.

This simple example provides an intuitive illustration for the motivation behind the above definitions of quality of warranty policy. Depending on the length of the warranty periods related to malfunctioning and misinforming, both parameters – expectation and variation – must be considered to distinguish the quality of different policies.

ASSESSMENT OF THE WARRANTY POLICY PARAMETERS

The two parameters in a mixed warranty policy $W_p=\{t^R,t^M\}$, represent the warranty coverage with respects of two different risks.

How to select the "best" values of t^R and t^M from producer's point of view?

First, we will consider selection of t^M. Figure 1 represents the clients' (assuming optimist) learning curve during the warranty (trial) period. The trial period starts with an initial level of certainty, $\hat{p}$, on whether the product is suitable for accomplishing his/her expected works and satisfies client's needs. The assessment of $\hat{p}$ is subjectively made by the client at the time of making the purchase decision based on provided information. During the trial period, the client's knowledge regarding the actual feature/capabilities of the product regarding the works and to satisfy client's needs approaches the real, objective capability of the product, which is estimated to be equal to p. The learning time t is proportional to the level of information asymmetry ia, which is defined (see Christozov D., Chukova S., Mateev P. (2007)) as $ia = abs\left(\hat{p} - p\right)$. Obviously, the larger the information asymmetry is the longer learning time is needed. The shapes of the learning curves of different clients could be similar in approaching p. The time to reach complete understanding regarding the suitability of the product depends on the value of the information asymmetry and efforts invested in learning.

In the case of a wrong decision, made by an optimist, i.e., $p < q < \hat{p}$, learning means that the assessment regarding capability of the product decreases and crosses the level of acceptance q (as illustrated on Fig. 4.2.1) at time t_c. This shape of the learning curves represents our understanding that learning is a logarithmic function on time. For more on the definition/estimation of the level of acceptance q see Chapter 2.3. At time t_c, due to the dissatisfaction with the product performance, the client may decide to make a claim against the product. The trial period should be long enough to allow the client to make a claim at time t_c. For this type of client extending the trial period will support their purchase decision.

In the case of a client, who is an optimist, but who made a correct decision, i.e., $q < p < \hat{p}$, as well as for all other types of clients - pessimists and realists – extending the trial period will lead only to extra time of using the product potentially for free and the warranty servicing cost may be unnecessary increased.

In general, the parameter t^M has to be selected according to the proportion of optimists in the clients' population, the level of their risk of misinforming, and the level of corresponding information asymmetry.

Figure 1. The optimists' learning curve during the trial period

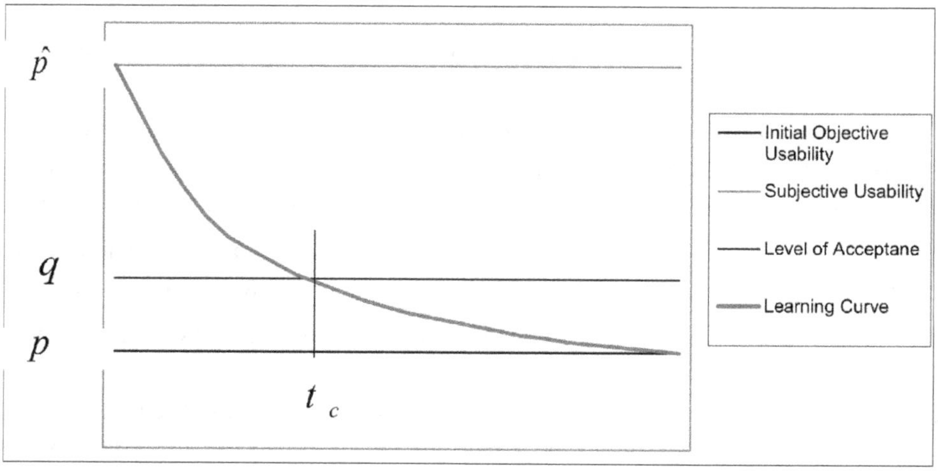

The second parameter t^R represents the warranty coverage related to malfunctioning of the product. It is based on the evaluation of the length of the three sub-periods within the product's life cycle:

- Decreasing Failure Rate sub-period (DFR) - early failures due to manufacturing defects, (infant mortality).
- The sub-period of a constant failure rate.
- Increasing Failure Rate sub-period (IFR) – failures caused by product's increasing age, consumption, or use.

A typical curve representing the three periods of failure rate is shown on Figure 2. The parameter t^R definitely has to cover the DFR sub-period or $t^R>t_0$ and in addition it should be a such that the inequality $t^R<t_1$ is valid. The failure rate in the interval

$[t_0,t_1]$ is a constant and the warranty cost will be proportional to its length. So overall, we would like to minimize the length of t^R. On the other hand, the promotional value of the warranty policy is also proportional to the length of t^R and we would like to maximize this value, which is equivalent of maximizing t^R. For example, selecting $t^R = t_1$ may give certain competitive advantages. Therefore, it is essential to find a value of t^R that assures the best balance between these two opposite trends.

Figure 2. Malfunctioning failure rate function over product's life cycle

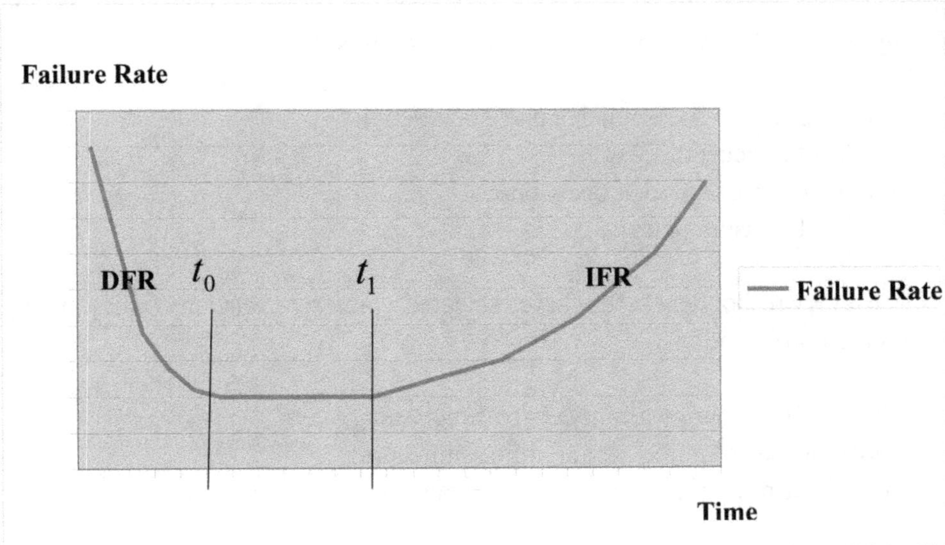

Onwards, we will assume that the "best" value of t^R is known. Further comments on the issue of selecting t^R are given in our concluding remarks and it is not among the main objectives of this book.

In addition, the determination of the parameter of misinforming warranty t^M one need a careful study of clients' population and their risk of misinforming. Next the measures of the risk of misinforming are used to identify the notion of the "quality" of a warranty policy from producer's point of view. To illustrate the ideas are using an example drawn from an empirical study (see Attachment 2 for surveys used throughout the study).

QUALITY OF WARRANTY POLICY AS A FUNCTION OF THE RISK OF MISINFORMING

To illustrate a way allowing to assess the quality a warranty policy one of the two data sets collected in a survey conducted at Victoria University of Wellington, Wellington, New Zealand in 2006 (see Attachment 2) are used. The data includes the feedback of the group of respondents who had a choice between three possible warranty strategies. This sample set consists of 54 data points, students responded to the survey. The survey was designed and conducted to collect information regarding warranty related parameters, utilized by a client in his/her purchasing decision making process. We were interested on the responses regarding:

- the needs n_{ij} for accomplish a particular activity.
- the level of acceptance q_{ij}.
- the indicator of a wrong decision r_{ij};
- the level of asymmetry ia_{ij}.

Also, every respondent in the survey selected a preferred warranty policy among the three possible options:

- three years of pure warranty of malfunctioning.
- three months of pure warranty of misinforming.
- mixed warranty with parameters t^R = one year and t^M = one month.

We use the survey information and consider the following cases, summarized in Table 1., $W_i(t^R,t^M)$ denotes the warranty policy for clients with risk level i, where $i = \{low, medium, high\}$.

Table 1. Options of warranty policies in the 2006 survey

		Correctness of the purchase decision		
		Low risk	**Medium risk**	**High risk**
		$r_j > r_u$	$r_l \leq r_j \leq r_u$	$r_j < r_l$
Preferred warranty policy	$W_p(36,0)$	$W_l(36,0)$	$W_m(36,0)$	$W_h(36,0)$
	$W_p(0,3)$	$W_l(0,3)$	$W_m(0,3)$	$W_h(0,3)$
	$W_p(12,1)$	$W_l(12,1)$	$W_m(12,1)$	$W_h(12,1)$

In Table 1, r_j denotes measures of the risk of misinforming as defined in Chapter 2. The values of the bounds of the risk of misinforming – the lower bound r_l and the upper bound r_u – are selected in a way to represent suitably of this risk for the respondents.

The ratios of respondents falling in each of the above nine categories will allow us to assess the quality of the warranty policy with respect to each particular target group. The average adjusted risk for the group of 54 respondents was evaluated at 0.296. Within this group the minimum computed risk was 0.030 and the maximum computed risk was equal to 0.573. We consider the range [0, 0.6] of the risk, and define the lower and upper bounds uniformly across the range as r_l=0.2 and r_u=0.4. Using the survey data and the selected values for the risk boundaries, results for estimated entries as of Table 4.2.1 are presented in Table 2.

Table 2. Summary of warranty related data, according 2006 survey

		Correctness of the purchase decision							
		Low risk		Medium risk		High risk		Total	
		r_j<0.2		0.2$_l$≤ r_j ≤0.4		r_j>0.4			
		No	%	No	%	No	%	No	%
Preferred warranty policy	W_p(36,0)	7	20.5	19	56.0	8	23.5	34	63.0
	W_p(0,3)	0	0.0	0	0	1	100.0	1	2.0
	W_p(12,1)	6	31.6	12	63.2	1	5.2	19	35.0
	Total	13	24.0	31	57.4	10	18.6	54	100

Table 2 shows that for 34 of the respondents, the corresponding distribution of importance is V_a(1,0) and they selected W_p(36,0). For one of the respondents, who selected W_p(0,3), the corresponding distribution of importance is V_a(0,1) and for the remaining 19 respondents, who selected the mixed warranty strategy W_p(12,1), we assume that the corresponding distribution of importance is V_a(0.5,0.5). Based on this information, using the approach sketched above, the quality of the warranty strategies, from client's point of view, could be evaluated.

The group of respondents is dominated by the sub-group of optimists – they are 38 out of 54 and the average risk of misinforming for this group is 0.337. This value is close to the upper bound of the medium level risk range. The other two sub-groups of respondents are the sub-group of pessimists – 4 out of 54, with the average risk of misinforming 0.311; and the sub-group of realists – 12 out of 54, with the average risk of misinforming 0.159. The average value of information asymmetry for the whole group is 0.19, with information asymmetry computed only for the sub-group of optimists equal to 0.24.

To assess the quality of the three warranty policies, from producer point of view, we will apply the following criteria:

1. Assess whether the policy supports clients' purchase decision making process. Looking at the above data, we may consider that the pure strategy $W_p(0,3)$ serves less than two percent of the population in their decision-making process. Obviously, this strategy cannot meet this quality criterion. The two other strategies – $W_p(36,0)$ and $W_p(12,1)$ – are supporting decision of significant number of respondents.
2. Assess the effect of the offered warranty on the reputation of the seller. The cost of misinforming on the reputation of the seller/producer with the first pure warranty strategy is defined as the proportion of unsatisfied clients who cannot claim full reimbursement on their product. For the above data, only 20% of clients would be "fully satisfied" (low risk), 56% will experience medium dissatisfaction and 23% will be extremely disappointed by their purchase. Therefore, nearly 80% of the customers will experience significant dissatisfaction, which may have a considerable negative impact on the reputation of the seller. Thus, the pure strategy $W_p(36,0)$ cannot be considered as a high-quality warranty policy.

Based on the above discussion, we may conclude that the data obtained in our empirical study supports our intuition that the mixed warranty policy is of higher quality, from the producer's point of view, than the two pure warranty policies. At least for the given population, dominated by optimists.

CONCLUSION

This chapter discusses ideas on the design of a composite warranty policy, combining coverage of malfunctioning and misinforming risks.

Nowadays, the awareness of the role of information in companies' operation management is one of the major criteria in assessing companies' effectiveness. All inward and outward information flows regarding the company's production (or services) impact significantly on the overall business performance. These flows are closely monitored by the information managers. Also, a rational attitude toward the warranty of misinforming, not only as a tool for promotion, but also as a product attribute that affects the overall business performance is necessary. This rational approach toward the warranty of misinforming will include the assessment of appropriate cause-and-effect relationships, estimating related costs, cash flow planning, etc. Also, this rational attitude will require a systematic approach for collecting, processing, and exploring data regarding the design and dissemination of the outward information and its impact on the receivers / customers, or its interpretation and implementation in practice. Setting up such an information monitoring system can be considered, according to Gartner's EIM classification (see Newman D., Logan D. 2008), as an indicator of moving from reactive to proactive stage of company's maturity. This type of information monitoring system is not a by-product of the "naturally" created and collected data within different departments of the company. Its design and implementation require the launching of special monitoring tools and development of special data processing procedures.

An early model for identifying the notion of "quality of a warranty policy" is proposed for mixed warranty contracts, to combine the effect of warranty of malfunctioning and warranty of misinforming. The quality of a warranty policy is considered from two different viewpoints: client's viewpoint and producer's point of view. This study is more at conceptual level attempting to identify the concept of "quality" of a warranty policy and to define approaches and criteria to measure and compare different policies and to open discussion on rational assessment and management.

REFERENCES

Christozov, D., Chukova, S., & Mateev, P. (2006). A Measure of Risk Caused by Information Asymmetry in e-Commerce. *Journal of Issues in Informing Science and Information Technology*, *3*, 147–158. doi:10.28945/879

Christozov, D., Chukova, S., & Mateev, P. (2007). On the Relationship between Warranty and the Risk of Information Asymmetry. *Journal of Issues in Informing Science and Information Technology*, *4*, 235–249. doi:10.28945/946

Christozov, D., Chukova, S., & Mateev, P. (2008). Warranty and the Risk of Misinforming: Evaluation of the Degree of Acceptance. *Journal of Issues in Informing Science and Information Technology*, *5*, 667–677. doi:10.28945/1035

Christozov, D., Chukova, S., & Mateev, P. (2010). Assessment of Quality of Warranty Policy. *Interdisciplinary Journal of Information, Knowledge, and Management*, *5*, 62–72.

Newman, D., & Logan, D. (2008). *Gartner Introduces the EIM Maturity Model.* Semantic Scholar. https://www.semanticscholar.org/paper/Gartner-Introduces-the-EIM-Maturity-Model-Newman-Logan/ca3b13f65a37d7b0a4428789971 0112e2c5afc4e

Chapter 18
Warranty of Misinforming as an Option in Product Utilization Process

ABSTRACT

The option is a term used in finance to mark a buyer's right, but not obligation, to acquire a product or service in preliminary agreed conditions. The chapter views the warranty of misinforming as an option, by offering the client rights to return the product after given period for utilization. The warranty of misinforming provides rights but not obligations of the client to use the service. As in the options of finance, the client needs to pay for the right to use the service in the future.

"Trial and error is freedom." -N. Taleb, Antifragile, p.246

INTRODUCTION

The following definition of "option" is given in Wikipedia - "In finance, an option is a contract, which gives the buyer (the owner or holder) the right, but not the obligation, to buy or sell an underlying asset or instrument at a specified strike price on or before a specified date, depending on the form of the option." Option as a risk management (mitigation) tool is broadly used in finance and trades. At the same time, it introduces asymmetry in the sense that, probabilistically, it limits the level

DOI: 10.4018/978-1-6684-8800-3.ch018

of losses (e.g., the price of the option) and allows for unlimited gains. In the market for sophisticated devices (as smart phones, tablets, etc.), where technologies are rapidly advancing, customers usually do not have the experience to use all features of the device at the time of the purchase. Due to the lack of appropriate expertise, the risk of misinforming leading to not purchasing the "right" device is high but given enough time to learn the capabilities of the device and map these to the needs and works that device will be used for, could provide the client with substantial long-term benefits. Warranty of misinforming is a mechanism that provides the client with the opportunity to explore the device and master its features under limited risk of financial losses. Thus, the warranty of misinforming could be considered as an option - the customers buy it (at a fixed cost) and may gain (theoretically) unlimited benefit by realizing (within the terms of warranty) that the device can be used to solve variety of problems not envisaged at the purchase time. This chapter is dedicated to discussion on the idea of treating the warranty of misinforming as an option in a similar manner as in finances. The chapter presents ideas, developed in Christozov D., Chukova S., Mateev P. (2016).

The market for complex, technologically advanced, devices is growing quickly offering many challenges to all involved parties. The major challenge is that many new features are included in the next generation devices and these new devices show up on the market almost on a daily basis. This quick turnaround does not allow the customers to learn how to fully utilize the device's built-in features. Additionally, smart devices allow an easy extension of their capabilities by adding a variety of on-line applications.

The circumstances in the nowadays market of technological products, but not only, as described above significantly affect the risk of misinforming by increasing the likelihood of becoming disappointed by a purchasing in long or even short-term. Usually, at the time of purchase the seller is not familiar with the problems, works, or activities the customers aim to solve or accomplish with the device and therefore is not able to provide comprehensive advice. Also, the advertising message cannot cover the variety of cases of how to use the device and what is possible to accomplish by adding additional applications. The customer must gain experience of using the device on his or her own and by mapping its features to the problems s/he faces. Also, often it is difficult to realize that a newly encountered problems can be addressed with the same device and the customer has not been aware of this possibility at the time of the purchase, and, of course, s/he doesn't include those problem in her/his purchasing motivation and selection criteria regarding the product's property.

This shows that there might also be some positive outcomes of misinforming. Smart phones can be used as a GPS navigator, which represents such an option adding positive effect to original motivation to purchase it. When it comes to such positive outcomes, the information asymmetry between the seller and buyer is not critical for quantifying the risk of misinforming, and moreover the information asymmetry cannot be reduced by improving the communication process between these two parties. In addition, even clients' training on original usage of the product would not necessarily reveal the hidden potential of the product and reduce the misinforming. The full benefit of the device for a particular client is usually understood, often by chance, via trials and errors and it is highly dependent on client's ability to adopt quickly the incoming technical advances for the device.

Nowadays the purchase decisions must incorporate a new source of uncertainty. Whether to buy a more advanced and expensive device, or to limit the purchase to a device that will allow accomplishing only the set of activities, as identified at the time of purchase?

In other words, the client is facing the following dilemma: buying a low-price device with limited opportunity for extra future benefits Vs. paying a higher price for a device with unknown potential benefits. This is a typical scenario that motivates buying options in trade and finance.

A Case to Illustrate the Use of Warranty of Misinforming as an Option

To illustrate the idea of considering the warranty of misinforming as an option, let us explore the case of buying a smart phone. The initial objectives, according to the originally identified needs, are to obtain a device which will allow the client to make calls and to exchange text messages. The customer has many options, from relatively cheap to extremely expensive devices, which allow him/her to accomplish these works. Let us also assume that the price corresponds to the device's properties (for example, the size of the screen). After buying a smart phone, the client discovers that there is a huge set of applications, developed by various vendors, available on-line. Installing an appropriate application enriches the device's capability to address different sets of problems. Let us assume that the customer has installed an application which allows for the smart phone to be used as a GPS navigation system and that the business of the client includes driving to unknown areas for delivering goods. The new navigation system will increase the client's productivity by decreasing the time needed to locate the required destinations. Unfortunately, the client realizes that s/he bought not the best device to address this newly identified usage, because the device's screen is too small. At the purchase time the screen was chosen according to the initially recognized needs (see the cartoon on Figure 1.) and the newly added objective of using it for "navigation" was not taken into account.

Figure 1. Smartphone jobs
(Downloaded from: http://fastler.net/p/0q1)

Typically, the warranty of misinforming provides the client with a "free" trial period for familiarizing himself/herself with the device. The price client pays for this "free" trial period is the charge for the warranty and the time spent learning the features and capabilities of the device. In the case of a smart device, its capabilities can be supplemented by apps and add-ins produced by a huge number of vendors. Obviously, the primary producer of the device is not in a position to comprehensively "inform" the clients about all these additional capabilities in the context of an individual's way of using the device. Moreover, at the purchase time even the client does not know what the most beneficial usage of the devices will be. In the above example, the navigation property of a smart phone turned out to be very beneficial for our specific customer. This additional utility of the device has been discovered by learning and installing an appropriate additional application well after the initial purchasing decision is made.

Therefore, purchasing a warranty of misinforming for a device could be considered to be equivalent to purchasing an option in financial context. One may decide to purchase more complex and technically advanced device with better properties and higher quality (e.g., larger screen) and to explore it during the trial period, so, to learn whether it can be beneficial for accomplishing works beyond the originally recognized set of activities. In the example above "the navigation" is an extra activity, beyond the initial set of "making calls and exchanging text messages".

WARRANTY OF MISINFORMING AS ANALOGUE TO THE "OPTION" IN FINANCE WITHIN PRODUCT'S UTILIZATION PROCESS

The warranty of misinforming could be interpreted as an analogue of the "option" as used in finance. At the time of purchasing the product it provides the buyer with the opportunity of trying and experimenting with the device with low-risk conditions. Or warranty of misinforming ensures some opportunities regarding the possibility to extend the usability of the device. The cost of this "option" is the learning time – time spent in exploring the device, plus the cost of purchasing the warranty. Depending on the warranty policy the later cost might be refundable or ignored.

"The warranty of misinforming" is understood here as the tool providing the client a "risk free" period to verify the usefulness of received information, as well as how the received information is understood, within the context of buyer's own faced problems. The warranty of misinforming is especially applicable within a commercial Selling-Buying transaction in acquiring a new product.

This study maps the option's risk mitigation principles to warranty as a form of mitigation the risk of misinforming. The chapter explores the specific properties of warranty of misinforming when considered it as an analogue of the option in finance. In general, we elaborate on the following idea: the warranty of misinforming for a smart device has pre-specified limited cost, but advanced utilization of the device may bring unlimited potential benefit.

Next section discusses the misinforming hazard in its both aspects – negative and positive, emphasizing the positive impact it may offer. Comparing with the "option" in finance the analogue is made according to existence of asymmetry in both circumstances.

The section "Model" maps warranty of misinforming as an option to risk of misinforming, discussing the sources of costs and benefits, and relate the properties of this concept to the properties of this risk identified in Chapter 2.

Further, we discuss the case of "warranty of misinforming" as an option from several different aspects. It is well known that the clients' major benefit from this warranty is the opportunity to study the features of the device with no or low risk. In addition, the learning opportunities are not limited only to the properties of the given device, but extend to mapping the client's problems or needs to solutions enhanced by the available technical advances for the device, e.g., apps, add-ins, etc. Offering of such learning opportunities is the main effect of positive misinforming: firstly, the buyer underestimates the potential of the device, and secondly, while the buyer utilizes the product to solve his/her initially recognized set of problems, s/he realizes that the product – the smart device – is suitable to address problems of larger scale than initially thought but may need a device with a bit different property.

Considering warranty of misinforming as an option enriches the understanding of this business practice as a factor for enhancing informing quality not only by reducing the negative aspects of misinterpretation, but also by serving as a learning tool for acquiring more comprehensive understanding of the meaning and impact of provided message. The misinforming hazard, viewed from this perspective, has a positive impact on buyers.

OPTIONS - RISK ASYMMETRY: POSITIVE VS. NEGATIVE MISINFORMING

Due to misinforming, it is possible that the client buys a product with much richer set of functionalities and/or properties with usage opportunities that go well beyond the initial set of problems intended to be solved with the product. In many cases, this happens because of misunderstanding of applicability of the product as described to the buyer's needs. Often a buyer is purchasing a product with propertied extended the originally assumed as the minimally acceptable, because of inability to exactly judge about it. The benefit of this positive aspect of the information asymmetry reveals itself during the learning process in the utilization phase of product adoption. One can buy a product to address a set of particular, originally identified, needs, but it may turn out (during the product adoption) that the product is suitable for solving a set of client's additional advanced problems, not even considered initially. The client was not aware of these additional, advanced problems at the time of purchasing, or the client was not aware that these types of problems can be solved by using the same device – overall, the benefit from product's full utilization may dramatically exceed (theoretically/potentially unlimited) the initial expectations for the product, which motivate for the positive purchase decision.

Option, as a tool to mitigate the market risks, has the following important property – it is risk asymmetric – a fixed loss, which is the price to purchase the option and (theoretically/potentially) unlimited gain. The potential gain, in case of misinforming, requires learning by trying and experimenting. Also, it requires expertise or wisdom to recognize that a given problem can be solved with a particular device, or a device from the same category of products. Even more, if the problem cannot be solved with the available device - what type of device, or what are the properties of a device that are needed to target the problem successfully.

Taleb, 2014, p. 190: "...all we need is the ability to accept that what we have on our hands is better than what we had before—in other words, to recognize the existence of the option (or "exercise the option" as people say in the business, that is, take advantage of a valuable alternative that is superior to what precedes it, with a certain gain from switching from one into the other, the only part of the process where rationality is required). And from the history of technology, this ability to use the option given to us by antifragility is not guaranteed: things can be looking at us for a long time."

Taleb, 2014, p. 192 continuous: "Trial and error has one overriding value people fail to understand: it is not really random, rather, thanks to optionality, it requires some rationality. One needs to be intelligent in recognizing the favorable outcome and knowing what to discard." Taleb (2014), p. 246 concludes: "Trial and error is freedom."

The warranty of misinforming provides risk free trial and error period and encourages exploring and discovering product's capabilities.

THE MODEL

The model of warranty of misinforming as an option, presented here, extended notations as presented in Part 2. The model describes relationship between the following categories (entities):

- Product

A product $d \in D$ (device) is described by a set of properties, $P=\{\{p_i, v_i\}, i=1,2,\ldots,k\}$, where every property is described by a pair p_i – the name of the property, and v_i

–descriptor – a numerical value describes the property. For example, the property "screen size" is presented as {"screen size", 5 inches}. *D* is the category of similar devices that can be used to perform the same or similar set of functions.

- Client

A client or buyer *b*∈*B* is described by a set of her or his needs *N*, s/he intends to solve or accomplish by using a product of a particular type. This set of needs motivates the client to buy the product *D*, which provides the best option in satisfying her/his needs:

- The purchase of the product *d*∈*D* has been motivated by the initial set of needs $N_0(A_b)$ – a set of problems or works the client *b* faces and wants to acquire a device or other product, that will allow her or him to satisfy those needs. To accomplish her/his works, the product must possess a set of properties $P^b_{N_0} = \{\{p_i, v_i\}, i = 1, \dots k^b_{N_0}\}$, that satisfy the minimal level of acceptance (quality) $Q^b_{N_0} = \left\{\left\{p_i, q_i^{min}\right\}, i = 1, \dots, k^b_{N_0}\right\}$. (Example: If the client needs a phone to make calls and to send/receive SMS: (1) the property "screen size" is relevant, and (2) the minimal level of acceptance - the minimal value of the property "screen size" - is 2 inches.)
- After the purchase of the product, a trial period starts and the set of needs evolves, so that they became N_t after a trial period of length *t*. The set N_t is an extended set of problems or works, identified by the client during the trial period, that are (1) recognized as needed and (2) potentially solvable with a product of the given type. The works of the set N_t are not necessarily solvable with the already purchased product, because the values of its properties do not satisfy the quality requirements (minimal acceptance levels) of the newly identified or updated needs. For example: the purchased smart phone allows for navigation via GPS, but to make practical use of it, the property – screen size – must be at least 5", whereas the purchased product has a screen size of 2".

Add-In Applications

Consider the set of applications $Ap = \left\{\left\{a_j, P^{a_j}, Q^{a_j}\right\}, j = 1, 2, \dots n\right\}$ which includes additional software tools (not provided by the producer at the time of purchasing), developed by different vendors, that are available on-line by producer's store and can be installed on the product to enrich its usability. Where a_j is the activity or work, the application is developed for; P^{a_j} is the set of properties of the device that are required to install and use the application; and Q^{a_j} is the set of minimal values required for these properties.

Suppose that an application *a*∈*Ap* requires a set of properties of the product $P^a = \left\{ p_i^a, v_i^a \right\}$ with qualities $Q^a = \left\{ p_i^a, v_i^a \geq q_i^{min} \right\}$. For applications, quality means the level of usability expressed by the property value. (For example: On a smart phone with 2 inches screen one can run navigation software, but its practical use while driving speed is very low – let us say only in 10% of cases. For the same smart phone, but with 5 inches screen, the usability could be much higher – say in 90% of cases.)

Process

The process would follow two phases, first purchasing and second – traying and learning, as shown in Figure 2. below. It is an illustration of the process of learning and can be elaborated as the follows:

First phase – purchasing: The purchasing decision is made according to N_0. We make the following assumptions:

- Assumption 1: the price of the product resembles the product quality level, which represents the product properties, unrelated to a specific client,
- Assumption 2: the client tends to minimize the price, i.e., chooses a product that satisfies $Q_{N_0}^b$ on the minimal level of v_i of relevant properties.

The client makes decision based on subjective assessment of product's properties $\widehat{P_0}(d) = \widehat{P}(m(P_d))$, as understood by buyer's interpretation of $m(P_{db})$– the message describing the product as provided by the producer to promote purchasing.

Second phase – learning: The learning includes "trial and error" time during a period *t*. It is identified by the triple $\left(\widehat{P_t}, \widehat{A_t}, \widehat{N_t}\right)$ describing the newly obtained knowledge regarding own needs, including an extended set of activities, and also the properties of product that can satisfy them. This phase discovers what really (sort of) the product allows the client to do with it. This may require reassessing the set of relevant product properties and related levels of qualities - $\widehat{P_t(D)}$. Also, a subset $\widehat{A_t}$ of available applications *A* might be tested by the client during the trial period *t* and recognized as useful. This testing might result in adding problems or works that were not initially considered as appropriate to be attempted with the product of this category – $\widehat{N_t}$. During this phase, the client may learn about applications, which would require properties at a higher quality than currently available and adjust his/her purchasing criteria (for the above example: to gain full benefit from the navigation application, the size of a smart phone screen must be at least 5 inches).

Figure 2. Illustration of the process of learning

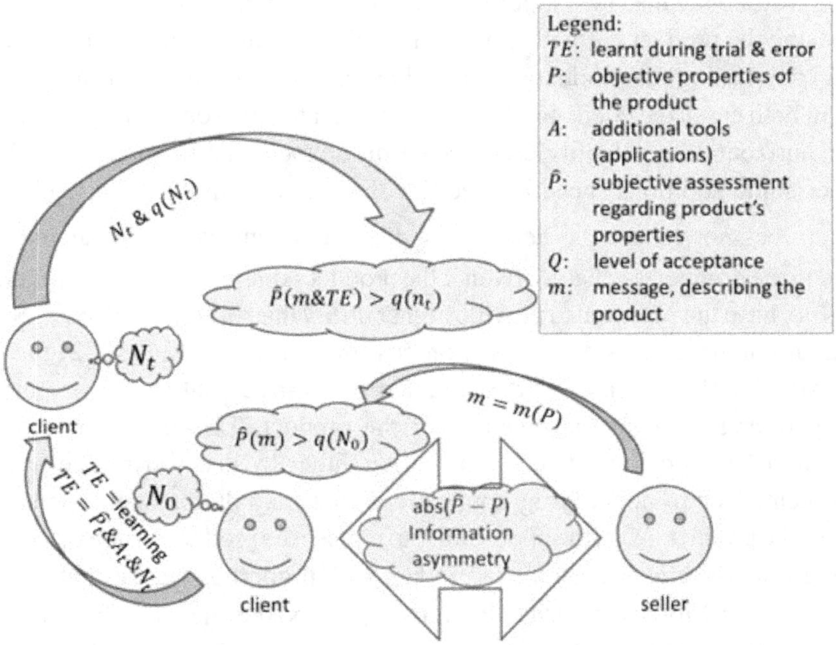

Utility

The benefit client b will obtain by using the product $d \in D$ to satisfy her/his needs is the value of his/her utility U_d^b.

The initial expected utility at the time of purchasing is

$$U_d^b(N_0) = U(N_0, D)$$

where $D = \min_{d \in D} \widehat{P}_0(D) > Q_{N_0}^b$ The purchase decision is based on selecting a product, with assumed minimal properties, corresponding to minimal price, that satisfies the initially needs and to ensure expected utility. This is illustrated in figure

4.3.3 by showing the relationship between utility and gained benefit. The optional (possible) utility at time *t*, which is at the end of the trial-and-error period (the learning phase), is

$$U_d^b(N_t) = U(N_t, P_t, A_t)$$

To illustrate the idea (see Figure 3.), let us consider the following two cases: (1) purchasing the product without applying the misinforming warranty (the blue line) and (2) purchasing the product with an additional misinforming warranty (the red line). In both cases the client purchases the product to gain some utility, represented by the horizontal line "Utility". The client may expect that the product will bring him/her some additional benefits (see the "Expected utility"). In case (1), if the product does not satisfy the needs ($P > \widehat{P_0}$), the client will be incurring losses related to the product purchased. Even if the product satisfies the initial expectations, it does not have the potential to provide higher utility than initially expected, because the client purchase decision is based on cost minimization. In case (2) the client pays extra for the warranty and is granted a risk-free trial-and-error period to investigate and discover the potential of the product. This may provide a very beneficial (theoretical/unlimited gain) option either by discovering the product's own potential or by identifying applications that may dramatically increase the utility of the product. Also, the opportunity to replace the product during the warranty period allows the client to acquire a product with properties that fits better her/his extended needs. Moreover, during the warranty period the client has the opportunity to adjust his/her understanding of what can be done with this type of product and what product properties are most valuable in aiming to fully utilize the product. In both cases, by purchasing a warranty of misinforming, the client de facto is purchasing an option, which may allow him/her to benefit beyond the initial expectations. The case of the second scenario the client has the right to alter and adjust her/his decision after a given trial, defined by warranty contract, period.

Figure 3. Illustration of the relationship between utility and gained benefit

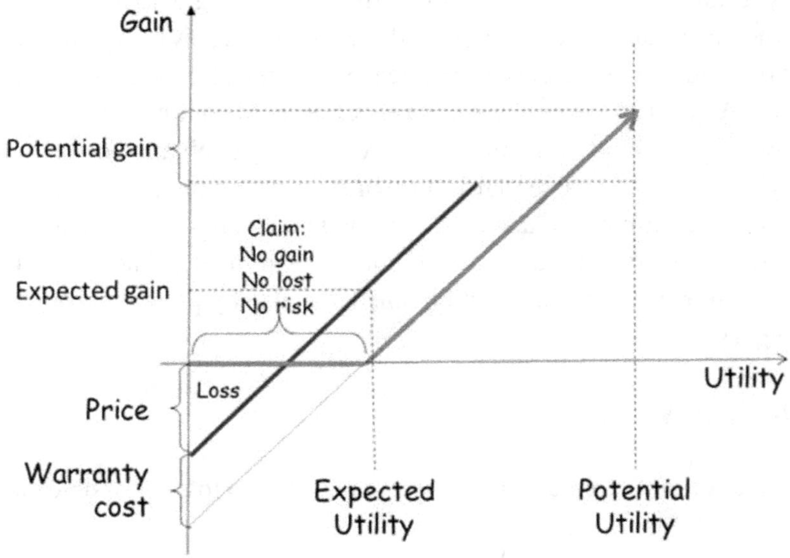

Investing in warranty of misinforming at the time of the product purchasing, will provide the client with a risk-free option to explore the extendable potential of the product including some of its increased properties and functionalities also by adding appropriate applications. The risk-free option to obtain and explore a higher quality product, due to the added applications, allows the client to determine her/his utility and fully benefit from the product. Theoretically this benefit/gain may be infinitely large.

DISCUSSION

In this discussion we address some open issues of the following three aspects of warranty of misinforming as an option:

(1) Utility – the objectives of a customer in obtaining a product, especially a smart device, always includes expectation for receiving some benefit. In principle, the actual benefit received becomes visible only after obtaining and experimenting with the product. Warranty of misinforming, represented as a slogan "if you are not fully satisfied - money back", originally addresses the case when obtained product doesn't bring the expected utility.

(2) Gain curves – acquiring the potential utility a product is able to provide may follow different processes of learning, including discovering of initially unknown product's properties, how these properties may bring value, and what are particular requirements, as physical parameters, for them to bring maximal value. As well as learning what is needed extra to gain maximal utility.
(3) Continue learning – is an ongoing process aiming to obtain the maximal value of given product is essential in utilizing a new product, especially a smart device. The learning includes enriching understanding of both what the product can do for the client, but also, and equally important, what utility the client may gain by using the product obtained and also by products from the given category.

Nominal Utility

The examination and exploration of the product may lead to two possible outcomes:

1. The product satisfies only the initial needs and does not show any potential for solving any additional problems during the period covered by the warranty of misinforming. Under this scenario, the client has two possible scenarios:
    - To claim the warranty and to replace the product with a cheaper one, which is suitable only for the initial needs N_0 – the case of further optimization of initial decision.
    - To keep the product, paying the margin between "optimal" product and the purchased one. The rationale of the second outcome is based on the following arguments: the limited trial time may not be long enough to identify fully the potential utility; the cost of the time and efforts to learn how to use the product is taken into account; and in addition, there is always a possibility that the product could turn out to be suitable for solving some extra problems that are not currently identified but could appear in the future.
2. The product shows potential to provide extra utility and it is not worth keeping it, but by exploring the warranty contract the client may acquire a higher range product that will allow her/him to benefit from solving an extended set of problems.

Variety of Gain Curves

The learning during the warranty period may progress in two directions answering to the following two questions:

- What are the properties of the product and how one can use the product, so that the properties are fully utilized?
- What are the additional problems or works in the costumer's domain area, such that the product is suitable to address them – identification of new problems to try to solve with the product. Learning may allow overcoming the initial bias regarding the suitability of the product. In this case the learning allows adjusting the client's initial understanding of the idea of what the "perfect" product is.

The actual gain of product utilization follows the learning progress and different learning curves may lead to different gain curves.

Importance of Learning

Learning progress is the main key in acquiring the utility, potentially embedded in the product. The learning is usually done through a trial-and-errors approach, because the customer has to learn how to use the product in order to address her/his own problems and to build her/his own skills and competences to use it. Some technical assistance during the learning period is not only possible, but desirable, but major efforts have to be invested by the client to avoid misleading, misinterpretation and, in general, misinforming.

CONCLUSION

In comparison with the classical use of options in finance and trade with the use of warranty of misinforming as an option, we can observe the following similarities and differences:

Similarities

- Options and warranty of misinforming provide the client with some rights, which can be exercised only under particular circumstances.
- To obtain these rights one has to invest some resources – the price of the option in finance and the prices of purchasing the warranty of misinforming.

Difference

- In the case of options in finance and trade, if the client decides not to use the option, s/he loses only the price paid for the option; in the case of warranty of misinforming the price, as a monetary value, is reimbursable, but the "value" obtained via investing time and efforts to explore the product – the knowledge, understanding, expertise, and even recognizing a set of additional problems of interest – remains as benefit to the client in extending her/his overall skills.
- In the case of options in finance and trade the market conditions are the same for all participants and everybody who bought the option gets the same benefit. The owners of an option either all will use it, or all will not use it. In the case of warranty of misinforming as an option, some clients may use it, and others may decide not to use it.
- In the case of options in finance and trade the market conditions are the same for all participants and everybody who bought the option gets the same benefit. In the case of warranty of misinforming as an option – the cost in monetary terms is the same for everybody, but the benefit is strictly individual to the particular client.

Having in mind all of the above, we believe that considering the warranty of misinforming as an option will provide some sound theoretical and practical background and a new research direction to study, in a more formal and deeper level, by addressing the warranty of misinforming using the well-developed methods and approaches employed for studying options in finance and trade.

Practical Implications

Understanding that,

- On one hand, the warranty of misinforming could address and remedy the negative aspects of the information asymmetry naturally affecting the communication process between sellers and buyers.
- On the other hand, the warranty of misinforming could have a positive impact on the seller–buyer relationship by providing some opportunities to expand the usefulness of the considered product. This aspect of the warranty may bring significant benefit also to the sellers.

Despite the financial uncertainties related to the warranty of misinforming, this new understanding of misinforming may encourage the sellers to provide and promote in their businesses the risks sharing mechanisms rooted in warranties.

Also, there are significant theoretical implications of the proposed work – more systematic analysis of the warranty of misinforming could be attempted by employing theoretical, well developed, and tested approaches and techniques from financial options.

REFERENCES

Christozov, D., Chukova, S., & Mateev, P. (2016). Warranty of Misinforming as an Option in Product Utilization Process. *Informing Science: the International Journal of Emerging Transdiscipline, 19.*

Taleb, N. (2014). *Antifragile: things that gain from disorder*. Random House Trade Paperback.

Chapter 19
The Role of Warranty of Misinforming for New Product Adoption

ABSTRACT

The utilization of a product is intended to highlight all possible forms of using the product. This is a learning process which results in reaching the stage of efficient and effective use of the product. In some cases, the learning may expose unsuitability of the product with acquired properties to perform some later identified benefits. A warranty for misinformation allows a replacement of the product on no cost and to increase its usability. The chapter considers the warranty of misinforming as a learning tool.

INTRODUCTION

The previous chapter presented the use of "warranty of misinforming" as an analogue of the role of "option" played in finance and trade. This section extended the idea of using it to promote learning during the process of adoption of a new product.

The current development of worldwide markets can be characterized by an increasing complexity and multi-functionality of their goods. Smart phones replaced the old-fashioned mobile devices, which very recently replaced the traditional land phones. Selection, purchasing and utilization of a new device are no longer simple, routine tasks. The increased product complexity requires relevant customer expertise to make proper use of modern devices. Research on consumers' behavior in adopting a new product is well presented in the literature in the last more than 50 years. The

DOI: 10.4018/978-1-6684-8800-3.ch019

adoption process of new products has attracted the attention of researchers, and it has been studied from different perspectives. The following are just a few examples of research addressing adoption. Eng & Quaia (2009) review the findings about new performance in the literature and conceptualize a framework and its related propositions for improving new product adoption process. Manchanda P. et al (2008) identified that the two main influences leading to adoption at the individual consumer level are marketing communication and interpersonal communication. Bhagat, S. et al (2012) presented a problem formulation to study the impact of user's experience (or projected experience) with a product in the adoption process. Sethi S.P. et al. (2008) proposed a model for new-product adoption that incorporates price and advertising effects. An optimal control problem that uses the model as its dynamics is solved explicitly to obtain the optimal price and advertising effort over time. Parry, M.E. et al (2011) dealt with forecasting the adoption of innovative products. They examined the usefulness of a probabilistic neural network algorithm for forecasting new product adoption success and compared their approach with the standard forecasting methods. Devos, J. et al (2012) consider the problem of small- and medium-sized enterprises with their lack of IT proficiency and dependence on external IT expertise, and the role of information asymmetry in the acquisition of strategic IT.

This chapter explores the role of warranty covering misinforming risk in consumer's adoption of a new product. The increased complexity and multi-functionality of the products lead to an increased level of information asymmetry during the purchasing process, which may mislead customers in making their purchase decision. Often, the customer buys a product, which he/she doesn't need or pays for product features that are not needed and will never be used. On the other hand, new devices provide not only challenges, but also opportunities for extending the set of problems the customer may wish to solve with. Nowadays, every purchase of a new product requires deciding under uncertainty.

The risk of misinforming is caused by the information asymmetry in interpreting the message describing the product's properties and usability. It is based on the inability of the customers to acquire complete, accurate, and sufficient understanding regarding the features and constraints of a new product in the context of her or his personal problem domain.

Here, the role of warranty of misinforming is considered in an "ideal" case, when the consumer optimizes the purchase decision led by rational assessment of her/his needs, product's price and some supplementary costs. Also, in this "ideal" case, the product's quality is positively correlated with the product's price. Under these assumptions, the role of warranty during product adoption process is discussed by addressing the following questions:

- What are the misinforming risks and how the warranty of misinforming may affect the adoption process?
- What is the adoption cost and how to optimize the adoption process based on this cost?

BASIC CONCEPTS OF NEW PRODUCT ADOPTION

New Product Adoption Process

The process of adoption of a new product includes two phases - acquiring and utilization, which can be further divided into a set of activities. The phase of acquiring of a new product, presented in terminology used in this book, includes the following stages:

a) Identification of the set of works the customer expected to accomplish with the product, including of the level of customer's needs.
b) Setting criteria for product acceptance, including the quality thresholds.
c) Collecting information regarding the alternative options on the market.
d) Selecting the most appropriate option.
e) Product purchasing.

The phase of the product utilization includes the following stages:

a) Learning how to accomplish the intended set of works with the new product. Acquiring skills to efficiently perform with the new product.
b) Learning what additional work can be accomplished with the new product.
c) Learning which works cannot be accomplished with the new product, or at least to not accomplish as expected.

During the first phase information asymmetry may cause misunderstanding of the actual properties of the product, which may lead to wrong purchase decisions in two aspects:

- To buy a product, which doesn't allow to accomplish the intended works and does not meet customer's needs.
- Not to buy a suitable for the customer's needs product.

The role of warranty in acquiring a new product was introduced in the previous chapters. The purchase decision is a tradeoff between the product's quality and the product's price. The natural assumption is that a higher quality means a higher probability that the product will address the customer's needs, but also implies higher product price.

During the utilization phase the customer learns how to use the new product. The risk in this phase is two-fold. Firstly, the customer may recognize that the product is not suitable for accomplishing all initially identified works and also the additional works identified in the process of adoption. Also, there are other products in the market that are more suitable, than the chosen one.

Informing Aspects of New Product Adoption: Misinforming

In general, the phases of the product adoption, as outlined above, are itself an informing process. The first phase can be considered as a process of learning via communication (talking to the seller, reading messages regarding the product, view demos, etc.) and the second phase – as learning via accumulating own experience while using the product, a process of learning via trials-and-errors. From this point of view, the second phase can be considered as a verification of what was learned during the first phase regarding the customer's needs and whether the selected product, as understood, is suitable for accomplishing needed works.

THE ROLE OF WARRANTY OF MISINFORMING IN THE PRODUCT ACQUIRING PROCESS

Success in the phase of acquiring a new product depends on the successful communication between sellers, offering their products, and buyers examining how suitable the product is for their needs. The buyer's decision is always influenced by the uncertainty regarding the product specifications as well as his/her "wish list" set of activities to accomplish by using the product. The buyer doesn't know exactly what additional opportunities the new product may offer, e.g., what additional works could be supported by the product and what product's "quality" properties will be needed for successful accomplishment of these new, unknown at the time of the purchase, works.

In the phase of new product acquiring, the initial four stages from a) to d) as listed above are influenced by information asymmetry as follows:

a) In the first stage, in order to identify her/his own needs, the customer have to be aware what is offered on the market and what activities those kinds of products can support. Identifying the own needs of a buyer is equivalent to matching the buyer's problems to products' specifications as described in the seller's advertisements.

b) During the second stage a set of criteria with corresponding quality thresholds are identified, so that the product which satisfies them is acceptable for the buyer. The successful completion of the second stage requires that the customer is able to understand most of the technical details regarding how his/her activities can be accomplished with the product. Identifying the acceptable price is among the important criteria for products' suitability.

c) The stage of collecting information regarding alternative options requires matching of the products' advertised specifications with the criteria of product suitability and selecting the options that satisfy the pre-specified "quality" thresholds. This is the stage of creating the "short list" of products for possible purchase.

d) Choosing the product which provides the best match for the set of buyer's product suitability criteria is equivalent to solving an optimization problem, which reflects the buyer's uncertainty in purchase decision making.

Quite often, the uncertainty in purchase decision making is not fully understood by the customers, because of disregarding the impact of misinforming hazards in obtaining and interpreting information. And, because the decision is motivated by such factors as emotion, fashion, or to follow "others", etc. – aspects of decision making not in the scope of the book, and not considered here. If the impact of information asymmetry, as resulted in inability to correct interpret the information, is disregarded, the risk of being misinformed is underestimated and often ignored in purchase decision making. In data collected in an empirical study conducted in 2006, published in Christozov, Chukova, Mateev (2007), among 65 respondents only 6 recognized their uncertainty of whether the product is suitable for their needs. The data revealed that the overall risk of making a wrong decision was above 40%.

A warranty of misinforming provides the customer with a risk-free trial period when an unsuitable product could be returned with no penalties. During this trial period the uncertainties regarding the suitability of the product can be resolved to some extent. The existence of warranty of misinforming allows the customers to choose the cheapest product from the "short list" of suitable products, and if it meets the customer's needs, then this purchase decision is the best (optimal) one from customer's viewpoint.

THE ROLE OF WARRANTY OF MISINFORMING IN THE PROCESS OF UTILIZATION OF A NEW PRODUCT

The process of learning about the actual properties and features of the newly acquired product and how this product can be efficiently utilized is usually quite lengthy. It includes consulting and reading about product specifications, but mostly it is a sequence of trials and errors while experimenting with the product. The goal of this process is to reduce uncertainty regarding usability of the acquired product and to gain skills and competences to how to use the device in executing its full potential in solving the problems user faces. During this phase there are two groups of activities and consequently two sources of risks:

- Learning how to accomplish initially identified works in an efficient manner with the new product. The discovery that the product is not suitable for some of the intended works or at least learning that this cannot be done as efficiently as expected is one of the major outcomes, indicating the failure in the process of acquisition. On one hand, this activity leads to reducing the uncertainty regarding the properties of the product, and on the other hand – it reduces the uncertainty regarding the actual qualities needed for accomplishing efficiently the intended works.
- Learning about the additional opportunities the new product is able to support. The realization that there are additional options that the new product may provide could lead to dissatisfaction with the purchase decision made if the properties of the obtained product do not allow to gain the benefit fully. For example, the next generation gadget may allow the accomplishment of numerous additional tasks, not identified at the time of purchase. This reduces the uncertainty regarding the customer's own needs and extends the understanding of the product quality needed, and related price criterion.

The warranty of misinforming promotes the emphasis on the evolving, potential needs when making purchase decision. It offers opportunities to adjust customer needs to the best practice and to select the product with best suitability for accomplishing the initially identified works as well as for possibilities evolved during the trial period.

The Framework

Any rational, informed, optimal purchase of a new product decision making should aim to minimize costs and maximize profit. The cost components that we will consider are as follows:

- Direct costs – the price of the product.
- Indirect costs – time and efforts for learning the product features and how to use it in an efficient manner, utilization. This cost is recovered by the future usage of the product.
- Sunk costs (retrospective cost) – time and efforts for identifying the needs and the set of the product acceptance criteria; mapping products' properties to the acceptance criteria to use when making the purchase decision. These are the preliminary costs spent in preparing to make the purchase decision. In case of not purchasing, these costs are not recovered, otherwise they can be considered as part of learning costs.

Also, the benefits of the purchase decision that must be taken into account are as follows:

- Monetary benefits or profit – savings for accomplishing works with the product, which otherwise will be carried out by an external service for higher cost.
- Non-monetary benefits – the ability to accomplish the work independently, without relying on external services or by working more effectively and saving time and effort.

The aim of a product purchase decision is to accomplish a certain set of works. The learning aspect during the adoption process identifies a set of additional new tasks that can be done with the product, as well as a set of works that cannot be reasonably accomplish with the new product.

The following simple example illustrates this idea. Let us consider purchasing a home printer. The printer's productivity, measured by number of printed pages per minute, is the "quality" measure of this product. At the time of the purchase, the customer plans to print her/his printing jobs, which are in up to 20 pages. The purchased printer allows printing all kinds of printing jobs, which do not exceed 100 pages per job in a reasonable time. Any printing job with more pages may take too long, so that its completion at home is inconvenient. For large jobs, the customer could use external services incurring associated charges. The purchased printer suits fully the initially identified needs (printing up to 20 pages) and use external service when need to print more than 100 pages. In case the later doesn't happen frequent enough – the purchased printer suits perfectly, otherwise it could be better to purchase more expensive printer.

Costs of Product Adoption

Costs of Product Adoption Quality of Acceptance and Buyer's Cost

In general, the optimization problem of making a purchase decision can be defined by following notations developed in Part 2 (see Appendix 1) as follows:

A customer (buyer) b (the index j is omitted here) needs to perform a set of activities $\left\{a_i^k\right\}$, where i corresponds to the categories of activities $\{A_i\}$ the product $d \in D$ is suitable for, and k is the index for the different activities within the category A_i the buyer b needs to address. For each of these a_i^k tasks b needs a product with given quality level q_i^k. The parameter q_i^k can be normalized, so that its values are within the interval [0, 1]. The properties or features of product d can be measured by the probability that it allows the buyer to accomplish a work at a given quality level.

A product d is characterized by a parameter p_i that represents the actual quality level of d with respect to category A_i. Then for a given set $\left\{a_i^k\right\}$ from A_i, d could be suitable for some of these and not suitable for others. For the case, illustrated in Fig. 4.4.1, the product d is suitable for accomplishing works with the following quality levels - q_i^1, q_i^5 and q_i^3 and not suitable for activities with quality levels q_i^2 and q_i^4 for b's needed works from category A_i.

Figure 1. An illustration of the suitability of product d to accomplish tasks a_i^k

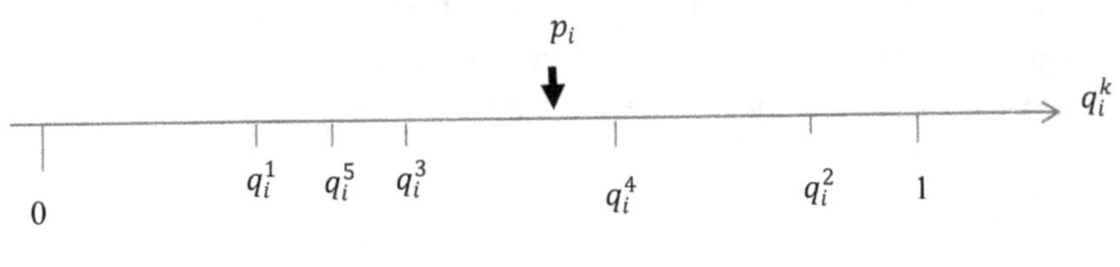

We call the parameter p_i the "quality level of product d for category A_i" and $q_i = \max\{q_i^k : q_i^k < p_i\}$ the "quality level for category A_i for the customer b". Also, we assume that c_i is the cost (price) to get this quality level q_i.

For Figure 1, c_i is the price of a product capable of accomplishing all tasks, which require quality p_i and therefore can accomplish all tasks, which need quality less than p_i, i.e., tasks – a_i^1, a_i^5, and a_i^3. On the other hand, this product is not suitable for accomplishing tasks, which require quality q_i^4, q_i^2 or higher. We denote the price of product d by $c_d = c_{p_i}$, i.e., the price of the product is equivalent (or measured by) to the price of quality level of tasks the product is suitable for. Next, we denote by C_i^k the quality cost (price) needed to accomplish a task the product d is not suitable for. The cost C_i^k corresponds to the price of quality required for a task a_i^k, which accomplishment requires quality higher than the quality of d, i.e., a task a_i^k such that $q_i^k > p_i$.

Assume that at the time of making the purchase decision, the buyer's subjective assessment of the quality p_i of d regarding her/his tasks is $\widehat{p_i}$. This assessment is based on the content of the message describing the product, which is provided by the seller. Byer's purchase decision is based on the relationship between q_i and $\widehat{p_i}$, where q_i is the quality level the buyer is ready to pay for, say c_q. Final assessment of the correctness of the buyer's purchase decision depends on estimation of $\widehat{p_i}$ and the ordering of p_i, q_i and $\widehat{p_i}$.

The utilization process, i.e., finding out the true properties of the product, brings $\widehat{p_i} \rightarrow p_i$ and the cost of this learning is denoted by c_u. This cost is smaller for "user friendly" products.

Note that this cost can be used to assess the property "user-friendliness" of the product. In the case of software application justification of this property of User Interface is often tricky. This cost can be used to measure "user experience" satisfaction.

The quality needed to accomplish different tasks from category A_i varies, i.e., for a certain quality level p_i of d, there are some tasks, which can be accomplished by using d, and some tasks that the buyer will not be able to perform with d. For the second group of tasks, the buyer must find another way for accomplishing them by paying extra for external service, denoted by

$$C_D = \sum_{q_i^k > p_i} C_i^k .$$

The cost structure of the works' portfolio of b, is composed by the price c_d of the product d and the extra costs for external service C_D (the cost for using an external product from the group of D that outperform $d \in D$). Next, based on the above notations and discussion, we can formulate an optimization problem to address the buyer's optimal purchase decision.

OPTIMIZATION PROBLEM

The buyer's optimal purchase decision aims to minimize the following objective function over all available products on the market:

$$\min_D(c_D + C_D + c_u + c_{sunk}) \quad (4.41.)$$

where c_{sunk} is the cost of all preliminary actions, such as rejecting all inappropriate products, identifying tasks and related quality levels; and assessing the acceptable prices. We may ignore this cost, because it prepares the customer for the decision making and it is not relevant in the product comparison. In function (4.4.1.) the term c_{sunk} is a constant and will not affect the finding of the optimal product choice.

Each of the other three components of function (4.4.1.) is composite and plays different role in the two phases of the new product adoption process:

- The price of the product c_d can be considered also in relation to the cost of the works the product d is suitable for, say $c = \sum_{q_i^k < p_i} c_i^k$ (this is the cost that could have need incurred for accomplishing these works without using d), i.e., this is the buyer's benefit from having and using the product $d \in D$. The buyer's actual benefit is the difference $c_b = c - c_d$. The value of c_b may change over the two phases of the product adoption process. During the acquiring phase the buyer is fully aware of the product's price and the tasks he/she intends to accomplish with a product from the category D, so denote the value of c_b during the acquiring phase by c_b^1, i.e., c_b^1 is the initial measure of c_b. During the utilization phase this value may change because: (1) it may include costs of works the buyer initially (at the time of purchase) had not intended to accomplish with $d \in D$, but the product d is suitable for them, and (2) it may exclude costs of works, which the buyer had intended to accomplish with a product from category D, but $d \in D$ is not suitable for. Denote the value of c_b during the utilization phase by c_b^2 i.e., c_b^2 is the updated measure of c_b.
- The cost of the works, which the product is not suitable for is C_D. Here again, similarly to the previous discussion, we have initial and updated sets of works with corresponding costs C_D^1 and C_D^2.
- In the case of making decision to place a warranty claim of misinforming leading to a replacement of the product (the initially purchased product $d^1 \in D$ proves to be unsuitable to the buyer) the utilization cost c_u will include the

utilization of the replaced product $d^2 \in D$ or we may have again initial and updated utilization costs c_u^1 and c_u^2.

Therefore, the optimal purchase decision will be based on maximizing the benefits, i.e., $\max_D(c_b)$ and minimizing the costs, i.e., $\min_D(C_D + c_u)$.

At the time of making the purchase decision, the buyer b optimizes with respect of the initial measures - $\max_D(c_b^1)$ and $\min_D(C_D^1)$. The utilization cost c_u is unknown at that time and it doesn't affect the decision-making process.

Often during utilization phase, in the case of provided warranty of misinforming, the buyer faces a decision whether to file a warranty claim. This decision is based on solving the max-min problem again, but now based on the updated measures and including the utilization cost. The utilization cost is important and may affect the buyer's decision to make a warranty claim leading to a product replacement. If this cost is too high, the buyer may infer that it will take additional significant time and effort to utilize the newly obtained (via replacement) product and may decide not to make the claim and incur this cost again.

CONCLUSION

The role of the warranty of misinforming in new product adoption is very important as it provides protection for the customers to examine the product, they are interested in through reassuring them that they can return the product if it is not suitable for their needs. At the same time, it plays a promotional role for the seller because it attracts customers who are not entirely sure what they are looking for or their expertise does not allow them to make a definite decision as to which product to buy. It allows customers to make purchase decisions close to the optimal according to a set of pre-specified criteria. Warranty of misinforming allows customers to assume the risk for purchasing a product with low acceptability. This increases the probability of making a correct, near optimal purchase decision under uncertainty.

The above observation on the utilization process reveals the following interesting fact: for products with high usability (especially learnability) the probability of making a claim under the warranty of misinforming is also high. One possible explanation of this fact is as follows: if the product has high usability, especially learnability, the customer gains expertise in using the product and advances her/his skills in utilizing not only this product, but more advanced products of the same range, which may lead to a decision to return the purchased product (which is acceptable under the warranty terms) and aim for a product with improved functionalities. Therefore, a warranty of misinforming has an addition effect on the customers – it stimulates their learning and enhances their technical skills.

On the other hand, better understanding how a customer makes purchase decisions in acquiring a new product, the process and risks associated with the utilization of this product allows producers to provide more effective product service and support. The warranty of misinforming serves as a tool for collecting customers' feedback and plays a significant role in the overall improvement of customer service and customer satisfaction.

REFERENCES

Bhagat, S., Goyal, A., & Lakshmanan, L. V. S. (2012). Maximizing product adoption in social networks *WSDM 2012 - Proceedings of the 5th ACM International Conference on Web Search and Data Mining*, (pp. 603-612). ACM.

Blischke, W., & Murthy, D. N. P. (1996). *Product Warranty Handbook*. Marcel Dekker.

Christozov, D., Chukova, S., & Mateev, P. (2006). A Measure of Risk Caused by Information Asymmetry in e-Commerce. *Journal of Issues in Informing Science and Information Technology*, *3*, 147–158. doi:10.28945/879

Christozov, D., Chukova, S., & Mateev, P. (2007). On the Relationship between Warranty and the Risk of Information Asymmetry. *Journal of Issues in Informing Science and Information Technology*, *4*, 235–249. doi:10.28945/946

Christozov, D., Chukova, S., & Mateev, P. (2009). On two types of warranties: Warranty of malfunctioning and warranty of misinforming. *Asia-Pacific Journal of Operational Research*, *26*(3), 399–420. doi:10.1142/S0217595909002274

Christozov, D., Chukova, S., & Mateev, P. (2011). Assessment of Risk of Misinforming: Dynamic Measures. *Interdisciplinary Journal of Information, Knowledge, and Management*, *6*, 163–176. doi:10.28945/1374

Christozov, D., Chukova, S., & Mateev, P. (2012). Market Segmentation Based on Risk of Misinforming Reduction. *Issues in Informing Science and Information Technology*, *9*, 253–265. doi:10.28945/1620

Christozov, D., Chukova, S., & Mateev, P. (2013). The role of Warranty of Misinforming in New Product Adoption. *Journal of Issues in Informing Science and Information Technology*, *10*, 111–120. doi:10.28945/1799

Devos, J., Van Landeghem, H., & Deschoolmeester, D. (2012). SMEs and IT: Evidence *for a* Market for "Lemons". *Electronic Journal Information Systems Evaluation, 15*(1), 2012.

Eng, Y., & Quaia, G. (2009). Strategies for improving new product adoption in uncertain environments: A selective review of the literature. *Industrial Marketing Management, 38*(3), 275–282. doi:10.1016/j.indmarman.2008.01.003

Manchanda, P., Xie, Y., & Youn, N. (2008). The Role of Targeted Communication and Contagion in Product Adoption. *Marketing Science, 27*(6), 961–976. doi:10.1287/mksc.1070.0354

Parry, M.E., Cao, Q. & Song, M. (2011). Forecasting new product adoption with probabilistic neural networks. *Journal of Product Innovation Management, 28*, 78-88.

Sethi, S. P., Prasad, A., & He, X. (2008). Optimal advertising and pricing in a new-product adoption model. *Journal of Optimization Theory and Applications, 139*(2), 351–360. https://www.marketing91.com/new-product-adoption/. doi:10.100710957-008-9472-5

Chapter 20
Warranty of Misinforming:
An Overview of Applicability

ABSTRACT

This chapter summarizes different aspects of warranty of misinforming from point of view of its applicability in business practices nowadays. In the case of e-commerce, a regulation is launched that guarantees the rights of the clients to return the product purchased on-line. This corresponds to the implicit form of warranty. The chapter provides a general discussion on applicability of warranty of misinforming by adopting the standard assessment techniques as feasibility studies and SWOT analysis.

INTRODUCTION

This part of the book introduces some ideas related to warranty as a business practice by emphasizing the warranty of misinforming. This form of risk-sharing can be represented by the slogan "if not fully satisfied, money back guaranteed". Very recently, with the introduction of online trades, were recognized various additional aspects of this slogan. On the one hand the growth of on-line commerce increases the importance of such practice, but on the other hand increases the volume of the eligible claims of unsatisfied clients. The slogan above deserted from pure promotional role toward a real valuable business policy of sharing risks. As a relatively new phenomenon, economically reasonable application of warranty of misinforming desires careful rational and data driven management and appropriate models to support feasibility evaluation.

DOI: 10.4018/978-1-6684-8800-3.ch020

Combining traditional warranty – warranty of malfunctioning, with warranty of misinforming is major concept discussed in the previous chapters. Several issues were presented as:

How to decide whether it is worth introducing a pure or mixed warranty for a particular business?
How does one can define "the best" parameters of such a practice or policy, especially in the case of a pure warranty of misinforming and of the mixed warranty policy?
How to predict what is its effect on the business and how to quantify and measure this effect?

The increased volume of product warranty returns, due to the clients being "not fully satisfied" and, because this type of warranty often is a default coverage for the indirect commerce, makes the Strengths, Weaknesses, Opportunities, and Threats (SWOT) analysis of the warranty of misinforming an essential tool in evaluating its effectiveness. It requires a careful analysis of feasibility, cause-and-effect analysis and possibly other techniques used to improve rationality and justification of any business decision.

The four components of SWOT - Strengths, Weaknesses, Opportunities, and Threats - are the common components of any methodology aiming to answer to the following question "Should the option/decision be enforced or neglected?" Or, in other words, what are the break-even values of the decision parameters that will make it beneficial from a business point of view. The common practice in making any important business decisions is to clearly understand and provide a proper interpretation of these main four aspects of their implementation, i.e., clarify the strengths, weaknesses, opportunities, and threats of any potential effect of the decision on the "health" of the business and to assess the set of business parameters, which makes the decision feasible.

The use of promotional slogans like "if not fully satisfied money back guaranteed" used for promotion has been a common business practice for years. It represents a special kind of warranty coverage, and as the classical warranty serving sharing risks needs a careful assessment of expected cost. On the one hand the growth of on-line commerce in the last 20 years increases the importance of such a practice, but on the other hand increases the volume of the eligible warranty claims. National and international regulation of business practices also addressed this kind of risk by providing protection for customers who have bought on-line goods that doesn't meet their expectations as understood by the advertisement.

The increased volume of product warranty returns, due to the clients being "not fully satisfied" and, because this type of warranty often is a default coverage for the indirect commerce, makes the need of careful assessment and the SWOT analysis of the warranty of misinforming is the essential tool in evaluating its effectiveness. Applicability of warranty of misinforming requires a careful "cost-benefit" analysis, analysis of feasibility, cause-and-effect analysis, and possibly other techniques used to improve rationality and justification of this business decision.

The four components of SWOT – Strengths, Weaknesses, Opportunities, and Threats – are the common components of any methodology aiming to answer to the following question "Should the option/decision be enforced or neglected?" Or, in other words – what are the break-even values of the decision parameters that will make it beneficial from the business point of view.

In this chapter we discuss specific information sources for the four SWOT components for making a decision "*to apply warranty of misinforming to a specific business or not*". Some approaches to research and quantify them are presented throughout the book. Here, the data collection, data analysis, and discussion on how to infer rational business decisions using these results are commented.

The chapter is organized as follows. A brief introduction of the idea of the risk of misinforming and warranty of misinforming, as well as a description of the process of decision making and aspects of related feasibility study are presented in the first section "Background" by refereeing to the previous chapters in this part of the book. Assessment of a given business decision is made usually by evaluation of its feasibility, which also includes assessment of resources needed to implement the decision. Discussion on how to perform the four components of SWOT are made under the "umbrella" of feasibility study. Separate sections are dedicated to the four components of SWOT analysis associated with the warranty of misinforming. In the last two sections we discuss the methodology and applicability of the proposed approach, as well as our concluding remarks.

BACKGROUND

Misinforming

Misinforming is a hazard, which may influence every process of communication. It happens when one of the parties – the receiver – is misled by the message provided by the other party – the sender. The many factors influencing the likelihood and of misinforming are discussed in Part 1 of the book. In brief, the term "misinforming" in our natural language has two different meanings (1) when the correct message of the sender is misinterpreted or misunderstood by the receiver, and (2) when the sender provides intentionally a wrong message to mislead the receiver. In the second interpretation the term "intentionally" refers better to "disinforming" and it is not considered in this book.

The major source of misinforming is the "information asymmetry" in it broader context – when one of the parties involved in a communication process knows more on the subject than the other party. In the case of business communications, we may observe the so-called two-sided asymmetry. The sender knows more about the content of the message – properties of the advertised product; whereas the receiver knows more about the problems he faces and aims to address by using the product.

In the case of indirect trade, the risk of misinforming could be quite high. The empirical studies, presented in Part 2 of the book, shows that there is a high probability/risk that a client is misled and makes a wrong purchase decision by the seller's properly and correctly formulated message regarding the product of interest.

Warranty

A warranty is a contract between the client and the seller/producer, which allows for sharing the risk of a given hazard among all customers of a particular product. Through the warranty the related price component is included in the product price, the customers harmed by the hazard are compensated on the expense of customers who did not have this experience. This requires a proper evaluation of the expected cost to cover the warranty risk for the entire population of customers and to include an appropriate share of this cost in the price of the product. The most common warranty coverage is for the risk of product malfunctioning (see Chapter 4.1). This part of the book is dedicated to warranty as business policy addressing risk of misinforming.

Warranty Policy

The warranty policy as a risk sharing tool includes the following two components – Warranty of Malfunctioning and Warranty of Misinforming (see Chapter 16). The "mixed warranty policy" is defined to combine coverage of the two categories of risks, while the "pure policy" covers only one of these risks. Defining the warranty policy, usually is done by specifying the periods of warranty coverage and terms of the risks coverage (see Chapter 17). There are well developed tools for studying the warranty of malfunctioning, which are based on estimating the reliability of the product, i.e., estimating the probability that the product will fail to perform as expected while aging. It is not so straightforward when it comes to the warranty of misinforming because it addresses the failures in communication between sellers and buyers. Evaluating the probability of malfunctioning is entirely under the control of the producer, which is not the case if aiming to assess the customers' exposure to the risk of misinforming.

Warranty of Misinforming

The promotional slogans like "if not fully satisfied, money back guaranteed" was firstly interpreted as a warranty contract covering the risk of misinforming or as the Warranty of Misinforming in Christozov, Mateev (2003). The different aspects of warranty of misinforming were further explored in multiple papers, including identifying the major factors influencing the risk of misinforming; approaches to quantify it in different circumstances; exploring learning opportunities provided by the warranty and viewing the warranty as an option, similarly to options in finance and trade. These aspects of warranty of misinforming are presented in the previous chapters of this part of the book.

Decision Making

The decision making (or decision cycle), as introduced by Simon (1960), is described as a well-structured process including three main phases: intelligence, design, and choice. Information, relevant to the identification and description of the problem, is collected and assessed early in the process during the intelligence phase. If a significant misinforming occurs during this phase, the entire process will be corrupted and will lead to wrong or less effective decisions. This form of misinforming is quite often observed during the process of making purchase decisions. As a result, any unsatisfied customers may become a source of negative information, which is harmful for the producer's reputation. The warranty of misinforming may help in mitigating this risk, but at the same time, it is important to assess the cost associated with related product warranty returns. The applicability of offering a warranty policy with specific parameters needs careful, rational and driven by data analysis and justification.

Feasibility study as well as SWOT analysis is the most reliable approach in justifying the rationality of such a decision. They also provide some useful clues regarding the decision's implementation as well as a set of indicators on whether the implementation of the decision is expected to become a success or a failure.

Feasibility Study

Feasibility study as a more comprehensive method for analysis of applicability of a business policy. It includes SWOT analysis as a systematical approach in justifying the rationality of a business decision by assessing the four critical factors – strengths, weaknesses, opportunities, and treats. Well-developed SWOT also provides some useful clues regarding the decision implementation as well as a set of indicators on whether the implementation of the decision is more likely to lead to success or failure. Cost-benefit analysis is the other tool to justify feasibility of a policy, which addresses in an explicit form the resources needed and the returns expected.

The first question a marketing manager needs to answer is whether to use/apply warranty of misinforming as a marketing tool/policy or not and why – only as a promotional tool or in its role as sharing the risk. If the answer is positive, then there are several additional problems that must be addressed such as:

- What is the reasonable time of the warranty coverage?
- What are the expected costs of the policy per one sell?
- How to justify this policy to the company principles, i.e.,
- What are the expected benefits?
- How reliable this justification is?

Moreover, there are some additional aspects of this decision that also have to be considered such as:

- What part of the achieved results are actually achieved by applying this policy?
- Whether this policy increases the clients trust toward the company and the product?
- Whether this policy increases the company market share, etc.

The difficulty of this decision is based on the complexity of the communication process between producer/seller and the potential clients. A possible segmentation of clients' population and an attempt to define different policies to address different clients' categories were discussed in Chapter 6.

In all of these studies, the proposed approaches explore reactive, post-factum assessment. The policy is already in place and the proposed methodologies provide an insight of what type of data should be collected and studied to assess the effect of the policy, how to collect these data, and what techniques to use for their analysis. Making a decision to either implement or not to implement a warranty of misinforming requires prediction, assessment of what to expect, i.e., what are the future positive and negative aspects of the decision on the business success. In summary, such a decision needs to be based on a carefully performed SWOT analysis.

There are two major and contradictory aspects in making the decision to introduce a warranty of misinforming for a particular product – financial arguments and promotional arguments. From a financial point of view, offering a warranty of misinforming for a new product in its early stages of adoption, or at the stage of the "peak of inflated expectations", is not feasible because of the expected significant number of “unsatisfied” customers. On the other hand, this is the time when the innovation enters the market and encouraging the customers to try the new product could be beneficial and contribute to building the market. From point of view of benefits, the warranty of misinforming may serve as a tool promoting a successful market distribution of the new product – risk free trial may encourage innovators and early adopters to experiment with the product and increase the understanding of the usefulness and applicability of the new product. Also, the accumulated user experience results in reducing information asymmetry.

The market study for collecting information regarding warranty of misinforming and performing SWOT analysis requires a careful design in identifying target groups and specifying how to approach them for collecting relevant data.

There are two categories of factors (see Figure 1.) in considering SWOT analysis – specific and universal. Specific factors are related to a particular product and the particular population’s segment of the clients. The universal factors are more abstract, relevant to a larger set of products. We will address mostly universal factors influencing the risk of misinforming or factors associated with the informing process. For every one of these factors, we are looking for answers to the following questions:

1. What is the importance of the given factor in the marketing of the product?
2. What data are needed to assess the importance of a specific factor?
3. How to collect data useful in assessing the actual effect of the factor for marketing success?
4. How to process the collected data so that to increase the understanding regarding the effect the given factor; what are the constraints and limitations of this effect?

In the following section we will address these issues in the context of the four components of the SWOT analysis.

Figure 1. Attributes of the four components of SWOT analysis

	Positive	Negative
Internal	**Strengths:** What are the factors that contribute to acquiring the benefits?	**Weaknesses:** What are the factors that may challenge acquiring benefits?
External	**Opportunities:** What are the factors that may increase the benefit?	**Threats:** What are the risks, that may decrease benefit or increase costs?

Strengths

1. A warranty of misinforming provides benefits in two ways – (1) encourages the purchase of the product, and (2) reduces the chances of having clients unsatisfied with the product.
2. Warranty of misinforming allows the producer to collect first-hand information/ data regarding:
    - The actual usage of the product.
    - The problems or activities the clients are trying to solve or accomplish with the use of the product.
    - The properties of the product resulted in preventing clients in accomplishing activities as initially expected.
3. Warranty of misinforming supports market promotion and distribution of a new product.

Weaknesses

1. It is not easy to evaluate the cost-benefit parameters of the warranty of misinforming.
2. Any inappropriate clustering of the clients' population could lead to addressing the clusters with an unsuitable information message, which may increase the risk of misinforming and related warranty costs to cover for this risk.

Opportunities

1. The warranty of misinforming provides learning opportunities for the clients and, due to its limited coverage period, encourages them to invest fully in mastering the features and use of the product.
2. The warranty of misinforming provides some learning opportunities for the producer as well. An analysis of the warranty claims could be a valuable source of information regarding the problems clients aim accomplishing with the product. Also, this information obtained via warranty may provide better understanding regarding the newly identified or emerging problems the clients are facing and could inspire some ideas for the design of new products in a way to address them.

Threats

1. The product could be inappropriate for coverage with warranty of misinforming. In this case, the warranty cost will exceed the warranty benefits. The product is usually inappropriate for warranty of misinforming coverage when it is well established on the market, and it is useful in addressing well-defined problems. The benefits of the implementation of the warranty of misinforming in such cases are solely based on its promotional role.
2. The learning opportunities provided by the warranty of misinforming may highlight the shortfalls of the product in comparison to its competitors and could serve as anti-promotion.

Assessing the Feasibility of Warranty of Misinforming

To make decision whether to provide or not a warranty of misinforming policy for a particular product the producer needs to find answers of the following issues:

a. Whether customers are aware of their own needs to use the product?
b. What problems or works do they expect to solve or accomplish with the product?
c. What is the customers' attitude toward adoption of a new product?
d. Whether the customers possess competencies to recognize that they have made a wrong purchase decision and their willingness to activate the warranty of misinforming?

Performing SWOT analysis requires investigating the market to answer those questions related to the population of potential customers. Also, the dynamics of the market and customers' awareness must be taken into account.

The two sides of such an analysis need careful design and planning:

- How to collect relevant and useful information/data? and
- How to analyze these data and draw an action plan driven by the insight provided by the data?

A systematic market study is needed to collect information for making a rational decision whether to cover a product with a warranty of misinforming. Such a study must highlight whether (1) such a policy is feasible and (2) what are the parameters of the warranty contract that will make this policy feasible.

A methodology to conduct a meaningful market study to reveal the needed information may consists of the following steps:

1. Preparation stage:
    - Identify the set of problems that the product is suitable to address or the set of activities the use of the product may bring benefit to clients.
    - Identify the populations of potential clients of the product. Who may need to accomplish works identified as suitable for accomplishing with the product.
    - Apply existing knowledge and or use historical data to identify the main clusters of clients on the Attitude/Expertise domain (see Chapter 7 and clusters presents on Figure 1.)
2. Stage 2. Compose an appropriate set of product description message(s) targeting customers in different clusters (see Table 1 on Chapter 7.)
3. Stage 3. Select two representative or large enough random samples of clients from each of the clusters. Include warranty of misinforming in the purchase agreement only for the first sample and leave the clients in the second sample without this option. After a several periods of product usage collect reactions from the two sets of customers:
    - From the second set: data on the product's satisfaction – subjective by using questionnaires.
    - From the first set: data on the product's satisfaction (subjective) and the number of cases when the warranty option has been applied, including time and circumstances of the claim.

The collected warranty data will allow us to trace the learning process related to the product features and to identify any specifics in respondents' attitude towards the proposed warranty.

4. Stage 4: Estimate the following indicators:
    - The percentages of satisfied customers using the data from the first and second samples in separate (with/without warranty of misinforming option); than () are the percentages of dissatisfied customers in the first and second samples.
    - The percentages () of satisfied/dissatisfied customers of the first sample who claim the warranty of misinforming. Satisfied customers claim the warranty of misinforming when they realize, during the adoption process, that they need a better product. Unsatisfied customers claim the warranty when they realize, during the warranty coverage period, that the product doesn't meet their initial expectations. Then () are the percentages of satisfied/dissatisfied customers who was given but did not use the warranty option.
5. Stage 5. Analyze results:
    - Compare ρ_1 and ρ_2:
        i. If : the warranty could be considered as a product attribute with positive contribution to the customer satisfaction – the warranty of misinforming is an appropriate option for this product.
        ii. If : the warranty does not have the desired impact on the customer satisfaction - the warranty of misinforming option is not needed for this specific product.
    - Compare and :
        i. If (the symbol ">>" means much larger): the warranty option increases the customer satisfaction. The message is correct, and the warranty allows customers to identify additional benefits they can acquire by using one of the products from given category. The warranty of misinforming is an appropriate option for this product.
        ii. If (the symbol "" means approximately equal): the data do not provide a clear indication regarding the impact of the warranty option on the customer satisfaction and about the message. Keep the warranty of misinforming but aim to improve the product description message for the customers in this cluster.
        iii. If is large: the message is not informative to the customers in the cluster and must be re-written. Additional training for the sales representatives will be useful as well.

6. After a pre-specified period of time (the length of which depends on the product type) repeat the procedure from Step 3 by applying the adjusted messages. The periodical repletion of the research will allow us to increase the reliability of obtained data, but also will allow us to identify the changes in the market. Obtaining reproducible results in repeating studies indicates that information collected correctly represents customers attitude toward the product and the warranty.

DISCUSSION

SWOT analysis is a tool supporting decision-making based on the balance between its four components. It is quite often that while making anticipative decisions, the decision maker overestimates either the costs or profits related to the outcomes, thus limiting the effect of the decision only to its financial impact. In many cases, intangible benefits, such as the learning opportunities provided by the warranty of misinforming, may play a significant positive role in the long-term market success of the product. On the other hand, before reaching such a success, the product has to pass through earlier stages of its launching, introduction, and establishing in the market and secure its niche. Product adoption is maybe the most important of these early stages. Success in product adoption creates the "name" and visibility of the product. The early stages are associated with costs, including the cost related covering the warranty of misinforming claims. The two opposite points of view – short-term costs and long-term benefits – need to be considered and properly balanced out while making a marketing decision regarding the inclusion of the product warranty of misinforming. Also, the process of introduction and establishing is associated with raising competences regarding usability of the product and provided messages, describing the product, need periodical adjustment to reflect the changed structure of the market.

The four components of the SWOT analysis and the methodology proposed above provide practical support for making decisions regarding the warranty of misinforming.

The iterative nature of the methodology allows (1) how to use the past experience regarding market acceptance of similar products; (2) predicting, by using currently collected data about how the customers will adopt the new product and how the warranty of misinforming encourages this adoption; and how to organize repeating research to guarantee reliability of the conclusion. This is the most challenging part of the application of SWOT analysis is the requirement of repeatedly collecting data needed for the SWOT steps outlined earlier.

CONCLUSION

In this chapter an approach on how to justify the need to provide a warranty of misinforming for a particular product is outlined. The feasibility of this decision needs a careful analysis and rational, data driven approach in making decision.

This study is an initial effort to consider the option of offering (or not) the product warranty of misinforming as a decision based on systemic study of the product market and potential customers. We believe that this is a line of research that will provide a deeper and clearer understanding of the incentives in offering this type of warranty. The algorithm discussed in this study is quite "naïve" and will be an initial point in extending the data-based approach in justifying decisions related to warranty of misinforming.

In this study we have outlined an approach on how to justify the need or otherwise of providing a warranty of misinforming for a particular product. We believe that the four components included in the SWOT analysis outline an approach for developing a well-balanced point of view on the feasibility of introducing a warranty of misinforming in the promotional marketing package for a new product. We sketched an algorithm, based on the analysis of appropriate data, aiming to support the decision maker attempting to justify the introduction (or unsuitability) of warranty of misinforming for his/her product.

REFERENCES

Christozov, D., Chukova, S., & Mateev, P. (2007). On the Relationship between Warranty and the Risk of Information Asymmetry. *Journal of Issues in Informing Science and Information Technology*, *4*, 235–249. doi:10.28945/946

Christozov, D., Chukova, S., & Mateev, P. (2008). Warranty and the Risk of Misinforming: Evaluation of the Degree of Acceptance. *Journal of Issues in Informing Science and Information Technology*, *5*, 667–677. doi:10.28945/1035

Christozov, D., Chukova, S., & Mateev, P. (2009). On two types of warranties: Warranty of malfunctioning and warranty of misinforming. *Asia-Pacific Journal of Operational Research*, *26*(3), 399–420. doi:10.1142/S0217595909002274

Christozov, D., Chukova, S., & Mateev, P. (2010). Assessment of Quality of Warranty Policy. *Interdisciplinary Journal of Information, Knowledge, and Management*, *5*, 62–72.

Christozov, D., Chukova, S., & Mateev, P. (2012). Market Segmentation Based on Risk of Misinforming Reduction. *Journal of Issues in Informing Science and Information Technology*, *9*, 253–265. doi:10.28945/1620

Christozov, D., Chukova, S., & Mateev, P. (2014). Warranty of Misinforming: An Overview. *Issues in Informing Science and Information Technology*, *11*, 31–46. doi:10.28945/1978

Christozov, D., Chukova, S., & Mateev, P. (2015). Risk of Misinforming and Message Customization in Customer Related Management. *Issues in Informing Science and Information Technology, 12*, 47-61.

Christozov, D., Chukova, S., & Mateev, P. (2016). Warranty of Misinforming as an Option in Product Utilization Process, *Informing Science: the International Journal of Emerging Transdiscipline, 19*, 75-87.

Christozov, D., & Mateev, P. (2003). Warranty as a Factor for e-Commerce Success. *Informing Science and IT Education Conference*, Pori, Finland. https://www.informingscience.org/Publications/2641?Type=ConferenceProceedings&ConferenceID=33)

Fenn, J., & Raskino, M. (2011). Understanding Gartner's Hype Cycles. *Gartner Research.* Harvard. http://isites.harvard.edu/fs/docs/icb.topic1360759.files/understanding_gartners_hype_214001.pdf

Robinson, L. (2009). A summary of Diffusion of Innovations, in Changeology.

Simon, H. A. (1977). *[1960]. The new science of management decision* (Revised ed.). Prentice-Hall.

Section 4 Conclusion

The world of business and trade is moving more and more rapidly to digitization and indirect trade. Communication via the Internet is becoming dominant and "old" forms of ensuring trust and mutual understanding as body language, environment, etc. are becoming less applicable. They are gradually replaced by more formal and regulated instruments. A warranty, as the risk sharing instrument, is one of the valuable business policies with a growing impact on the market success. To react to the changed way of establishing seller-customer relationship, the risk of becoming misinformed is growing. This part of the book is dedicated to the warranty policies developed to address the risk of misinforming. Traditionally, this kind of guarantee serves solely for promotion but nowadays it starts obtaining economical value and impacts the financial and overall success of the business. With the growing impact of e-commerce, the need for more comprehensive research on assessment of the outcomes of misinforming and building models to allow mitigation of this risk will become inevitable. Warranty, as one of the widely used risk mitigation techniques, deserves special attention and development as theory and practice.

There are many possible directions for extending the research on warranty by considering the risk of misinforming one can consider. For example:

- Formulating and solving the optimization problem for determining the "best" warranty period(s) under restricted budget. The formulation of this type of problem usually is based on manufacturer utility function along with the client utility function. The problem of optimizing parameters in the mixed warranty strategy requires development of a measure of the risk covered by the warranty via combining the two risks – the risk of malfunctioning and the risk of misinforming.
- Minimizing clients' dissatisfaction could be among the priorities for the manufacturers. The dissatisfaction with the product could be due to unappropriated or imprecise advertising messages. Warranty models to include penalty function for client dissatisfaction will improve manufacturers'

advertising strategy and improve product description as conveyed to potential customers.

- Developing an approach on data collection and processing in a way to evaluate the model parameters, i.e., what type of data are needed for the estimations of the product suitability with respect to different activities and how to collect such data. This is always an open, but critically important, issue.

Issues discussed in the chapters of this part of the book aim to initiate systematic study of the warranty as risk sharing tool addressing the phenomenon of misinforming as a hazard. This hazard occurs when there is a failure in communication between parties and therefore is not under the control of either of the parties. Comparing with classical form of warranty – warranty of malfunctioning, where the probability of a failure can be evaluated well by the producer and assessment of the expected cost for covering the claims over the life of the product is done for various of products and circumstances – the expected cost associated with covering the warranty addressing misinforming is on its very early stage.

Appendix 1. Symbols, Notations, Definitions, Formulae

This appendix summarizes all symbols used, their meaning throughout the book, and assumptions associated with their usage.

Table 1. Sets of objects used throughout the book

Notation/Symbols	Definition/Meaning	Comments
Parties		
Buyers: $B=\{b_j, j=1,2,\ldots,J\}$	Potential customers making purchase decision based on information provided in the advertisement.	In more general meaning – the users of information.
Seller/Producer: $S=\{s\}$	The group of sellers or producers.	Only one seller is considered here. In the case of competing devices, the difference of producers is not accounted.
Object of communication / informing:		
Devices: $D=(d_i, i=1,2,\ldots,I\}$	Concurrent products, promoted to customers. Objects of purchase decision.	In most of the cases this set includes only one member and the index *i* is omitted.
Characteristics: $C=\{c_l, l=1,2,\ldots,L\}$	Properties of the group of devices, described in the message.	A particular device d_i can be described only by a subset of C_D.
True probability: $P_i=\{p_{ik}, k=1,2,\ldots,K\}$	Level of performance of device d_i in accomplishing activity from category A_k.	Assumption is that a category of activities has variable levels of complexity. Some devices may accomplish only simple works, but other the full range of activities.
Subject of communication / informing:		
Activities: $A=\{\cup A_k, k=1,2\ldots K\}$	Complete set of activities or works that all buyers may expect to accomplish with any product $d\in D$.	As assumed by the producer of the product.
Activities*: $A^*=\{\cup A_k, k=1,2\ldots K\}$	Categories of works that can be accomplished with any device from "Devices" set, according to expectations of the buyers.	As assumed by users of the product. Every buyer may want to accomplish only a subset of these categories of activities $A_j^*=\{a_{kj}, k=1,2,\ldots,K_j\}$. This set may include activities that are not assumed originally by the producer in the scope of the device purpose.
Buyer's works: $A_j=\{a_{jk}, k=1,2,\ldots,K_j\}$	Set of activities or works the customer b_j needs to accomplish by using a product $d\in D$.	The buyer may not expect to use the device to accomplish the entire set of activities or even activities from any category.
Properties for activity: $C^A=\{c_k^A, l=1,2,\ldots,L^A\}\subset C$	Characteristics of the device essential for accomplishing a category of activities.	Different buyers may have different expectations for the list of relevant characteristics that allows meaningful performance in executing the work.
Message: $C_i=\{c_{li}\}$	Components of the message describing properties of device d_i.	In case the message describing device d_i doesn't present a value for characteristic c_l the value of $c_{li}=0$.
Subjective probability: $\hat{P}_{ji}=\{\hat{p}_{jik}, k=1,2,\ldots K\}$	Level of performance of device d_i in accomplishing activities a_{jk} in the list of needed works as assessed by buyer b_j.	Subjective probability is the assessment of suitability of the device to accomplish works as assessed by the buyer.
Indicator of wrong decision: $r_j=\{r_{jk}, k=1,2,\ldots,K)$.	Correct or wrong {1,0} decision. Indicator of the decision $r_{jk}=0$ if the decision is correct; $r_{jk}=1$ if the decision is wrong.	A binary parameter {0,1}. The decision could be wrong related to one activity and correct for another.

Continued on following page

Table 1. Continued

Notation/Symbols	Definition/Meaning	Comments
Needs: $n_j=\{n_{jk}\}$	Priority of buyer b_j to accomplish activity a_k.	If a buyer doesn't expect to do work from a given category the need is set to zero. In case the activity is defining one – the buyer is purchasing the product because of this work the need is set to one. The need for other activities is in interval (0,1).
Information asymmetry: $ia_j=\{ia_{jk}\}$	Difference between actual probability of the product to accomplish activity a_k and the assessment made by the buyer b_j.	The parameter is calculated as $ia = \| p_k - \hat{p}_k \|$.
Degree of acceptance: $q_j=\{q_{jkl}\}$	The minimal quality (a threshold), which the product must possess in order to meet the customer's b_j expectations regarding product characteristic c_l, regarding the activity a_{jk}.	Degree of acceptance is a value reflecting subjective minimal expectations of product quality.
Measures of risk of misinforming:		
Models of risks: {M1, M2, M3}	• M1 – simple – r^s or R^s • M2 –needs – r^n or R^n • M3 –needs and information asymmetry – r^a or R^a	Selection of model to use depends on available data. Capital *R* refers to the risk of Seller (the risk associated with the group of buyers); *r* refers to the risk of an individual.
"Simple" measure of risk: $r_j^s(r_{ij})$	The measure depends only on whether the purchase decision is correct or not.	The value is either zero or one.
Measure of risk based on buyer's needs: $r_j^n(r_{ij}, n_{ij})$	The measure depends on whether the decision is correct or not and the needs.	This measure accounts only wrong decisions when they are relevant to buyer's needs.
Measure of risk based on buyer's needs and level of information asymmetry: $r_j^a(r_{ij}, n_{ij}, ia_{ij})$	The measure of the risk incorporates the indicator for correctness of the purchase decision, the needs, and the measure of information asymmetry.	This measure accounts only wrong decisions when they are relevant to buyer's needs, and also use the difference in actual properties with buyers' assessment as a weight measuring the degree of misunderstanding.
"Simple" measure for group *B:* $R_j^s(r_{ij})$	The "simple" measure of the risk in a purchase decision for group *B*, depends only on whether the decision is correct or not.	This measure aggregates risks of the group of buyers as viewed by the seller/producer of the device.
Measure of risk for the group *B* accounting the needs: $R_j^n(r_{ij}, n_{ij})$	The measure of the risk in a purchase decision for group *B*, depends on whether the decision is correct or not; and the needs.	This measure aggregates risks of the group of buyers as viewed by the seller/producer of the device.
Measure of risk for the group B accounting the needs and level of information asymmetry: $R_j^a(r_{ij}, n_{ij}, ia_{ij})$	The measure of the risk in a purchase decision for group *B*, which incorporates the indicator for correctness of the decision, the needs and the measure of information asymmetry.	This measure aggregates risks of the group of buyers as viewed by the seller/producer of the device.
Dynamic measures: $r(t)$ and $R(t)$	Measures of the risk at certain time *t* for an individual buyer b_j and for the entire group of buyers *B*.	This measure accounts for changes of client's understanding regarding suitability of the product over the time of usage.
Indicator of the risk leading to warranty claim: $r_{ji}^{wc} = \{r_{jik}^{wc}, k = 1, 2, \ldots, K_j\}$	Wrong decision to buy d_i leading to warranty of misinforming claim.	The purchase decision regarding d_i is positive, but wrong, and the buyer b_j is not satisfied.
Indicator of the risk leading to missing purchases of suitable product: $r_{ji}^{ms} = \{r_{jik}^{ms}, k = 1, 2, \ldots, K_j\}$	Wrong decision to buy d_i leading to reject purchasing.	The purchase decision is negative, but wrong. The buyer assess that the product is not suitable for at least one of the b_j activities, but this assessment is wrong – d_i is perfectly suitable for the needs of b_j.

Continued on following page

Table 1. Continued

Notation/Symbols	Definition/Meaning	Comments
Warranty		
Warranty policy: $W_p = W(t)$	Warranty period t– the time of coverage when the client has rights to claim reimbursement or free replacement.	Time is defined in the context of the product usage.
Warranty covering malfunctioning: $W_R(t^R)$	Warranty contract covering risk of failures or in general malfunctioning of the product.	This is a standard warranty covering the risk of low reliability or the case the product doesn't perform as promised.
Warranty covering misinforming: $W_I(t^I)$	Warranty contract covering the risk of misinforming or the risk that the buyer will obtain a not suitable product.	Slogan like "if you are not fully satisfied – money back" describes this policy.
Mixed warranty coverage: $W_p = \{t^R, t^I\}$	Warranty contract covering the two types of risks: risk of malfunctioning and risk of misinforming.	The two time-parameters of coverage must be different from zero: $t^R \neq 0$ and $t^I \neq 0$
Pure warranty policies: $W_p(t^R,0)$ or $W_p(0,t^I)$	Warranty contract covering only one out of the two types of risks: risk of malfunctioning and risk of misinforming.	One of the two time-parameters is zero.
Importance of the two warranty parameters: $V_b(q^b, m^b)$ for a customer $b=b_j$.	$0 \leq q^b \leq 1$ and $0 \leq m^b \leq 1$ $q^b + m^b = 1$	Here with "q" is marked reliability parameter of warranty of malfunctioning, and with "m" – the parameter of warranty of misinforming.
Seller's preference regarding mitigation of the two kinds of risks: $\tau = [0,1]$	The parameter defining Seller's mixed warranty policy.	The Seller's attitude toward the two types of risks $\left\{ r_{ji}^{ms}, r_{ji}^{wc} \right\}$ are $(\tau, 1-\tau)$, where $0 \leq \tau \leq 1$. When τ is zero or one, the warranty policy is not mixed.
Buyer attitude regarding misinforming warranty: $\{\mu j_{kj}$	Subjective assessment of importance of the misinforming warranty policy for making purchase decision by b_j in respect to activity a_{jk}.	μj_k indicates the level of buyer's trust regarding her or his competence. Whether bj expects that could be "unsatisfied". $0 \leq \mu jk_{\leq} 1$
Warranty policy coverage: $B\left(W_P\left(b_j\right)\right) = \mu_{jk} t^I + \left(1 - \mu_{jk}\right) t^R$	"Balanced" value – represents the effective coverage of a warranty policy to b_j.	The warranty policy that accounts clients' attitude.
Symbols related to warranty survey		
Results of survey regarding satisfaction: $(\rho 1\ \rho 2)$	Percentages of satisfied customers from those who are offered warranty of misinforming $(\rho 1_)$ and those, who are not offered $(\rho 2)$.	Satisfaction is indicated by answering a questionnaire.
The percentages of satisfied or dissatisfied customers who claim the warranty of misinforming: $(\delta s_{w_i} \delta w_j$	Percentages of customer who were given the option of warranty of misinforming and who use their right to claim it and to reimbursed money ("money back") or to replace the product.	Satisfied customers claim the warranty of misinforming when they realize, during the adoption process, that they need a better product. Unsatisfied customers claim the warranty when they realize, during the warranty coverage period, that the product doesn't meet their initial expectations.

Table 2. Indices

Symbol	Meaning
b_j, j=1,2,…,J	j marks one random buyer
d_i, i=1,2,…,I	i marks one random product
a_k, k=1,2,…,K	k marks one random activities
c_l, l=1,2,…,L	l marks one random characteristic of product

Table 3. Measures of static risk of misinforming

scenario	Models		
	M1	M2	M3
	Buyer (Receiver) b_j		
1:1	$r_j^s = \frac{1}{I}\sum_{i=1}^{I} r_{ij}$	$r_j^n = \frac{1}{\sum_{i=1}^{I} n_{ij}} \sum_{i=1}^{I} n_{ij} r_{ij}$	$r_j^a = \frac{1}{\sum_{i=1}^{I} n_{ij}} \sum_{i=1}^{I} n_{ij} r_{ij} ia_{ij}$
2:N	$r_j^s = \frac{1}{I}\sum_{i=1}^{I} \max({}^1r_{ij}, {}^2r_{ij})$	$r_j^n = \frac{1}{\sum_i n_{ij}} \sum_{i=1}^{I} n_{ij} \max({}^1r_{ij}, {}^2r_{ij})$	$r_j^a = \frac{1}{\sum_i n_{ij}} \sum_{i=1}^{I} n_{ij} \max({}^m r_{ij}, {}^m r_{ij}) \max_{{}^m\widehat{p}_{ij}}(abs({}^m\widehat{p}_{ij} - {}^m p_i)), \quad m = 1,2$
N:M	$r_j^s = \frac{1}{I}\sum_{i=1}^{I} \max_{m=1,2,\ldots N}\left({}^m r_{ij}\right)$	$r_j^n = \frac{1}{\sum_i n_{ij}} \sum_{i=1}^{I} n_{ij} \max_{m=1,2,\ldots,N}\left({}^m r_{ij}\right)$	$r_j^a = \frac{1}{\sum_i n_{ij}} \sum_{i=1}^{I} n_{ij} \max_{m=1,2,\ldots,N}\left({}^m r_{ij}\right) \max_{{}^m\widehat{p}_{ij}}(abs({}^m\widehat{p}_{ij} - {}^m p_i)), \quad m = 1,2$
	Seller (Sender)		
1:N	$R^s = \frac{1}{IJ}\sum_{j=1}^{J}\sum_{i=1}^{I} r_{ij}$	$R^n = \frac{1}{IJ}\sum_{j=1}^{J}\left(\frac{1}{\sum_{i=1}^{I} n_{ij}}\sum_{i=1}^{I} n_{ij} r_{ij}\right)$	$R^a = \frac{1}{IJ}\sum_{j=1}^{J}\left(\frac{1}{\sum_{i=1}^{I} n_{ij}}\sum_{i=1}^{I} n_{ij} r_{ij} ia_{ij}\right)$
2:N single problem	${}^k R_i^s = \frac{1}{J}\sum_{j=1}^{J} {}^k r_{ij}, \quad k = 1,2.$	${}^k R_i^n = \frac{1}{J}\sum_{j=1}^{J} n_{ij} {}^k r_{ij}, \quad k = 1,2.$	${}^k R_i^a = \frac{1}{\sum_j n_{ij}}\sum_{j=1}^{J} n_{ij} {}^k r_{ij} (abs({}^k\widehat{p}_{ij} - {}^k p_i)), \quad k = 1,2.$
2:N overall	${}^k R^s = \frac{1}{IJ}\sum_{j=1}^{J}(\sum_{i=1}^{I} {}^k r_{ij}), \quad k = 1,2.$	${}^k R^n = \frac{1}{J}\sum_{j=1}^{J}(\frac{1}{\sum_i n_{ij}}\sum_{i=1}^{I} n_{ij} {}^k r_{ij}), \quad k = 1,2.$	${}^k R^a = \frac{1}{I}\sum_{i=1}^{I}(\frac{1}{\sum_j n_{ij}}\sum_{j=1}^{J} n_{ij} {}^k r_{ij} (abs({}^k\widehat{p}_{ij} - {}^k p_i))), \quad k = 1,2.$

Appendix 1. Symbols, Notations, Definitions, Formulae

scenario	Models		
	M1	M2	M3
N:M single problem	${}^{m}R_i^s = \frac{1}{J}\sum_{j=1}^{J} {}^{m}r_{ij}, \quad m = 1,2,\ldots,N$	${}^{m}R_i^n = \frac{1}{J}\sum_{j=1}^{J} n_{ij}\, {}^{m}r_{ij}, \quad m = 1,2,\ldots,N$	${}^{m}R_i^a = \frac{1}{\sum_j n_{ij}}\sum_{j=1}^{J} n_{ij}\, {}^{m}r_{ij}(abs(\widehat{{}^{m}p_{ij}} - {}^{m}p_i), \quad m = 1,2,\ldots,N$
N:M overall	${}^{m}R^s = \frac{1}{IJ}\sum_{j=1}^{J}(\sum_{i=1}^{I} {}^{m}r_{ij}), \quad m = 1,2,\ldots N$	${}^{m}R^n = \frac{1}{I}\sum_{i=1}^{I}(\frac{1}{\sum_j n_{ij}}\sum_{j=1}^{J} n_{ij}\, {}^{m}r_{ij}), \quad m = 1,2,\ldots,N$	${}^{m}R^a = \frac{1}{I}\sum_{i=1}^{I}(\frac{1}{\sum_j n_{ij}}\sum_{j=1}^{J} n_{ij}\, {}^{m}r_{ij}(abs(\widehat{{}^{m}p_{ij}} - {}^{m}p_i))), \quad m = 1,2,\ldots,N$

Table 4. Measures of dynamic risk of misinforming

Model	Topology	
	1:1	1:N
M1	$r_j^s(t)=\frac{\sum_{i=1}^{k} r_{ij}(t)\left(\mu_{ij}t^I+\left(1-\mu_{ij}\right)t^R\right)}{\sum_{i=1}^{k}\mu_{ij}t^I+\left(1-\mu_{ij}\right)t^R}$	$R^s(t)=\frac{\sum_{j=1}^{J}\sum_{i=1}^{k} r_{ij}(t)\left(\mu_{ij}^a t^I+\left(1-\mu_{ij}^a\right)t^R\right)}{\sum_{j=1}^{J}\sum_{i=1}^{k}\left(\mu_{ij}^a t^I+\left(1-\mu_{ij}^a\right)t^R\right)}$
M2	$r_j^n(t)=\frac{\sum_{i=1}^{k} n_{ij}(t)r_{ij}(t)\left(\mu_{ij}t^I+\left(1-\mu_{ij}\right)t^R\right)}{\sum_{i=1}^{k} n_{ij}(t)\left(\mu_{ij}t^I+\left(1-\mu_{ij}\right)t^R\right)}$	$R^n(t)=\frac{\sum_{j=1}^{J}\sum_{i=1}^{k} r_{ij}(t)n_{ij}(t)\left(\mu_{ij}^a t^I+\left(1-\mu_{ij}^a\right)t^R\right)}{\sum_{j=1}^{J}\sum_{i=1}^{k} n_{ij}(t)\left(\mu_{ij}^a t^I+\left(1-\mu_{ij}^a\right)t^R\right)}$
M3	$r_j^a(t)==\frac{\sum_{i=1}^{k} n_{ij}(t)r_{ij}(t)ia_{ij}\left(\mu_{ij}t^I+\left(1-\mu_{ij}\right)t^R\right)}{\sum_{i=1}^{k} n_{ij}(t)\left(\mu_{ij}t^I+\left(1-\mu_{ij}\right)t^R\right)}$	$R^a(t)==\frac{\sum_{j=1}^{J}\sum_{i=1}^{k} r_{ij}(t)n_{ij}(t)ia_{ij}\left(\mu_{ij}^a t^I+\left(1-\mu_{ij}^a\right)t^R\right)}{\sum_{j=1}^{J}\sum_{i=1}^{k} n_{ij}(t)\left(\mu_{ij}^a t^I+\left(1-\mu_{ij}^a\right)t^R\right)}$

Appendix 2. Data Collection Surveys

This appendix presents forms used in surveying potential customers to collect data suitable to verify applicability of models developed through the book. The presented surveys reflect the history of developed models. The possibility to collect relevant data is essential to apply the models developed in Part 2 of the book. This appendix includes all forms of questionnaires used to survey respondents' attitude toward misinforming risk and associates warranty coverage.

Surveys were conducted to students at American University in Bulgaria, Bulgaria (in English); of Victoria University of Wellington, New Zealand (in English; and at State University of Library Studies and Information Technologies, Bulgaria (in Bulgarian). All forms presented in this appendix are in English.

Appendix 2.1. History of Developed Surveys

Table 1. Summary of history of surveys

Year	Objectives	Type of responses	Applicability	Comments	Respondents
2001-2003	Illustrating existence of misinforming	Y/N	Easy	Not designed to allow quantifying the risk. Designed to illustrate importance of user-oriented MIS interface.	Sophomore students in AUBG[1] MIS course.
2006	Allowing basic measures	Likert scale	Easy	The survey allows evaluation of the basic measures of the risk of misinforming.	Offered to two different categories of students: 1. Sophomore students in OR course in Victoria University[2]. 2. First year students in IB course of SULSIT[3].
2008	Evaluation of degree of acceptance	Likert scale	Complicated	The survey was done in two stages with one week break to exclude self-plagiarism. The first one addressed degree of acceptance, and the second to assess applicability of device.	Offered to two different categories of students: 1. Sophomore students in OR course in Victoria University. 2. First year students in IB course of SULSIT.
2008	Addressing competing messages	Likert scale	Over complicated	The survey was done in two stages with one week break. The same respondents were approached twice.	Offered to First year students in IB course of SULSIT.
Next surveys, conducted in 209 and 2010 replicated the one 2008 survey addressing the degree of acceptance.					

Notes:

1. Every survey includes the same part for assessing basic measures of the risk.
2. The second survey at 2008 was conducted only with students of SULSIT, and complexity of answering, as well as logistic to conduct it makes unfeasible to replicate it to VUW.
3. The last survey shows that increasing further complexity of surveys to collect the needed data is not practical.

Appendix 2.2. Surveys Forms

Appendix 2.2.1. Surveys Conducted in 2001-2003 to Illustrate the Existence of Misinforming[4]

Please, consider the following configuration of a PC:

ASUS A7V333/RA sA, VIA KT333, 266, ATA 133, RAID, 3DDR, AGP 4x, USB 2.0, IEE 1394, ATX
AMD XP PALOMINO 2100PR/1.75 GHz
DDRAM 512 MB DDR, PC 333MHz, SAMSUNG
80 GB MAXSTOR / 7200 / ATA 133/2MB
PCI ATI 1MB
17'' SAMSUNG 753S 1280x1024/65Hz 1024x768/85 Hz BW
keyboard, mouse, midi tower case

Please, evaluate what is your need to use a PC, and whether the above PC will satisfy your need for given application:

Application	**Needs Yes/No**	**Assessed ability of the PC Yes/No**
Word Processing		
Computation		
e-mail		
Internet		
Personal data		
Games		
Movies		

Table 3. Please, choose which one of the two warranty option you prefer in a way to purchase the above PC

Warranty contract	**Choice Yes/No**
Three-years warranty if the product fails	
One-month probation	

Appendix 2.2.2. Surveys Conducted in 2006 to Allow Evaluation of Basic Measures of Misinforming[5]

Dear students,

We are investigating the impact of information asymmetry on business transactions and purchase decisions. Our main goal is to assess the relation between information asymmetry and warranty assigned to the product.

Thank you for being part of our study. Your response will contribute significantly in developing a methodology for assessing the risk of information asymmetry and warranty settings.

Description of the experiment:

You are offered to buy a personal computer (PC) with a highly attractive price. In addition, you are asked to select the warranty policy you consider to be the best for your purchase decision.

AMD 64 Entertainer Pack: AMD Athlon 64 4800+ Dual Core

Hardware

- 107S 17" Flat Screen Beige or Black
- PowerColour X300SE 128MB PCI Express Video Card
- 512 MB DDR 400 RAM
- Seagate 160GB Serial ATA Hard Drive
- Samsung Internal IDE 52/24/52 CDRW
- 3.5" Floppy Drive
- 56 kbps V92 PCI Fax Modem
- Integrated 10/100 Network Card
- Microsoft Multimedia Keyboard
- Microsoft Optical Wheel Mouse
- Microsoft Windows XP Home Edition OEM - Supplied on Genuine Microsoft Original CD's

Bundled Software

- Microsoft Windows XP Home OEM supplied on genuine Microsoft original CD's
- Open Office ver 2 consisting of:
- Calc - MS Excel-compatible spreadsheet
- Writer - MS Word-compatible word processor
- Impress - MS Powerpoint-compatible presentations
- Draw - Drawing program
- AVG Antivirus

2006 survey, continue.

Support

- One Year return-to-store parts and labor warranty on base computer unit
- One Year free telephone support during business hours within Wellington free dial area
- Three Years onsite warranty on Philips Monitors. three years return-to-store on AOC monitors
- 90 days support on bundled software supplied with PC through Quay Computers
- All PC Servicing to the computer base unit is carried out in store

1. Please fill in the table below by ticking the box that represents the best your needs and your opinion on whether the offered computer configuration is capable to satisfy them.

Task	Degree of needs						Degree of capability					
	0	1	2	3	4	5	0	1	2	3	4	5
Using word processing												
Using spread sheets (e.g., MS Excel)												
Using e-mail												
Surfing Internet												
Solving complicated math problems												
Playing Games												
Watching movies												
Listening Music												

0 – lowest, not at all, i.e. "NO",
5 – highest, definitely "YES"

2. Choose one of the options listed below, by ticking the box:

I am not interested in buying this PC at all.	
I will buy it if the warranty policy is:	
The PC is replaced or repaired if it fails within the first three years after purchasing	
You will get full refund if you are not fully satisfied with the PC within the first three months after purchasing	
You will get a full refund if you are not fully satisfied with the PC within the first month after purchasing. AND The PC is replaced or repaired if it fails within the year after purchasing	

Appendix 2.2.3. Survey Conducted in 2008 to Evaluate the Degree of Acceptance[6]

Part 1 of the survey consists of eight identical tables, one for each of the type of works assumed relevant. Here, only two of these tables, for word-processing and for using spreadsheets are shown.

Dear students,

We are studying the impact of information exchange on business transactions and purchase decisions and the way this exchange affects the customer choice.

We are running the following experiment:

Firstly, we need information about your needs and applications, you are going to use, as well as the minimal configuration of the PC you need to run the application in a way suitable to your needs.

Second, assume that you are offered the opportunity to buy a personal computer (PC) at a **highly attractive price** (say, the sale price is 30% less than you would expect to pay). You have to assess the level the given PC configuration meets your needs to run applications you need as well as the warranty policy, which suits the best to your purchase decision.

Part 1. Assessment of needs

Form 1: Please, select the minimal configuration of the PC to meet your needs for using it for:

Table 6. Using word processing

PC property	Low				High
	0	**1**	**2**	**3**	**4**
CPU	0.35 GHz	1 GHz	1.6 GHz	2.4 GHz	4.8 GHz
RAM	256 MB	512 MB	1 GB	2 GB	4 GB
HDD	20 GB	40 GB	80 GB	120 GB	240 GB
VRam	16 MB	64 MB	256 MB	512 MB	1 GB
Ethernet	56 Kbs	10 Mbs	100 Mbs	1 Gbs	10 Gbs

How often you use PC for word processing	Low				High
	never	yearly	monthly	weekly	daily
	0	1	2	3	4

Table 7. Using spreadsheets, (e.g. Excel)

PC property	Low				High
	0	**1**	**2**	**3**	**4**
CPU	0,35 GHz	1 GHz	1.6 GHz	2.4 GHz	4.8 GHz
RAM	256 MB	512 MB	1 GB	2 GB	4 GB
HDD	20 GB	40 GB	80 GB	120 GB	240 GB
VRam	16 MB	64 MB	256 MB	512 MB	1 GB
Ethernet	56 Kbs	10 Mbs	100 Mbs	1 Gbs	10 Gbs

How often you use PC for spreadsheets	Low				High
	never	yearly	monthly	weekly	daily
	0	1	2	3	4

Part 2. Assessment of degree of acceptance

Form 1: Please, select the minimal configuration of the PC to meet your needs for using it for:

Table 8. a) Using word processing

PC property	Low				High
	0	**1**	**2**	**3**	**4**
CPU	0,35 GHz	1 GHz	1.6 GHz	2.4 GHz	4.8 GHz
RAM	256 MB	512 MB	1 GB	2 GB	4 GB
HDD	20 GB	40 GB	80 GB	120 GB	240 GB
VRam	16 MB	64 MB	256 MB	512 MB	1 GB
Ethernet	56 Kbs	10 Mbs	100 Mbs	1 Gbs	10 Gbs

How often you use PC for word processing	Low				High
	never	yearly	monthly	weekly	daily
	0	1	2	3	4

Table 9. b) Using spreadsheets, (e.g., MS Excel)

PC property	Low				High
	0	**1**	**2**	**3**	**4**
CPU	0,35 GHz	1 GHz	1.6 GHz	2.4 GHz	4.8 GHz
RAM	256 MB	512 MB	1 GB	2 GB	4 GB
HDD	20 GB	40 GB	80 GB	120 GB	240 GB
VRam	16 MB	64 MB	256 MB	512 MB	1 GB
Ethernet	56 Kbs	10 Mbs	100 Mbs	1 Gbs	10 Gbs

How often you use PC for spreadsheets	Low				High
	never	yearly	monthly	weekly	daily
	0	1	2	3	4

Part 2. Assessment of degree of acceptance (continue).

Form 2: Consider the following PC:
AMD 64 Professional Pack: AMD Athlon 64 4800+ Quad Core
Hardware

- 107S 17" Flat Screen Beige or Black
- PowerColour X300SE 64MB PCI Express Video Card
- 2 GB DDR 400 RAM
- Seagate 160GB Serial ATA Hard Drive
- Samsung Internal IDE 52/24/52 CDRW
- 3.5" Floppy Drive
- 56 kbps V92 PCI Fax Modem
- Integrated 10/100 Network Card
- Microsoft Multimedia Keyboard
- Microsoft Optical Wheel Mouse
- Microsoft Windows XP Home Edition OEM

Bundled Software

- Microsoft Windows XP Home

- Open Office ver 2 consisting of:
- Calc - MS Excel-compatible spreadsheet
- Writer - MS Word-compatible word processor
- Impress - MS Powerpoint-compatible presentations
- Draw - Drawing program
- AVG Antivirus

We need your input on the following:

1. **Please fill in the table** below by ticking the box that best represents your needs in order to perform the stated task (listed in the first column) and your opinion on the extent to which the offered computer is capable of satisfying them.

Task	Degree of your needs					The PC degree of capability				
	Low High					Low High				
	0	1	2	3	4	0	1	2	3	4
Using word processing										
Using spreadsheets, (e.g. Excel)										
Using e-mail										
Surfing Internet										
Solving complicated problems										
Playing Games										
Watching movies										
Listening to Music										

Part 2. Assessment of degree of acceptance (continue).

Note: these forms are split into groups to reveal respondents' attitude toward warrant.

Form 3: Specific part: Survey provided to group 1.

Which warranty option would you prefer for your purchase? Please, choose **ONE** of the options listed below, by ticking the box on the right:

The PC is replaced or repaired free of charge to the customer if it fails within the first **THREE years** after the sale date.	
The customer will get full refund if he/she is not fully satisfied with the PC within the **first THREE months** after the sale date.	

Form 3: Specific part: Survey provided to group 2.

Which warranty option would you prefer for your purchase? Please, choose **ONE** of the options listed below, by ticking the box on the right:

The PC is replaced or repaired free of charge to the customer if it fails within the first **THREE years** after the sale date.	
The customer will get full refund if he/she is not fully satisfied with the PC within the **first THREE months** after the sale date.	
The customer will get full refund if he/she is not fully satisfied with the PC within **the FIRST month** after purchasing AND The PC is replaced or repaired free of charge to the customer if it fails within **ONE year** after the sale date.	

Note: The two parts of the survey were offered to respondents in two stages with one-hour break. Firstly, the respondents were asked to fill in Form 1, which addresses the degree of acceptance and how often they need to do the given activity . After approximately one hour, the second part of the survey was given out. The time gap between the first and the second part of the survey was introduced to allow reduce the direct dependence between the information used to evaluate the degree of acceptance for the different PC components and the configuration of the particular PC given in the second part of the survey. In this way the degree of acceptance is evaluated for the group of respondents.

Appendix 2.2.4. Survey Conducted in 2008 to Evaluate the Risk of Misinforming in the Case of Competing Messages[7]

Note: This survey extended the survey designed to collect data for measuring degree of acceptance by adding a third part to compare two competing products. The third part was offered to the same students who responded to the above survey after one week. Here is presented only the third part.

Part 3: Evaluation in case of competing messages

Table 10. Configuration of the two competing products

PC 1	PC 2
AMD 64: AMD Athlon 64 4800+ Quad Core **Hardware** • 107S 17" Flat Screen Beige or Black • PowerColour X300SE 64MB PCI Express Video Card • 2 GB DDR 400 RAM • Seagate 500 GB Serial ATA Hard Drive • Samsung Internal IDE 52/24/52 CDRW • 3.5" Floppy Drive • 56 kbps V92 PCI Fax Modem • Integrated 10/100 Network Card • Microsoft 101 Keyboard • Microsoft Optical Wheel Mouse **Software** • Microsoft Windows XP Professional • Open Office ver. 2 • AVG Antivirus	**AMD 64: AMD Athlon 64 4800** **Hardware** • 107S 21" Flat Screen • PowerColour X300SE 512MB PCI Express Video Card • 2 GB DDR 400 RAM • Seagate 160GB Serial ATA Hard Drive • Samsung Internal IDE 52/24/52 DVDRW • 256 kbps V92 PCI Fax Modem • Integrated 100/1000 Network Card • Microsoft Multimedia Keyboard • Microsoft Optical Wheel Mouse **Software** • Microsoft Windows XP Home • MS Office Professional • AVG Antivirus

Table 11. Survey form for direct comparison of the two products

Applicatione	Degree to which the given PC 1 satisfies your needs					Degree to which the given PC 2 satisfies your needs				
	low High					Low High				
	0	1	2	3	4	0	1	2	3	4
Word processing										
Spreadsheets, (Excel)										
e-mail										
Internet										
Complex computational problems										
Games										
Movies										
Music										

Appendix 2.2. Surveys Forms

Appendix 2.2.1. Surveys Conducted in 2001-2003 to Illustrate the Existence of Misinforming[8]

Please, consider the following configuration of a PC:

ASUS A7V333/RA sA, VIA KT333, 266, ATA 133, RAID, 3DDR, AGP 4x, USB 2.0, IEE 1394, ATX
AMD XP PALOMINO 2100PR/1.75 GHz
DDRAM 512 MB DDR, PC 333MHz, SAMSUNG
80 GB MAXSTOR / 7200 / ATA 133/2MB
PCI ATI 1MB
17'' SAMSUNG 753S 1280x1024/65Hz 1024x768/85 Hz BW
keyboard, mouse, midi tower case

Please, evaluate what is your need to use a PC, and whether the above PC will satisfy your need for given application:

Application	Needs Yes/No	Assessed ability of the PC Yes/No
Word Processing		
Computation		
e-mail		
Internet		
Personal data		
Games		
Movies		

Please, choose which one of the two warranty option you prefer in a way to purchase the above PC

Warranty contract	Choice Yes/No
Three-years warranty if the product fails	
One-month probation	

Appendix 2.2.2. Surveys Conducted in 2006 to Allow Evaluation of Basic Measures of Misinforming[9]

Dear students,

We are investigating the impact of information asymmetry on business transactions and purchase decisions. Our main goal is to assess the relation between information asymmetry and warranty assigned to the product.

Thank you for being part of our study. Your response will contribute significantly in developing a methodology for assessing the risk of information asymmetry and warranty settings.

Description of the experiment:

You are offered to buy a personal computer (PC) with a highly attractive price. In addition, you are asked to select the warranty policy you consider to be the best for your purchase decision.

AMD 64 Entertainer Pack: AMD Athlon 64 4800+ Dual Core

Hardware

- 107S 17" Flat Screen Beige or Black
- PowerColour X300SE 128MB PCI Express Video Card
- 512 MB DDR 400 RAM
- Seagate 160GB Serial ATA Hard Drive
- Samsung Internal IDE 52/24/52 CDRW
- 3.5" Floppy Drive
- 56 kbps V92 PCI Fax Modem
- Integrated 10/100 Network Card
- Microsoft Multimedia Keyboard
- Microsoft Optical Wheel Mouse
- Microsoft Windows XP Home Edition OEM - Supplied on Genuine Microsoft Original CD's

Bundled Software

- Microsoft Windows XP Home OEM supplied on genuine Microsoft original CD's
- Open Office ver 2 consisting of:
- Calc - MS Excel-compatible spreadsheet
- Writer - MS Word-compatible word processor
- Impress - MS Powerpoint-compatible presentations
- Draw - Drawing program
- AVG Antivirus

2006 survey, continue.

Support

- One Year return-to-store parts and labor warranty on base computer unit
- One Year free telephone support during business hours within Wellington free dial area
- Three Years onsite warranty on Philips Monitors. three years return-to-store on AOC monitors
- 90 days support on bundled software supplied with PC through Quay Computers
- All PC Servicing to the computer base unit is carried out in store

3. Please fill in the table below by ticking the box that represents the best your needs and your opinion on whether the offered computer configuration is capable to satisfy them.

Task	Degree of needs						Degree of capability					
	0	1	2	3	4	5	0	1	2	3	4	5
Using word processing												
Using spread sheets (e.g., MS Excel)												
Using e-mail												
Surfing Internet												
Solving complicated math problems												
Playing Games												
Watching movies												
Listening Music												

0 – lowest, not at all, i.e. "NO",
5 – highest, definitely "YES"

Table 15. 4.Choose one of the options listed below, by ticking the box:

I am not interested in buying this PC at all.	
I will buy it if the warranty policy is:	
The PC is replaced or repaired if it fails within the first three years after purchasing	
You will get full refund if you are not fully satisfied with the PC within the first three months after purchasing	
You will get a full refund if you are not fully satisfied with the PC within the first month after purchasing. AND The PC is replaced or repaired if it fails within the year after purchasing	

Appendix 2.2.3. Survey Conducted in 2008 to Evaluate the Degree of Acceptance[10]

Part 1 of the survey consists of eight identical tables, one for each of the type of works assumed relevant. Here, only two of these tables, for word-processing and for using spreadsheets are shown.

Dear students,

We are studying the impact of information exchange on business transactions and purchase decisions and the way this exchange affects the customer choice.

We are running the following experiment:

Firstly, we need information about your needs and applications, you are going to use, as well as the minimal configuration of the PC you need to run the application in a way suitable to your needs.

Second, assume that you are offered the opportunity to buy a personal computer (PC) at a **highly attractive price** (say, the sale price is 30% less than you would expect to pay). You have to assess the level the given PC configuration meets your needs to run applications you need as well as the warranty policy, which suits the best to your purchase decision.

Part 1. Assessment of needs

Form 1: Please, select the minimal configuration of the PC to meet your needs for using it for:

Table 16. a) Using word processing

PC property	Low				High
	0	**1**	**2**	**3**	**4**
CPU	0.35 GHz	1 GHz	1.6 GHz	2.4 GHz	4.8 GHz
RAM	256 MB	512 MB	1 GB	2 GB	4 GB
HDD	20 GB	40 GB	80 GB	120 GB	240 GB
VRam	16 MB	64 MB	256 MB	512 MB	1 GB
Ethernet	56 Kbs	10 Mbs	100 Mbs	1 Gbs	10 Gbs

How often you use PC for word processing	Low				High
	never	yearly	monthly	weekly	daily
	0	1	2	3	4

Table 17. b) Using spreadsheets, (e.g. Excel)

PC property	Low				High
	0	**1**	**2**	**3**	**4**
CPU	0,35 GHz	1 GHz	1.6 GHz	2.4 GHz	4.8 GHz
RAM	256 MB	512 MB	1 GB	2 GB	4 GB
HDD	20 GB	40 GB	80 GB	120 GB	240 GB
VRam	16 MB	64 MB	256 MB	512 MB	1 GB
Ethernet	56 Kbs	10 Mbs	100 Mbs	1 Gbs	10 Gbs

How often you use PC for spreadsheets	Low				High
	never	yearly	monthly	weekly	daily
	0	1	2	3	4

Part 2. Assessment of degree of acceptance

Form 1: Please, select the minimal configuration of the PC to meet your needs for using it for:

Table 18. a) Using word processing

PC property	Low				High
	0	**1**	**2**	**3**	**4**
CPU	0,35 GHz	1 GHz	1.6 GHz	2.4 GHz	4.8 GHz
RAM	256 MB	512 MB	1 GB	2 GB	4 GB
HDD	20 GB	40 GB	80 GB	120 GB	240 GB
VRam	16 MB	64 MB	256 MB	512 MB	1 GB
Ethernet	56 Kbs	10 Mbs	100 Mbs	1 Gbs	10 Gbs

How often you use PC for word processing	Low				High
	never	yearly	monthly	weekly	daily
	0	1	2	3	4

Table 19. b) Using spreadsheets, (e.g., MS Excel)

PC property	Low				High
	0	1	2	3	4
CPU	0,35 GHz	1 GHz	1.6 GHz	2.4 GHz	4.8 GHz
RAM	256 MB	512 MB	1 GB	2 GB	4 GB
HDD	20 GB	40 GB	80 GB	120 GB	240 GB
VRam	16 MB	64 MB	256 MB	512 MB	1 GB
Ethernet	56 Kbs	10 Mbs	100 Mbs	1 Gbs	10 Gbs

How often you use PC for spreadsheets	Low				High
	never	yearly	monthly	weekly	daily
	0	1	2	3	4

Part 2. Assessment of degree of acceptance (continue).

Form 2: Consider the following PC:
AMD 64 Professional Pack: AMD Athlon 64 4800+ Quad Core Hardware

- 107S 17" Flat Screen Beige or Black
- PowerColour X300SE 64MB PCI Express Video Card
- 2 GB DDR 400 RAM
- Seagate 160GB Serial ATA Hard Drive
- Samsung Internal IDE 52/24/52 CDRW
- 3.5" Floppy Drive
- 56 kbps V92 PCI Fax Modem
- Integrated 10/100 Network Card
- Microsoft Multimedia Keyboard
- Microsoft Optical Wheel Mouse
- Microsoft Windows XP Home Edition OEM

Bundled Software

- Microsoft Windows XP Home

- Open Office ver 2 consisting of:
- Calc - MS Excel-compatible spreadsheet
- Writer - MS Word-compatible word processor
- Impress - MS Powerpoint-compatible presentations
- Draw - Drawing program
- AVG Antivirus

We need your input on the following:

2. **Please fill in the table** below by ticking the box that best represents your needs in order to perform the stated task (listed in the first column) and your opinion on the extent to which the offered computer is capable of satisfying them.

Task	Degree of your needs					The PC degree of capability				
	Low High					Low High				
	0	1	2	3	4	0	1	2	3	4
Using word processing										
Using spreadsheets, (e.g. Excel)										
Using e-mail										
Surfing Internet										
Solving complicated problems										
Playing Games										
Watching movies										
Listening to Music										

Part 2. Assessment of degree of acceptance (continue).

Note: these forms are split into groups to reveal respondents' attitude toward warrant.

Form 3: Specific part: Survey provided to group 1.

Which warranty option would you prefer for your purchase? Please, choose **ONE** of the options listed below, by ticking the box on the right:

The PC is replaced or repaired free of charge to the customer if it fails within the first **THREE years** after the sale date.	
The customer will get full refund if he/she is not fully satisfied with the PC within the **first THREE months** after the sale date.	

Form 3: Specific part: Survey provided to group 2.

Which warranty option would you prefer for your purchase? Please, choose **ONE** of the options listed below, by ticking the box on the right:

The PC is replaced or repaired free of charge to the customer if it fails within the first **THREE years** after the sale date.	
The customer will get full refund if he/she is not fully satisfied with the PC within the **first THREE months** after the sale date.	
The customer will get full refund if he/she is not fully satisfied with the PC within **the FIRST month** after purchasing AND The PC is replaced or repaired free of charge to the customer if it fails within **ONE year** after the sale date.	

Note: The two parts of the survey were offered to respondents in two stages with one-hour break. Firstly, the respondents were asked to fill in Form 1, which addresses the degree of acceptance and how often they need to do the given activity . After approximately one hour, the second part of the survey was given out. The time gap between the first and the second part of the survey was introduced to allow reduce the direct dependence between the information used to evaluate the degree of acceptance for the different PC components and the configuration of the particular PC given in the second part of the survey. In this way the degree of acceptance is evaluated for the group of respondents.

ENDNOTES

1 AUBG: American University in Bulgaria, Blagoevgrad, Bulgaria

2 VUW: Victoria University of Wellington, Wellington, New Zealand

3 SULSIT: State University of Library Studies and Information Technologies, Sofia, Bulgaria

4 Offered to sophomore students in the BUS 270 "MIS" course at American University in Bulgaria, Blagoevgrad, Bulgaria

5 This survey was offered twice to students at two different categories:International students' body – sophomores in Operations Research course at Victoria

University, Wellington, New Zealand, and Bulgarian first-year students in Information Brokerage course at University of Library Studies and Information Technologies, Sofia, Bulgaria.

6 Offered to first-year students in Information Brokerage course at University of Library Studies and Information Technologies, Sofia, Bulgaria (the survey form was in Bulgarian and an English translation is presented here).

7 Offered to first-year students in Information Brokerage course at the University of Library Studies and Information Technologies, Sofia, Bulgaria

8 Offered to sophomore students in the BUS 270 "MIS" course at American University in Bulgaria, Blagoevgrad, Bulgaria

9 This survey was offered twice to students at two different categories: International students' body – sophomores in Operations Research course at Victoria University, Wellington, New Zealand, and Bulgarian first-year students in Information Brokerage course at University of Library Studies and Information Technologies, Sofia, Bulgaria.

10 Offered to first-year students in Information Brokerage course at University of Library Studies and Information Technologies, Sofia, Bulgaria (the survey form was in Bulgarian and an English translation is presented here).

Compilation of References

Agrawal, R., Kadadi, A., Xiangfeng, D., & Adres, F. (2015). Challenges and Opportunities with Big Data Visualization. *7th International Conference on Management of computational and collective IntElligence in Digital EcoSystems (MEDES)*, (pp. 169–173). ACM. 10.1145/2857218.2857256

Akerlof, G. (1970). The Market for "Lemons": Quality Uncertainty and the Market Mechanism. The Quarterly Journal of Economics, 84(3). Oxford University Press.

Anzilotti, E. (2017). *How Mastercard's "Data Philanthropy" Program is Tackling the Global Financial Information Gap.* Fast Company. (https://www.fastcompany.com/40457902/how-mastercards-data-philanthropy-program-is-tackling-the-global-financial-information-gap)

Apostel, L. (1972). *Seminar on Interdisciplinarity in Universities.* Lib. https://lib.ugent.be/catalog/rug01:000175104

Arrow, K. (1963). Uncertainty and Welfare Economics of Medical Care. *The American Economic Review*, *53*(5), 942–973.

Ashby, W. (1963). *Introduction to Cybernetics*. John Willey & Sons.

Asimov I. (1961). The Machine That Won the War. *The Magazine of Fantasy & Science Fiction.*

Asimov, I. (1940). *I, robot.* SFU. https://www2.cs.sfu.ca/~vaughan/teaching/415/papers/I,%20Robot%20Ch1-3.pdf

Barton A. (2022). Grade Inflation: What Goes Up Must Come Down. *The Harvard Crimson.*

Bella, A., Ferri, C., Hernández-Orallo, J., & Ramírez-Quintana, M. J. (2009). Negotiation with price-dependent probability models. *CEUR Workshop Proceedings*, *635*, 9–20.

Bhagat, S., Goyal, A., & Lakshmanan, L. V. S. (2012). Maximizing product adoption in social networks *WSDM 2012 - Proceedings of the 5th ACM International Conference on Web Search and Data Mining*, (pp. 603-612). ACM.

Blischke, W., & Murthy, D. N. P. (1993). *Warranty Cost Analysis*. Marcel Dekker.

Blischke, W., & Murthy, D. N. P. (1996). Product Warranty Handbook, Marcel Dekker Chang-Tseh Hseih, Fujun Lai, and Weihua Shi, (2006), Information orientation and its impact on information asymmetry and e-business adoption: Evidence from China's international trading industry. *Industrial Management & Data Systems, 106*(6), 825–840.

Blischke, W., & Murthy, D. N. P. (1996). *Product Warranty Handbook.* Marcel Dekker.

Box, G. E. P., & Draper, N. R. (1987). *Empirical model-building and response surfaces.* John Wiley & Sons.

Brammar, S., & Millington, A. (2008). Does it pay to be different? An analysis of the relationship between corporate social and financial performance. *Strategic Management Journal, 29*(12), 1325–1343. doi:10.1002mj.714

Brandenburger, A., & Nalebuff, B. (1996). Co-opetition: A Revolution Mindset that Combines Competition and Cooperation, Harvard business Press, Cambridge.

Brandenburger, A., & Nalebuff, B. (1996). Co-opetition: A Revolution Mindset that Combines Competition and Cooperation. Harvard business Press, Cambridge.

Buckland, M. (1991). Information and Information Systems. Praeger.

Buckland, M. (1991). *Information and Information Systems.* Praeger.

Chomsky N. (1957), Syntactic Structures, *Mouton & Co.*, 1957

Chomsky N. (1964), Current Issues in Linguistic Theory, *Mouton & Co.*, 1964

Christozov D., Reeves-Ellington R. (1995). *Measures for Culture's Influence in Managerial Area.* SDA'95, Varna, Bulgaria.

Christozov, D. (1999). Evaluation of the Quality of an Option Compare to Its Alternatives, in Polis, Dontchev, Kall, Lasiecka, Olbrot Systems Modelling and Optimization. *Proceedings of the 18th IFIP TC7 Conference (Research Notes in Mathematics Series).* CRC Press.

Christozov, D., & Mateev, P. (2003). *Warranty as a Factor for e-Commerce Success.* Informing Science and IT Education Conference, Pori, Finland. http://InSITE.nu

Christozov, D., & Mateev, P. (2003). Warranty as a Factor for e-Commerce Success. *Informing Science and IT Education Conference*, Pori, Finland. https://www.informingscience.org/Publications/2641?Type=ConferenceProceedings&ConferenceID=33)

Christozov, D., & Nikolova, I. (2001). Infobroker – an Emerging Profession of Informing Mediators? *Proceedings Informing Science 2001.* Information Science. (http://proceedings.informingscience.org/IS2001Proceedings/pdf/Christozov.pdf)

Christozov, D., & Toleva, S. (2013) Knowledge diffusion via social networks: The 21st century challenge, International Journal of Digital Literacy and Digital Competence (IJDLDC). IGI-Global. 2013

Christozov, D., Chukova, S., & Mateev, P. (2015). Risk of Misinforming and Message Customization in Customer Related Management. *Issues in Informing Science and Information Technology, 12*, 47-61.

Christozov, D., Chukova, S., & Mateev, P. (2016). Warranty of Misinforming as an Option in Product Utilization Process, *Informing Science: the International Journal of Emerging Transdiscipline, 19*, 75-87.

Christozov, D., Chukova, S., & Mateev, P. (2016). Warranty of Misinforming as an Option in Product Utilization Process. *Informing Science: the International Journal of Emerging Transdiscipline, 19.*

Christozov, D., Toleva-Stoimenova, S., Rasheva-Yordanova, K., & Vukarski, I. (2016). Developing Big Data Competences in the Digital Era, Proceedings of "Big Data, Knowledge and Control Systems Engineering - BdKCSE'2016. Sofia.

Christozov, D., Chukova, S., & Mateev, P. (2006). A Measure of Risk Caused by Information Asymmetry in e-Commerce. *Journal of Issues in Informing Science and Information Technology, 3*, 147–158. doi:10.28945/879

Christozov, D., Chukova, S., & Mateev, P. (2007). On the Relationship between Warranty and the Risk of Information Asymmetry. *Journal of Issues in Informing Science and Information Technology, 4*, 235–249. doi:10.28945/946

Christozov, D., Chukova, S., & Mateev, P. (2008). Warranty and the Risk of Misinforming: Evaluation of the Degree of Acceptance. *Journal of Issues in Informing Science and Information Technology, 5*, 667–677. doi:10.28945/1035

Christozov, D., Chukova, S., & Mateev, P. (2009). Informing Processes, Risks, Evaluation of the Risk of Misinforming. In *Foundations of Informing Science* (pp. 323–356). ISI.

Christozov, D., Chukova, S., & Mateev, P. (2009). On two types of warranties: Warranty of malfunctioning and warranty of misinforming. *Asia-Pacific Journal of Operational Research, 26*(3), 399–420. doi:10.1142/S0217595909002274

Christozov, D., Chukova, S., & Mateev, P. (2009). The risk of misinforming for competing messages. *Journal of Issues in Informing Science and Information Technology, 6*, 351–364. doi:10.28945/1064

Christozov, D., Chukova, S., & Mateev, P. (2010). Assessment of Quality of Warranty Policy. *Interdisciplinary Journal of Information, Knowledge, and Management, 5*, 62–72.

Christozov, D., Chukova, S., & Mateev, P. (2011). Assessment of Risk of Misinforming: Dynamic Measures. *Interdisciplinary Journal of Information, Knowledge, and Management, 6*, 163–176. doi:10.28945/1374

Christozov, D., Chukova, S., & Mateev, P. (2012). Market Segmentation Based on Risk of Misinforming Reduction. *Journal of Issues in Informing Science and Information Technology*, *9*, 253–265. doi:10.28945/1620

Christozov, D., Chukova, S., & Mateev, P. (2013). The role of Warranty of Misinforming in New Product Adoption. *Journal of Issues in Informing Science and Information Technology*, *10*, 111–120. doi:10.28945/1799

Christozov, D., Chukova, S., & Mateev, P. (2014). Warranty of Misinforming: An Overview. *Issues in Informing Science and Information Technology*, *11*, 31–46. doi:10.28945/1978

Christozov, D., Chukova, S., & Mateev, P. (2015). Risk of Misinforming and Message Customization in Customer Related Management. *Issues in Informing Science and Information Technology*, *12*, 47–61.

Christozov, D., Denchev, S., Toleva-Stoimenova, S., & Rasheva-Yordanova, K. (2008). Training Information Brokers: A Curriculum Model. *Journal of Issues in Informing Science and Information Technology*, *5*, 87–94. doi:10.28945/997

Christozov, D., & Mateev, P. (2005). Assessment of Information Asymmetry. *Pliska Studia Mathematica Bulgarica*, *17*, 27–38.

Christozov, D., & Mitreva, E. (2020). Trust in Learning from Big Data: The Two Sides of the Same Coin. *Issues in Information Systems*, *21*(1), 147–152.

Christozov, D., & Rasheva-Yordanova, K. (2017). Data Literacy: Developing Skills on Exploring Big Data Applications. [IJDLDC]. *International Journal of Digital Literacy and Digital Competence*, *8*(2), 14–38. doi:10.4018/IJDLDC.2017040102

Christozov, D., Rasheva-Yordanova, K., & Toleva-Stoimenova, S. (2018). *Analytical Competences in Big Data Era: Taxonomy. Proceedings of ICERi2018*, Seville, Spain. 10.21125/iceri.2018.2731

Christozov, D., Rasheva-Yordanova, K., & Toleva-Stoimenova, S. (2019). Challenges in Designing Curriculum for Trans-Disciplinary Education: On Cases of Designing Concentration on Informing Science and Master Program on Data Science. *Informing Science*, *22*, 19–30. doi:10.28945/4300

Christozov, D., & Toleva-Stoimenova, S. (2015). Big Data Literacy - a New Dimension of Digital Divide: Barriers in learning via exploring Big Data. In J. Girard, K. Berg, D. Klein, & I. G. I. Global (Eds.), *Strategic Data Based Wisdom in the Big Data Era* (pp. 156–170). doi:10.4018/978-1-4666-8122-4.ch009

Chukova, S., Arnold, R., & Wang, D. (2004). Warranty Analysis: An Approach to modelling Imperfect Repairs. *International Journal of Production Economics*, *89*(1), 57–68. doi:10.1016/S0925-5273(03)00200-7

Chukova, S., Dimitrov, B., & Rykov, V. (1993). Warranty Analysis. A survey. *Journal of Soviet Mathematics*, *67*(6), 3486–3508. doi:10.1007/BF01096273

Devos, J., Van Landeghem, H., & Deschoolmeester, D. (2012). SMEs and IT: Evidence *for a* Market for "Lemons". *Electronic Journal Information Systems Evaluation, 15*(1), 2012.

Dimitrov, B., Chukova, S., & Khalil, Z. (2004). Warranty Costs: An Age - Dependent Failure/ Repair Model. *Naval Research Logistics, 51*(7), 959–976. doi:10.1002/nav.20037

Duncan, D. (1998). *The Calendar: The 5000 Year Struggle To Align The Clock and the Heavens, and What Happened To The Missing Ten Days*. Fourth Estate.

Eng, Y., & Quaia, G. (2009). Strategies for improving new product adoption in uncertain environments: A selective review of the literature. *Industrial Marketing Management, 38*(3), 275–282. doi:10.1016/j.indmarman.2008.01.003

Fenn, J., & Raskino, M. (2011). Understanding Gartner's Hype Cycles. *Gartner Research*. Harvard. http://isites.harvard.edu/fs/docs/icb.topic1360759.files/understanding_gartners_hype_214001.pdf

Frankfurt, H. (2005). *On bullshit*. Princeton University Press.

Freedman, M. (2016). *Using Data as a Force for good* (TED talk). TED. (https://splvers.ups.com/what-if-2016/Using-Data-as-force-for-good-ted-ups-video)

Friedman, M. (2007). *The social responsibility of Business is to increase its profit, Corporate Ethics and Corporate Governance*. Springer.

Gackowski, Z. (2006). Quality of Informing: Credibility Provisional Model of Functional Dependencies. *2006 Informing Science and IT Education Joint Conference*, Salford, UK. 10.28945/3017

Gill, G. (2013). Culture, Complexity, and Informing: How Shared Beliefs Can Enhance Our Search for Fitness. *Informing Science, 16*, 71–98. doi:10.28945/1778

González Díaz, V., Barberá Martínez, L., Gómez Fernández, J. F., & Crespo Márquez, A. (2012). The management of a warranty assistances program: A suggestion as reference framework. *Advances in Safety, Reliability and Risk Management, Proceedings of the European Safety and Reliability Conference*. Research Gate.

González-Prida, V., Gómez, J., Barberá, L., & Crespo, A. (2012). The customer relationship in the warranty management of distribution network service providers, *11th International Probabilistic Safety Assessment and Management Conference and the Annual European Safety and Reliability Conference, ESREL*. Research Gate.

Haidt, J. (2006). The happiness hypothesis Finding modern truth in ancient wisdom. Perseus Books Group.

Haidt, J. (2001). The emotional dog and its rational tail: A social intuitionist approach to moral judgment. *Psychological Review, 108*(4), 814–834. doi:10.1037/0033-295X.108.4.814 PMID:11699120

Han, K. Pei (2011). Data Mining: Concepts and Techniques, (3rd ed.). Morgan Kaufmann Publishers.

Heller, J. (1961). *Catch-22*. Simon & Schuster.

Hofstede, G. (1984). *Culture's Consequences: International Differences in Work-Related Values* (2nd ed.). SAGE Publications.

Hofstede, G. (1984). Culture's Consequences: International Differences in Work-Related Values. *Sage (Atlanta, Ga.)*, 1984.

Hseih, C.-T., Lai, F., & Shi, W. (2006). Information orientation and its impact on information asymmetry and e-business adoption: Evidence from China's international trading industry. *Industrial Management & Data Systems, 106*(6), 825–840. doi:10.1108/02635570610671506

Huang, Y.-S., Lin, Y.-J., & Ho, J.-W. (2013). A study on negative binomial inspection for imperfect production systems. *Computers & Industrial Engineering, 65*(4), 605–613. doi:10.1016/j.cie.2013.05.017

Ifrah, G. (1998). *Universal History of Numbers: From Prehistory to the Invention of the Computer.* Harville Press.

Kahneman, D. (2011). *Thinking fast and slow*. Farrar, Straus and Giroux.

Kamburova, E., & Christozov, D. (1998). Assessment of and comparison between Bulgarian and International standards for quality control of evaluation of the element composition of geological samples. Sofia.

Karim, R., & Suzuki, K. (2004), Analysis of warranty claim data: A literature review. In *Proceedings of the 2004 Asian International Workshop on Advanced Reliability Modeling.* World Scientific. 10.1142/9789812702685_0030

Keahey, T. A. (2013). Using visualization to understand big data. *IBM Business Analytics Advanced Visualisation*, 16. IBM.

Kim, D. (2010). The interactive effects of colors on visual attention and working memory: in case of images for tourists attraction, *International CHRIE conference.* University of Massachusetts. https://scholarworks.umass.edu/cgi/viewcontent.cgi?article=1487&context=refereed

Kulkarni, V., & Shau-shiang, J. (2002). Warranty Reserves for Non-stationary Sales Processes. *Naval Research Logistics, 49*(5), 499–513. doi:10.1002/nav.10023

Kullback, S., & Leibler, R. A. (1951). On Information and Sufficiency. *Annals of Mathematical Statistics, 22*(1), 79–86. doi:10.1214/aoms/1177729694

Kyvykaite, R., Dovaliene, A., & Navickiene, L. (2009). Impact of package elements on consumer's purchase decision, *Ekomomika ir vadyba.* file:///C:/Users/dgc/Downloads/9405-Article%20Text-30522-1-10-20150210.pdf

Lotrecchiano, G. (2017). Personal communication during InSITE-2017.

Lotrecchiano, G., & Misra, S. (2017). Observational and Analytic Features for the Study of Transdisciplinary Teams. InSITE 2017: Informing Science & IT Education Conferences: Vietnam, 063-064.

Lotrecchiano, G., & Misra, S. (2018). Transdisciplinary knowledge producing teams: Toward a complex systems perspective. *Informing Science*, *21*, 51–74. doi:10.28945/4086

Lotrecchiano, G., & Misra, S. (2019). Transdisciplinary knowledge producing teams: Toward a complex systems perspective. *Informing Science [InformingSciJ]. The International Journal of Emerging Transdiscipline*, *21*, 41–50.

Loundon, K., & Laudon, J. (1996). *Management Information Systems*. Prentice Hall.

Lumina Foundation. (2014). *The degree qualification profile*. Lumina Foundation. https://www.luminafoundation.org/files/resources/dqp.pdf

Magnuson-Moss Warranty and Federal Trade Commission Improvement Act of 1975, Pub. Law No 93 – 637 (15 U.S.C. 2301)

Manchanda, M. (2018). Web Usage Mining: Dynamic Methodology to Preprocessing Web Logs. *Helix*, *8*(5), 3810–3815. doi:10.29042/2018-3810-3815

Manchanda, P., Xie, Y., & Youn, N. (2008). The Role of Targeted Communication and Contagion in Product Adoption. *Marketing Science*, *27*(6), 961–976. doi:10.1287/mksc.1070.0354

Marsden, S. (n.d.). *How Do Search Engine Crawlers Work?* DeepCrawl. https://www.deepcrawl.com/knowledge/technical-seo-library/se arch-engine-crawling/

Mehra, J., & Thakur, R. S. (2018). An Effective method for Web Log Preprocessing and Page Access Frequency using Web Usage Mining. *International Journal of Applied Engineering Research: IJAER*, *13*(2), 1227–1232. http://www.ripublication.com

Mercier, H. (2011). Reasoning serves argumentation in children. *Cognitive Development*, *26*(3), 177–191. doi:10.1016/j.cogdev.2010.12.001

Mercier, H. (2012). Looking for arguments. *Argumentation*, *26*(3), 305–324. doi:10.100710503-011-9256-1

Mercier, H. (2016). The argumentative theory: Predictions and empirical evidence. *Trends in Cognitive Sciences*, *20*(9), 689–700. doi:10.1016/j.tics.2016.07.001 PMID:27450708

Mercier, H., & Sperber, D. (2009). Intuitive and reflective inferences. In J. St. B. T. Evans & K. Frankish (Eds.), *In two minds: Dual processes and beyond* (pp. 149–170). Oxford University Press. doi:10.1093/acprof:oso/9780199230167.003.0007

Mercier, H., & Sperber, D. (2017). *The Enigma of Reason*. Harvard University Press.

Mobasher, B., Dai, H., Luo, T., Sun, Y., & Zhu, J. (2000). Combining Web Usage and Content Mining for More Effective Personalization. Lecture Notes in Computer Science (Including Subseries Lecture Notes in Artificial Intelligence and Lecture Notes in Bioinformatics), 1875, 165–176. doi:10.1007/3-540-44463-7_15

Mooers, C. (1950). Information retrieval viewed as temporal signaling. *Proceedings of the international congress of mathematicians*. Information Science.

Mooers, C. (1950). Information retrieval viewed as temporal signaling. *Proceedings of the international congress of mathematicians*. ISI.

Mooers, C. N. (1952). Information retrieval viewed as temporal signaling. *Proceedings of the International Congress of Mathematicians* 1, (pp 572-573). IEEE.

Murthy, P. D., & Djamaludin, I. (2002). New product warranty: A literature review. *International Journal of Production Economics*, *79*(2), 236–260.

Naisbitt J. (1982). Megatrends – Ten New Directions Transforming Our Lives. *Warner Books Inc.*

Naisbitt, J. (1982), *Megatrends*. Warner Books. https://www.brainyquote.com/quotes/john_naisbitt_382513)

Newman, D., & Logan, D. (2008). *Gartner Introduces the EIM Maturity Model*. Semantic Scholar. https://www.semanticscholar.org/paper/Gartner-Introduces-the-EIM-Maturity-Model-Newman-Logan/ca3b13f65a37d7b0a4428789971 0112e2c5afc4e

Niazi, M., & Hussain, A. (2009). Agent-Based Tools for Modeling and Simulation of Self-Organization in Peer-to-Peer, Ad-Hoc and Other Complex Networks. *IEEE Communications Magazine*, *47*(3), 166–173. doi:10.1109/MCOM.2009.4804403

Nonaka, I., & Takeuchi, H. (1995). *The Knowledge-Creating Company: How Japanese Companies Create the Dynamics of Innovation*. Oxford University Press. doi:10.1093/oso/9780195092691.001.0001

Orlitzky, M., Schmidt, F. L., & Rynes, S. L. (2003). Corporate Social and Financial Performance: A Meta-Analysis. *Organization Studies*, *24*(3), 403–441. doi:10.1177/0170840603024003910

Owen, C. B. (2008). *Parameter Estimation for the Beta Distribution*. [MSc thesis, Brigham Young University, Utah, USA].

Parry, M.E., Cao, Q. & Song, M. (2011). Forecasting new product adoption with probabilistic neural networks. *Journal of Product Innovation Management*, *28*, 78-88.

Pham, H., & Wang, H. (1996). Imperfect maintenance. *European Journal of Operational Research*, *94*(3), 425–439. doi:10.1016/S0377-2217(96)00099-9

Piscini, E., Guastella, J., Rozman, A., & Nassim, T. (2016). *Blockchain: Democratized trust. Distributed ledgers and the future of value*. Deloitte University Press.

Rathi, P., & Vishwavidyalaya, G. K. (2019). An Efficient Algorithm for Data Pre-Processing and Personalization in Web. *International Journal of Computer Sciences and Engineering Open Access An Efficient Algorithm for Data Pre-Processing and Personalization in Web Usage Mining*, *7*(May), 160–164. Advance online publication. doi:10.26438/ijcse/v7i5.160164

Robinson, L. (2009). A summary of Diffusion of Innovations, in Changeology.

Schoderbek, P., Schoderbek, C., & Kefalas, A. (1990). *Management Systems: Conceptual Considerations*. BPI IRWIN.

Sethi, S. P., Prasad, A., & He, X. (2008). Optimal advertising and pricing in a new-product adoption model. *Journal of Optimization Theory and Applications*, *139*(2), 351–360. https://www.marketing91.com/new-product-adoption/. doi:10.100710957-008-9472-5

Simon, H. A. (1965). *The Shape of Automation for Men and Management*. Harper Torchbooks.

Simon, H. A. (1977). *[1960]. The new science of management decision* (Revised ed.). Prentice-Hall.

Slovac, P. (1993). Perceived Risk, Trust, and Democracy. *Risk Analysis*, *13*(6), 675–682. doi:10.1111/j.1539-6924.1993.tb01329.x

Sprenger, G. (2016) Structured and unstructured misunderstandings: Towards an anthropological theory of misunderstanding. *Civilizations: Rue internationale d'anthropologie et de sciences humaines*, 21-38. https://journals.openedition.org/civilisations/4050

Syed Fiaz, A. S., Asha, N., Sumathi, D., & Syed Navaz, A. S. (2016). Visualization: Enhancing big data more adaptable and valuable. *International Journal of Applied Engineering Research: IJAER*, *11*(4), 2801–2804.

Taleb, N. (2014). *Antifragile: things that gain from disorder*. Random House Trade Paperback.

U.S. Code Collection. (n.d.). Cornell University. http://www.law.cornell.edu/uscode/html/uscode15/usc_ sup_01_15_10_50.htm

Ugarchinsky, B., Christozov, D., Denchev, S., Hicova, T., & Deneva, L. (1987). Information Service in Technology Transfer: Basic Sources and Channels of Technological Information. *ICTT "Informa."* Sofia.

UPS. (2014). *Before, During and After: Disaster Preparedness and Recovery*. UPS. https://www.ups.com/assets/resources/media/en_US/UPS_disaster.pdf

Vinge, V. (1993). *Technological singularity*. CMU. https://frc.ri.cmu.edu/~hpm/book98/com.ch1/vinge.singularity .html

Wang, H., & Qian, C. (2011). Corporate Philanthropy and Corporate Financial Performance: The Role of Stakeholders Response and Political Access. *Academy of Management Journal*, *54*(6), 1159–1181. https://www.gartner.com/it-glossary/big-data/ https://en.wikipedia.org/wiki/Data_philanthropy. doi:10.5465/amj.2009.0548

White, M., & Eiser, R. (2005). Information Specificity and Hazard Risk Potential as Moderators of Trust Asymmetry. *Risk Analysis, 25*(5), 1187–1198. https://en.wikipedia.org/wiki/Disintermediation. doi:10.1111/j.1539-6924.2005.00659.x PMID:16297224

Wilensky, U. (1999). *NetLOGO*. Northwestern University, Evanston.

Wilensky, U. (2002). *Netlogo PD N*. Person Iterated.

About the Author

Dimitar Christozov is a Professor of Computer Science at the American University in Bulgaria, since 1993. He has more than 35 years of research and education experience in areas as computer science, applied statistics, information systems. His recent interests are in the field of business analytics and data science. He graduated Mathematics from Sofia University "St. Kliment Ohridski" in 1979. He completed his Ph.D. thesis "Computer Aided Evaluation of Machine Reliability" in 1986 and D.Sc. thesis "Quantitative measures of the quality of informing" in 2009. At Central Institute of Mechanical Engineering (1979-1986) Dimitar Christozov was engaged in numerous software development projects. His major contribution was design and development of "Relia-Soft", a software application to support research on evaluation machine reliability, for different platform widely used by Bulgarian industry. At Information Center for Technology Transfer "Informa" (1986-1993) Dr. Christozov was involved in establishing the national information network for technology transfer and lead the research in the areas of technologies assessment, integral quality measures and developing information systems in support of quality management. In these areas he was recognized as one of the leading experts in Bulgaria. At the American University in Bulgaria, he was the leading person in curriculum development of the majors of Computer Science (1993) and Information Systems (2008). In the period 2015-2017 he was appointed as the representative of Mathematics and Computer Science in the Executive Board of the Bulgarian Science Fund. Professor Christozov has more than 100 publications as separate volumes, journal papers and papers in refereed proceedings. He is a founding member and Fellow of Informing Science Institute and chair of Bulgarian Informing Science Society. For his contribution to the ISI he was awarded Zbigniew Gackowski Memorial Award for excellent and the advancement of Informing Science. He is founding member and fellow of Applied Knowledge Management Institute; founding member of the Bulgarian Statistical Society; and the Bulgarian Telework Association. He had chaired and served as member of Program and Organizing Committees of many international conferences and other scientific events.

Index

N

P

Q

R

T

U

W

www.ingramcontent.com/pod-product-compliance
Lightning Source LLC
LaVergne TN
LVHW080600300926
849162LV00005B/1004

* 9 7 8 1 6 6 8 4 8 8 0 0 3 *